PATERNOSTER THEOLOGICAL MONOGRAPHS

Theology After Neo-Pragmatism

PATERNOSTER THEOLOGICAL MONOGRAPHS

PATERNOSTER THEOLOGICAL MONOGRAPHS

Theology After Neo-Pragmatism

Adonis Vidu

WIPF & STOCK · Eugene, Oregon

Wipf and Stock Publishers
199 W 8th Ave, Suite 3
Eugene, OR 97401

Theology After Neo-Pragmatism
By Vidu, Adonis

ISBN 13: 978-1-60608-471-7
Publication date 2/6/2009
Previously published by Paternoster, 2008

"This Edition Published by Wipf and Stock Publishers
by arrangement with Paternoster"

SERIES PREFACE

In the West the churches may be declining, but theology—serious, academic (mostly doctoral level) and mainstream orthodox in evaluative commitment—shows no sign of withering on the vine. This series of *Paternoster Theological Monographs* extends the expertise of the Press especially to first-time authors whose work stands broadly within the parameters created by fidelity to Scripture and has satisfied the critical scrutiny of respected assessors in the academy. Such theology may come in several distinct intellectual disciplines—historical, dogmatic, pastoral, apologetic, missional, aesthetic and no doubt others also. The series will be particularly hospitable to promising constructive theology within an evangelical frame, for it is of this that the church's need seems to be greatest. Quality writing will be published across the confessions—Anabaptist, Episcopalian, Reformed, Arminian and Orthodox—across the ages—patristic, medieval, reformation, modern and counter-modern—and across the continents. The aim of the series is theology written in the twofold conviction that the church needs theology and theology needs the church—which in reality means theology done for the glory of God.

SERIES EDITORS

For my parents, Peter and Geta

Contents

Acknowledgements

Writing on theology and neo-pragmatism from Romania presents a variety of challenges: first, Anglo-American philosophy is not at all at home in this context; secondly, the paucity of bibliographical resources available in this particular geographical area. The first of these obstacles was partially surmounted with the help of academics and friends who have given magnanimously of their time in replying to my emails and making comments on my work. Terry F. Godlove and Kevin Schilbrack have made available hard to find resources and provided encouragement along the way. Dirk-Martin Grube of Utrecht University provided useful insight and made valuable comments, including drawing my attention to more continental sources. Among these, the Norwegian theologian Ulf Zaccariason kindly supplied both published and unpubished work. Lastly conversations with Kevin Vanhoozer have been a rich mine of invaluable insights. Nothing that is in the least objectionable in this essay can be in any way blamed on these colleagues.

The second of these hurdles was overcome by the financial support of dear friends who made research possible. Brother Don Church sponsored a summer research at Wheaton College; my friend, Billy Breland, purchased books on neo-pragmatism; my uncle, Lucian Coltea, covered the expenses of several trips to the United States. Without such incredible support, this sort of research would have been unthinkable. I am deeply grateful to them.

For the past eight years, I have been blessed with the most wonderful, loving and supportive wife, Adriana. Her contribution to this book is hard to overestimate, ranging from her constant encouragement, to stimulating conversations on the nature of, e.g., legal interpretation. She is the source of my joy, energy, and fulfilment.

Parts of chapters 2 and 4 have been published as articles elsewhere and I am thankful to the editors for permission to include them here. These are: 'The Place of the Past in Theological Construction', *Theology Today* 64/2 (July, 2007); 'Bruce D. Marshall and Realism', *Journal for Christian Theological Research* 10 (2005); and 'Bruce D. Marshall and Donald Davidson on Epistemic Justification', *Heythrop Journal* 47/3 (July, 2006).

Abbreviations

ITI	Donald Davidson, *Inquiries into Truth and Interpretation* (Oxford: Oxford University Press, 1984).
SIO	Donald Davidson, *Subjective, Intersubjective, Objective* (Oxford: Oxford University Press, 2001).
TLH	Donald Davidson, 'Meaning, Truth, and Evidence', *Truth, Language, and History* (Oxford: Oxford University Press, 2005).
TDE	Willard v. O. Quine, 'Two Dogmas of Empiricism', in Quine, *From a Logical Point of View* (Cambridge, MA: Harvard University Press, 1980).
WO	Quine, *Word and Object* (Cambridge, MA: MIT Press, 1960).
EPM	Wilfrid Sellars, *Empiricism and the Philosophy of Mind* (http://www.ditext.com/sellars/epm.html).
PMN	Richard Rorty, *Philosophy and the Mirror of Nature* (Princeton: Princeton University Press, 1979).
MW	John McDowell, *Mind and World* (Cambridge, MA: Harvard University Press, 1996).

Introduction

In *Postliberal Theological Method*, we drew on Donald Davidson to expose the postliberal over-confidence in the unity, stability and visibility of the Christian vocabulary, as something distinct from other 'external' discourses, such as science, art, politics, philosophy. The argument was that narrativists tended to regard meanings as being fixed quite apart from an investigation into the truth of sentences. The natural result was a quasi-fideism which eventually wore down the supporters of narrative theology. What Donald Davidson contributed was the notion that meaning and truth form a pair. The immediate impact of this was to undermine the postliberal semantic poise, but also to suggest that fideism is spent as a theological option.

But now the question became: what is the role of tradition, of Christian practices? Have we not thrown out the baby with the bath water? Even at that time, we were aware that a better epistemic account of the function of conventional traditions had to be offered, but also (more intuitively) of some drawbacks of Davidson's extensional approach to meaning. This called for an engagement and analysis, which eventually prolonged over a period of four years, of Davidson's possible contribution to theology. Such a discussion could not be carried out independently of an assessment of the encompassing neo-pragmatic philosophy. Thus, *Theology After Neo-Pragmatism*!

Far from being of a purely regional interest, neo-pragmatism is an important conversation which draws quite a number of thinkers which are frequently quoted by theologians today. We said 'conversation', because instead of a substantive unity of perspectives, we find a range of related philosophical subjects being pursued in a similar style. Susan Haack draws on Papini's analogy to speak of pragmatism as a hotel in which each philosopher works on his own theme, in his own room, although they all arrived through the same corridor.[1] Much the same is true about neo-pragmatists: they are not all antirealists, they do not all embrace naturalism, their attitudes to science are different and they disagree about the role of theory. But what is it that unites them? Cornel West explains:

---

[1] Susan Haack, ed., *Pragmatism, Old and New: Selected Writings* (Amherst, NY: Prometheus Books, 2006).

> Much of the excitement about neopragmatism has to do with the antifoundationalist epistemic claims it puts forward. The idea that there are no self-justifying, intrinsically credible or ahistorical courts of appeal to terminate chains of epistemic justification calls into question positivistic and formalistic notions of objectivity, necessity and transcedentality. In this sense, all neopragmatists are antifoundationalists; that is, the validation of knowledge claims rests on practical judgments constituted by, and constructed in, dynamic social practices. For neopragmatists, we mortal creatures achieve and acquire knowledge by means of self-critical and self-correcting social procedures rooted in a variety of human processes.[2]

The positivism and the formalism mentioned by West are in fact descriptions of the two schools of thought that dislodged pragmatism from the American cultural and academic life in the first quarter of the twentieth century: neo-orthodoxy and logical positivism. The old pragmatism, with its optimistic ideology, had been discredited by the Depression and the horrors of war, as Morris Dickstein notes.[3] The attendant liberal theology suffered the same fate and saw itself retreating before the onslaught of the continentally imported Neo-orthodoxy, which soon dominated American theological schools. (Neo-orthodoxy bequeathed to postliberalism, not without the indispensable contribution of Hans Frei, its formalistic approach to Scripture and religion generally.) While Neo-orthodoxy was beginning to capture the imagination of theologians, academic philosophers turned to logical positivism, fascinated by its rigor. As Rorty recounts,

> It was as if pragmatism had been crushed between Tillich and Carnap, the upper and the nether millstones. Carnap, with his return to hard-edged empiricism, became the hero of the philosophy professors, but most American intellectuals turned their back on pragmatism and on analytic philosophy simultaneously. They began to look to Tillich, or Sartre, or Marcuse, or some other philosopher who sounded deeper and more intellectually ambitious than the Deweyan anti-ideological liberalism on which they had been reared. Liberalism had come to strike them as, at best, boringly platitudinous, or, at worst, a defensive apologia for the status quo.[4]

This was a case of one frontier being taken up into another: the fresh, practical, goal- and problem-solving-oriented approach which characterised both American puritan theology of the sort advocated by Jonathan Edwards as well as pragmatism was swallowed up by the continental émigrés turning American academic departments into their own frontier! In a very real sense, the

---

[2] C. West, 'The Limits of Neopragmatism', in Cornel West, ed., *The Cornel West Reader* (New York: Basic Civitas Books, 2000), pp. 183f.

[3] M. Dickstein, The Revival of Pragmatism: New Essays in Social Thought, Law, and Culture (Durham, NC: Duke University Press, 1998), p. 1.

[4] R. Rorty, *Objectivity, Relativism and Truth: Philosophical Papers 1* (Cambridge and New York: Cambridge University Press, 1991), p. 64.

philosophical and theological disputes between the old (pragmatism and liberal theology) and the new (logical positivism and Neo-orthodoxy) is a clash of cultures, a dispute about conceptual immigration, as some pragmatic commentators have been quick to point out.[5] The American academic establishment was becoming colonized by European intellectual fashions.

Interestingly, though, the two currents were antithetical to each other. It was only a matter of time before they clashed with each other. Or so it would seem. But something happened. To cut a long story short, the energy of logical positivism did not obliterate pragmatism, but actually gave it a second life which eventually led to the formation of what we call neo-pragmatism. It was not as if logical positivism was a problem free movement. Trouble brewed already on the old continent. While the common emphasis remained a purification of philosophy from pseudo-issues, such as metaphysics, cracks began to show in the understanding of empirical evidence, but also in other quarters.

As Alan Janik and Stephen Toulmin explain in their masterful *Wittgenstein's Vienna*, one of the driving motivations behind the Vienna Circle was a dissatisfaction with the conventional ossification of Austrian cultural language and discourse. The meaning of ethical, religious, metaphysical and generally philosophical discourse was under scrutiny. The idea was that, by subjecting language to close analysis, we could get rid of certain pseudo-problems of philosophy by showing them to be mere consequences of linguistic confusion.

But since all scrutiny takes place from a certain vantage point, this one too had a blind spot, i.e. it's own unproblematically assumed meanings. Carnap *et al* had critiqued the language of metaphysics, religion and ethics *by presupposing the unproblematic status of logic and analyticity*. Carnap purported to show that the problem of the existence of metaphysical entities was in fact an issue about which conceptual framework to use, rather than a real existence issue. He distinguished between internal questions, i.e. questions of existence which can be asked only once we have accepted a given framework (e.g. for the framework of numbers, we may ask: is there a prime number between 7 and 11?) and external questions, like: 'are there such things as numbers?'. For Carnap the latter question is actually a question about whether our use of the number framework is felicitous or not, *and that is a pragmatic question*. This is the first sign of the logical positivist Carnap nodding in the direction of pragmatism. But such pragmatic criteria could only be employed in the external questions. Internal questions are settled by appeal to analyticity (definitions) and the rules of logic. This is the blind spot: inside the language or the framework, meanings are considered to be settled, fixed, stable. Dagfin Føllesdal and Michael Friedman reflect on this:

---

[5] For example, William Dean and John E. Smith.

> While the influence of ideas from American pragmatism undoubtedly played a significant role in the development of Carnap's later view, at the same time, it is clear that a fundamental difference between his orientation and that of American pragmatism remained. For the entire point of Carnap's mature philosophy was to persist in a sharp distinction between formal and factual questions – both of which are adjudicable, at least in principle, on the basis of previously adopted logical rules – and practical or evaluative questions – which are adjudicable by no such rules.[6]

The obvious question, which Quine will later ask: how do these meanings get fixed? How is a new conceptual scheme introduced? How can we accept a framework prior to asking hard empirical questions? Quine's verdict regarding Carnap's 'pragmatism' was that it 'leaves off at the imagined boundary between the analytic and the synthetic.' It is precisely this boundary which Quine makes problematic, as the first section will show. But if Carnap hesitantly approaches pragmatism, Quine too had stopped mentioning pragmatism by the time he was composing *Word and Object*, as Tom Rockmore points out.[7] Nonetheless, Quine, but also Sellars, Davidson, and Rorty, while all sharing some (though not all, and not the same) logical empiricist presuppositions, decisively advance beyond it and, by drawing on pragmatism, strike out in the direction of its non-identical repetition: neo-pragmatism.

Thus the energy of logical positivism was entirely spent on correcting its own difficulties, leaving pragmatism, as Joseph Margolis points out, with a decisive advantage.[8] Whether or not this resurgence of pragmatism is accidental, as he sometimes implies,[9] the undisputed reality is that theology can no longer afford to pass pragmatism and neo-pragmatism by.

While the two European currents were essentially antithetical, the drift of logical empiricism towards pragmatism also affected the conversation between theology, pragmatism, and neo-pragmatism. As Giles Gunn notes, communication between these has been reviving since the 1970s.[10] Part of the burden of this essay is to suggest that the addition of Donald Davidson's voice

---

[6] Follesdal and Friedman, 'American Philosophy in the Twentieth Century', *Daedalus*, 135 (2006).

[7] Tom Rockmore, 'Analytic Philosophy and the Hegelian Turn', *Review of Metaphysics* 55/2 (2001).

[8] Joseph Margolis, 'Pragmatism's Advantage', in *Ars Disputandi*, 3 (2003).

[9] J. Margolis, *Reinventing Pragmatism: American Philosophy at the End of the Twentieth Century* (Ithaca: Cornell, 2002), p. 2: 'Had not Rorty and Putnam identified themselves as pragmatists *in* the process of reviewing and disputing the professional prospects or realism, relativism, knowledge under the condition of history, public and private responsibility and value, no one would have envisaged such a "revival."'

[10] Giles Gunn, 'Religion and the Recent Revival of Pragmatism', in Dickstein, *The Revival of Pramatism*, p. 406.

to this conversation promises good things for Evangelical theology, while it also requires a theological supplement. Following is a short outline of the book.

The first chapter introduces some of the epochal conceptual landmarks that frame the current neo-pragmatic discussion of the themes of meaning, justification, and ontology. Quine strays from Carnap's line with his critique of analyticity. Whatever there is about meaning it is not simply given, but related to our experience of the world, modelled after science. However, as Sellars points out, any appeal to experience must avoid the notion of the Given. Our experience of the world is conceptual through and through. Despite Quine's rejection of empiricism, Davidson does not think he goes far enough. As a result, he attempts to purify the notion of a conceptual experience from the idea that we are presented with bits of 'content' which we then organise into concepts. But if the notion of evidence falls down, dragging with it Quine's 'stimulus meaning', how is the relationship between meaning and the world to be constructed? Davidson suggests that a theory of meaning must take the form of a truth theory. We conclude the first chapter with Rorty's claims that the ontological consequences which derive from this enlarged picture leave no room for a distinction between what exists and how we should speak. There is no perfect description of reality. It has no preferred self-description and we have no way of checking the referential success of our language save by seeing whether it helps us achieve our purposes.

Chapter 2 sets out to discuss some of the ways in which theologians have appropriated pragmatic and neo-pragmatic ideas. We pursue three generic themes throughout the essay: justification, meaning (including the meaning of orthodoxy), and ontology.

The third chapter more closely discusses Davidson's contribution to our understanding of meaning and justification. In a certain sense the unelaborated thesis throughout the book is that there are significant differences between Davidson and other neo-pragmatists, which render his philosophy more fertile for a theological dialogue.

Chapter 4 exploits the insight that Davidson offers some important corrections of some neo-pragmatic tendencies such as the drive towards revisionism. We argue that he offers resources to combat the recent tendency in religious studies to neglect first person authority. However, these resources are seriously limited by his extensionalist and truth-conditional approach to meaning. These will surface in the work of Bruce Marshall, one of the first theologians to see the theological benefit of Davidsonian semantics. While Davidson's notion of interpretive charity effectively blocks any form of fideism (and incommensurability), it is nevertheless liable to introduce a form of epistemic subordinationism.

The severe drawbacks highlighted to this point suggest the need for a theological supplement, which is the task of the final chapter. Once again the discussion follows the three guiding lanes. In *justifying* religious claims we have to once again lay claim to experience, but without resurrecting the Myth of the Given. Experience generically denotes the external friction that should be felt by our system of beliefs. However, a right disposition, or orientation, is a requirement for the epistemic use of religious experience. Deliverances of experience are genuine components or reality, yet without being separable from certain normative dispositions towards reality. The second supplement relates to *meaning*: the normative dispositions required for theological knowledge are laid out for us in Scripture, which is a primordial performance and embodiment of a disposition, having become a script for the Church. Where neo-pragmatism tends to consider the past, Scripture, and tradition to be, at best, material for playful experimentation, we argue that we have no other insight into the mystery of God save by the disposition-forming Scriptures. These provide an irreducible intensional context which, as God's word, gives the meaning of the historical events of revelation by rightly disposing us. The final section elaborates on our concept of *aspectival realism*. We argue that there is no single perfect description of reality, but rather a plenitude of such perfect descriptions. These depend precisely on disposition and practical orientation. But in order to make sense of the notion that these dispositions bring out real aspects of the world and not just manufactured illusions, we need to view the world as God's creation. The nature of the truth of these descriptions does not consist in their correspondence to reality, but in their correspondence to the plenary, perfect and infinite mind of God. God alone has perfect knowledge of the world because he created it. We have limited knowledge of reality, but we do have knowledge of those things *we* create, such as art, texts, and conventional constructions such as mathematics. Yet our knowledge of God and his created reality depends on our participation in the divine intellect.

Chapter 1

Themes in Neo-Pragmatic Philosophy

Quine's Rejection of Analyticity

Quine's readily admits his debt to Carnap: 'I was very much his disciple for six years. In later years his views went on evolving, and so did mine, in divergent ways. But even when we disagreed, he was still setting the theme; the line of my thought was largely determined by problems that I felt his position presented.'[1] It is not only Carnap's influence which left an enduring mark upon Quine's development, but the whole intellectual atmosphere of the Vienna Circle seems to have been an inspiration for most neo-pragmatists. The occasion for such an emulation arose with Quine's 1933 trip to Vienna, but it was especially the emigration of several prominent Austrian intellectuals to the United States that created a new context in which European logical-positivist themes and styles gestated with American pragmatist ideas.[2] Alan Janik's and Stephen Toulmin's vivid portrait of the Viennese intellectual life highlights a common critical stance towards the conventionally ossified Austrian culture. The conditions there have become appropriate for a thoroughgoing critique of language. Neo-pragmatists, beginning with Quine, imported the mandate of a linguistic criticism to the United States. Although, as Cornel West and others have complained, the neo-pragmatic style is more of the armchair variety, the significance of its outlook for life, meaning, society and religion are sometimes underestimated. Quine's critique of meaning and analyticity and Davidson's deconstruction of linguistic convention represent important departures from the notion that meanings are fixed, self-contained and trustworthy. Part of the burden of this book is to show just why the neo-pragmatic philosophy of meaning, truth and reality bears upon the meta-level of the very intelligibility of our speech, and consequently our theological talk. Sometimes it may appear that such a detached, a-historical style gets in the way of truthful insight, especially because of a penchant for logical regimentation. It is equally true,

---

[1] Quoted in Hans-Johann Glock, *Quine and Davidson on Language, Thought and Reality* (Cambridge: Cambridge University Press, 2003), p. 15.

[2] For more on this see Murray G. Murphy, 'American Philosophy', in Luther S. Luedtke, *Making America: The Society and Culture of the United States* (University of North Carolina Press, 1992); Rom Harré, *One Thousand Years of Philosophy* (Oxford: Blackwell, 2000).

however, that this is most of the time a failure of nerve, rather than of substance and intention.

Quine accepts many of the central claims of the logical positivists. He accepts, for instance, the verificationist doctrine that meaning is determined by empirical evidence, the positivist insistence that sensory experience provides evidence for our beliefs. The logical positivist suspicion of metaphysics was also inherited by Quine, although perhaps not as radically. For Quine, metaphysical and abstract entities can be postulated under certain stringent conditions. Most importantly, however, he shares in their scientism, i.e., the claim that science is the final arbiter of truth claims.

Perhaps it is this very scientific and empirical orientation which accounts for his ultimate dissatisfaction with Austrian analytic philosophy. The ambition of the logical positivists was to provide a distinctive role for philosophy, but without making dubious appeals to God, metaphysics, or Kant's non-empirical preconditions of experience. All meaningful talk is restricted to either empirical and observational discourse (subject to verification and falsification), or to the necessary truths contained in analytic propositions like 'all bachelors are unmarried'. The doctrine of linguistic necessity provided a distinctive space which philosophy could explore and have as its sole jurisdiction. This line of thought was explored and developed in one direction by Carnap, as we have seen, and in another by Wittgenstein and ordinary language philosophers. Now the task of philosophy is analysis, as second-order reflection upon language.

Celebrations were short lived, however, for G. E. Moore had already pointed out the so-called 'paradox of analysis': 'This paradox results from supposing that any correct philosophical analysis consists of nothing but analytic statements. For analytic statements can be transformed into logical truths. Logical truths, however, were supposed to be tautologies and tautologies are trivial. So philosophical analysis is correct only if its results are trivial.'[3] Carnap had already drawn the consequences of the demarcation between philosophy and science and understood that philosophy had to be refigured as a 'logical analysis of the language of philosophy.' In Carnap's vision, the task of philosophy is to investigate the inner logic of a conceptual scheme, while external questions about its adequacy must be governed by pragmatic considerations. While the scientist assumes a given conceptual scheme and acquires knowledge about the world inasmuch as that conceptual scheme permits it, the philosopher *cum* logician lays bare the necessary structure of that conceptual scheme. The considerations which bear upon the philosopher's work are not of an empirical and scientific nature, but of a necessary kind. The philosopher cannot draw on the resources of the scientist in dealing with his problems, which belong to the very structure of thought. Scientific tools can

---

[3] Herbert Schnädelbach, 'Two Dogmas of Empiricism: Fifty Year After', in Hans-Johann Glock, Kathrin Gluer, Geert Keil, *Fifty Years of Quine's 'Two Dogmas'* (Amsterdam: Rodopi, 2003), p. 8.

only be put to contingent use, while what is truly interesting for the philosopher is necessity.

Quine radically overturns this picture. Using Neurath's famous metaphor, he insists that 'the philosopher and the scientist are in the same boat.'[4] It is a mistake to disjunct between a realm of necessity and one of contingency, one belonging to philosophy proper, the other to science. Questions of language are themselves empirical questions. The burden of showing this was taken up in 'The Two Dogmas of Empiricism', where Quine attacked the two foundational pillars of logical positivism: the distinction between the analytic and the synthetic and the dogma of reductionism. We shall be concerned in this section with the first of these attacks, Quine's rejection of analyticity, leaving the second to the next.

It is widely agreed within analytic philosophical circles that the rejection of the analytic synthetic distinction restored philosophy on its right path. Herbert Schnädelbach is enthusiastic: 'Erasing the borderline between the analytic and the synthetic meant releasing analytic philosophy from its man-made prison.'[5] Davidson also voices his gratitude: 'In my view, erasing the line between the analytic and the synthetic saved philosophy of language as a serious subject.'[6] While Schnädelbach and Davidson praise Quine for bringing philosophy within the influence of empirical science, Rorty has a different appreciation of Quine's accomplishment: 'Given Quine's doubts (buttressed by similar doubts in Wittgenstein's *Investigations*) about how to tell when we are responding to the compulsion of "language" rather than that of "experience", it became difficult to explain in what sense philosophy had a separate "formal" field of inquiry and thus how its results might have the desired apodictic character.'[7] While these are all positive receptions of Quine's first attack, there are also less enthusiastic appraisals, as we shall see momentarily. Before we get to that, let us look more closely at what is entailed by the rejection of analyticity and how Quine hopes to pull it off.

Quine attacks the distinction from two directions, which are in fact attacks on the two dogmas of empiricism. There is a semantic/ontological argument which is itself composed of two separate arguments. Briefly stated, first it is claimed that analyticity belongs to a cluster of obscure 'intensional' notions and is dependent on these for its explanation (the circularity argument); secondly, these *intensions* are dubious entities with no clear criteria of identity,

---

[4] W. v. O. Quine, *Word and Object* (Cambridge, MA.: Technology Press of the Massachusetts Institute of Technology, 1960), p. 3.

[5] H. Schnädelbach, 'Two Dogmas', pp. 8-9.

[6] Donald Davidson, 'A Coherence Theory of Truth and Knowledge', in Donald Davidson, *Subjective, Intersubjective, Objective* [*SIO*] (Oxford: Oxford University Press, 2001), p. 145.

[7] R. Rorty, *Philosophy and the Mirror of Nature* [*PMN*](Princeton: Princeton University Press, 1979), p. 169.

hence it is philosophically and scientifically improper to ascribe existence to them. The second main strand of Quine's attack belongs to the epistemology of scientific method. We shall devote more attention to this, the so-called holist aspect of Quine's epistemology in another section, but it boils down to the fact that given the holist nature of epistemic verification, it makes no sense to distinguish between statements which are true in virtue of experience and statements which are true come what experience may. No statement within the 'web of beliefs' is immune to revision. The qualitative distinction between analytic statements which are true in virtue of their meaning and synthetic ones whose truth is contingent upon experience vanishes.

Inheriting the logical positivist suspicion of metaphysical entities, Quine affirms his preference for an extensional language, rather than an intensional one. The distinction between extension and intension was introduced in Carnap's 1956 *Meaning and Necessity*.[8] An extension denotes what an expression stands for and is a generalization of reference. The extension of a singular term is the object it refers to; the extension of a predicate is a set of objects of which it is true. Finally, the extension of a declarative sentence is its truth value. On the other hand, an intension is an aspect of what an expression means. Hence the intension of a singular term is a description which singles out its referent, the intension of a predicate denotes the attributes possessed by the object referred to and the intension of a declarative sentence is the thought/proposition expressed by it.

It is not difficult to see what bothers Quine about intensions. Talk about these seems to presuppose that entities such as 'propositions', or 'thoughts' actually exist. Hence Quine's semantic argument against analyticity is that it is part of a cluster of intensional notions like synonymy, self-contradiction, necessity, definition, semantical rule, that cannot be reduced to purely extensional ones like reference and truth. Hence they are disreputable. We can only explain these concepts by relying on other members of the family. Thus all possible explanations would be circular.[9] Glock helpfully points out that the 'circularity charge' only has force once one accepts Quine's strict demands placed on 'explanation'. Moreover, what Quine requires explanation to do rests in fact on his covert employment of an intensional notion, viz. when he requires that an extensional explanation give the *meaning* of an intension. This is itself circular. In addition, as Grice and Strawson point out, while it may be granted that the notion is poorly explained, it does not follow that we cannot and do not

---

[8] Rudolf Carnap, *Meaning and Necessity* (Chicago: University of Chicago Press, 1956).

[9] See H. –J. Glock, *Quine and Davidson*, pp. 72ff., for a discussion of what he calls the 'circularity charge.'

in fact reliably distinguish *in most cases* between statements which are analytic and statements which are synthetic.[10]

There is no need to dwell more on the circularity charge. As Glock observes, Quine himself seems to have quietly dropped it as early as 1953.[11] Yet Quine has at least a couple of other ways to defend his prejudices against intensions. First is his slogan, 'no entity without identity.' In order to posit entities of any kind, what is required is that we have clear identity criteria for them. Unlike abstract extensional objects, intensions (or meanings) lack such criteria.[12] This is sufficient to motivate a flight from intensions, in Quine's view.

It is hard to overestimate the importance of this discussion for our larger project. As we mentioned earlier, Quine does not simply do away with all abstract entities. Whether a notion, say the notion of number, is kept in our ontological vocabulary depends on two main factors: whether the theory that we use depends on the existence of that entity and whether the entity resists reduction to another vocabulary (logical paraphrase). Again, this position was formulated in explicit opposition to Carnap, but also to the ordinary language philosophy's absolutisation of language: what we admit in our ontological repertoire is a scientific and empirical question. Indeed, Quine thought that Carnap's distinction between the external and the internal was so intimately related to the distinction between the analytic and the synthetic that the former effectively collapses with the latter. The question of whether an entity such as 'colour' exists depends on whether our theory (that is, our best scientific theory of the world) employs it and depends on its existence and, secondly, whether it is immune from logical paraphrase. It will have to be seen what sort of equivalence logical paraphrase aims for and whether Glock is right in saying that if something explains it does not necessarily also replace.[13] The significance of this for our larger project bears on the question of God's existence. Does God exist independently of religious conceptual and symbolic schemes? Can God talk be reduced to questions of, say, intra-textual coherence? Is God simply a convention? *Quine's merit is to have pointed out the proximity between questions of existence, of reality and questions of meaning.*

We need to return to the question of analyticity, however. Strawson objects to Quine's logical paraphrase on the grounds that simply changing the way we speak does not always change the way we think: 'committed in thought to what we shun in speech, we should then seem like people seeking euphemisms in

---

[10] H. P. Grice and P. F. Strawson, 'In Defense of a Dogma', in L. W. Sumner, John Woods, eds., *Necessary Truth: A Book of Readings* (New York: Random House, 1969).

[11] H. –J. Glock, *Quine and Davidson*, p. 77.

[12] See H. –J. Glock, *Quine and Davidson*, pp. 47ff.

[13] H. –J. Glock, *Quine and Davidson*, p. 66.

order to avoid explicit mention of distasteful realities.'[14] We seek such euphemisms, perhaps, because we have ridiculously strict standards of admissibility, ending up with what, together with Grice, Strawson calls the philosopher's paradox: 'Instead of examining the actual use that we make of the notion of meaning the same, the philosopher measures it by some perhaps inappropriate standard (in this case some standard of clarifiability), and because it falls short of this standard, or seems to do so, denies its reality, declares it illusory.'[15] The notion of 'meaning the same' does not necessarily presuppose that we have reified meanings and turned them into metaphysical entities. But while Quine's criteria for what we may posit as an entity are too narrow to permit the existence of even important aspects of reality for which we do not have clear and precise criteria of identity, *it is quite another thing to say that questions of meaning have to be precise*. Glock proposes that such a precision should not be determined by *criteria of identity*, but by the notion of identifiability.[16] By Quine's lights, since we have no way of *counting* the attributes of, for instance, Rheims cathedral, it follows that there are no such things as attributes. One important difficulty with this, as Glock notes, is that innumerability is a question of regimentation, not one of reality.[17] The fact that we cannot count how many propositions there are in this present book does not *necessarily* mean that there are no such things as my propositions. Conversely, if we could count them, as in fact we can do with some things, it only serves to show that the theory that we use provides clear criteria of counting. We have ways of counting, say, the attributes of Bohr's electron only because the theory itself draws precise distinctions in these objects. On the other hand, if we have no agreed way of counting mountains, it does not mean that they do not exist. It only means that we have not come up with a consensual method of enumerating.

We must also recognize at this point the existence of an objection coming from a direction quite opposite to Quine's. It goes something like this: both criteria of identity and criteria of identifiability are a case of confusion between ontology and epistemology. The existence of meanings and intensions is logically independent of the ability to tell whether these exist. Ontology is prior to epistemology. Such a line of inquiry should sound familiar to theologians and is in fact quite at home in many a theology. We shall come across it on a number of occasions and it is generally a warranted complaint. It boils down to the fact that theology must beware of epistemising God's reality. Take for

---

[14] P. F. Strawson, *Entity and Identity* (Oxford: Clarendon, 1997), quoted in Glock, *Quine and Davidson*, p. 68.

[15] Grice and Strawson, 'In Defense', p. 147.

[16] H. –J. Glock, *Quine and Davidson*, p. 51.

[17] H. –J. Glock, *Quine and Davidson*, p. 51.

example Flew's famous illustration of the mysterious gardener.[18] The believer insisted on the existence of such a gardener even if he was unable to distinguish between the conditions which obtained if he existed from the conditions which obtained if he did not. *The correct theological complaint against this antirealism of verificationism is that we cannot hang God's existence upon human ways of verifying this existence.* This is quite right.[19]

However, at the level of the intelligibility of our discourse, such considerations are important. At this meta-level, they do not necessarily bear upon questions of existence, but upon questions of meaningfulness. There can be true or false answers to questions about whether entities of all kinds of types exist only if these questions are meaningful to begin with. *The question of intelligibility, we argue, determines the one of the primordial zones of contact and cross-fertilization between theology and neo-pragmatism.*

Quine's criteria of identity are needlessly restrictive and betray an *a priori* negative stance with respect to intensions generally. Rorty disagrees with Quine's preference for extensional languages. It is a mistake, he says, to assume that the extensional vocabulary is superior to the intensional one. These are simply different ways to approach language and communication and it is wrong to give undue privilege to either one of them, as Quine does. The ironic implication of setting up such oppositions between an extensional language which 'limn[s] the true and ultimate structure of reality' (Davidson's words) and an intensional one which is ontologically disreputable, is to return philosophy to its role of guardian. The two vocabularies, as all such explanatory devices, are irreducible one to the other, hence 'To abandon the notion that in philosophy we have a discipline which guards against "irresponsible reification" and systematizes our "scruples about what objects one may assume" would be to take irreducibility in our stride and thus to judge each such vocabulary on pragmatic and aesthetic grounds alone.'[20] Now it is conceivable that Rorty goes too far in the aesthetic direction. But he is right to spot an disingenuouity between Quine's insistence that the fate of the scientist and of the philosopher are knit together and his 'armchair' attitude with respect to intensions. Rorty also argues that his polemic against intensions is not really of a piece with his rejection of analyticity. He 'should have said that concepts and meanings are harmless if posited to give explanations of our behaviour, and

---

[18] Anthony Flew, 'Theology and Falsification,' in Anthony Flew and Alasdair MacIntyre, eds., *New Essays in Philosophical Theology* (New York: Macmillan, 1955), p. 96.

[19] Interestingly, as Randal Rauser points out, Quine's rejection of necessity has been read by theologians such as Colin Gunton, but especially William Placher as congenial to preserving God's sovereignty and freedom. See Randal Rauser, 'Can There Be Theology Without Necessity?' *Heythrop Journal* XLIV/2 (2003): 131-146.

[20] R. Rorty, *PMN*, p. 208.

become harmful only when treated as a source of a special kind of truth and of a special sort of authority for certain assertions.'[21]

The analytic-synthetic distinction only becomes problematic when it is taken to express the necessary structure of a conceptual scheme taken in the wrong sense as mediating our epistemic relationship to the world. It is one thing to posit the existence of meanings for explanatory purposes and quite another to isolate a set of such meanings which mediate our relationship to truth necessarily. Even the analytic-synthetic distinction can be given a respectable neo-pragmatic interpretation, once its explanatory pretensions have been toned down. The problem is not so much with a qualitative difference between the propositions which are analytic and those which are synthetic. Grice and Strawson have given us much reason to continue accepting that there is a strong intuitive difference between these. This is merely a case of 'itching,' and it understandably gives rise to philosophically interesting questions. The moment we begin answering these in a way which sets up our conceptual scheme against the world as an intermediary, whose necessary structure is given by analyticity, then we have made a mistake. In other words, the problem is not with the itching, it is with a certain type of scratching. We go wrong, Rorty warns us, when we begin treating these analytic sentences as premises for a foundational argument, when we imbue them with an authority of a special kind.[22]

A new line of thought seems to be developing within neo-pragmatism and it has very much to do with Davidson, while it unites diverse figures such as Rorty, John McDowell, Barry Stroud, Hilary Putnam, Paul Boghossian and others. While plenty of dissenting voices remain, these philosophers regard the analytic-synthetic distinction with much less suspicion than initially. In the face of critique, Quine himself has substantially altered his views on analyticity. In *The Roots of Reference* he writes: 'language is social, and analyticity, being truth that is grounded in language, should be social as well. Here then we may at least have a line on the concept of analyticity: a sentence is analytic if everybody learns that it is true by learning its words. Analyticity, like observationality, hinges on social uniformity.'[23] More recently, Quine spoke of the 'germ of a plausible analyticity' which 'contributes one worthwhile general insight: that some truths are learned by learning words.'[24] This constitutes no threat if it is taken to apply to 'verbal' rather than to 'substantive' issues. Rorty continues this line of thought which connects analyticity with language, while stressing, again with Quine and Davidson, that language is a social art: 'Behaviourism in epistemology is a matter not of metaphysical parsimony, but

---

[21] R. Rorty, *PMN*, p. 194.

[22] Rorty, *PMN*, p. 177.

[23] W. v. O. Quine, *The Roots of Reference* (La Salle: Open Court, 1974), p. 79.

[24] W. v. O. Quine, 'Reply to Critics', in E. Hahn, A. Schillp, eds., *The Philosophy of W. v. O. Quine* (LaSalle, IL: Open Court, 1986), p. 95

of whether authority can attach to assertions by virtue of relations of "acquaintance" between persons and, for example, thoughts, impressions, universals and propositions.'[25] If, as Rorty suggests, Quine has taken his behaviourism in a far too radically eliminative and reductionist direction, then meanings must not be eliminated. Rather, *we have to clarify what we are up to when we persist in our talk about 'meaning the same as'*. Or, as Glock put it, '"Ontological" problems are solved not by positing or depositing entities. Instead, they are solved by clarifying what our various existential claims amount to.'[26]

How might this revised analyticity be described? John McDowell, to whom we shall return, argues that analytic truths are those which delineate the necessary structure of what Jonathan Lear calls 'our mindedness'.[27] As we shall observe, this 'mindedness' denotes a human conceptual scheme conceived in an un-problematic way, i.e., not as a *tertium* between human beings and the world, but as 'constitutive of our unproblematic openness to the world.'[28] Such a conceptual scheme is embodied in languages and traditions. Languages have necessary structures and it is these structures which analytic truths point to. Grice and Strawson have made a similar point in their reply to Quine's 'Two Dogmas': 'It is one thing to admit this ['that there is no absolute necessity about the adoption or use of any conceptual scheme whatever'] and quite another thing to say that there are no necessities within any conceptual scheme we adopt or use.'[29] Glock touches a similar note: 'the most promising suggestion is that necessary propositions do not *follow* from the meanings of their component signs, rather they partly *determine* or *constitute* these meanings.'[30]

It can be concluded that Quine's dissolution of the analytic-synthetic distinction, while initially persuasive and extremely influential, has suffered serious qualification. Quine himself has been soft-pedaling since 1974, and more recently philosophers of language insist upon retaining a 'soft' analyticity. But it is now inconceivable to return to a pre-Quinean naiveté. Discussions around meaning, most everyone now agrees, cannot be dissociated from empirical discourse. While Quine and his followers may have gone too far in naturalizing and behaviourising meaning, *it is difficult not to accept the insight that meaning, behaviour and empirical engagement with reality are issues that cannot be treated in isolation from each other.* After Quine, especially through Davidson's influence, the philosophy of language starts in

---

[25] R. Rorty, *PMN*, p. 177.

[26] H.–J. Glock, *Quine and Davidson*, p. 69.

[27] J. McDowell, *Mind and World* [*MW*] (Cambridge, MA: Harvard University Press, 1996), p. 158.

[28] J. McDowell, *MW*, p. 155.

[29] Grice and Strawson, 'In Defense', p. 158.

[30] H.–J. Glock, *Quine and Davidson*, p. 84 (original italics).

the jungle rather than in a Harvard or Oxford armchair. Furthermore, Quine's provocative insight that questions about meaning and necessity are intimately related to the best scientific theory of the world is still tremendously influential. The very imagination of a realm of the conceptual, where necessity is at home, is only possible from within a present theory of the world – and that theory is empirical.

What is the significance of this for theology? Chapter II introduces and discusses various theological engagements with the work of neo-pragmatists, including Quine's. Randal Rauser has managed to praise Quine, in an otherwise critical article: 'there is much that is initially appealing with his rejection of the analytic-synthetic distinction. To begin with, Quine's radical epistemological egalitarianism has a claim to respect the integrated and communal nature of human knowledge more faithfully than the strong foundationalism he was reacting against.'[31] Moreover, 'it offers a means to reintroduce theological knowledge into the discussion. Put in Barthian terms, we may say that on this view God remains absolutely "free" to reveal himself in any way he desires, and thus to challenge our beliefs at whichever point he chooses.'[32] That is as far as the praise goes, on Rauser's reading: 'but contingentism [...] would lead to skeptical implications'[33] and this would mean that we as theologians would lose the ability to affirm anything about God and thus it would critically undermine the very possibility of theology. That is, of course, theology conceived in a certain manner.

The present chapter does not deal specifically with the theological employment of neo-pragmatic modes of thought. That task is taken up in the next chapter. In the next section it will become clear that the holism to which Rauser hints poses further special problems for the task of justification. In fact, the holist argument forms the second main strand of Quine's attack on analyticity. John McDowell argues that, of the two attacks against empiricism, 'the rejection of the second dogma is the fundamental point.'[34] It is to that attack that we now turn.

The Given

The elimination of the analytic-synthetic distinction finds further support in Quine's attack on the so-called second dogma of empiricism, namely that all meaningful statements should be translated into statements about immediate experience. Quine purports to show that the logical positivist programme of reducing talk of objects to talk of sense data ultimately fails because there is no piece-by-piece matching between individual statements and individual

---

[31] R. Rauser, 'Can There Be Theology Without Necessity?', p. 137.

[32] R. Rauser, 'Can There Be Theology Without Necessity?', p. 137.

[33] R. Rauser, 'Can There Be Theology Without Necessity?', p. 143.

[34] J. McDowell, *MW*, p. 130.

experiences. On the contrary, 'statements about the external world face the tribunal of sense experience not individually but only as a corporate body.'[35] This section introduces Quine's understanding of the relationship between reason and experience, as well as Wilfrid Sellars' account of the so-called myth of the given, especially as rendered in his seminal essay, 'Empiricism and the Philosophy of Mind.' These two thinkers lay the foundations for the neo-pragmatic embrace of epistemic holism. Together they help inculcate an image of the relationship between mind and the world which demarcates an inside realm of conceptuality from an outside world. This picture is of tremendous importance for understanding what theology might look like in the wake of neo-pragmatism. A sustained critique of this picture will have to be postponed until later chapters in the book.

Quine's 'Two Dogmas of Empiricism' presents a head-on attack on the notion that we can distinguish, at the level of individual statements, between a linguistic component and a factual component. Analytic statements are those for which the factual component is null, while synthetic statements depend for their truth on both language and what the world is like. The image of science that derives from such a distinction is one of straightforward accumulation of data via sense experiences, which are then neatly added to our existing body of knowledge, the assumption being that there is an unproblematic correlation between individual sense experiences and propositional knowledge. Thus, each experience contains its own propositional claim which is non-inferential with respect to other statements and beliefs. If such a view is correct, then the task of science is conceived foundationally, as anchoring our larger body of theoretical knowledge, by way of reliable epistemic procedures of inference, to those observation statements which are basic. On such a view, warrant is reliably transferred from observation statements to theoretical statements with the help of an already existing logical apparatus. This logical apparatus must itself be *a priori*, i.e. independent of whatever experience might deliver. For the logical positivist programme of 'radical reductionism', it was absolutely essential that such an apparatus must somehow be immune from external disturbances. Hence the persistence of a doctrine of analyticity and the vision of the new task of philosophy, namely to investigate the a priori conditions which make knowledge and science possible.

But if there is no such epistemically relevant distinction between the analytic *a priori* and the synthetic *a posteriori*, then there can be no such distinction as that between what we learn from experience and that by way of which we learn, no absolute distinction between fact and value. The 'how' of knowledge (the logical apparatus) is not immune to revision. It follows that the process of transferring warrant from observation statements towards the theoretical centre

---

[35] W. v. O. Quine, 'Two Dogmas of Empiricism' [*TDE*], in Quine, *From a Logical Point of View* (Cambridge, MA: Harvard University Press, 1980), p. 135.

(or supra-structure, depending on the metaphor) relies on a mechanism which is itself a product of science.

This is Quine's seminal claim, original not in itself but in the way in which it is brought to bear on epistemology: that mathematics and logic are not a God-given flawless and transcendental mechanism for the smooth flow of knowledge through the system. Being themselves the product of the system, it becomes difficult to polarise between the beginning of the system and its development. Quine deplores the foundationalist ambitions of epistemology, and both the doctrine of analyticity and the doctrine of reductionism should plead guilty. Philosophy cannot claim the right to guard and police the birth place of knowledge, not because science has that right, but because there is no such place. It is instructive that Quine prefers Neurath's nautical metaphor to describe the condition of epistemology: we have to make do with whatever we have at hand, with the possibility of stepping outside the boat or docking being forever denied.

Mathematics and logic are themselves revisable and even, in principle, abandonable. We should not commit the mistake, argues Quine, of confusing our enduring reluctance to do so with any epistemologically interesting quality that these sciences might have. If the apparatus can be abandoned in principle it means that we have no reliable ways to transfer knowledge within the system, from the empirical edges (to use one of Quine's metaphors) to the theoretical centre. If we cannot transfer warrant, neither can we then say that a certain type of statements is more fundamental and 'germane' to experience than others. The difference is only one of degree and it is measured by our reluctance to revise the apparatus, which is what Quine calls the 'maxim of minimum mutilation'. Our natural tendency is to disturb the system as little as possible. The system remains stable not because it is securely anchored, or because an adequate 'chain of command', to shift metaphors, is in place, but because of pragmatic considerations. Once we realise the pragmatic sustainability of the system, we stop asking interesting philosophical questions about it.

In the face of recalcitrant experience, any claim anywhere in the system might be abandoned. 'But the total field is so underdetermined by its boundary conditions, experience, that there is much latitude of choice as to what statements to re-evaluate in the light of any single contrary experience. No particular experiences are linked with any particular statements in the interior of the field, except indirectly, through considerations of equilibrium affecting the field as a whole.'[36] This is Quine's epistemic holism: the claim that warrant is not transferred smoothly and reliably from observation statements to theoretical statements, thus being grounded on experience. Now the difference between claims which are closer to the centre and claims closer to the periphery is only one of degree. 'Physical objects are conceptually imported into the situation as convenient intermediaries – not by definition in terms of

[36] *TDE*, p. 136.

experience, but simply as irreducible posits, comparable epistemologically to the gods of Homer. [...] in point of epistemological footing the physical objects and the gods of Homer differ only in degree and not in kind.'[37] Both, Quine continues, are cultural posits.

The difference between the various items present in our discursive system of knowledge, items such as 'table', 'electron', 'God', is not one of kind, but one of degree. These are 'only differences in the degree to which they expedite our dealings with sense experience.'[38] We tend to accept or reject their existence depending on their usefulness in helping us predict our future experiences. However, our access to tables as opposed to our access to gods is only one of degree, not of essential kind. *It can hardly be said that the empirical content of 'God' is minimal by comparison with the empirical content of 'table'*. The very point of Quine's arguments is that 'it is misleading to speak of the empirical content of an individual statement'.[39] On the other hand, the unit of empirical significance is the whole of science. The divergence with Carnap is very clear at this point as well: while Carnap maintains that the question of the existence of abstract entities – or, we might add, extra-empirical ones such as God – is a question not of matters of fact, but of choosing a convenient language or conceptual scheme, Quine holds that any reply to such a question is of the same kind with a reply to the question 'are there tables in this room?' Furthermore, Quine adds, 'Carnap has recognised that he is able to preserve a double standard for ontological questions and scientific hypotheses only by assuming an absolute distinction between the analytic and the synthetic.'[40] Quine accuses Carnap of abandoning his pragmatism at the borderline between the analytic and the synthetic. Conversely, he views his own epistemology as moving in a pragmatic direction.

What remains of empiricism in Quine? Although experience no longer keeps a foundational function, Quine nevertheless insists on speaking in terms of the 'tribunal of experience'. Yet this tribunal judges only the whole of science, not its individual statements. Roger Gibson argues that there are two sides to Quine's new empiricism: a doctrinal side which holds that whatever evidence there is for science is sensory evidence; and a conceptual side, to the effect that all inculcation of meanings of words must rest ultimately on sensory evidence. The goal of epistemology is 'to provide a factual account of the link between observation and theory', "between the meager input and the torrential output."'[41] This is no longer epistemology as traditionally conceived. Quine is

---

[37] *TDE*, p. 138.

[38] *TDE*, p. 138.

[39] *TDE*, p. 136.

[40] *TDE*, p. 139.

[41] Roger F. Gibson, *Enlightened Empiricism: An Examination of W. V. Quine's Theory of Knowledge* (Gainesville, Fl.: University Presses of Florida, 1988), pp. 29-30, quoting Quine's 'Epistemology Naturalized'.

after a 'naturalised epistemology', that does not deal with concepts such as normativity or justification, but is content to observe regularities between sensory input and theoretical output. This would be an empirical study of how sensory stimulation leads to the formation of belief. How might such a study proceed?

> [Naturalized epistemology] studies a natural phenomenon, viz. a physical human subject. This human subject is accorded experimentally controlled input – certain patterns of irritation in assorted frequencies, for instance – and in the fullness of time the subject delivers as output a description of the three dimensional external world and its history. The relation between the meager input and the torrential output is a relation that we are prompted to study for somewhat the same reasons that always prompted epistemology; namely in order to see how evidence relates to theory, and in what way one's theory of nature transcends any available evidence.[42]

Theory is underdetermined by evidence because for any evidence we have, there is a number of possible theories which all do justice to the evidence. The deeper reason behind this is given by Hume's critique of causality. For Quine, 'the Humean predicament is the human predicament'. Causes are not out there to be known, they can only be inferred as regularities in patterns of interaction. Similarly, the only correlation we can make between an experience which causally impinges upon our system of beliefs and the stirring of the system is in terms of regularities. The only scientifically respectable option is to observe these regularities and postulate patterns. To take but one example, physical objects are precisely such regularities in observed relationships. Although Quine considers them to be of paradigmatic importance, they are nevertheless mere posits, on a par with the gods of Homer.

Quine's epistemological holism leads to a semantic holism *via* his verificationist theory of meaning. According to this theory, the meaning of a sentence is in principle determined by the evidence that would count for or against it. However, if empirical evidence is not in a one-by-one relationship to individual statements, neither will empirical meaning attach to individual statements. Individual sentence meaning is made out to depend on the meaning of the whole, leading some critics to fear that we cannot be confident of the meaning of any single sentence, or word. *The dissolution of the analytic-synthetic distinction further means that there is no difference between revising a definition and changing a postulate.* If such is the case, can we say that at any given time we know what a theory is about? This is not the time to address such issues, and our own suspicion with regard to holism will be voiced in due course.

---

[42] Quoted from 'Epistemology Naturalized', in Jaegwon Kim, 'What is "Naturalized Epistemology"?', *Philosophical Perspectives*, vol. 2: Epistemology (1988): 381-405, p. 390.

It does have to be pointed out that Quine retains a notion of 'stimulus meaning' which seems to grant empirical content to certain individual sentences. This is Quine's way of accounting for sameness of meaning in behavioural terms. The stimulus meaning of sentences is determined by the neural stimulations that would prompt speakers to assent to them.[43] However, what this notion is not supposed to do is to create another entity, similar to old 'meaning' which is somehow in the head. Quine's position is precarious, for he wants his talk of stimulus meaning to retain all the advantages of older talk of meanings, while skipping out on all its disadvantages. Thus, stimulus meaning is said to be *cognitively significant*, which means that it must concern evidence that the speaker understands and which is therefore relevant to his beliefs. On the other hand, however, in Glock's opinion, 'a consistent behaviourist *ersatz* would lack the conceptual connections with epistemic concepts like belief, knowledge, etc. Quine repudiates our intensional concepts in the name of an austere behaviourism. But he must tacitly rely on these concepts, if his discussion is to have the implications he assigns to it.'[44] That is to say, if stimulus meaning is to be serviceable for the purposes of radical interpretation, it must be connected with belief and other intensional notions, which is something that Quine denies.

The predicament can be restated as follows: *a concept such as stimulus meaning must be behavioural enough to avoid the assumed pitfalls of intensional notions, while it must be somehow connected in a normative way with belief so that it may be used to kick-start radical interpretation.* To use a language with which we shall engage immediately below, in order for such a stimulus meaning to be evidence, it must already be in the 'space of reasons', beliefs and justification.

Let us summarise this introduction to Quine's rejection of the second dogma of empiricism by introducing his notion of 'conceptual sovereignty'. In *Word and Object*, he writes that

> We cannot strip away the conceptual trappings sentence by sentence and leave a description of the objective world; but we can investigate the world, and man's part in it, and thus find out what cues he could have of what goes on around him. Subtracting his cues from his worldview, we get man's net contribution as the difference. This difference marks the extent of man's conceptual sovereignty – the domain within which we can revise the theory while saving the data.[45]

Quine's epistemology denies access to experience in a way in which it could justify one's beliefs about the world. Epistemology is restrained to a mere description of regularities in our interaction with the world. Conceptual

---

[43] W. v. O. Quine, *Word and Object* [*WO*] (Cambridge, MA: MIT Press, 1960), pp. 31-4.

[44] H. –J. Glock, *Quine and Davidson*, p. 181.

[45] *WO*, p. 5.

sovereignty is seen in the 'torrential' way in which we make sense of that relationship, by 'swelling ontology to simplify theory.'[46]

In the remainder of the section, we shall introduce the thought of Wilfrid Sellars. 'The Two Dogmas of Empiricism' and 'Empiricism and the Philosophy of Mind' are the two seminal essays which set the neo-pragmatic philosophical agenda on the question of givenness and experience. It will be Sellars' argument that experience, when taken as deliverances of sense data cannot constitute a ground for justification. Sellars also moves away from Kantian rationalism, but not as far as Quine was prepared to go. Thoughts as intentional inner episodes have no place in Quine's philosophy because these presuppose intensional notions such as beliefs and meanings which cannot be translated into an extensional idiom. Sellars, on the other hand, never abandoned this classical notion of thoughts as intentional inner episodes, but denied that their role is anything other than a causal-explanatory one vis-à-vis overt behaviour. He approaches the issue from a completely different direction from Quine, from bottom up, as it were. The latter's starting point is scientifically testable behaviour. Thoughts and sensations need not be introduced into the picture, for regularities in behaviour can be accounted by way of dispositions to respond differentially to a variety of stimuli. However, as we saw above, this creates a difficulty for Quine, since a mere dispositional inclination to respond to given stimulations, although real enough, does not adequately account for that which is characteristically human as opposed to animal. Moreover, there is a logical gap between such a quasi-natural inclination and the cognitive, rational supra-structure which somehow rests on it. Parking sensor automobiles are capable of discriminating between stimulations, but they do not form beliefs about what goes on around them. How do we transition from quasi-physical impingements on our nerve endings to the rational belief structure which constitutes our knowledge?

Philosophers have expressed a significant worry that Quine's naturalist approach to epistemology drops, together with normativity, even the notion of belief and knowledge.[47] The border between inside (the linguistic system, the conceptual scheme) and outside (world) is not drawn a priori; it is diffuse and the general area it approximates shifts together with science. Even the judgments we make within the system are characterised by the provisionality of being mere posits which help expedite our dealings with our sensory influx. This is one of the important things that sets Quine apart from Carnap. The epistemological implications for this are enormous, as we saw. *Normativity does not merely retreat inside the system, as with Carnap, but it disappears altogether.*

---

[46] *TDE*, p. 138.

[47] See for example, Jaegwon Kim, 'What is "Naturalized Epistemology"?', pp. 389-393.

Sellars refuses the reduction of inner intentional events to behaviour after the fashion of Quine. This does not mean that we can know these in ways relevant to grounding knowledge. He replaces Quine's behaviourist austerity with another kind of austerity which sharply distinguishes between two logical spaces. On the one hand we have the logical space of causes, on the other there is the 'logical space of reasons.'[48] There must be a clear distinction, he urges, between characterising something that belongs to the realm of causes and characterising something which belongs to the space of reasons. The space of reasons is *sui generis,* and it is characterised by freedom and spontaneity. Sellars urges that in accounting for this spontaneity, we cannot simply deny intensional facts: 'Now the idea that epistemic facts can be analyzed without remainder – even "in principle" – into non-epistemic facts, whether phenomenological or behavioural, public or private, with no matter how lavish a sprinkling of subjunctives and hypotheticals is, I believe, a radical mistake – a mistake of a piece with the so-called "naturalistic fallacy" in ethics.'[49] This is precisely what Quine intended and what Sellars denies. Spontaneity has to be taken seriously.

In effect Sellars regains some of the territory lost by Carnap to Quine. The line is redrawn as to distinguish two ways of characterising events, neither of which can be reduced to the other. McDowell also uses the territorial metaphor: Sellars' 'master thought, as it were, draws a line: above the line are placings in the logical space of reasons, and below it are characterizations that do not do that.'[50] Territory is regained because there is something of a clearer line that distinguishes the realm of reasons, i.e. a conceptual scheme, a language, a belief system etc. from the world, nature, the space where causal descriptions are at home. Inside the territory demarcated by the line we can speak of normativity, reasons, beliefs and justification. Outside it we can only make causal inferences. As we shall explain momentarily, the line between inside and outside the space of reasons is broadly the line between pre-linguistic awareness and linguistic conceptualisation, between infanthood and training into language.

But causes are not reasons. To say that they are is to invoke the Given and kick-start foundationalism, argue neo-pragmatists. *Quine strands very far indeed from the given, so far in fact that he has serious difficulty accounting for knowledge.* In naturalized epistemology, there are no such things as reasons, but only patterns of discriminating responses to stimuli. Conversely, 'The idea of the Given is the idea that the space of reasons, the space of justification or

---

[48] Wilfrid Sellars, *Empiricism and the Philosophy of Mind* [*EPM*], (http://www.ditext.com/sellars/epm.html), §36.

[49] *EPM*, §5.

[50] John McDowell, 'Having the World in View: Sellars, Kant, and Intentionality. Lecture I: Sellars on Perceptual Experience', *The Journal of Philosophy*, XCV, no. 9, Sept. 1998, pp. 431-450, p. 433.

warrants extends more widely that the conceptual sphere. The extra extent of the space of reasons is supposed to allow it to incorporate non-conceptual impacts from outside the realm of thought.'[51] McDowell is very much aware that the correct intuition behind this thought is that we want our spontaneity, our structure of belief, conceptually sovereign as it is, to be rationally accountable to the way things are. The fear is that 'frictionless spinning in the void' lies behind this myth of the given. Yet the cure given by proponents of the myth is hopelessly incoherent, as Sellars shows. He argues that the classical concept of a sense datum, an exemplary bearer of the Given, is a mongrel resulting from crossbreeding two ideas: the idea that there are conceptual inner episodes without which it would be in some sense impossible to see and which are active prior to concept formation; and the idea that there are certain inner episodes which are non-inferential knowings that certain items are, for example red, and that these inner episodes are a necessary condition for empirical knowledge.[52] What results from this conflation is a notion of the accumulation of knowledge which treats these inner episodes as authoritative even though they are prior to the formation of concepts, i.e. not in the space of reasons. To return to our metaphor, somebody has opened the border for the free traffic of sensations into the space of reasons. Now knowledge is on the right track if we pursue deontology: 'if observation reports are construed as actions, if their correctness is interpreted as the correctness of an action, and if the authority of an observation report is construed as the fact that making it is "following a rule" in the proper sense of the phrase, then we are face to face with givenness in its most straightforward sense.'[53] This is a confusion between an explanation and a justification. Saying that a belief is at the receiving end of a causal chain leading from world *via* sensations *via* concepts is not justifying it. It isn't because causal characterisations and rational characterisations are of a completely different order from each other. One belongs to the realm of law, the other to the realm of freedom. In addition, 'to be the expression of knowledge, a report must not only have authority, this authority must in some sense be recognized by the person whose report it is.'[54] In that case, the person giving the report must not only have the concept, say, 'green', but also the concept of uttering 'this is green', indeed, the concept of certain conditions of perception, and the list could continue. Sellars brings out an important point: *epistemological authority is epistemic. In other words, it makes no sense to speak of an authority that is unacknowledged.* Epistemic authority, in order to be authority, must be capable of being recognized as such. For that to be the case, it cannot be something private, but must be in the public space. Once we accept this, it becomes clear, at least by Sellars' lights, that 'one cannot have

[51] J. McDowell, *MW*, p. 7.
[52] W. Sellars, *EPM*, §6.
[53] W. Sellars, *EPM*, §34.
[54] W. Sellars, *EPM*, §35.

observational knowledge of *any* fact unless one knew many other things as well', and this 'requires an abandonment of the traditional empiricist idea that observational knowledge stands on its own feet.'[55]

These self-authenticating episodes are what Sellars calls the '"unmoved movers" of empirical knowledge'.[56] It follows that there are no solid foundations to science, because the whole system, or at least large chunks of it, is presupposed in making even the simplest observational report. However, Sellars does not do away with sensations. He keeps them in a humble causal role.[57]

The line which separates the space of causes from the space of reasons is drawn together with language-acquisition. Sellars' psychological nominalism holds that having a concept is having a linguistically acquired concept. This prevents him from ascribing concepts to infants. Yet for a critic such as Roderick Firth, ascribing concepts to infants is possible, while ascribing linguistic concepts to them isn't. In 'Coherence, Certainty, and Epistemic Priority', Firth suggests that Sellars unwarrantedly conflates words and concepts. He says, 'it is at least logically possible to have the concept "looks red" *before* we acquire the concept "is red."'[58] We have concepts because we can discriminate between stimuli even before we learn a language, holds Firth. What happens when we learn our first language is that we are able to 'baptise' the concepts of our initial pre-linguistic awareness with the names of the concepts that our first language teaches us. He calls these pre-linguistic concepts, 'primitive concepts' and warns that 'we must not suppose that the child somehow *loses* his primitive concept when he acquires a more sophisticated one.'[59] Firth thinks this point has the important philosophical implication that allows us to break out of the conceptual coherentist circle. The threat of such circularity is real enough and it does indeed worry philosophers like Sellars, McDowell and Davidson.

But is Firth's solution helpful? Sellars does not think it is. He challenges Firth to explain 'just what features of the sophisticated concepts expressed by our mature "looks" and "seems to see" locutions are to be found in ur-concepts that the child is able to share with us, in spite of his lack of mastery of our sophisticated vocabulary?'[60] This is a strong point against any appeal to givenness: if you say that you have access to a primitive concept which is

---

[55] W. Sellars, *EPM*, §36.

[56] W. Sellars, *EPM*, §38.

[57] See McDowell's comments on the reasons why Sellars holds on to sensations, in 'Having the World in View', pp. 442-5.

[58] Roderick Firth, 'Coherence, Certainty, and Epistemic Priority', *The Journal of Philosophy*, LXI, no. 19 (1964): 545-557, p. 547.

[59] R. Firth, 'Coherence', pp. 547f.

[60] W. Sellars, 'Givenness and Explanatory Coherence', *The Journal of Philosophy*, 70/18 (1973), pp. 612-624, p. 614.

somehow not linguistic, how do you know with which linguistic concept to pair it? Firth anticipates this critique but his pre-emptive response, namely that 'the scientist [upon learning a sophisticated new language of science, with its own ontology] does not necessarily forget how to use words in their non-technical senses; and for the same reason there is no inconsistency in maintaining that even as adults we continue to have a concept "looks red" which is logically prior to our concept "is red"'[61], is ultimately unsatisfactory because the difference is not between two linguistic usages but between a linguistic usage and a pre-linguistic 'usage'. Traditional empiricists wanted to fasten on raw feels, but these raw feels had to have their own special connection with 'primitive concepts'.

Sellars must not be interpreted as giving a theory of how the concepts which we acquire linguistically hook on sensations, impressions, inner mental events. To do so would be to repeat the illusion that we can know (in the proper sense of 'know') how mind touches on the world. His point is *post factum*: *once* we have acquired concepts, we no longer have the means to return to those primitive concepts (whether or not we can still accept that we have sensations, which Sellars actually accepts) and put them in rational contact with elements in our linguistic system. Rorty helpfully explains what Sellars is up to:

> It is not as if we might be *mistaken* in thinking that a four-year-old has knowledge but that no one-year-old does, anymore than we might be *mistaken* in taking the statutes word for the fact that eighteen-year-olds can marry freely whereas seventeen-year-olds cannot. It may be *injudicious* to take the prattle of certain four-year-olds seriously, just as it may have been injudicious to have set the age of legal responsibility so low, but no greater understanding of how knowledge (or responsibility) "works" will decide such matters.[62]

It is therefore not as if once we figure out where language begins we can also figure out what it is that constitutes knowledge, but that once language has begun there is no other way to justify knowledge than by using the linguistic concepts we have.

Let us now attempt to pull together some of the various lines of thought that were mentioned. Both Quine and Sellars reject the so-called myth of the given. For both, knowledge forms a web which must be presupposed on the whole in order to make individual statements about matter of fact. The naturalism and behaviourism which Quine espouses leads him to a naturalised account of epistemology, according to which reasons and thoughts are made into secondary explanations of patterns of response to sensory stimulation. Although Quine needs his talk of 'conceptual sovereignty' to match his talk of 'tribunal of experience', the space of reasons itself is not *sui generis* as such. It is itself a posit based on a naturalistic interpretation of behaviour. Some of

---

[61] R. Firth, 'Coherence', p. 548.

[62] This is Rorty's take on Sellars, which seems persuasive (*PMN*, p. 187).

these implicit tensions within his work are brought out with devastating force by Donald Davidson, as we shall see below. On the other hand, with Sellars we have a return to a well established sphere for rationality. 'Empiricism and the Philosophy of Mind' gives a clearer sense of the border between the space of reasons and the space of causes, while at the same time sharing Quine's Humean suspicion about causal explanations. As McDowell argues, tracing causal relations only offers us exculpations when we really needed justification. What we need is evidence, but there is no evidence that is not propositional.

The Dualism of Scheme and Content

The work of Donald Davidson is of central importance to the present essay. Although we shall devote a separate chapter to the examination of his contribution to neo-pragmatic philosophy, it is useful at this point to briefly introduce one aspect of his work: the deconstruction of the scheme-content dualism, which he dubs the 'third dogma of empiricism'. Chapters III and V show that, while Davidson can help theology understand several aspects of meaning and interpretation, there are other aspects of his work which have to be severely qualified before it is of any use to Christian theology. At this point in the argument we want to show how Davidson's argument against the third dogma of empiricism advances the neo-pragmatic agenda of giving a thick account of meaning, truth and rationality.

One major prong of Quine's attack on the analytic-synthetic distinction has been to focus on criteria of identity for meanings. Since intensions lack such identity criteria it is doubtful that they exist, let alone do any work in the theory of interpretation. Quine quickly realised that in order to substantiate this claim he would have to give more attention to translation as an empirical project. As a result of Quine's turn to translation and Davidson's transformation of his project of radical translation into one of radical interpretation, the neo-pragmatic philosopher has come very close to becoming a field linguist. However, it is important to keep things in perspective, since, contrary to Rorty's appraisal, Quine's and Davidson's philosophies do not derive from an ethnographic perspective. Rather, as Glock points out, 'Quine and Davidson use the idea of anthropological encounters as a "thought experiment" [...] or "conceptual exercise". [...] The purpose of the heuristic device is to enforce the austere approach to language and meaning that Quine and Davidson deem proper.'[63] The hope was that by focusing of cases of radical translation/ interpretation, where no prior knowledge of meanings and beliefs is presupposed, it can be shown, first, that meanings have no clear identity criteria, and second, that we do not need to appeal to entities like meanings in order to explain communication and translation.

[63] H. -J. Glock, *Quine and Davidson*, p. 167.

The fact that there are no clear identity criteria for meanings results from the fact that translation is indeterminate. Given all the evidence that there is available in a given situation, an interpreter can come up with a variety of diverging theories about what an interpretee means. Davidson is Quine's faithful student up to this point. He thinks Quine's huge contribution is in showing that all that can be learnt about meaning is learnt from studying how one learns language.[64] Although he does not wish to eliminate meanings from the ontological registry, as Quine does, Davidson remains austere with regard to their usefulness or necessity for a theory of interpretation. If such entities will have a legitimate role it is only if they play a useful role in the construction of an adequate theory. However, 'There is no reason to believe in advance that these entities will be any help, and so it cannot be an independent goal of a theory or analysis to identify the meanings of expressions or the objects of belief.'[65]

A further complication for the interpreter arises from the fact that 'beliefs and meanings conspire to account for utterances. A speaker who holds a sentence to be true on an occasion does so in part because of what he means, or would mean, by an utterance of that sentence, and in part because of what he believes.'[66] Beliefs and meanings form an intricate web into which we must somehow break if we are to make sense of the utterances of others. Davidson's and Quine's austerity forbids them from presupposing knowledge of an interpretee's beliefs, for to know what one believes is to know what one means and vice versa. Quine's and Davidson's common suggestion is that such a situation calls for the so-called principle of charity. Quine applies this principle with more reserve than Davidson, to the overall logical apparatus of the native speakers. Davidson, on the other hand, takes it to mean that speakers are generally true in their perceptual beliefs.

Assuming charity, we have to find a form of evidence which is describable in non-semantic, non-linguistic terms. Moreover, this must be the sort of evidence that the linguist has without being in possession of the theory that it is supposed to be evidence for. Here Davidson introduces a distinction between the utterance of an expression and a certain attitude towards expressions, namely that of *holding true*. Davidson then argues that we can describe the external circumstances under which such an attitude holds or fails to hold. Crucially, these are 'behavioural or dispositional facts that can be described in ways that do not assume interpretations, but on which a theory of interpretation can be based'.[67] If we could now correlate assent or dissent to a specific

---

[64] D. Davidson, 'Empirical Content', *SIO*.

[65] D. Davidson, 'Belief and the Basis of Meaning', *Inquiries into Truth and Interpretation* [*ITI*] (Oxford: Oxford University Press, 1984), p. 149.

[66] D. Davidson, 'Belief and the Basis of Meaning', *ITI*, p. 142.

[67] D. Davidson, 'Belief and the Basis of Meaning', *ITI*, p. 148.

utterance, on the one hand, with specifiable external stimulations, on the other, we have a way of ascribing both beliefs and meanings to the interpretee.

So far Quine and Davidson are on common ground. But they do diverge on a key point – the nature of the evidence required for a theory of interpretation. Whereas Quine takes sensory stimulations to provide the evidence for such a theory, Davidson gives the theory of interpretation an explicitly semantical shape, the form of a theory of truth. Quine argues for a *proximal* whereas Davidson calls for a *distal* theory of meaning. It will emerge that this difference is of crucial importance.

The only acceptable evidence for Quine is in the form of neural stimulations. Naturalised epistemology is restricted to giving an account of how, given the sensory evidence we have, we are able to form a satisfactory account of the world, to give an account of how we move from the 'meagre input' to the 'torrential output'. Davidson says that 'It is easy to remember what prompts this view: it is thought necessary to insulate the ultimate sources of evidence from the outside world in order to guarantee the authority of the evidence for the subject.'[68] For Quine, as we pointed out in the last section, distal objects are simply ways of coping with the regularities in the causal chain of stimulation. They cannot form the basis for a theory of meaning because they are themselves the object of that theory. Sensory stimulations provide a kind of evidence which can be described without reference to what it is evidence for. All that we have, according to our best science, are these patterns of stimulation. On the basis of these we must build our theory of the world, as well as our theory of interpretation. What Quine thinks he has found is a form of evidence which is not itself a belief, but upon which beliefs are built.

Although Quine is not a reductionist, he nevertheless thinks a real distinction is to be made between the invariant content (sensory stimulations) and the variant conceptual strappings, or between cues and conceptualisation. For Davidson this poses a double problem, for epistemology as well as for a theory of interpretation. Epistemologically speaking, to speak about sensory stimulation as a form of evidence which is not a belief introduces a logical gap between our subjectivity and objective externalia, and this makes for skepticism. The hypothesis of brains in a vat is a frightening possibility which becomes real when we remove thought from the world the way in which Quine does. Semantically speaking, on the other hand, we have the problem of inaccessible evidence for a theory of interpretation.

Davidson believes that theories of interpretation which rely on the notion of evidence rather than, as his does, on the notion of truth all lead to skepticism. He targets Hilary Putnam and Michael Dummett at this point and we shall engage in this debate later on. What drives these philosophers, as well as Quine's, is the 'much more general idea that empirical knowledge requires an epistemological step between the world as we conceive it and our conception of

[68] D. Davidson, 'The Myth of the Subjective', *SIO*, p. 42.

it, and this idea is at the heart of Quine's proximal theory.'[69] Dummett, Putnam and Quine all agree on the 'basic principle, which is that whatever there is to meaning must be traced back to experience somehow, the given, or patterns of sensory stimulation, something intermediate between belief and the usual objects our beliefs are about.'[70] The possibility, which this *step* between the accessible intermediaries and the 'constructed' worldview opens up, is that we conceptualise reality in radically different and incommensurable ways.

However, this is an incoherent outcome by Davidson's lights. As we shall see, to speak of a conceptual scheme is at the same time to speak of a language. But the notion of a conceptual scheme which is true but nonetheless incommensurable boils down to the possibility of a language which is untranslatable. But why should anyone suppose that a language which is untranslatable is a language nonetheless? Davidson finds no good reasons for this claim, hence the notion that there are incommensurable conceptual schemes is incoherent. *Davidson's account of knowledge and interpretation demonstrates that attitudes are already connected, causally, semantically, epistemically with real objects and events in the world.* In what follows we will attempt to present Davidson's critique of the third dogma of empiricism.

In 'On the Very Idea of a Conceptual Scheme', Davidson's unmasks Quine's reliance on a distinction between un-interpreted content and conceptual scheme. A conceptual scheme is then taken to do either of two kinds of things: a) it organises, systematises, divides up experience; or b) it fits, predicts, accounts for experience.[71] A conceptual scheme is a way of organising the content of experience (the evidence provided by the sensory stimulation). 'Something is a language, and associated with a conceptual scheme, whether we can translate it or not, if it stands in a certain relation (predicting, organising, facing, or fitting) experience (nature, reality, sensory promptings).'[72] Inasmuch as they seek to anchor knowledge on 'non-verbal rocks', both Quine and Dummett are in fact foundationalists.[73] Once we accept that we have such rocks, the possibility of constructing upon them radically diverging theories of the world becomes real.

A pivotal point in Davidson's rejection of the third dogma is the association of the notion of a conceptual scheme with that of a language. He writes

> We may accept the doctrine that associates having a language with having a conceptual scheme. The relation may be supposed to be this: where conceptual

---

[69] D. Davidson, 'Meaning, Truth, and Evidence', *Truth, Language, and History* [*TLH*] (Oxford: Oxford University Press, 2005), p. 57.

[70] D. Davidson, 'A Coherence Theory of Truth and Knowledge', *SIO*, p. 144.

[71] P.M.S. Hacker, 'On Davidson's Idea of a Conceptual Scheme', *Philosophical Quarterly* 46/184 (1996). See Davidson, 'On the Very Idea', *ITI*, p. 191.

[72] D. Davidson, 'On the Very Idea', p. 191.

[73] D. Davidson, 'A Coherence Theory', *SIO*, p. 144. More will be said about Dummett's semantics in chapter IV.

> schemes differ, so do languages. But speakers of different languages may share a conceptual scheme provided that there is a way of translating one language into the other. *Studying criteria of translation is therefore a way of focusing on criteria of identity for conceptual schemes.*'[74]

Whereas Quine focuses on the indeterminacy of translation to show that meanings have no identity criteria, Davidson focuses on the notion of translation to elucidate identity criteria for conceptual schemes. The assumption that a conceptual scheme must somehow be 'associated' (note the ambiguity here) with a language (or sets of inter-translatable languages) derives from Davidson's insistence that there is no thought without talk.

It is possible, argues Davidson, that the rejection of the analytic-synthetic distinction may still leave room for the distinction between total scheme and content. We may be tempted, he argues, to keep the notion of an empirical content. Giving up the distinction means in this case that we have rejected reductionism and we see such empirical content as being distributed across science and our total body of sentences. But the fact is that it remains a meaningful notion. The analytic-synthetic distinction deconstructed the dualism of concept and content, but it is possible to put in its place a distinction between conceptual *scheme* and un-interpreted content. Giving up the first distinction means abandoning the notion that we can clearly distinguish between theory and language. But the conclusion which Feyerabend seems to draw from this unsettles Davidson:

> Our argument against meaning invariance is simple and clear. It proceeds from the fact that usually some of the principles involved in the determinations of the meanings of older theories or points of view are inconsistent with the new … theories. It points out that it is natural to resolve this contradiction by eliminating the troublesome … older principles, and to replace them by principles, or theorems, of a new … theory. And it concludes by showing that such a procedure will also lead to the elimination of the old meanings.[75]

We have made a transition from the unrealistic supposition that we can tell for individual sentences when a change in belief entails a change in meaning or not, to the equally unrealistic idea that we must now assume that such new beliefs entail a whole set of meanings for the entire conceptual scheme.

> We get a new out of an old scheme when the speakers of a language come to accept as true an important range of sentences they previously took to be false (and, of course, vice versa). We must not describe this change simply as a matter of their coming to view old falsehoods as truths, for a truth is a proposition, and what they come to accept, in accepting a sentence as true, is not the same thing that they rejected when formerly they held the sentence to be false. A change has

[74] D. Davidson, 'On the Very Idea', *ITI*, p. 184.

[75] P. Feyerbend, quoted by Davidson, 'On the Very Idea', pp. 187-8.

> come over the meaning of the sentence because it now belongs to a new language.'[76]

Quine takes the view that new and better schemes result from better science. That is, we have to let our beliefs take their cue from science and, as the result of the new conceptuality, change the way we talk. But what would warrant us, as interpreters, in believing that a certain number of people's talk is governed by a radically untranslatable conceptual scheme? We may all take up Quine's advice and change our speech, but 'For all I know, the shiny new phrases, though stolen from the old language in which they refer to physiological stirrings [instead of emotions, feelings and thoughts], may in his mouth play the role of the messy old mental concepts.'[77]

In effect, Davidson brings to bear a radically third person perspective upon meaning and interpretation. Ironically, it is the same perspective that Quine espouses. The only available clues which can guide us in interpretation are clues having to do with publicly observable behaviour. The question of whether or not one employs a different conceptual scheme (and thus a radically untranslatable set of meanings) is not one which is to be answered in one way by the speaker and in the other by the interpreter. What we as interpreters use to fix the meaning of someone else's speech is identical with what she uses to fix the meaning of her own words.

The retention of some or all of the old vocabulary is of no help. For all I know, the speaker may intend this vocabulary in a radically different way from my own, for he has an utterly different set of beliefs about what is the case. It is his beliefs about some given element, his interpretation of that element, his conceptualisation of (as we will see momentarily) experience, which determine a new conceptual scheme. The very notion of a conceptual scheme is possible because we have retained the notion of an empirical content. This is the raw input of experience, to which we have non-conceptual access, but which we organise into a conceptualisation. Since for Quine the gap between meagre input and torrential output is vast, it seems only natural that our conceptualisations diverge as radically as they do. This, Davidson seminally argues, is the third dogma of empiricism.

Quine fails to exorcise this dualism and he is in the grip of the notion of the relativity of truth not simply to languages but to conceptual schemes. Moreover, he retains a notion of the given, an un-interpreted something which stands in an evidential relationship to the conceptual scheme: '"The totality of our so-called knowledge or beliefs ... is a man-made fabric which impinges on experience only along the edges..." [...] "As an empiricist I ... think of the conceptual scheme of science as a tool ... for predicting future experience in the light of past experience."'[78] Something is a conceptual scheme in that it is

[76] D. Davidson, 'On the Very Idea', p. 188.
[77] D. Davidson, 'On the Very Idea', p. 189.
[78] Quotes from Quine in Davidson, 'On the Very Idea', p. 191.

taken to do two sorts of things with the 'meagre input': it either organises it, or it fits it. The two metaphors are put forward as 'criteria of languagehood'. Both are problematic. First the metaphor of 'organising' experience is deficitary because one can only organise something which is plural. In other words, the content, the experience has already to be divided in order to be organised in a certain way. When an interpreter infers that the speaker is organising reality, nature, the world, in a particular way, he has to base this inference on the assumption of an ontology common to the two languages. If the ontologies massively differed, the interpreter would have no way of knowing what precisely the speaker's conceptual scheme organises, thus *a fortiori* he could not infer *that* it organises anything.

The metaphor of fitting is somewhat more difficult to reject. The case is made by the likes of Quine, that 'A sentence or theory fits our sensory promptings, successfully faces the tribunal of experience, predicts future experience, or copes with the pattern of our surface irritations, provided it is borne out by the evidence.'[79] This should be familiar territory already, for Quine's epistemology turns on the fact that all we have to go on is given by the best results of science and it is these best results that we have to work out into a 'torrential' worldview. Our worldview must fit the facts, it must cope with the data, it must serve a predictive role. For Davidson, on the other hand, this is to have things upside down:

> The point is that for a theory to fit or face up to the totality of possible sensory evidence is for that theory to be true. [...] The trouble is that the notion of fitting the totality of experience, like the notion of fitting the facts, or of being true to the facts, adds nothing intelligible to the simple concept of being true. To speak of sensory evidence rather than the evidence, of just the facts, expresses a view about the source or the nature of evidence, but it does not add a new entity to the universe against which to test conceptual schemes.[80]

The full force of Davidson's argument is evident here: Quine is wrong to come up with a special kind of entity against which a conceptual scheme is tested: sensory promptings. There is no other way to test a conceptual scheme, if we were to grant that notion, than from within a conceptual scheme, from within the body of our already existing beliefs. This is Davidson's unhappily self-described 'coherentism'. The point is that nothing can count as a justification or evidence for something if it is not a belief.[81] The whole idea of a conceptual scheme turns on the fact that we have, on the one hand, access to special un-interpreted entities like sensory promptings, which, being insulated from our cognitive apparatus, maintain a special status and authority; on the other hand, we have a conceptual scheme, which is the constructive, imaginative

---

[79] D. Davidson, 'On the Very Idea', p. 193.

[80] D. Davidson, 'On the Very Idea', pp. 193-4.

[81] See 'A Coherence Theory', p. 144, 'Empirical Content,' *SIO*, p. 164.

construction upon those bare sources of evidence. But to speak of fitting *just these* is to impose unwarranted restrictions on knowledge. On the other hand, to include all possible evidence – from sensory promptings, to facts, to everything that is taken as true given what we know so far, is to render the notion of 'fitting' secondary to the notion of truth. Davidson again:

> Our attempt to characterise languages or conceptual schemes in terms of the notion of fitting some entity has come down, then, to the simple thought that something is an acceptable conceptual scheme or theory if it is true. Perhaps better say largely true in order to allow sharers of a scheme to differ on details. And the criterion of a conceptual scheme different from our own now becomes: largely true but not translatable. The question whether this is a useful criterion is just the question how well we understand the notion of truth, as applied to language, independent of the notion of translation. The answer is, I think, that we do not understand it independently at all.[82]

Davidson goes on to say that we can only understand the notion of truth, for a given language, by connecting it to the notion of translation. To go into that argument here would require too wide a detour for our present purposes. But it should not take too much reflection to understand the weight of this argument. The very notion of a language which is largely true, but untranslatable is incoherent. If there was an incommensurable conceptual scheme (i.e. largely true but untranslatable), we would have no way of testing it, precisely because a positive test would involve accepting its truth without being able to translate it.

There is one more argument for the notion of an incommensurable conceptual scheme: partial un-translatability. If the notion of a total untranslatability is incoherent, what about partial failure of translation? Here again Quine is turned on his head. The fact that belief and meaning conspire to account for utterances allows us to a) associate conceptual scheme with languages,[83] but it also forces us to accept that without a great deal of common knowledge and assumptions, there would be no communication. 'Charity is forced upon us', writes Davidson, 'whether we like it or not, if we want to understand others, we must count them right in most matters.'[84] The only way into the web of meaning and belief is provided by counting others true on most things. Yet if we count them true, it follows that disagreement and failure of translatability can only occur and make sense on the background of massive agreement and understanding.

We may return here to a difference between Quine and Davidson already touched on. The commonality that we have to assume as a methodological requirement of interpretation is not stimuli-identity. What we have to do is 'that we must, in the plainest and methodologically most basic cases, take the objects

---

[82] D. Davidson, 'On the Very Idea', p. 194.
[83] D. Davidson, 'On the Very Idea', p. 195.
[84] D. Davidson, 'On the Very Idea', p. 197.

of a belief to be the causes of that belief. And what we, as interpreters, must take them to be is what they in fact are. Communication begins where causes converge: your utterance means what mine does if belief in its truth is systematically caused by the same events and objects.'[85] Later Davidson explains the requirements of interpretation in terms of his notion of 'triangulation':

> until the triangle is completed connecting two creatures, and each creature with common features of the world, there can be no answer to the question whether a creature, in discriminating between stimuli, is discriminating between stimuli at the sensory surfaces or somewhere further out, or further in. Without this sharing of reactions to common stimuli, thought and speech would have no particular content – that is, no content at all.[86]

For Quine, physical objects are the contingent result of our own coping with experience. They are conceptualisations and posits, based upon the meagre input of experience. They are 'reifications' which are 'decidedly part of the plot, not to be passed over as part of the setting.'[87] For Davidson, on the other hand, to assume that they are part of the plot and that the plot can be distinguished from the setting is to affirm the third dogma of empiricism, with the result of privileging one form of evidence – in the case of sensory promptings – as being the foundation upon which a conceptual scheme rests. Instead, we should refuse any such role to these 'intermediaries', since we cannot swear them to truthfulness. Their position in our body of knowledge is no more epistemically or semantically interesting than the role of other things we take to be facts.

What does the elimination of the scheme-content dichotomy mean? It all depends on whom we ask. Davidson thinks it is of a piece with the rejection of empiricism. Throughout his later work he will bring it to bear on, or against, the notion of language, of convention, of foundationalism and so on. Chapter III is dedicated to a more detailed description and discussion of Davidson's philosophical project. Thus far, we have identified three characteristics of neo-pragmatism, all of them defined in terms of rejections of so-called dogmas: the rejection of the analytic-synthetic distinction, the rejection of reductionism and the myth of the Given, and finally the rejection of the scheme-content dualism. The next section introduces the thought of Richard Rorty, who makes more explicit connections between neo-pragmatism and religion.

---

[85] D. Davidson, 'A Coherence Theory', p. 151.

[86] D. Davidson, 'Three Varieties of Knowledge', *SIO*, p. 212.

[87] Quoted in Piers Rawling, 'Radical Interpretation', in Kirk Ludwig, ed., *Donald Davidson* (Cambridge: Cambridge University Press, 2003), p. 98.

Richard Rorty on Pragmatism and Religion

For Rorty, there is no principled difference between philosophy and the history of philosophy. In *Philosophy and the Mirror of Nature*, the narrative of philosophy is interpreted through the lens of an alleged fascination with a number of unfortunate metaphors, mostly of an ocular kind. These images make it seem natural that knowledge should be conceived as 'mirroring' the world and *representing* in thought and language a reality which exists independently of our knowing, believing and desiring. Although, as Michael Williams notes,[88] Rorty's increasing scepticism with regard to the analytic tradition had been evident in his essays written during the seventies, *Philosophy and the Mirror of Nature* fell like a bombshell on the field of professional American philosophy. It would not be too much of an overstatement to say that the American academic philosophy is still not over Rorty's impact, complemented by the translation of Derrida into English.

On Rorty's reading, the history of philosophy witnessed a series of fateful turning points, ever since Descartes' turn to the subject. While Kant gives us a first real taste of what it means to do epistemology, Frege's turn to logic was an attempt to rescue philosophy as a normal discipline. Carnap continues this project with his demarcation of the internal from the external. What made possible all these attempts to view knowledge as a representation is the distinction between conceptual scheme and content. It was the concerted efforts of philosophers like Quine, Sellars, Wittgenstein, Austin, but supremely Davidson, which showed the mythical character of this distinction. The common denominator of these thinkers is a form of methodological behaviourism, according to which the only way to get at the presumed 'essence' of our beliefs, meanings, or ways of justification is by a study of how human beings come to acquire and use these concepts, meanings and justifications. This reintroduced a decisively historicist philosophical method. It is not difficult to see how foreign this might look to professional analytical philosophers. Yet Rorty himself continued to employ the tools of the analytic trade, even though he considers himself one of its undertakers. Philosophy should instead be reconfigured as another kind of literature, rather than continue in the illusion that it had some privileged access to truth. Quine had not gone far enough in his critique of Carnap's fundamental demarcation of philosophy from science.[89]

The dissolution of the scheme-content dualism prohibits us from finding a space between the world and our language (something like Quine's stimulations), from which we could sort out the contribution of our spontaneity or creativity from the world's. Such a demarcation is, for Rorty, not only a futile attempt to ground knowledge in something which does not exist in itself,

---

[88] Michael Williams, 'Rorty on Knowledge and Truth', in Charles Guinon and David R. Hiley, eds., *Richard Rorty* (Cambridge: Cambridge University Press, 2003), pp. 61f.

[89] *PMN*, p. 208.

a return to the implausible notion of *das Ding-an-sich*, but a religious and infantile attitude of deference before a non-human authority. Realists will argue that this orientation towards something outside our conceptual framework is the result of an important intuition. Rorty rubbishes this by saying that it is an obsession rather than an intuition. It is incoherent, after Davidson, to speak of a world as having intrinsic properties. To speak of properties is only possible given a certain way of speaking. Remember Davidson's arguments against notions like the 'organising' of experience. To speak of organising is already to assume that a plurality exists, but to assume a plurality is already to *count* in a certain manner. It is on other words already to possess an ontology. What this shows for Rorty is that ontology and epistemology cannot be hierarchised.

The moral of the unmasking and destruction of the third dogma of empiricism is that we cannot separate what we talk about (the Given, experience, the world, what exists) from how we talk about it (what he will later label as 'cultural politics'). While in *PMN* the obvious heroes were Quine and Sellars, there is a visible shift in preference to Davidson, coupled with an increasing identification with pragmatism. Quine remains enthralled in a kind of empiricism that is dubious for both Davidson and Rorty. Sellars on the other hand 'cannot quite get over the thought that philosophy deals with conceptual issues'[90] Both retain sympathy for what Williams calls 'demarcational projects', namely to prioritise philosophy among other discourses. On this view, philosophy is superior to literature or, say, politics because it affords us access to either what there is or to what we can speak while remaining confident of the meanings of our terms. *If philosophy is able to do that, than the question 'what is there?' is prior to the question 'what should we write about?', which would itself be prior to the question 'how should we write about it?'*

To reject the scheme-content dichotomy is to deny philosophy, according to Rorty at least, this privileged position. Sellars is nevertheless on the right track with his distinction between the space of reasons and the space of causes. Davidson takes it over from where Sellars left it to argue that nothing justifies a belief except another belief.

Now consider these two principles: the one just enounced, plus the principle that there are no 'areas of culture' with a privileged access to reality. Rorty unites these two ideas into a single whole by way of another principle which he takes over from William James: there is no hard distinction between beliefs and desires. Let us enounce the synthesis at the very outset, before we further consider it: *different areas of culture should not be ranked according to the sort of access they have to reality. Their difference lies in the specific interests and purposes that they serve.* James held that beliefs are habits of action. We always form such beliefs as ways to expedite our dealings with the world, or, as Rorty likes to say, in order to 'cope'. Inquiry is another name for problem

[90] M. Williams, 'Rorty on Knowledge and Truth', p. 67.

solving,[91] and beliefs form an important part of problem solving inasmuch as they help predict future experiences and solve past and possibly future problems. 'Attributions of reality and truth are, on the view I share with James, compliments we pay entities or beliefs that have won their spurs…'[92] There is a certain similitude to the view taken by Quine, that physical things are mere posits that we make in order to organise our sensory input into patterns. Of course, Rorty rejects the implicit assumption of a scheme-content dualism which is present in this Quinean view. Yet he retains the notion that it is impossible to speak about the things in the world except by at the same time drawing on our own dealings with them. Hence, 'On a pragmatist account, the only point of having beliefs in the first place is to gratify desires'.[93]

Again, the realist might be expected to respond: but we form desires in response to what is 'objectively there'. Rorty's preferred way of responding to this kind of critique is to place the burden of proof on the realist: to imagine that we can have an epistemic access to the world independently and prior of our passions, desires, and interests is to suppose that we could get out of our own skins and have a view from nowhere. What Quine has decidedly shown is that we have no piecemeal access to reality, which then we could map unto individual propositions to check them for correspondence to reality. The whole notion of truth as correspondence to reality has to go. Although Rorty has somewhat attenuated his rhetoric against truth (in *PMN*, truth is not something we should be talking about), partly as a result of criticisms by Charles Taylor, but also as a result of an ongoing debate with Davidson, he continues to think that the only plausible way in which the metaphysical realist can hold his view is by continuing to talk of intrinsic properties. These are properties that things have independently of any description and prior to any descriptions. If there were no people in the world, it would still make sense to say that these things have such properties.

This is precisely the view from nowhere that Rorty objects to. It is this view which held philosophy captive and gave rise to epistemology. But, Rorty asks, what sense does it make to speak of properties prior to somebody's speaking about them? 'We do not know how to find a way of describing an enduring matrix of past and present inquiry into nature except in our own terms', and 'our present view about nature are our only guide in talking about the relation

---

[91] Richard Rorty, 'The Decline of Redemptive Truth and the Rise of a Literary Culture', [http://olincenter.uchicago.edu/pdf/rorty.pdf]

[92] Richard Rorty, 'Cultural Colitics and the Question of the Existence of God', in Nancy Frankenberry, ed., *Radical Interpretation in Religion* (Cambridge: Cambridge University Press, 2002), p. 57.

[93] Richard Rorty, 'Religious faith, intellectual responsibility, and romance', *American Journal of Theology and Philosophy* 17/2 (1996), p. 126.

between nature and our words.'[94] There are no 'theory-independent' descriptions of things.

Implicit in this account common to Sellars, Davidson and Rorty is a certain 'disenchanted' view of nature, as the realm of law. As a realm of law, nature does not possess its own self-description. It is contradictory to ascribe such a description to nature, for that would amount to returning to a baneful Platonism. To hold on to a 'metaphysical realism' is to say 'that we are successfully representing according to Nature's own conventions of representation'.[95] Of course, from within a quasi-naturalist, atheistic worldview, it is difficult to entertain such a view.

If there is no such view, neither can there be areas of culture, or intellectual discourses which represent what there independently exists better than others. The upshot of this refusal to demarcate is that we no longer need to ask, 'which is true? Science or religion?'. Cultural projects cannot be categorised according to how well they represent reality, i.e., how true they are. Given that beliefs are only to be judged in relation to the sorts of different actions that they serve, we should resist the urge to unify them into a coherent whole. 'To ask "which of the their two accounts of the universe is true?" may be as pointless as asking "is the carpenter's or the particle physicist's account of tables the true one?" For neither question needs to be answered if we can figure out a strategy for keeping the two accounts from getting in each other's way.'[96] This is quite astounding, given Rorty's earlier dismissals of religion, his atheism, and his judgment against religious attitudes to life in general. But the fact remains that in his later writings Rorty has begun to develop a more positive attitude to religion, an attempt to carve out a place for religion which, as was just quoted, would not get in the way of other cultural endeavours.

His later acceptance of religion, moreover, seems to flow directly from his critique of representationalism. He argues that an advantage of the anti-representationalist view of belief which views beliefs as habits of action, is that it frees us from the responsibility to unify all our beliefs into a single world-view.[97] There need be no single world view, for there is no nature's preferred way of representation. It is partly this hegemony of nature, or any other non-human source of authority, which upsets Rorty. Yet, inasmuch as we can entertain a religious faith which does not force us into any obligation before an authority non-human, it will pass muster by Rorty's standards.

The idea of polytheism is precisely the thought that there need be no single all-encompassing description of reality. According to Rorty, we have to embrace polytheism in order to disabuse ourselves of the notion of a single

---

[94] *PMN*, p. 276.

[95] *PMN*, p. 298.

[96] R. Rorty, 'Religious Faith, Intellectual Responsibility, and Romance', p. 127.

[97] Richard Rorty, 'Pragmatism as Romantic Polytheism', in Stuart Rosenbaum, *Pragmatism and Religion* (Urbana: University of Illinois Press, 2003), p. 118.

redemptive truth. This is the conviction that a set of beliefs which can be justified to all human beings will also fill all the needs of all human beings. But, Rorty pleads, that idea was an inherently unstable compromise between the masochistic urge to submit to the non-human and the need to take proper pride in our humanity. Redemptive truth is something which is not made by human beings, but to which human beings have a special, privileged relation, not shared by animals.[98]

It is hard to miss the similarity with Kant's understanding of Enlightenment as growing to maturity and the daring to take responsibility for belief. Rorty detests earlier attempts to seek redemption from non-human sources, whether God, or nature or whatever. The image of philosophy and human culture which is embraced by Rorty is thoroughly humanistic and historicist. The great virtue of pragmatism, ventures Rorty, is that is shows us how to break the traditional link between the religious impulse (to stand in awe of something greater than oneself) and the infantile need for security, the childish hope of escaping from time and chance. Another way to put the contrast is between 'panic' (even 'guilt', a sentiment sometimes expressed by William James, to whom, for precisely this reason, Rorty prefers John Dewey), and 'healthy mindedness'.[99] Sometimes, as in the last case[100], this contrast is deployed historically, in quasi-Hegelian fashion. William James' deferent and guilt-laden attitude to the religious object is characteristic to a past phase of religious development, characterised by the turn to a belief in another being, not helped by the fact that things looked so hopeless 'in the past ages of the world'. But, thank God (sic!) 'things are different now 'because of human beings' gradual success in making their lives, and their world, less wretched. Non-religious forms of romance have flourished –if only in those lucky parts of the world where wealth, leisure, literacy, and democracy have worked together to prolong our lives and fill our libraries.'[101] It appears that not only is Rorty's philosophical methodology consciously ethnocentric, but its results are also decidedly 'white'.

The connection between religious faith and human flourishing is not at all incidental here. As was pointed out, beliefs hang together with desires and must be judged according to the interests they serve. Dewey is sometimes preferred to James for two reasons, both of which shall be discussed briefly.

First, Dewey does not have the sense of guilt which affects James. There is nothing wrong about us as we naturally stand. We have no duty before any extra-human reality. Indeed, all that is wrong with us is that the Christian ideal of fraternity has not yet been achieved, but this is not something that can be solved by recourse to a higher authority, but by human effort alone.[102] In

---

[98] Richard Rorty, 'The Decline of Redemptive Truth', p. 10.

[99] R. Rorty, 'Religious Faith, Intellectual Responsibility, and Romance', pp. 137f.

[100] But see also 'The Decline of Redemptive Truth'.

[101] R. Rorty, 'Religious Faith, Intellectual Responsibility, and Romance', p. 137.

[102] R. Rorty, 'Pragmatism as Romantic Polytheism', p. 121.

connection to this Dewey argues that even if Jesus told you something, this would only be revelation, when embodied in a life. Rorty loves this: 'even if a nonhuman authority tells you something, the only way to figure out whether what you have been told is true is to see whether it gets you the sort of life you want.'[103] There is no telling of truth in isolation from ones desires and wants. Again, the Kantian connection is strong: if something is to have authority over us, it can only do so by our appropriating it in furthering our own projects of flourishing. This is a very significant aspect of Rorty's interpretation of religion and it will receive further comment below.

The second significant aspect where Dewey is to be preferred to James is in his non-intellectualism. Although James is the first to point out the passional character of beliefs, he sometimes tries to go beyond the subjective element and make inquiry into the intellectual content of the faith itself. But to suspect that one could sort out the passional component from the intellectual component is to be once again tempted by projects of demarcation: the serious from the frivolous, the literal from the symbolic, the cognitive from the non-cognitive. We should replace all these distinctions, argues Rorty, by the distinction between projects of social cooperation and projects of individual self-development. Both kinds of projects involve the passions, yet the latter is distinguished from the former by its private character. Religion is one such private project. Instead of going after the intellectual content of religious faith, James should have been content with what he said in 'The Will to Believe', namely that we are free to believe whatever we want in our free time, but when we engage in projects of cooperation, we abandon this right.[104] Since religion is a private project, we should not allow its intellectual content to get in the way of other social projects. In religion, redemption does not and should not come from justifying oneself in front of others.

Religion is such a project of self-development. Like with Dewey, it does not matter what is the source of the material which helps one flourish. The object of belief does not matter. To have matured means to have understood that redemption does not come from outside oneself, or from a non-human reality, or from one's ability to defend oneself before others. As Nicholas H. Smith puts it, 'Redemption involves a self-developing, self-transforming, and in a manner of speaking "self-completing" encounter with something larger than oneself. The desire for redemption can be made good by the participation in the life of this awe-inspiring thing.'[105] Central to this contention is that it is what the relation *does* to one's development that is important for redemption, rather than the propositional content of the faith.

---

[103] R. Rorty, 'Pragmatism as Romantic Polytheism', p. 121.

[104] R. Rorty, 'Pragmatism as Romantic Polytheism', p. 121.

[105] Nicholas H. Smith, 'Rorty on Religion and Hope', *Inquiry* 48/1 (2005): 76-98, p. 82.

Rorty tries to explain the specific difference of religion by describing it as a relation to an awesome being, a relationship which *should not* involve the claim of knowing that being's will.[106] Only by preserving this distinction can religion be kept in the private realm. This relation, whether of adoring obedience, or ecstatic communion, or quiet confidence, or some combination of these,[107] is not something which should be mediated by a creed. Indeed, Rorty at times seems to encourage a non-cognitive approach to religious faith. This is not exactly to say that the objects of religious belief should be treated instrumentally. Quite the contrary, God is as real as tables, electrons and quarks.[108] Following James, this time, the question is not whether religion is cognitive or non-cognitive, because there is no precise line of demarcation between these as we have seen. Now it is a question whether the sorts of beliefs we entertain in our projects of individual self-development (e.g., religion) can be held in good conscience, 'even after I realize that I cannot justify this belief to others.'[109] The point is not that some religious beliefs have to be abandoned because we have realised that they have no objective referent. No beliefs, whether scientific, or religious, should be subjected to that sort of analysis. The only analysis which counts is whether the beliefs that I have help me live the life I want. The only restriction, when it comes to beliefs of the private sort is whether or not they get in the way of other beliefs, serving other purposes and areas of culture, especially those of mutual cooperation.

What should partly characterize religious beliefs, then, is that they are not the sort of beliefs that we have to justify to other people. This is essential for Rorty's armistice between religion and science. Yet Rorty renders this characteristic in three very different manners: religious beliefs a) do not stand in inferential relationships to other beliefs; or, b) are unjustifiable;[110] or c) do not have to be justified. These three descriptions are used inter-changeably and seem to be regarded by Rorty as equivalent. Yet they are certainly not equivalent and their differences are quite important. Further, Rorty uses the analogy of *love* in order to explain the peculiar character of religious faith and its quasi non-propositional character. 'Our intellectual responsibilities are responsibilities to cooperate with others on common projects designed to promote the general welfare [...] and not to interfere with their private projects. For the latter projects - such as getting married or getting religion – the question of intellectual responsibility does not arise.'[111] Along these lines, we have to distinguish sharply between faith and belief, just as we distinguish

---

[106] R. Rorty, 'Religious Faith, Intellectual Responsibility, and Romance', p. 122.
[107] R. Rorty, 'The Decline of Redemptive Truth', p. 6.
[108] R. Rorty, 'Religious Faith, Intellectual Responsibility', p. 130.
[109] R. Rorty, 'Religious Faith, Intellectual Responsibility', p. 129.
[110] R. Rorty, 'Religious Faith, Intellectual Responsibility', p. 134.
[111] R. Rorty, 'Religious Faith, Intellectual Responsibility', p. 128.

between loving someone and the beliefs one might have about that person. Rorty should be allowed to speak at length here: '

> People often say that they would not be able to go on if it were not for their love for their spouse or their children. This love is often not capable of being spelled out in beliefs about the character, or the actions, of these beloved people. Further, this love often seems inexplicable to people acquainted with those spouses and children – just as inexplicable as faith in God seems to those who contemplate the extent of seemingly unnecessary human misery. But we do not mock a mother who believes in her sociopathic child's essential goodness, even when that goodness is visible to no one else.[112]

The essential characteristic implied here is that religious faith seems to obtain despite all of these other beliefs a person might have. The central point for Rorty is that faith, as faith rather than belief, is not in inferential links with other beliefs.

This creates an obvious problem for Rorty: 'can we disengage religious belief from inferential links with other beliefs by making them too vague to be caught by a creed – by fuzzying them up in Tillichian ways – and still be faithful to the familiar pragmatist doctrine that beliefs have content only by virtue of inferential relations to other beliefs?'[113] *If beliefs get their content by their relations to other beliefs (rather than by direct contact with reality), and if religious beliefs do not stand in such relations to other beliefs, how can we be confident of the meaning that they have?* Rorty's solution is that there is a practice, other than justification, by which such private utterances have their content. This is the practice of ascribing beliefs in order to make sense of behaviour, to 'explain what is going on'. Then,

> We can give content to an utterance like "I love him" or "I have faith in Him" by correlating such utterances with patterns of behaviour, even when we cannot do so by fixing the place of such utterances in a network of inferential relations. For such utterances do help us figure out what the utterers are likely to do in various situations, and hence help us figure out how to coordinate our own actions with theirs.[114]

This is definitely too simple. Rorty is right that love cannot be explained by a given number of beliefs that we might have about the loved person, or about ourselves, indeed about anything. But that is not to say that it can be explained in isolation from these. To say that the affection we call love comes *despite* all sorts of belief that we have is not at all to say that it is *not* in inferential relationships to these. If it weren't we could not even say that it comes *in spite* of these, for that would take away the force of 'despite'. A further aspect is relevant here, but since it presupposes a future discussion of Davidson, only a

---

[112] R. Rorty, 'Religious Faith, Intellectual Responsibility', p. 133.
[113] R. Rorty, 'Religious Faith, Intellectual Responsibility', p. 133.
[114] R. Rorty, 'Religious Faith, Intellectual Responsibility', p. 134.

very short-hand version can be given here. Davidson's theory of interpretation instructs interpreters to ascribe beliefs and meaning at the same time, by correlating the (un-interpreted) beliefs and meanings of the native with the beliefs and meanings that we have in the same situation. In order for an interpreter to be able to ascribe beliefs, at least two sorts of things need to be shared: the causes which prompt the native to hold his beliefs – these must be the same causes that prompt the interpreter to form his beliefs; secondly, the speaker and interpreter must share an overwhelming majority of beliefs, in order for the interpreter to be able to ascribe to the native the beliefs that he has formed as a result of interacting with the common causes. Hence, the only way in which we can attribute anything on the basis of behaviour – in this case a faith or love – is if we can correlate it with similar behaviour that we have, similar causes and indeed shared beliefs. We are forced to assume inferential relations if we want to keep any hope of attributing beliefs to others.

Rorty complicates his case by commending the Tillichians for thinking that they can get away without beliefs, because 'they think the point of religion is not to produce any *specific* habit of action, but rather to make the sort of difference to a human life that is made by the presence or absence of love.'[115] The implicit admission here is that religion can be conceived in such an individualist-private fashion only at the cost of losing its purchase on life, of renouncing the notion of a specifically religious behaviour. The obvious question is: *if there is no specifically religious behaviour, on what basis can we ascribe specifically religious beliefs*?

Privatising religion like this comes at a great cost. Descriptively speaking, it fails to take account of the fact that, as Gregory L. Reece puts it, religious people justify their religious beliefs to other people all the time, hence, 'Rorty's proposal to find a place for religious beliefs in society comes at a high cost: cutting them off from the communities in which they have their home.'[116] *The social and communitarian aspect of religious faith is integral to its content.*

Another consequence of this understanding of religious faith is a '*deflation of the ontological stature of "God-talk*"'[117] All sorts of contrary signals are being emitted at this point too. On the one hand, Rorty denies he is being an instrumentalist, while on the other he proposes a demythologization or resymbolisation of certain centrally Christian symbols: 'Pragmatist theists, however, do have to get along without Personal Immortality, Providential Intervention, the efficacy of the sacraments, the Virgin Birth, the Risen Christ, the Covenant of Abraham, the authority of the Koran, and a lot of other things which many theists are loath to do without. Or, if they want them, they will

---

[115] R. Rorty, 'Religious Faith, Intellectual Responsibility', p. 132.

[116] Gregory L. Reece, 'Religious Faith and Intellectual Responsibility: Richard Rorty and the Public/Private Distinction', *American Journal of Theology and Philosophy*, 22/3 (Sept 2001), p. 213.

[117] N. Smith, 'Rorty', p. 80 (our emphasis).

have to reinterpret them symbolically'.[118] What should prompt religious believers to drop these beliefs? According to Rorty's theory, it should not be science, for it deals with different purposes. The only other possible source of critique is whether continuing to talk about these things helps or hinders human flourishing.

For Rorty, the question of the existence of God and the question of whether and how we should continue to talk about Him are inextricable from one another. 'Cultural politics should replace ontology', he writes. To this extent, talk of God is like talk of 'human rights' or 'race'. It makes no sense to separate inquiry into the existence of these notions from the question of whether we should continue to speak about human rights or race, and if it helps us create a better society if we do. Rorty thinks the question of how do we tell (if ever) when a question about what exists should be discussed independently of our socio-political goals – is a rhetorical one. This flows directly from the notion of beliefs which he inherits from James. Thus, the ontological priority of God, nature, world and so on, is replaced with the priority of the 'social', following Robert Brandom. We have not discussed the latter's inferentialism, but the arguments are very similar to Davidson's. There is, Brandom argues, no authority beyond that of society. It is useless to invoke divine authority, or the authority of mother nature because the reality of the conflict of interpretations. Given such a conflict, what will decide the issue is precisely what will have authority. For Brandom, assertions are assumptions of social responsibilities. The authority attributed to the non-human can be explained sociologically, with no need to invoke mysterious beings such as God, the intrinsic nature of reality and so on. This should be a familiar position by now: it is an argument that for something to be authoritative, it must be epistemic. Since God, allegedly, is not in such a position, nor is nature, the authority that we think derives from these concepts actually derives from social norms. Although we invoke their authority in support of our assertions, they serve no real, but only an illusory role. Concepts like God and nature are disguised moves in the game of cultural politics, and that is 'the only game in town'.[119] Such concepts figure in the machinery of our justification-talk, *but they turn no wheels*, they serve no purpose. The actual wheels are turned by something else, and that is society.

What Dewey has said about testing the truth of Jesus' claims by seeing whether it gets you the sort of life you want, drives home the same point. In neo-pragmatism, authority has shifted from 'objective' reality, from ontology, not to epistemology, but to society. The present essay is a sustained argument against this epistemising of authority. But a fuller deployment of countermeasures will have to await further chapters. Given the introductory nature of this first chapter, not much space could be reserved to critical debates, but some salient points do need to me made.

---

[118] R. Rorty, 'Religious Faith, Intellectual Responsibility', p. 130.

[119] R. Rorty, 'Cultural Politics', p. 58.

There is a certain disanalogy between talk about race and human rights, on the one hand, and talk about God, on the other. Although the disanalogy is perceived from the religious perspective, it is nonetheless persuasive, even if only for interpretative reasons. While the concepts of 'race' and 'human rights' are reifications of abstract realities, the concept of God designates a personal reality. Rorty could and should grant this much, or his analogy of love would lose most of its force, though conceivably not all.[120] In terms of ontological commitment, Rorty puts God on the same level as tables, chairs, electrons and so on. Talk about their existence is part of our attempts to cope with the world and create a better life. While Quine talked about these notions as posits necessary for the organisation of our stimulatory input, this is too empiricist for Rorty and it assumes the scheme-content dualism. But Rorty, just as much as Quine, subordinates our ontological talk about such entities to our pragmatic talk about their usefulness. Moreover, it will appear at some point in the history of inquiry that some of these notions 'turn no wheels', hence we can and perhaps should dispense with them.

Here is the problem. Brandom argues that we should apportion no authority to those items over which conflicts of interpretation arise. But on that logic, we should ascribe no more authority to people than we ascribe to nature, or God, simply because conflicts of interpretation are bound to arise when we interpret the speech of others. This would amount to saying that a general has no authority over his troops simply because his orders are always subject to distorted understanding. Putnam and Cavell make this point brilliantly: my statements about, say, Caesar, are not simply statements that I make in relation to my attempts to cope, but are utterances about another human being. I cannot simply think of Caesar, or any other name, as another language-game, one which enables me to cope. Putnam views this as a kind of scepticism which is 'infinitely remote from our actual form of life'.[121] This is a kind of scepticism and, someone like Charles Taylor might say, solipsism, because it takes its starting point with the human subject and his attempts to cope. *Such an attitude would displace the whole question of whether it is acceptable to hurt other people. Hence, there is a difference between scepticism about other people and scepticism about 'middle sized dry goods'.*

The point we have laboured is that the criteria according to which we cannot allot authority to God and nature (conflict of interpretations) should also prohibit us from recognising the authority of other human beings. But to say that these human beings have authority, at least in respect of clarifying for us what they mean, is part of a picture with an enormous human weight. Possible

---

[120] R. Rorty could retreat into speaking of a supra-human reality, i.e. society, which is not necessarily personal.

[121] H. Putnam, 'Does the Disquotational Theory of Truth Solve all Philosophical Problems?', in Putnam, edited by James Conant, *Words and Life* (Cambride, MA: Harvard University Press, 1994), p. 276.

mis-understandings, even undecidability, should not count against that authority. Neo-pragmatism, with its relocation of meaning in the public space between speaker and interpreter misses out on part of that picture.[122]

This concluding section of our first chapter introduced Richard Rorty's philosophy of religion. Some of the conspicuous themes which Rorty develops, which could not be adequately addressed due to lack of space, themes like historicism, cultural politics, the epistemic nature of authority, the public/private distinction, the importance of democracy, figure prominently in American pragmatic theology. The next chapter discusses various theological appropriations of the pragmatic, but especially the neo-pragmatic tradition in the American context. We shall trace the way in which major neo-pragmatic emphases are employed theologically.

[122] See our discussion of Davidson's notion of first-person authority in chapter 5.

Chapter 2

Pragmatic and Neo-Pragmatic Theological Options

Neo-Pragmatic Justifications of Religious Belief

With this chapter we advance to a more specifically theological and religion-philosophical discussion of the bearing of neo-pragmatism. One major assumption of this study is that significant differences divide neo-pragmatists like Rorty, Putnam, Goodman, Fish and others from Donald Davidson. It will also be suggested that these differences are significant from a theological standpoint. In order to clearly demarcate these two different strands of neo-pragmatic influence, we are proposing two separate discussions, the first of which is the task of the present chapter, the second being the object of chapter IV. More to the point, this chapter engages with the work of a variety of theologians who take their philosophical bearing from Rorty, besides some of the classical pragmatists like James and Dewey. Divisions are not always neat and they can sometimes more closely resemble dissections. This case is no different, but there is a very good reason for that. While we argue that significant divergences set Rorty *et. comp.* apart from Donald Davidson, this view is not shared by many theologians who tend to lump them together. This is understandable given Rorty's own insistence on enlisting Davidson for his own project. To be sure, a significant overlap exists between the two philosophers, which is why Davidson is also considered to be a neo-pragmatist. But it is rather the differences between these prominent figures that we are more interested in; and we will argue that these differences are theologically significant. Thus, for example, our discussion of J. Wesley Robbins as a theologian from the Rortian camp is not a wilful concealment of the fact that he is, perhaps in an equal measure, claiming the support of Donald Davidson. If the argument is correct, Robbins reads Davidson through Rorty and tends to minimize the differences between them.

Thus, as a matter of methodological clarification, the theologians which form the object of analysis in this chapter, are those who more readily endorse a Rortian neo-pragmatism (including a Rortian reading of Davidson). Three sets of issues will be discussed. The first section discusses the bearing of neo-pragmatism on questions of theological justification. The second and third sections respectively deal with the issue of revisionism and the meaning of orthodoxy, and the deflation of the ontological stature of God-talk.

Pragmatic and neo-pragmatic theology[1] is a radical rejection of foundationalism. If Rorty is right that we must drop the distinction between knowledge by acquaintance and knowledge by description, then neither can theology find a resting place in some certain knowledge, e.g. revelation, on which to base the rest of its beliefs. The image of Neurath's boat has become something like a guiding analogy for neo-pragmatists. For Rorty, we cannot separate what we talk about from how we talk about it. The moral he draws from this claim is that we should simply concentrate on cultural politics. We should not waste our time looking for skyhooks for our language, something which could then guide the rest of our epistemic efforts. Knowledge is simply a matter of experimenting with different vocabularies and seeing how far these take us into creating a better life, achieving our purposes, our country etc. There is nothing ahistorical by reference to which a certain cultural politics is either good or bad, true or false.

Theological claims and religious beliefs should be no different. Theology and religion, as a specific area of culture, is not inferior to philosophy or science. Formerly such an alleged inferiority was postulated on the basis of the difference in the degree in which these cultural discourses are based upon experience. But science, just as much as theology, is justified according to the efficiency with which it can expedite our dealings with the world. In his own way, Rorty continues the tradition of Schleiermacher and Ritschl, namely their quest to carve out a safe haven for religion, and implicitly theology. Whereas for Schleiermacher religion was romantically assigned to feeling, the feeling of ultimate dependence, and Ritschl attempts to correct his predecessor's hopeless subjectivism by turning to practical life and ethics, Rorty returns to the former's emphasis upon individuality. If religion is that private hope which helps one entertain one's dreams and forge one's identity, without getting in the way of public life, it is an entirely legitimate discourse. But the way in which religious claims are to be tested is not by recourse to public norms and criteria – for it is an entirely private affair – but by judging how useful it is for one's private hopes.

Ritschlian theology oscillated and eventually split, under the tension between two different attitudes to the past, especially to Jesus. Dogmatic Ritschlians sought to keep both the practical and valuational aspects of Ritschl's theology, as well as the normativity of Jesus' teaching. An essence from the past had to be kept, by reference to which theological claims had to be tested. On the other hand, theologians more influenced by the *Religionsgeschichtlicheschule* conceived religion entirely in socio-historical terms. This more radical historicism gave up treating the past as a source of truth, a tribunal before which we are responsible. In Rorty's words, the past was beginning to be treated 'as material for playful experimentation rather than

---

[1] As will become clear, these designations are not synonymous.

as imposing tasks and responsibilities upon us.'[2] Theology's task became more descriptive, with respect to the past. This socio-historical sensibility was one of the hallmarks of the Chicago School of theology, which is one of the precursors of today's neo-pragmatic theology. One of the pioneers of the new historicism at Chicago, George Burman Foster, taught that 'the validity of a category of any kind, including a religious category, is not rightly determined by referring to some hypothetical cause, but rather by observing its value to the life of the human spirit.'[3] What theologians must do is to analyze the deep history of religious ideas, charting their path through history, mining the cultural and political influences which led to their formation. This was, however, not to remain a strictly descriptive exercise. It was a keen sense of value which qualified this historicism, inasmuch as the theologian must not only describe the life-history of an idea, but also *judge* its felicity and propriety for today. Gradually, an analysis of the usefulness of an idea was substituted for an analysis of its historical pedigree. Foster's distinction between 'hypothetical causes' and 'value to the life of the human spirit' can be seen to prefigure the neo-pragmatic distinction between causes and reasons. Yet for Foster this distinction was not motivated by something like Sellars' and Davidson's critique of the myth of the given. It was rather embedded in an eminently practical, non-dogmatic and specifically American attitude to life.

While Foster had certain reservations about the application of historicism to Christian theology, insisting that metaphysical questions still had to be asked, Shirley Jackson Case had no such misgivings. He maintained that the test for religious truth is functional significance, not the source from which it derives. The meaning of 'God', 'atonement' and other Christian theological notions can only be discovered by reconstructing the social settings in which these concepts were employed throughout history and they can have meaning for modern people only if they are translated into modern concepts. Religion was for Case the communal reconstruction of the past in order to meet new social needs. While supernaturalism was true for the ancient church because it worked for that age, it does not work today, hence it must be abandoned. Newer forms have become 'more efficient in supporting the ideals and aims of Christian living in a modern world'.[4] Interestingly, for Case, there was such a thing as 'the ideals and aims of Christian living', which are worth preserving for their own sake. William Dean spots the problem with this dualism between the temporality of Christian doctrines, which must be evaluated in terms of their

---

[2] Quoted in Cornel West, *The American Evasion of Philsophy: A Genealogy of Pragmatism* (Madison: University of Wisconsin Press, 1989), p. 198.

[3] Gary J. Dorrien, *The Making of American Liberal Theology: Idealism, Realism, and Modernity: 1900-1950* (Westminster/John Knox Press, 2003), p. 171.

[4] Quoted from J. Case, in William Dean, *History Making History: The New Historicism in American Religious Thought* (Albany: State University of New York Press, 1988), p. 53.

socio-historical felicity, and the eternal nature of Christian attitudes, aims, values, which constitute the permanent element in religion. But this is a problem inherent to pragmatic, functionalist interpretations of religion.

The test for religious truth was no longer its historic source, but its significance for present human experience. The question which must be asked is, *what norms and criteria tell us whether an idea has been useful, or successful, or efficient*? To speak about the permanence of Christian values from within a historicist perspective poses the question about the normativity of those values themselves. Why should these attitudes and aims be regarded as somehow exempt from the test of usefulness? Yet if we subject them to the test, by what criteria are we to know whether they passed it? This problem of norms is a pressing one, for neo-pragmatist thinkers like Rorty suggest that they are able to speak of justification in terms of success. Yet *they fail to explain what success means and who is to tell us whether we have found it.* Rorty candidly acknowledges this: 'we do not know what "success" would mean except simply "continuance."'[5] This is candid indeed, but as we will hope to show, not candid enough, for we should not be so confident that we know even what 'continuance' would mean.

Sheila Greeve Davaney

So what are these norms by which pragmatic efficiency is judged? Clearly, normativity is something that all neo-pragmatists want. But can one still talk of norms if one is a new-, or radical-, historicist? Sheila Greeve Davaney thinks that one can. Davaney calls herself a 'pragmatic historicist'. Her theology draws equally on Rorty, Jeffrey Stout, and Cornel West in an attempt to secure a substantive notion of norms for pragmatic justification. She claims that 'for pragmatic historicists, we need to forego the notions of sites of authority and replace them with sites of responsibility. And for pragmatists, it is the present which is finally the locus of authority.'[6] To treat the present as the site of authority is not to absolutise it in a Hegelian fashion. The norms derived from the present are still historical norms, and not the end result of a process of rational evolution. Quite the opposite, 'Contemporary visions and norms are, like all others, thoroughly historical and hence partial, reflective of location, infused with interest and laden with power; they are transient, contingent, and eminently revisable, just as they are finally unavoidable.'[7] This does not mean that a pragmatic theology should rest content with the justifications and norms

---

[5] Richard Rorty, 'Pragmatism, Relativism, and Irrationalism', *Consequences of Pragmatism* (Minneapolis: University of Minnessotta Press, 1982), p. 172.

[6] Sheila Greeve Davaney, 'Judging Theologies: Truth In An Historicist Perspective', *Pragmatism, Neo-Pragmatism, and religion: Conversations with Richard Rorty*, ed. Charley D. Hardwick and Donald A. Crosby (New York: Peter Lang, 1997), p. 140.

[7] S. G. Davaney, 'Judging Theologies', pp. 140-141.

provided within one's own community. Davaney critiques Lindbeck's postliberalism for treating communities as self-enclosed systems, with a stable depth grammar, despite their changing vocabularies. 'Lindbeck finally presents a very undynamic, ahistorical interpretation of cultural-linguistic traditions.[8]' Davaney wants to find a way to refuse 'The unenviable choice for theologians [which] appears to be a retreat to the distinctive languages of their traditions hence gaining uniqueness but at the price of being ignored by their secular cohorts, or losing their distinctive voice, thus also courting irrelevance.'[9] Davaney attempts to imagine precisely such a third option. She proposes an 'expansive pragmatic historicism', which views traditions as porous rather than unitary and self-contained. If traditions are not unitary, it makes no sense to speak of an intra-textual approach. An expansive historicism 'must ask [its] questions not only at the centers of traditions but at their margins and of those who are not practitioners of a tradition, but experience its impact daily.'[10] Pragmatic testing must be carried out on 'the broadest field', rather than on local fields 'belonging' to particular traditions.

Yet what are these norms? Davaney admits that a more substantive description of the norms involved is necessary, but she immediately adds that such an analysis of norms can only be given in specific historical situations. In other words, we cannot and should not have a theory of norms with which to approach particular situations. Despite her plea for a more substantive notion of norms – by which she probably means one filled with some kind of content – Davaney eventually fails to spell out in concrete terms what those norms should be. But hiding behind the excuse that such norms must be decided in concrete relevant situations is the question of how do we know what those relevant practical situations and contexts are? In the absence of norms, or of a minimal theory, how do we sort what is relevant from what is unimportant for our debate? She makes a gesture in the direction of admitting this necessity by accepting a single 'general norm': 'namely, the substantive criterion of how well our visions, beliefs, or practices enhance or fail to enhance our historicized existence, an existence that is embedded in the thick web of natural and human history.'[11] Still further questions are begged by this requirement, of which we shall identify but two: *first, how would such a general norm be justified*? Does it itself derive from a historical experience, or does it covertly claim a justification which transcends history? Secondly, it is difficult to see in what its substantiveness consists, given that to speak of 'enhancing our historicized

[8] Sheila G. Davaney, *Pragmatic Historicism: A Theology for the Twenty-First Century* (Albany: State University of New York Press, 2000), p. 38. We have made the same point in our extensive critique of Lindbeck's postliberalism, *Postliberal Theological Method: A Critical Study* (Carlisle: Paternoster, 2005).

[9] S. G. Davaney, *Pragmatic Historicism*, p. 140.

[10] S. G. Davaney, 'Judging Theologies', p. 142.

[11] S. G. Davaney, 'Judging Theologies', p. 144.

existence' does not say anything specific about what an enhanced existence might consist in. Nonetheless, *Davaney's plea for normativity is praiseworthy, even while she ultimately fails to specify both the specific content of norms, and their source or justification.* Moreover, it is difficult to avoid the conclusion that *her distancing from postliberal insularism oversteers into a vaguely defined, almost universal context of inquiry and justification.* It is hard to notice the dividing line between seeking 'to ensure that as many voices as are relevant and possible are part of the process of framing the questions',[12] and an 'ideal community of inquiry'.

William Dean

We have suggested that, besides arguing that norms are important in a pragmatic inquiry, there is a stringent need to specify where those norms come from and why they should be regarded as such. One of Davaney's conversation partners, whose proposals she ultimately finds if not unsatisfactory then at least 'problematic', is William Dean. He argues that values can be accounted for in historical experience without violating either pragmatism or historicism. This is precisely what Davaney argues, but the difference consists in how Dean proposes to do the accounting. Davaney's problem is to reconcile a neo-pragmatism (she usually calls it 'historicism', while Dean calls it a 'new historicism') which insists on the maxim that justification is not a matter of appeal to eternal truths, or to bits of the Given, with a perceived need to hold for values and norms in pragmatic historicism. For Dean it is not neo-pragmatism that needs to be reconciled to normativity, for neo-pragmatism itself has taken a wrong turn. In *History Making History* Dean laments the Continental turn in Rorty's neo-pragmatism, at the cost of forgetting his American cultural and historical roots. By turning away from the 'empirical piety' of a James or Royce, the new historicists find it impossible to account for the values which permeate their own judgments. James' radical empiricism contrives to exhibit a religious naturalism, its attendant idea of God, and an experience of values in historical experience. Of course, it is this part of James that Rorty does not like, as we saw in the last chapter. 'When they [today's new historicists] do turn to them [classical American pragmatists], it is for their pragmatic method, not for their empiricism, and certainly not for their insights about the way this empiricism yields values.'[13] Interestingly, Davaney too opts

---

[12] S. G. Davaney, *Pragmatic Historicism*, p. 187.

[13] W. Dean, *History Making History*, p. 75. Dean's rebuke to Rorty is gentle, even congratulatory, by comparison with John E. Smith's harsh words: 'Like the Prodigal Son, Rorty, who has repented of his former views and discovered pragmatism, is rewarded with the fatted calf while those of us who stayed within the fold and upheld the insights of the pragmatists when it was not popular to do so are treated only to an opportunity to hear Rorty tell us what we already know.' (John E. Smith, 'Experience,

for a 'procedural pragmatism' which stops short of importing the radical empiricism of James.

According to Dean, the Chicago school of theology was fully historicist sixty years before the new historicism. Their historicism did not exclude a religious option, but complemented it, while it was also a value-laden historicism. Such an accounting for values is necessary, lest the new pragmatism be a 'floating pragmatism', given that it lacks its basis in empirical piety. The new pragmatism, charges Dean, speaks about the interaction between our discourses, beliefs, faiths and the environment, social history, culture and politics, without knowing the reasons for the interaction. Dean hits where it hurts the most: how does one know when an idea has proved satisfactory? What does it mean to cope with new environments?[14]

According to Dean, 'history yields criteria'.[15] History is not simply 'the stage and judge of facts, but of relations, qualities, and values as well.'[16] This view of history (and nature) is extremely significant, for it renounces a dualist view which juxtaposes the mind, with its organising categories of spontaneity, to the world, as something which is neuter and awaiting schematisation. As Dewey puts it, 'The live animal does not have to project emotions into the objects experienced. Nature is kind and hateful, bland and morose, irritating and comforting long before she is mathematically qualified or even a congeries of "secondary" qualities like colours and their shapes.'[17] The values themselves are derived from historical experience and not something imposed upon it.

Dean, like John E. Smith, is opposed to the neo-pragmatic insistence that it is language and texts all the way down. Such a preoccupation with language resulted in an exaggerated neo-pragmatic obsession with method, a 'historicist methodologism,'[18] to the neglect of saying something positive about God. Instead, theologians should have the courage to follow James and Dewey and say something positive about God, as the 'something urging the growth of value in the historical process.'[19] Yet despite all this resolve to say something positive about God, in the end Dean says precious little about it. God remains for Dean the source of value, something vague and fuzzy, something underlying the totality of experience.

It is not hard to anticipate why Davaney should be unhappy with Dean's radical empiricism. On the one hand, 'What Dean's position does not provide, however, is a way beyond the fallibility and partiality of the evaluative process

---

God, and Classical American Philosophy', *American Journal of Theology and Philosophy* 14/2, 1993, p. 135).

[14] W. Dean, *History Making History*, p. 82.

[15] W. Dean, *History Making History*, p. 83.

[16] W. Dean, *History Making History*, p. 105.

[17] Quoted in W. Dean, *History Making History*, p. 107.

[18] W. Dean, *History Making History*, p. 124.

[19] W. Dean, *History Making History*, p. 136.

and the values that shape it in any given moment.'[20] This is an entirely sensible judgment. Dean's radical empiricism is committed to taking experience at face value. But when it comes to experience, there are a number of factors should be brought to bear before it can be of any epistemic use. Neo-pragmatism is all too aware of this, as we shall see below. Davaney is again dead right: 'to say that history yields criteria, even if we could make them clear, does not solve our problems of judgment, for history yields *all* criteria, including conflicting ones.' But Davaney continues this with yet another blow: 'Explaining where criteria or values come from is not giving a justification (or indeed falsification) of them.'[21] We have separated the two quotations for they make different points, the last one being specifically neo-pragmatic: to allege that a norm has a certain historical filiation has no bearing on justification. It does not end the process of legitimation, but merely plays a part in it. To maintain, as Davaney does, that causes *do* play a part, if only a part, in the process of justification is to say that her distinction between causes and reasons is not exactly the same as the one found in Sellars, Rorty, and Davidson. For the notion of cause, as found in these philosophers, restricts those items which are causes from being in epistemic contact of any kind, including playing minor roles in justifications.[22]

Davaney's criticism of Dean leads her to seek an appropriate context of justification, and this context can only be historical, cultural and social. It is within such a context that we have norms, beliefs and reasons – and only these can play a part in the process of justification. It perhaps should be pointed out, in view of later discussion, that D. C. Macintosh voiced a similar criticism of experience-based theologies, himself being an empirical theologian. The empiricist subjectivism in the work of Schleiermacher and Ritschl had to be objectified. A pragmatic religious science must get beyond the critically-unverified religious common sense.[23] For Macintosh, experience is not the measure of religious value, but only the means by which to describe the object known to it. This critical stance towards experience led Macintosh to a critical realist position. Experience does not mediate its contents, especially its religious contents, *immediately*. One must possess a 'right religious adjustment'[24], before one is able to turn this experience into a basis for theological judgment. He then goes on to speak of *laws* according to which God responds and presents himself in experience to the person attuned in such a way. The right religious posture has nothing to do with any normative description of Christianity, whether it be found in Scripture, tradition, or the

[20] S. G. Davaney, *Pragmatic Historicism*, p. 184.

[21] S. G. Davaney, *Pragmatic Historicism*, p. 183.

[22] Davaney imports her distinction between causes and reasons from Sandra Harding, see *Pragmatic Historicism*, p. 151.

[23] See D. C. Macintosh, *Theology as Empirical Science* (New York: Macmillan, 1919), p. 24.

[24] D. C. Macintosh, *Theology as Empirical Science*, pp. 32, 41, 97.

teachings of Jesus Christ. Should the historical credibility of such former sources of authority be doubted, it should leave unchanged the reality of the religious experience.

Besides the obvious theological problems posed by the notion of *laws* according to which God might respond and be present in religious experience, Macintosh makes a valid point, namely that experience should not be taken at face value and stands in need of interpretation.[25] Whereas the fallibility of experience leads Davaney away from historical causes to a context of normative evaluations, the realm of reasons, the same fallibility leads Macintosh into a critical realism, where experience still plays a role in justification, although one of a certain religiously existential character.

J. Wesley Robbins

Macintosh, Dean and John E. Smith share a desire to have thought connected to the world. This is a legitimate desire from our standpoint, but it appears intractable from an authentically neo-pragmatic viewpoint. Jeffrey Wesley Robbins is a good representative of this philosophical suspicion with regard to the place of experience in justifying theology. His conviction that experience is seriously compromised as a source of justification generated an ongoing conversation with radically empiricist theologians like William Dean. This is what Dean had to say about Robbins in 2004:

> For at least three decades, Robbins has been a tough-minded, rigorous, well-published critic of many theologians' purported solutions to philosophical and social problems. In that period I am only one of many who has been the recipient of his philosophically based analysis. In a Darwinian manner, some of his ministrations saved us from continued pursuit of weak options and provoked us to better defend abiding commitments. For some of us would-be constructive theologians, at times he has been a kind of David Hume.[26]

The analogy with David Hume is not accidental. Just as Hume dismantled a certain understanding of causality as something residing in the world, neo-pragmatism insists that causation must not be confused with justification. If experience figures in the causal chain that leads to the formation of beliefs, that is well and good, but it does not mean that it also has a place in their justification.

The neo-pragmatic construal of this distinction between causes and reasons was already discussed in the previous chapter. What is its bearing upon religious justification? William Dean objects to what he perceives as the 'logicality' of the 'pure neopragmatic method'. The focalisation upon language

---

[25] We shall make a similar point in connection to John McDowell's notion of 'second nature' and 'habitus', in the last chapter.

[26] W. Dean, 'Response to Critics', *American Journal of Theology and Philosophy* 25/2 (2004), pp. 174-5.

is a kind of 'group subjectivism' in which human linguistic games are *cut off* from the world, nature, and the historical process. As a result of this separation, *neo-pragmatic philosophy is denying itself the means and the resources for a critique of ideological distortions within religion.* Post-modern philosophies, including neo-pragmatism, 'have lost most grounds for rejecting premodern authoritarianism and its supernaturalistic, biblically literal theological teachings.'[27] In the absence of a critical and rational relation between thought and the social, historical and natural environment from which it springs, thought itself is deprived of methods of self-critique.

Robbins objects to this understanding of neo-pragmatism. It does *not* fill the intermediary position left vacant by 'experience' with 'language', or 'practice', or anything else for that matter. Instead, it holds that no such intermediaries are required and that they do not serve any explanatory role whatsoever. They are useless in other words and should be abandoned. However, their abandonment does not amount to a linguistic idealism, which Dean and Bob Mesle suspect behind neo-pragmatism. Experience stands in a purely *causal* relation to our beliefs. This ensures that our beliefs are not disconnected from the world, yet neither does the world play a role in piece-by-piece justification of our claims to knowledge.

The Darwinian analogy is hardly accidental. While both Robbins and Dean lay a claim to the pragmatism of William James, Robbins thinks that James unfortunately lapses into worries about the problem of the knowledge of the external world, worries which should have been long assuaged given his evolutionary approach to knowledge. This is one piece of Cartesianism which James retained, but which neo-pragmatists like Robbins are happy to abandon: the distinction between knowledge by acquaintance and knowledge by description. Knowledge is not a matter of being able to connect bits of thought with chunks of reality. To assume that this is what knowledge is about is to return to dualism. But to hold that knowledge is about being able to manipulate sentences about this or that appropriately and not about something which enters the head and forces one to explain where it comes from, is not to disconnect language from the world. In Robbins' judgment, radical empiricist theology 'gives us a God we don't need to save us from a problem we don't have, that of epistemological separation of everything except ourselves.'[28] The allusion here is to John E. Smith's idea that men's separation from the world is a problem which can only be solved by someone not under the same condition.[29] This is a non-problem for Robbins. The task of language is not to represent something

[27] Quote in J. W. Robbins, 'Neo-pragmatism and the Radical Empiricist Metaphysics of Pure Experience', *American Journal of Theology and Philosophy* 14/1 (1993), p. 20.

[28] J. W. Robbins, 'Neo-pragmatism and the Radical Empiricist Metaphysics of Pure Experience', p. 23.

[29] Witness the implicit connection to the Christian doctrine of atonement, a doctrine creatively reconstructed in Smith's work.

external to it. Hence, 'the legitimacy of human language use thus devolves to the ideal values that we formulate in it, and how well these, our purposes are served by our various linguistic practices.'[30] In another context, Robbins declares that there is no secret to these words, there is just the terminology, the vocabularies, and how they have worked thus far.

The same theme of an instrumentalist justification of language recurs here. Since there is no God's eye view of the world, all we can do is see how far our vocabularies will take us in the direction of our goals. *Robbins gives no real thought to the question which not only interests Dean, but provides the basis for his claim that 'history yields values', namely where do our values come from? What is their legitimacy?* Following Rorty, the question of values and norms is merely one of cultural politics, not one of ontology. Our values emerge from the democratic process. Beyond this democratic and human conversation, there is nothing to be added to the question of the legitimacy of norms. While Dean thinks that some transcendent norms and grounds must be available for the distinction between good and bad consequences, Rorty and Robbins hold that no such grounds, other than what emerges out of the democratic process, are permissible. The distinction between good and bad consequences is one that can only be made after the community has decided one way or another. Similarly, 'Philosophical pragmatism, as Rorty notes, defers questions about ultimate justification to the future, instead of to extra-human authority'. Note that this is neither Davaney's 'expansive pragmatic historicism', nor Stout's bricolage and larger audience. The attitude which pervades Robbins' proposal is one of 'so what?': if the democratic community decides this, then there is no point in further asking, 'but is it right?' for no norms exist outside this democratic community, and these have already been drawn on in the process. Stout, but especially Davaney, are concerned with the possible 'bad' consequences of the best democratic process. For it is precisely the marginalised, the pariah which might suffer as a result. If there is no distinction to be made between the outcome of the democratic process and its morality, if the majority determines values, then what resources does a democratic society have at its disposal to denounce evil in other democratic societies? What about its own, endemic evil?

Cornel West has produced a penetrating critique of the political consequences of Rorty's philosophy. What he styles as Rorty's 'ethnocentric posthumanism'[31] is in fact politically inept, because while Rorty accepts the critical post-modern stance towards society, he simultaneously dilutes it by embracing the bourgeois capitalist liberalism of his own society. His parsing of democracy as the source of norms and values renders his philosophical

---

[30] J. W. Robbins, 'Neo-Pragmatism and the Philosophy of Experience', *American Journal of Theology and Philosophy* 14/2 (1993), p. 181.

[31] Cornel West, *The American Evasion of Philosophy: A Genealogy of Pragmatism* (Madison: University of Wisconsin Press, 1989), p. 206.

program devoid of political or social consequences. West diagnoses one of the major shortcomings of Rorty's project as being its distrust of theory. A purely pragmatic emphasis on practices and vocabularies, with no thought given to a morality which might transcend local norms, leads to a contentment with the *status quo*. Instead, 'a more refined pragmatism, one that preserves its historicist sense and genealogical aims, accents both consequences [of ideas] and specific practices in light of a set of provisional and revisable theoretical frameworks while it resists grand theories.'[32] West points out the possibility of a third way, which avoids both grand theories and a resigned utilitarian behaviourism. Working with theories need not imply that we treat these theories as irrevocable, unchangeable and eternally true. Yet such theories may provide us with ways of distinguishing between good and bad consequences, or as we pointed out with respect to Davaney, between trivial and relevant situations.

Returning to Robbins (and Dean), his belief that we can only discover which consequences are good or bad by letting the democratic process run its course, is an entirely un-pragmatic stance. For surely, the decision to create anti-Jewish laws in pre-war Germany needed not wait for the outcome of such laws in order to be rightly exposed as immoral. Or take the question of war: should we withhold judgment on the morality of, say, going to war against an 'innocent' and peaceful country, until the outcome of this action becomes clear? Why should we be in a better position to judge a practical outcome (looking to it, as it were, from the present to the past), then we might be able to judge it before its consequences unfold? The same norms which are lacking when we are told to wait upon the consequences will be lacking when these consequences have played themselves out. It might be cynical to suppose that what decides the matter is whether the president who sends the country to war will be re-elected. That is surely the impression given by Robbins in his exchange with Dean: good or bad consequences are determined by whoever wins the election: 'Philosophical pragmatists reply that answering questions about the objectivity of this political judgment involves waiting and seeing how it fares with future citizens.'[33]

The reason why Robbins feels pressed into this epistemological position, is a certain view about the relationship between mind and world. The mind is in a causal relationship to experience and the world and not in an epistemic one. Thus we cannot draw on the world in order to legitimate our beliefs about religion or politics. If this position does indeed lead to political cynicism, as we

---

32 C. West, *American Evasion*, p. 209. A similar point has been made in legal and political theory by Michael Sullivan and Daniel J. Solove, 'Law, Pragmatism, and Democracy', *Yale Law Journal* 113 (2003), mainly in response to the 'legal pragmatism' of Richard Posner.

33 J. W. Robbins, 'God-less Pragmatism', *American Journal of Theology and Philosophy* 25/2 (2004), p. 161.

have observed, Robbins argues that Dean's own position invites scepticism. In order to play a role in justification, the contents of experience must be specifiable independently of what it is supposed to be evidence for. 'Otherwise, whatever uncertainties pertain to what one might think about these latter things are liable to flood back into the experience on which those beliefs are supposed to be based.'[34] But if this independence holds, then what beliefs we might have could be utterly different from how things stand in the world. But if there is no fact of the matter as to how things stand in the world, but the world figures only in causal, rather than epistemic relationships to our beliefs, then this is a worry that need not detain us. For Dean, on the other hand, as for all empiricism, scepticism is invited by imposing unreasonable, unnecessary and un-fulfilable demands.

> This, in turn, dramatically changes how we go about assessing the epistemic value of religious vis-à-vis scientific beliefs. We can no longer divide beliefs into objective versus subjective ones, based on the role that experiential content does or does not play in their formation and validation. There is, then, no basis for an invidious distinction between objective beliefs which are robustly true because, through experience, they reproduce the world's own message and subjective, made-up beliefs whose "truth" is just a matter of courtesy. Instead, we will have to identify the relevant human interests that various respective beliefs are supposed to serve and ask how well those interests are being served by current beliefs versus how they might better be served by new beliefs.[35]

This interpretation is not altogether smooth. Dean would probably insist that he does not view experiences as being independently experienceable, and at a distance from beliefs. On the contrary, what radical empiricism holds is that one does not experience discrete objects of experience, but rather a totality, a sum of both objects, relations between them, relationships between objects and the experiencing agent and so on. To speak about discrete experiences does not capture the full wealth of the experience and is only possible as an abstraction.

Moreover, Dean's position only invites scepticism if it is assumed that justification is linear, rather than holistic. In a linear justification, the contents of experience would indeed have to stand independently of the contents of the beliefs to be justified. Should the uncertainties which pertain to beliefs filter down into the very contents of those experiences, then we would indeed have a problem. Here the assumption is that for experience to play a part in justification, it must provide us with indubitable contents. But this is not a requirement. It will be the burden of part of chapter III to show that experience can and must play a role in the justification of beliefs and that this need not imply a return to the so-called myth of the Given.

---

[34] J. W. Robbins, 'Donald Davidson and Religious Belief', *American Journal of Theology and Philosophy* (1996), p. 149.

[35] J. W. Robbins, 'Donald Davidson', p. 152.

A summary of this section's argument is in order now. Neo-pragmatic theological justification, espoused most faithfully in the writings of J. Wesley Robbins, and to a lesser extent by Sheila G. Davaney, leaves no room for experience in the process. While it accepts the socio-historical method of the early Chicago school theologians, it resists their empiricism and the turn towards the 'pure experience' of radical empiricism. Yet, *Dean's epistemology tends to treat experience and the God behind it as the source of value, as a self-interpreting source of knowledge; Davaney's call for more substantive norms eventually fails to deliver any particular norms; Robbins' neo-pragmatism leaves no critical room between our beliefs and what they are about to the point of inviting a cynical attitude towards politics, and perhaps even epistemology*. Despite their differences, however, all these thinkers, including D. C. Macintosh and John E. Smith, but also others which will be discussed presently, are united in their rejection of essentialism. There are no norms other than historical norms, there are no eternal ideas which claim our allegiance other than ideas as they have evolved through history in the process of human adaptation to environment. Christianity is no exception: it has no abiding essence, no self-contained unity, no self-assured truth. As a porous, developing tradition, it is not bound to the past, but its responsibility is defined by the present and its challenges. We now turn to the neo-pragmatic understanding of the importance of the past and tradition for theological construction.

The Meaning of Orthodoxy

If normativity is exclusively a matter of historical and cultural contingencies, does anything remain of the notion of orthodoxy? Can theology speak with confidence from a position it can call its own? Or, has theology lost its voice? This question, posed by Jeffrey Stout back in 1990, is still a live one today. The fate of academic theology, although not necessarily in doubt in secular contexts, seems deeply connected with the possibility of finding *the right balance between academic credibility and its proper distinctiveness*, usually rendered in terms of faithfulness to a past. However, while thirty years ago the empirical sciences and philosophy gave the uncontested meaning of 'academic credibility', today this meaning is no longer taken for granted. Neither, moreover, is the meaning of 'distinctively Christian theology'. The levelling of the qualitative distinctions between the hard and the soft sciences means that the public space itself is contested. There is no privileged definition of standards of public argumentation.

One such standard, however, seems to have gained increasing acceptance among contemporary theologians.[36] This is the view that, however committed

---

[36] After it enjoyed a period of quasi-dominance in the United States, neo-orthodoxy started to lose momentum as theologians became increasingly uncofortable with its

theology has to be to Christianity's own central symbols, it cannot bypass engagement with the other discourses which also shape the public sphere. The understanding of this engagement varies between conservatives, post-liberals, and liberals. For conservatives engagement usually takes the form of apologetics, whereby internal criteria of truth and meaning, specifically Christian doctrines and practices retain epistemic primacy.[37] Postliberals similarly privilege internal symbols and descriptions[38] whilst generally avoiding apologetics. In their view the latter project uncritically assumes a common epistemology with its secular counterparts, thus leading to a possible idolatry.[39]

This section focuses on three liberal approaches. A distinctive of the liberal approach to this 'negotiation' is that epistemic primacy is ascribed to secular notions of 'public', rather than to internal descriptions. While such internal descriptions may be held in common with conservatives or post-liberals, they are not normative and may be abandoned in the face of evidence available in the public sphere. Linell E. Cady, Delwin Brown, and Sheila G. Davaney all insist that *in order to carve out a place for theology in the public arena, what is normally understood by distinctiveness in relation to the past has to be redefined.* Tradition may have to be revisioned and restructured. Their respective attempts at this revision form an interesting test case for the possibility of revisionism generally.

Linell E. Cady

In her 1993 book, *Religion, Theology, and American Public Life*[40], Cady turns to a legal analogy for the burden of theological construction. The task of the theologian, she proposes, is similar to that of the judge who seeks to apply the law to a particular new situation. Much like the judge is compelled by a history of legal precedents, the theologian is responsible to what tradition has said before him on a given topic. For the judge the past is not codified in any fixed

---

apparent withdrawal from public justfication. See for example Sheila Greeve Davaney, *Pragmatic Historicism: A Theology for the Twentieth Century* (Albany: SUNY Press, 2000), pp. 14-16.

[37] We borrow this term from Bruce D. Marshall. It is especially apt to describe not simply what beliefs one may happen to hold at a given time (internal or external), but which of them are more likely to be abandoned in epistemic conflict. See his *Trinity and Truth* (Cambridge: Cambridge University Press, 2000).

[38] For a typology of theological methods in terms of how they relate internal to external description, see Hans W. Frei, *Types of Christian Theology* (New Haven: Yale, 1996). Frei is also the premier example of this type of engagement.

[39] In connection to idolatry, see especially William C. Placher, *Unapologetic Theology: A Christian Voice in a Pluralistic Conversation* (Westminster/ John Knnox, 1989), p. 168.

[40] (Albany: State University of New York Press, 1993).

canon, however. The faithfulness that is required of him is before a broader context of past legal decisions, none of which is privileged. Similarly, the theologian should reject an essentialist reading of the past, refusing to privilege any single text, symbol, or canon from that past. It should be the past '*as a whole*' that guides contemporary theology.

Borrowing from legal philosopher Ronald Dworkin, she identifies three possible models for the relationship to the past: conventionalism, extensionalism (Dworkin's naturalism), and instrumentalism. For the conventionalist, the past is a *deposit of unambiguous rules*. These can be found and then applied in a relatively straightforward way. Should such precedents not be found for a novel situation, the judge (and by analogy the theologian) is free to improvise, free to use his imagination and to draw on other intellectual discourses and norms in his decision.

The unintentional effect of this model, argues Dworkin, is precisely opposite from the one intended. Rather than making the past authoritative, it renders it irrelevant in licensing the judge to seek guidance in other sources rather than his own legal tradition. Moreover, failing to make explicit the complex ways in which we actually appropriate the past means that we keep our eyes closed to the possibility of distorted readings. Putatively objective readings turn out to be subtle imaginative creations under the guise of unambiguous exegesis.

Extensionalism meets these problems, first, by openly admitting that every interpreter brings to his texts a whole ballast of interests, values, and norms. Secondly, it rejects conventionalist essentialism, refusing to treat any single precedent as uniquely authoritative. It is rather the past *as a whole* which is normative. The judge should be aware that there is no precedent that applies strictly to his cases. Particular practical situations possess an inherent complexity which makes any such simple application impossible. In deciding which particular precedents apply, he or she is engaging in an ample interpretative process, to which he or she always brings a number of external constraints. We will return to this model presently.

While for the extensionalist, the past carries intrinsic normative weight, for the instrumentalist it is *only valuable inasmuch as it is instrumental in the creation of an optimal society*. We allow ourselves to be constrained by the past only if the benefits of doing so exceed those of readjusting our values according to other norms. Since in practice this creates a lot of disruption, it has proved pragmatically more advisable to stick with the old ways. However, what guides judicial decisions is not the past as a whole, nor particular elements from the past, but the current epistemic priorities of the judge. In other words, the judge is free to create whatever precedents he may wish, whilst keeping a minimal eye on the past for reasons described above.

Let us now return to extensionalism, which is obviously the type preferred by both Dworkin and Cady. To make his notion of treating the whole of the past as authoritative, Dworkin uses a literary analogy. The constraints under which a judge operates are similar to those which constrain the writer of a chain-novel.[41] Each chapter of a chain novel is written by a different author. Each writer, with the possible exception of the first writer, who begins the novel, is constrained by what has been written by those preceding him. Dworkin argues that what each writer must do is to continue the novel by making it the best it can be.[42] In his words, 'Each has the job of writing his chapter so as to make the novel being constructed the best it can be, and the complexity of this task models the complexity of deciding a hard-case under law as integrity.'[43] Both the judge and, as we will see, the theologian seek to be faithful to the past, yet both are aware of the creative and imaginative nature of their tasks. As the illustration of the chain-novel demonstrates, both judge and theologian treat the past as normative precisely in light of their present values and interests. *Extensionalism means recognizing that there is no simple repetition of the past, but that each repetition is itself (partly) forward-looking.*

The tension between backward- and forward-looking is beautifully captured by Cady's expression, 'in the best possible light'[44], which she believes is synonymous with Dworkin's 'the best it can be'. She suggests that since we are bound to bring our commitments to the interpretation of the past, what we should do is, by using the best knowledge we have to-day, so interpret the past as to make it the best it can be. Unquestionably Cady intends something like a face-lift job, as when she writes that the theologian/jurist 'may legitimately sacrifice the strictest continuity in order to articulate a more adequate story.'[45] It turns out that her interest is not simply to *interpret* a normative tradition, but to *prescribe* ways in which one should relate to it. *To see a tradition in its best light involves a certain amount of revision, of adjustment. One has to ask what has to be dropped in order to save the whole.*

The negotiation of our relationship to the past, according to Cady's extensionalist model, presupposes an adjustment of what we take to be the most fundamental insights and principles of a tradition (the whole) in light of what we might call our present worldview. This brings us to the heart of the matter, to a fundamental tension besetting the historicist theologians that we are discussing here. Cady, Brown and Davaney all want to hold on to both (a) all discourses, including the theological ones, are historical; they can have no justification beyond a merely local and conventional warrant; they can make no claim on absolute truth; finally, as a result of this, their history is fraught with

---

[41] He elaborates this analogy in 'How Law is Like Literature', to be found in his *A Matter of Principle* (Cambridge, Mass.: Harvard University Press, 1985) and *Law's Empire* (Cambridge, Mass.: Harvard University Press, 1986). We discuss this analogy in relation to Stanley Fish's criticism of objectivity in our *Postliberal Theological Method* (Carlisle: Paternoster, 2005), pp. 74-76.

[42] R. Dworkin, *Law's Empire*, p. 112.

[43] R. Dworkin, *Law's Empire*, p. 229.

[44] L. Cady, *Religion*, p. 54.

[45] L. Cady, *Religion*, p. 52.

mistakes, illusions, ideological distortions; but (b) it is still worth doing theology; a place can still be carved out for theology in the *academia*; 'Christian' tradition still needs to be reckoned with regardless of its past failures. Attempting to hold these two emphases in balance results, at least for these theologians, in holding (with their own particular emphases) that (c) the past, the tradition, what it means for a theological discourse to be called Christian, all these have to undergo a certain amount of revision, while still keeping continuity with tradition.

The way in which Cady attempts to hold (c) is by arguing that no continuity with tradition is strict continuity. Conventionalists, who advocate such strict continuity, fail to see how their own prejudgments condition their perception. As a result, their continuity is no less creative than the extensionalist's except that such creativity is not admitted.

Cady models her theological methodology along the lines of Lindbeck's cultural-linguisticism. It is only Lindbeck's formal model that she adopts, rather than his substantive theological application of that model in theology. A religion functions, according to Lindbeck, like a language which models perception. A religion is not, as in David Tracy's experiential-expressivist model, a symbolization of a pre-conceptual experience. Tracy follows Gadamer's aesthetic considerations about how truth is revealed in art and in the so-called 'classics'. Cady, on the other hand, follows a different strand in Gadamer, one pertaining to legal interpretation. In legal interpretation there is no strict demarcation between understanding the law and applying it. Gadamer relativises the difference between the legal historian and the judge. To understand a law is already to imagine how it might be applied. With each new application, therefore, a judge *adds* meaning to the law. By analogy, with each new theological decision one is both continuing the tradition (backward-looking) as well as adding new meaning to it (forward looking). Yet each such decision also involves the operation of the judge's present worldview, which is independent of his tradition.

This is an important theological difference from Lindbeck. For whereas Lindbeck would argue that religions tend to condition perception in such a way that they strive to make everything internal, Cady accepts the possibility that we might not be so heavily conditioned by tradition and that we might self-consciously invoke resources external to that tradition in the process of 'seeing it in the best light'. This sets the Christian tradition, for example, equally available as a resource with, say, modern science. Nothing should stop the theologian from drawing on the best insights in these external discourses. Should that process lead to abandoning central insights of the Christian tradition, it is all for the better.

How can Cady have her cake and eat it too? *Is it possible to claim that one might abandon the central ideas of a tradition and still hold that this is in continuity with that very tradition?* Cady would presumably reply that 'what is deemed as important and central [in a given tradition] will be determined in large part by the interpreter's current beliefs and values.'[46] 'This dialectic', she continues, 'is unavoidable given the current nature of interpretation, conventionalist denials notwithstanding.'[47]

In our opinion, the problem with Cady's view results from her combination of a quasi-monolythic view of tradition with her conception of what it means to continue a tradition (by revising it). Later we will argue that Brown and Davaney both move away from a unified notion of tradition, but that this lands them with another set of difficulties. Before we turn to these thinkers, we would like to point out in more detail where Cady's analysis and solution goes wrong. A similar tactic will be used for the other two theologians.

First, the legal analogy is extremely limited. Although Gadamer uses legal hermeneutics as an illustration for his wider claims about understanding and application, it is not clear whether he applies his conclusions to general hermeneutics as such. Even within the legal institution the statement that judges make new meanings for the law applies strictly in those countries where the doctrine of precedent, or *stare decisis* is normative. This is not the case in most francophone countries, where the statutes as such are considered absolute and normative and where, moreover, precedents do not have a normative role in decision making or even in the justification of judicial decisions. If Gadamer's conclusions apply to the regional hermeneutics he discusses, he makes it quite clear that they do *not* apply in theology. He writes 'Unlike a legal verdict, preaching is not a creative supplement to the text it is interpreting. Hence the Gospel acquires no new content in being preached that could be compared with the power of the judge's verdict to supplement the law.'[48] By itself, this reminder is not sufficient to undermine Cady's claims because Gadamer's distinction is based on a difference between the institution of law and that of interpreting the Gospel, while Cady's claims are precisely about understanding how this latter institution functions.

Given the importance of this topic it is surprising that she gives so little attention to the differences between the normative practice of judicial interpretation and the practices of the theological interpretation of Scripture. She merely notes that it is misleading to accept the analogy between biblical interpretation and constitutional interpretation. Isolated biblical passages are not like individual statutes. To say this would mean to misconstrue the character of the Bible. But the conventionalist readily accepts this. *In the so-called conventionalist camp there was never a question of treating biblical texts as normative in and of themselves, but only as part of the larger context in Scripture as God's communicative event.* But Cady denies this appeal to the whole of the Bible as analogical to the constitution. The reason she invokes is

---

[46] L. Cady, *Religion*, p. 53.

[47] L. Cady, *Religion*, p. 53.

[48] Hans-Georg Gadamer, *Truth and Method* (second edition, New York: Continuum, 1994), p. 330.

curious, to say the least: this fails to recognize fully the 'human and therefore corrigible roots of the text.'[49] To which the conventionalists might fairly reply: this is not a question of the *truth* of the theological construction based upon biblical interpretation, but a question of what within a given tradition is considered to be *warranted.* Cady's mentioned reply is doubly curious, for isn't the constitution itself 'human and therefore corrigible?'. The issue is not one of truth or falsity, but an institutional one of whether within a given social structure a canon is considered authoritative. Much like the constitution, although differences do remain, the Bible can be considered authoritative. Unless, that is, other considerations can be fruitfully brought to bear against it.

A second set of issues that reflect upon the above proposal concern the nature of interpretation. The extensionalist model is aware of the subjective implication in any act of understanding. This self-consciousness renders it superior, at least from this perspective, to the so-called conventionalist one. Yet Cady does not succeed in maintaining these distinctions sharply enough. For one thing, it will be very hard to run into such a conventionalist. If they exist, they are such a minority position as to be irrelevant to the discussion. However, we suspect it is not these fundamentalists that Cady has in mind, but theologians of a more 'Evangelical' bent. If the suspicion is misplaced, then it is Cady's fault to have omitted them from the discussion. If the guess is right, then her description is certainly simplistic. For such Evangelical interpreters of the Bible who are not aware of the role of prejudgments in their thinking are indeed rare. If Evangelical theology has any problem, it is certainly not this lack of self-awareness. It seems like there is an empty slot in Cady's typology which, if we might be able to fill in, it could prove quite successful even by Cady's lights. The representatives of such a position might argue that *while one does bring an entire symbolic horizon to understanding, a horizon composed of a variety of intersecting discourses, it is not the case that this horizon determines our reading of the past.*

Yet this is precisely what Cady holds: that what we take to be the central elements of a tradition are determined in light of our present values and interests. If this is an interpretative issue, it is surely wrong. For if that were so, should we even have such interests and values independently of the tradition we come from? Cady wants to retain both the possibility that we are not captives to our own tradition and thus are able to draw on other resources, as well as a unified notion of tradition as a project that we need to continue. To be fair to Cady, although she doesn't discuss this explicitly, she doesn't seem to frame the issue as one of interpretation. But, against her, it becomes an issue of interpretation the moment she argues that her revision, her theological decision is one which continues the tradition rather than brakes with it. It is an interpretive decision because in order to say the above you have first to demonstrate what is the meaning of the tradition. If one argues for continuity

[49] L. Cady, *Religion*, p. 62.

with the past, some sort of description of the past is required which is at least in principle different from a subjective take on it.

To say that we have to be aware of our own contribution to interpretation is commendable. Yet this does not mean that what is important and central in a given tradition will only be determined by our current beliefs and values (presumably external to that tradition). One may determine what is central to a tradition even while one rejects it.

Cady's insistence on the fact that even while I am rejecting (formerly) central aspects of a tradition I am nonetheless continuing it, raises the question of when is a non-identical repetition still a repetition? This is puzzling for two reasons: (a) it seems to ascribe agency to tradition, which is then denied when it appears that we decide what is central and what isn't, and (b) it is never explained why we should bother to remain faithful to our traditions. Cady's historicism appears to not be historicist enough. If her tradition is so unified, if it is a whole, then the revision she wants to undertake cannot conceivably count as one within the limits of that tradition. It would seem that *it is difficult to affirm a unified notion of tradition whilst having a revisionist agenda*. Delwin Brown, the theologian we shall discuss next, promptly drops a the unified view of tradition.

Delwin Brown

While for Cady the Bible as a whole is not normative because it is a human text and thus subject to mistake, for Delwin Brown, another historicist theologian, it isn't normative because it has no discernible meaning.[50] This argument goes deeper than Cady's, since it not only doubts credibility, but it attacks the very notion of a coherent whole which has a meaning. Brown's historicism, even more than Cady's, is influenced by continental traditions of thought, more particularly by the 'textualist' strand which builds on Gadamer's notion of hermeneutical experience. According to this strand, not easily discernible in Gadamer himself, however, human discourses are plurivocal. In each a variety of sometimes competing texts intersect. Naturally enough, for Brown a tradition is even less unitary than a text.

Brown's theory of tradition (and hence our relationship to the past) is articulated by elaborating on three fundamental concepts: culture, tradition, and canon. There is an intentional departure from the Geertzian notion of culture assumed by Lindbeck's and Cady's cultural linguisticism. To assume that a culture (and by implication a religion) functions much like a language which conditions perception is to ascribe an exaggerated unity to it. The notion of culture as a stable structure with a depth grammar disappears in favor of culture

---

[50] Delwin Brown, *Boundaries of Our Habitations: Tradition and Theological Construction* (Albany: SUNY Press, 1994), p. 123.

as 'struggle to create, maintain, and recreate individual and collective identities.'[51]

A tradition, on the other hand, is the particular specification of such identity. It is not static, but 'a continuously reformed and formative milieu, a dynamic stream of forces in which we live (or die), move (or stagnate), gain (or lose) our being.'[52] Tension and conflict is already a part of the very fabric of tradition, rather than an accident following which we break with it. Imagination and improvisation need not be seen as enemies of the identity specified by tradition. That would assume that such identity is fixed, its specification complete. On the contrary, both continuity and conflict are part of the formation of historical and traditioned identity.

At the heart of traditions are canons, which are 'complexes of myths, stories, rituals, doctrines, texts, or institutions'.[53] Canons ground and give shape to historical lineages. But they are complicated 'beings' and are not easily defined, or identified. Moreover, Brown turns to radical empiricism in denying that canons are simply textual or cognitive. They also encompass non-conceptual symbols, practices, rituals, bodily actions and so on. This renders the borders of canons very loose. It does not follow that canons are not identifiable, only that their perimeter is very loose and is always a matter of contested interpretation.

Together these notions compose a picture of what we have more loosely called tradition which is certainly different from Cady's. Being what they are, *faithfulness to a tradition cannot simply be translated in terms of conformity to the past.*

We are now in a better position to see the differences between Lindbeck, Cady and Brown. For Lindbeck faithfulness to the past is described in terms of intratextuality.[54] One follows if one allows oneself to be inscribed within a Scriptural universe where the grammar of the Bible rules reality. This type of repetition is too rigid by Cady's lights. For her tradition must be 'stylized', put in the best light, harmonized with what we take to be the good, the true and the beautiful. However, she is still presupposing that a tradition can be talked about as a whole. There is still a depth-grammar, only it has to be adjusted. The fact that her notion of tradition is not flexible enough, as was shown, generates problems when she argues that her own modification of tradition is still part of that very tradition. For Brown, on the other hand, this problem disappears, for a tradition is never unified anyway. The issue, therefore, is not one of arguing that one is still faithful to a tradition even while one rejects major parts of it. On

---

[51] D. Brown, *Boundaries*, p. 63.

[52] D. Brown, *Boundaries*, p. 4.

[53] D. Brown, *Boundaries*, p. 114.

[54] See Lindbeck's chapter entitled 'Faithfulness as Intratextuality', in his *The Nature of Doctrine* (Philadelphia: Westminster Press, 1984), pp. 113-123 .

the contrary, such rejections, shifts, conflicts are an integral part of each tradition: 'plurivocal canons, as such, cannot be conformed to.'[55]

Brown faces another difficulty, however. For the question of whether one is in fact faithful to a tradition remains even though he dismisses the notion of tradition as unitary. Now the question is, *if traditions are plurivocal, how does one know when one is being faithful to one?* Moreover, if unity is illusory why should we even continue to speak in terms of faithfulness? Hasn't Brown relativised tradition to such an extent that to speak of faithfulness (or revision) is question-begging?

What clarifies this issue for Brown is the notion that traditions possess *agency*. Canons themselves are not simply fields of play, writes Brown, they are also agents of play.[56] This is a familiar notion, in the entrenchment of which Gadamer played no small part. Although traditions are such dynamic fields, they nevertheless *condition* those who 'play' on them. Faithfulness is no longer a question of an *intentional defense* of the boundaries of tradition. One is faithful to a tradition whether one is aware of it or not.[57] *The agential nature of tradition means that conformity does not pertain to the intentionality of adherents.* To this extent, Brown thinks that the 'pious possessiveness' of conservatives is unwarranted: 'conservatism is stultifying because it fears the imagination. And it fears the imagination because it underestimates the power of canon to take care of itself, to criticize as well as to be criticized, to change as well as be changed – in short, to play those who play it.'[58]

Yet it is not clear whether this traditioned agency renders superfluous all efforts at conscious preservation. Brown gives all sorts of contradictory hints in this respect. Somehow contrary to what he said above, he insists that when we draw upon the insights of other discourses, these *have to be* 'integrated back into the reconstruction of Christianity's inherited resources.'[59] This seems to be an intentional appropriation, rather than something which goes on in the background regardless of the intentions of adherents. Why should we consciously strive to integrate these other values and interests into or inherited tradition, if our tradition is so plurivocal and non-unitary anyway? Or, if tradition subliminally always catches up with our various peregrinations, which should we intentionally return to it? Our efforts of integration make no difference anyway.[60]

---

[55] D. Brown, *Boundaries*, p. 126.

[56] D. Brown, *Boundaries*, p. 127.

[57] Gadamer's point that even in refusing to obey an order one is in fact applying it, or at least imagining its application, is to the point here. Gadamer involves application in all understanding.

[58] D. Brown, *Boundaries*, p. 127.

[59] D. Brown, *Boundaries*, p. 131.

[60] This type of argument is very similar to Stanley Fish's comment that 'theory has no consequences'. If one assumes such an agential notion of tradition as both Brown and

The closest Brown comes to an answer is when he reminds us that we can only work with what we have inherited. Our tradition, whether Christian or otherwise, is like a house we have inherited. 'But whatever we wish to do with the house we inherit, and whatever tools we use, we can succeed only by working on, precisely, that house – because to say that humans are historical means that our futures are built through the reconstruction of our pasts.'[61] This appeal to historicity misfires, for the architectural analogy implies plenty of structure and cohesion and these are precisely features that traditions have been denied. Historicity should only imply according to his lights, and to use the same analogy, that we are bound to work with whatever we find *around* the house, like planks, bolts, nails and so on, rather than with the house *itself*.

The same failure to reconcile the agential work of tradition, which implies a certain passivity of adherents, with the intentional 'caretaking' of its members is apparent in his discussion of authority. Continuing his point about the ability of tradition to take care of itself, he suggests that we see tradition as *formative* rather than *normative*, as *author* rather than as *authorizer*.[62] '[T]he authority of a canon is the creative power it manifests and therefore enables in those who inhabit it, and the authority of a tradition is the power of its canon again and again to author reconstructions, conceptual and affective, that yield visible individual and communal identities.'[63]

It would appear that the reply to the question: 'why should we still be faithful to *this* tradition?' is that we cannot help being so. Yet if we cannot help it, why should we *strive* to integrate new pieces of knowledge into the fabric of our inherited tradition? It seems that *Brown has succeeded in rendering entirely superfluous all talk about whether a given theological decision is in conformity or conflict with its 'host' tradition*. For the notion of authority is entirely non-epistemic, to borrow a term from another philosophical discussion. Brown has argued that tradition functions as a *cause* rather than as a *reason* in theological decisions. However, we would like to argue, unless causes can also be reasons, even invoking tradition in anything other than a very generic and non-specific case is unwarranted.

The distinction between causes and reasons makes sense on the assumption that traditions do indeed have agency. To view tradition as a cause, or as an

---

Fish do, it makes no difference to ask about faithfulness, or conscious reintegration. This always takes place regardless of how we adjust our theory. Interestingly, Fish's comment on Dworkin's chain-novel analogy is that even the first author is constrained by tradition, whether he thinks he is or not. See Stanley Fish, 'Working on the Chain Gang: Interpretation in Law and Literature', and 'Change', both in *Doing What Comes Naturally: Change, Rhetoric and the Practice of Theory in Literary and Legal Studies* (Durham: Duke University Press, 1989). See our discussion of the whole debate in *Postliberal Theological Method*, pp. 26-30, 39-42.

[61] D. Brown, *Boundaries*, p. 131.

[62] D. Brown, *Boundaries*, p. 144.

[63] D. Brown, *Boundaries*, p. 144.

author, means to view it as being determinative of the theological decisions made. It is crucial to the distinction to stipulate that this determination takes place non-epistemically, i.e., without our being aware of it. I can be determined, say, by my upbringing to do something, even though I think I have other reasons for doing that. What caused me to act is different from the reasons I gave for my actions. All this makes very good sense, but the problem appears when we try to hold both

(1) traditions are causes, rather than reasons for our decisions, and

(2) a tradition is composed of these doctrines, these canons, these symbols, actions, rituals etc.

If we accept that traditions act in non-epistemic ways upon us, it no longer makes sense to separate between tradition A, to which I belong because it acts upon me, and tradition B, to which I do not belong because it does not condition me. Since I have no idea about what conditions me, neither will I have any idea about what doesn't. But if that is the case, on what basis can we ever distinguish between traditions?

The problem, in short, is that once we accept a notion of tradition as cause and then deny that causes can be reasons, we have to surrender all attempt to flesh it out in any particular description. Tradition is something like a 'final cause', regardless of whether the notion makes much sense at all.[64]

Brown is left with two options: either he distinguishes between the senses of tradition so that on the one hand we have tradition as 'final horizon', which bears of no further description or distinction, or he accepts that faithfulness to tradition is a non-issue, since tradition is nothing definite. The first option would mean that his arguments against the normativity of tradition lose all force, given that he was using a different sense for tradition. Finally, his second option raises a further question: why even bother with theology? Why should theology be the caretaker of tradition, if traditions are so relative and indistinctive?

Sheila G. Davaney

Let us recapitulate the argument so far. The theologians we have discussed both struggle to articulate the place of the past in theological construction today. Their outlook is historicist and they assume the contextual character of all

---

[64] Davidson similarly insists that the world only acts causally upon our senses and is not in epistemic contact with these. As a result, the world is not normative in epistemology and it becomes a vague notion which allows of no distinctions. All the distinctions that we make are internal to a belief-system and do not mirror the world ('A Coherence Theory of Truth and Knowledge', in Donald Davidson, *SIO*, pp. 143-146).

intellectual reflection. However, both maintain a notion of faithfulness to one's tradition. While for Linell Cady it is difficult to reconcile her notion of the whole of a tradition with her 'revisionist' agenda, thus modifying the meaning of faithfulness, for Brown the very idea of a tradition suffers essential modifications. If our arguments hold, Cady loses her grip on the meaning of 'creative *extension*', while Brown relativises tradition to the point of rendering it entirely useless for theological reflection.

Some of the points we have made in relation to these theologians find echo in Davaney's affirmation of *Pragmatic Historicism*,[65] although from a different perspective and leading to different conclusions. Where Cady proposes that we see the past 'in its best light', and Brown argues that there is no canonical unity to the past such that no simple conformity is possible, Davaney wishes to drop any hint of debt to the past. It is not the past as such that we must conform to. This does not mean that we are free to ignore it. For Davaney, historicism means that the past *as such* is not normative either for our theological judgments or for our communal and individual identities. Rather the historicist task is to draw on the past as a depository of resources which must be brought to bear on the more important task of living meaningful lives today. Let me attempt to flesh out her position in more detail.

Davaney rebukes Cady, with good reason, for replacing an illegitimate essentialism with a stress on the whole of tradition. From a historicist perspective there is no such whole.[66] Brown has made a similar point, yet this did not prevent him from conceiving our relationship to the past in terms of continuing a tradition, extending an argument, as we integrate various 'external' discourses into the reconstruction of our inheritance. The relativising of tradition begun by Brown is deepened in Davaney's pragmatic historicism. Our identity, both individual and communal, need not be conceived on the background of a single tradition. The past as such is 'a vast stream of historical developments that embody not one thrust or set of principles, but multiple, contending ones.'[67] There is not a privileged set of doctrines, issues, symbols or practices which gives unity to such a past.

Rather than searching for such a depth grammar, the theologian should

> turn to particular developments within our tradition, claiming them as particularly relevant for today or perhaps as the best or most challenging the tradition has to offer. Our arguments for so doing should be predicated, however, on their viability for today, not on the suggestion that they somehow are the embodiment of either the "fundamental principles" of a tradition or of its general character.[68]

---

65 S. G. Davaney, *Pragmatic Historicism*.
66 S. G. Davaney, *Pragmatic Historicism*, p. 103.
67 S. G. Davaney, *Pragmatic Historicism*, p. 103.
68 S. G. Davaney, *Pragmatic Historicism*, p. 103.

This last sentence brings us to the thrust of her critique of Brown. Davaney puts her finger on what she identifies as Brown's (lingering) monotraditionalism'.[69] This shows up at a number of levels. First, at the level of the formation and development of traditions, Brown fails to appreciate fully their so-called hybrid character. Although he does underscore the fact that traditions are not unitary, he nonetheless employs notions which suggest otherwise, as we have also argued.[70] Brown's insistence on the integration of alien knowledge into a dominant tradition seems gratuitous, for 'it is not at all clear that the way [development] occurs is primarily through the recovery of past elements or the sublation of foreign elements into dominant traditions.'[71]

Critiquing Brown's integrative task makes sense, but not for the reason given by Davaney. She invokes an 'empirical' reason, i.e., that is not how traditions develop historically. It is true that syncretism plays a part, even an important part in the development of traditions. But to insist against integration into a dominant tradition makes sense not because it might be based on empirical data, but because it conflicts with Brown's other historicist assumptions. We have already stressed this much: Brown's own logic should *only* compel him to draw on 'planks' rather than 'structures'. There is no work of integration required once such a fragmentary conception of tradition is accepted.

At another level, Brown's monotraditionalism is reflected in his tendency to view personal and communal identity as emerging *within* dominant traditions, rather than at the intersection of these. This is obviously a related point, but it is more anthropological than sociological.[72]

Finally and more importantly (from the perspective of the present argument), Brown is monotraditionalist in that 'his [...] assumptions about traditions tend to encourage an excessive confidence in our inherited traditions and to discourage an interest in other traditions.'[73] This point is rather psychological: because theologians see their function as 'caretakers' of traditions, they would *tend* to be more concerned about their own tradition rather than about the resources available elsewhere. Now Davaney has to be careful not to forget her own historicism, for isn't this one of its very central points, namely that being human we are constructed by our traditions and cultures? It is only natural that this should be the case. However, she probes deeper: Brown's position lends 'support to a too easy leap from the plurality of resources to the adequacy of

---

[69] S. G. Davaney, *Pragmatic Historicism*, p. 108.

[70] The same holds for Cady, who does admit that traditions are very diverse (Cady, *Religion*, p. 61).

[71] S. G. Davaney, *Pragmatic Historicism*, p. 109.

[72] See Milbank's similar point in his response to Davidson's and Alasdair MacIntyre's assumption of a 'unified mental subject', *Theology and Social Theory* (Oxford: Blackwell, 1993), pp. 341, 342.

[73] S. G. Davaney, *Pragmatic Historicism*, p. 110.

such resources. While the past may contain potentialities for today, that recognition should not lead to the much more sweeping claim that they do so or that those resources are adequate to the task before us.'[74]

The simple fact that something is in the past should not mean that is valid today. We should remember the tension at the heart of Brown's program: between the agential function of tradition and the intentional actions of theologians that resolve to continue tradition. Davaney's notion of tradition is much more liberal than Brown's. If traditions do condition us, they do so even at a level of which we are entirely unaware. This fits the logic of Brown's position well, although he does not admit it. Nonetheless, although the identities of agents are shaped at the intersection of traditions, there is a sense in Davaney that we as agents have much more control over how precisely we integrate those traditions than either Cady or Brown allows. This has probably to do with the fact that she carries the dissolution of the notion of tradition to farther limits.

The site for normative judgment is the present.[75] Not only the present, but the present public sphere. This public sphere is the melting pot of all discourses, whether they concern norms of justification, direct truth claims etc. The past only has a function if we are able to locate within it resources[76] that can contribute to make our contemporary search for a meaningful life more successful.[77] But the decision as to the adequacy of those resources has to be justified according to present and public norms. Merely tracing the lineage of a belief or system of doctrines to the past is not sufficient to warrant it. Davaney invokes the same distinction between reasons and causes, which she borrows from Sandra Harding. '[B]ecause a current belief or practice resonates with or is faithful to some dimension of a tradition's history tells us about historical connectedness but does not settle issues of validity.'[78] It is readily visible that she does not employ this distinction to quite the same ends as Brown. She couldn't, for Brown is concerned with faithfulness, whereas this is precisely what she rejects as irrelevant. Proper belief pedigree might establish faithfulness (Brown would obviously disagree based on the very same distinction), but it says nothing about validity.

The task of theology cannot be Brown's caretaking. That implies monotraditionalism and this is irresponsible. Theology, no less than other intellectual discourses, must assume the burden of establishing the validity of its own views. Should one ask: 'validity in terms of what?', Davaney has a ready and somewhat counter-intuitive answer: theology is 'a fundamentally practical undertaking whose goal is the shaping of habitats of meaning, value,

---

[74] S. G. Davaney, *Pragmatic Historicism*, pp. 110-111.
[75] S. G. Davaney, *Pragmatic Historicism*, p. 152.
[76] S. G. Davaney, *Pragmatic Historicism*, p. 153.
[77] Davaney seems to fit Cady's instrumentalist profile rather well.
[78] S. G. Davaney, *Pragmatic Historicism*, p. 152.

and practice *so that contemporary persons might function in a universe construed to have significance and direction.*'[79] This is so counter-intuitive because it relies on a general characterization of what religions and theologies do.[80] Now, she does not agree with Rorty that generalizations are wrong. Quite rightly. But this conflicts with her historicism as well as her anti-essentialism. First, it is anti-historicist because it offers a sweeping generalization of what a religion is, quite independently of an empirical description of how adherents themselves might describe it. Not all religions are about the meaning of life. Christianity isn't primarily about the meaning of life, neither is Islam. Secondly, it is essentialist because she professes to have identified a *central* requirement of the public sphere, namely a certain construal of validity. But if the public sphere contains not only the discourses of liberal theology, of scientific positivism, or radical empiricism, but also those of Evangelical theology, fundamentalism, post-liberalism, Jewish theology and so on – each with their own conception of validity – is it not therefore wrong to privilege a single construal?

Once faithfulness is considered unnecessary and even immoral, what is the task of theology? It is 'the identification, examination, assessment, and reconstruction of historical traditions of interpretation and practice so that humans might more fruitfully and responsibly live within our complex and interdependent universe.'[81] Theology, in other words, must listen to only a number of imperatives, those which Davaney assumes are central to what 'public' means. These imperatives guide the archeological process by which adequate resources from the past are drawn on. Theology is very similar to what Delwin Brown has called an 'ethnography of belief', 'that is, the task of identifying the religious beliefs of particular communities, including general assumptions about humanity and the cosmos, and tracing their interconnection with other cultural beliefs, institutions, and practices such as economic realities, political configurations, and the distribution and deployment of power.'[82]

The frank admission that theology should simply be another ethnography of belief is not followed to its conclusion, however. Davaney thinks that this will permit theologians to have a distinctive voice in the academy, without retreating to communities of faith and their languages. But we already have departments of anthropology and sociology with their own ethnographers. How can theology justify a place for itself? The only reply that we can imagine is

---

[79] S. G. Davaney, *Pragmatic Historicism*, p. 85.

[80] See Tyron Inbody, 'Delwin Brown's Constructive Historicism as A Reconstruction of Empirical Theology', *American Journal of Theology and Philosophy*, 18/2 (1997), p. 163, who similarily criticizes Brown, while he also thinks this is a dilemma at the heart of any historicist theory.

[81] S. G. Davaney, *Pragmatic Historicism*, p. 114.

[82] S. G. Davaney, *Pragmatic Historicism*, p. 140.

that whereas a non-theological ethnography is merely descriptive, theological ethnography is prescriptive and normative.[83]

The Morale

Can anything be learnt from this extended discussion? Is the failure of these theologians indicative of a substantial difficulty, perhaps an impossibility? Can the logic of this triple failure be captured by any generalization? These are tempting questions, at least from this perspective. On the other hand, caution is preferable given the fact that traditions are after all what John Searle called *institutional realities or facts*. Their existence is a product of human conceptualization. We establish conventions according to which a certain body of texts, symbols, rituals and so on stipulated to form a 'tradition'. But before one should jump on the band-wagon of convention and cheerfully announce that we have been struggling with a pseudo-issue, one would do well to remember that although conventions themselves are indeed arbitrary, the similarities and the relations that they name are objective, at least in a soft sense of being there independently of our thinking. We usually say that something belongs to a tradition while something doesn't because of inherent features that are there whether we recognize it or not.

Caution does not mean that we arrest all thinking about the issue, but only that there are no clear-cut answers about notions like the boundaries of a tradition, criteria for belonging to one, faithfulness and so on. Contrary what some may wish, there is no simple calculus which demonstrates what belongs where and what doesn't.

This is the point where it has to be conceded to these thinkers that traditions are themselves human. Consequently, it is humans which decide what belongs and what doesn't. What these theologians should recognize, however, is that there are also matters of fact which *might* adjudicate the debate, at least in some of its particulars. To take but one extreme example, no one could argue coherently that the Quran actually belongs to the Christian tradition. Although traditions are conventions and although they change historically, there are matters of fact as to whether at some point one group of ideas ceases to belong to a tradition. Let's say this again: *the strength of revisionism is that there is no privileged, normative and absolute description of a tradition which we could read of some ahistorical dictionary.*

It is on the basis of this common-sense assumption that theologians such as Cady, Brown and Davaney set out to redefine what the Christian tradition means. What appeared to be privileged definitions of orthodoxy are nothing but interpretations which happen to have gained historical acceptance. But they involve historical, cultural, political decisions and have no inherent claim on the heart of the tradition.

---

[83] S. G. Davaney, *Pragmatic Historicism*, p. 140.

On the other hand, we have tried to argue that there are limits to the amount of revision one can get away with. Granted, there will never be a clear demarcation. But in each of these cases, certain problems accrue which might be instances of a more general impossibility, or simply mistakes from which one has to learn in order to offer a better solution. The first of our theologians, Linell Cady, found it difficult to harmonize a fairly strong notion of the 'whole' of a tradition with her revisionist impulse. Adopting a revisionist starting point, or in Bruce Marshall's words, having alien epistemic priorities, is hard to reconcile with a unified notion of tradition. Brown attempted to solve the difficulty by stressing that tradition is not in fact unified. This landed him with a different predicament: he could no longer make sense of the notion of tradition itself. Rather tradition becomes something like an ultimate horizon which conditions our thinking, but which is very hard to flesh out in particular terms. Faithfulness itself becomes a pseudo-issue when there is nothing in particular to be faithful to. Davaney accepts much of the present critique but insists that faithfulness is not what we should be after anyway. Faithfulness betrays a monotraditionalist anthropology which has been discarded. Human beings are shaped by a variety of traditions and discourses. We have to draw on these only to the extent that they help us live meaningful lives. The question we posed to Davaney, one which we suspect she would find important, is, why bother with theology?[84]

We have come full circle to a position which followed the logic of its predecessors to its ultimate conclusion: theology as ethnography. Evangelicals are bound to see in this the validation of their initial suspicions: that something important is surrendered and that revisionism is incompatible with Christian tradition. Liberals, on the other hand, would argue that this is theology's only hope of maintaining an academic profile. One thing is no longer claimed by this final liberal position: that it is faithfully continuing the Christian tradition. In this it is surely right.

Ontological Parsimony and God-talk

Pragmatism and neo-pragmatism, we saw, pose special problems for a Christian account of theological justification, but also for the very understanding of what it means to be bound to a past. This section engages with a perceived loss of ontological reference for God-talk. Naturally, this is a huge discussion, and we cannot hope to do justice to the full wealth of arguments deployed in the field. Neither can we hope to engage with every relevant critic. The point is not to give an exhaustive treatment of each issue, or thinker, but to chart and actual and possible conversation. It is our hope that a coherent

---

[84] See Jeffrey Stout, *Ethics After Babel: The Languages of Morals and their Discontents* (James Clarke, 1990), p. 189: 'Serious conversation with theology will be greatly limited if the voice of theology is not recognizably theological.'

argument and proposal will emerge, but inevitably the steps taken in that direction will sometimes be small, numerous, and selective.

We have identified *three major areas where theology is most likely to feel the weight of neo-pragmatic thinking: justification, the meaning of orthodoxy, and ontological reference.* As we deal with the last of these, three religious critics/ constructive theologians have caught our attention: Charley Hardwick, William Dean, and Eberhard Herrmann. While Hardwick and Dean will not easily accept to be called neo-pragmatists, Herrmann's drawing upon the thought of Hilary Putnam brings him closer to our target. Yet all of these authors engage in issues about the ontological reference of religious utterances, as well as theological beliefs. Hardwick is a self-styled physicalist-naturalist who wants to recast talk of God in terms of talk of values. Dean is a radical empiricist who suggests that we should speak of God in terms of a 'sacred social convention'. Last, Herrmann calls our attention to the interconnection between questions of divinity and questions about the goodness of life.

It will be seen that in a pragmatic and neo-pragmatic context, questions about the existence of God, and about the reference of theological concepts, tend to be cast in terms of the value of such talk for human life. Of course, this is very vague and various thinkers construe this significance in particular ways. At the origin of this refiguration stands a certain suspicion of metaphysics. In fact the history of liberalism, both on the European continent, as well as in America can be narrated as a series of attempts to secure a space for religion. Now and again, throughout this history, theologians have turned to values, ethics, the practical life as being the context in which religious claims are most at home. If Schleiermacher cleared a space for religion in the realm of subjective experience, it was Ritschl that turned explicitly to values and ethics. While Schleiermacher can only be classified as a subjectivist on pain of distorting his thought, on Ritschl's view his theology was painfully subjectivist and individualist. Religion is not so much about what an individual feels, but about a communal way of life. Having its proper home in a realm of ethics, religion is not, like science, about objective reality. It is about values. That is not to say that science itself is not informed by values. The crucial distinction is that whereas the scientist is guided by his values only in directing his thought and gaze to certain objects, these values do not play a part in constructing the solutions, i.e., they are without moral effects. For the religious believer and the theologian, on the other hand, values go, so to speak, all the way down. Ritschl's religion comes perilously close to utilitarianism. Its nature and content are given in terms of the function it serves. This is a subordinationist model, in that religion is subservient to a certain normative understanding of the relationship between man and nature. Ritschl insists that 'Knowledge of God can be demonstrated as religious knowledge only when He is conceived as securing to the believer such a position in the world as more than counterbalances its restrictions.'[85] Moreover, this *subordinationist* component is adjacent to a *universalist* one: 'in every religion, what is sought with the help of the superhuman power reverenced by man, is a solution to the contradiction in which man finds himself as both a part of nature and a spiritual personality claiming to dominate nature.'[86]

With modification this Ritschlian theology also found its way to the United States, especially to Chicago. The subordinationist component is abandoned in Wieman's realism, in response to the idealism of the social gospelers. True religion is not about fulfilling human ideals, but about a certain adjustment to God. We already mentioned Macintosh's insistence on a 'right religious adjustment'. Wieman's 'theocentric' understanding of religion, as opposed to the Ritschlian anthropocentric view, did not however entail the abandonment of the latter's valuational component. God is defined as 'this most subtle and intimate complexity of environmental nature which yields the greatest good when right adjustment is made.'[87] For Wieman, God is not personal, but this is not supposed to be detrimental to his being. In Wieman's metaphysics, ultimate reality is processual, it is events which are the most fundamental components of reality, rather than distinct objects or persons. God is not personal, but neither is he less than personal. To the obvious question, 'but can people love an event, an interaction, rather than a person?', Wieman hastens to reply: that is precisely what people love. When one loves another, one loves the fellowship with the other, one loves love itself. This understanding of God as an ordered process is also a de-supernaturalized view. While God is superhuman, God is not supernatural. If there is such a thing as God, he is within nature, history and experience.

The all important question is, if God is fully collapsed into history, what point is there to continue talking about God? Dewey's objections to both Macintosh and Wieman are instructive: the former's talk about 'right religious adjustment' only makes sense from the perspective of a Western liberal protestant. In other words, it does not do much to accommodate other religious views and experiences. As for Wieman, his talk about God is subjectivist in a very peculiar sense. It is one thing to say that people find in existence the support for the goods and values of living. It is quite another thing to say that these goods constitute a single unified object that rightly deserves human worship. This amounts to an abandonment of the empirical method, for while the first claim is empirical, the second – the religious one – isn't. Dewey's caution is a very important one and it will resurface in our discussion of Hardwick. It aims at the very heart of empirical theology, for empirical theology attempts to have it both ways: adopt a strictly empirical approach to

---

[85] Quoted by Claude Welch, *Protestant Thought in the Nineteenth Century*, vol. 1 (New Haven and London: Yale University Press, 1972), p. 7.

[86] Quoted by C. Welch, *Protestant Thought*, p. 8.

[87] Quoted in G. Dorrien, *The Making*, p. 267.

questions of value, on the one hand, but also resolve that a) value is unified, and b) that it tolerates a religious description, on the other hand.

Charley Hardwick's Events of Grace

Dewey was content to speak about value in purely secular terms, given his conviction that when theology advances beyond empirical experience it becomes subjectivist. Charley Hardwick's *Events of Grace: Naturalism, Existentialism, and Theology*[88] disputes precisely the assumption that a 'valuational theism' is incoherent and in fact subjectivist.

Hardwick's programme is impressive, for it attempts to combine into what he calls a 'valuational theism' both an austere physicalist naturalism, but also a rich description of religious experience in terms of some of the positive concepts of Christian theology, like grace, creation, redemption and so on. While this latter part of his project is especially interesting, there is not enough space to fully engage it here. Rather, what interests us is precisely Hardwick's confidence that theistic language can be interpreted as true even while physicalist naturalism holds that the term 'God' does not refer. The contention is that one can recast theistic religious talk entirely in naturalist terms, as referring to a 'valuational complex' and an 'attendant theistic seeing-as'.

Hardwick takes for granted that 'God' does not refer, at least not to that independently existing and autonomous being, which for Christians is personal. *If we want to keep the truth* of our theistic language, the truth of statements like 'God exists', or 'God loves the world', then we have to be prepared to relinquish the traditional meaning of God. Speaking about the revisionist effort that this implies, Hardwick loftily pontificates that 'It is true that many of the ontological references theologians make are compromised by this effort. But the day is very late for Western theism, and those references are already deeply compromised anyway.'[89] We shall not get into a debate on whether the issue is indeed settled in favour of a physicalist-naturalist denial of the reference of 'God'. In fact we will grant this point to Hardwick for the sake of argument and ask whether his proposal to change the meaning of 'God' works well within his own parameters. What are these parameters?

Hardwick insists, first, that his valuational theism is not noncognitivist. Although the traditional reference of God is made obsolete, the sentences in which this term of reference is present remain nonetheless true. Hardwick's proposal is that God refers to a 'subjunctive meta-assertion for a valuational complex' and an 'attendant seeing-as'. Speaking of God is in fact a roundabout way of speaking about a valuational complex. In other words, when religious adherents speak of God, they proclaim allegiance to a form of life, to a practice which is guided by certain values. This accounts for the 'valuational complex'

---

[88] (Cambridge: Cambridge University Press, 1996).

[89] C. Hardwick, *Events of Grace*, pp. 182-3.

component in Hardwick's valuational theism. Yet he knows very well that this is not enough: 'A seeing-as is required because *seemingly referential language* is used to constitute the religious form of life and must somehow be accommodated.'[90] Thus, the second component of Hardwick's valuational theism is a theistic seeing-as, a method by which religious believers view reality 'as if' all these theistic statements were true of it. Needless to say that these statements must not be interpreted literally, but only as make believe.

Let us point out that there are two different ways in which Hardwick's revisionary theism can be interpreted. One might suppose that this is an *interpretive thesis*, a proposal about the way in which the first-order speech of religious adherents should be understood. As an interpretive thesis, it runs into serious problems. Part of the contention of this volume is that Davidson's understanding of the relationship between truth and meaning leans heavily against such revisionist attempts. Chapter IV includes a detailed discussion of this implication. Yet Hardwick himself admits that if something is to be salvaged from theism, something must also be sacrificed. He speaks approvingly of Wieman's changing the entire religious problematic. It then appears that this is not simply a descriptive proposal, but a *normative thesis*, a positive suggestion about what theology should be about, after old orthodoxies are left behind.

In order to make such a normative proposal, some description of what adherents have been up to – the interpretive component – is still necessary. In this respect it is, we believe, illuminating that Hardwick looks favourably towards 'thick' sociologies of religion, like that of Geertz, for example. These sociologies are of a Durkheimian inspiration. They treat religions as mainly interpretive frameworks. Such frameworks are built of an outer husk – which is constituted by the myths, stories, symbols, practices of a community or society. When Hardwick deals with the first order religious beliefs, he insists upon setting these on the backdrop of the husk, i.e. they become secondary to the larger task, the meta-task which that particular religion is supposed to accomplish. We argue that *it is only by presupposing such a complexity behind the first order speech acts, a complexity of which naïve believers are understandably ignorant, that Hardwick and other revisionists is able to tell us that their utterances are really about a valuational complex, or whatever else.* He urges that 'we look not to claims about what exists but to a form of life and a practice to do justice to religious discourse.'[91] Curiously, he enlists both George Lindbeck and (with some hesitation) Stanley Hauerwas, as valuational theists. Lindbeck is the more obvious candidate, for he too builds on Geertz's work in arguing that theological claims are actually expressions of second order rules of grammar.

---

[90] C. Hardwick, *Events of Grace*, p. 62.

[91] C. Hardwick, *Events of Grace*, p. 63.

In appears, then, that *Hardwick's whole proposal rests on a disjunction between what religious adherents say, or understand themselves to be saying, and a religious framework, a form of life, a practice, which organizes these acts of reference in a fashion quite independent of believer's own intentions or awareness*. To us this looks like promoting a dualism of scheme and content, a dualism demolished by Davidson's critique.

Let us, however, return to the suggestion that it is still important and also cognitively significant to speak of God, even while the conditions of reference have drastically changed. Since there are two components to valuational theism, a valuational complex, plus an attendant seeing-as, these have to be defended.

Hardwick holds that a normative account of values is possible and rationally defensible. Needless to say, the existence of such values does not presuppose the existence of a separate world of values, an 'upper room' of eternal forms. He draws on the work of John Post's *Faces of Existence* to speak of values as supervening on physical characteristics, while not being reducible to these. Hardwick identifies this wider valuational stance with 'openness to the future understood as an existential mode of being.'[92] While this is an extremely important aspect of his work, we are more interested in the second defence, namely, that these values, which possess normativity, also require in some sense a theistic seeing-as. This is precisely where Dewey focuses his attack on Wieman: it is one thing to come up with a normative description of a valuational matrix, but it is quite another to infer that this complex bears a Christian theistic description. This is precisely what Hardwick wants to argue. But this is also where his proposal breaks down, in our opinion.

The task, therefore, is to move from a phenomenology of the human condition, which uncovers a normative set of values, to the possibility of a theistic expression of these values in terms of God's existence. As we saw, before such a transition is possible, the traditional ontological reference of God-talk has to be ruled out: 'Once we change our vision about what "God" *means*, then we can defend theism as integral to the articulation of a normative valuational stance.'[93] Hardwick believes that once this angle of sight is changed, the appropriateness of Christian theistic seeing-as becomes evident 'when the deepest issues regarding authentic human existence are brought to the surface.'[94] However, not much argument is presented as to why these values should be given a theistic rendering. It is simply assumed that it is appropriate to do so: 'We simply draw forth from an existentialist interpretation of faith an existentialist interpretation of God. A theistic seeing-as then becomes *appropriate* for expressing a normative valuational stance (authentic human

---

[92] C. Hardwick, *Events of Grace*, p. 197.

[93] C. Hardwick, *Events of Grace*, pp. 186-7.

[94] C. Hardwick, *Events of Grace*, p. 187.

existence).'[95] But to say that it is *appropriate* will surely not satisfy the critics. For what we wanted to know is why *these* symbols, *these stories and creeds* are needed to express a valuational stance. Yet Hardwick is candid about this: 'The question is whether such *appropriateness* is sufficient to establish normativity. This last question is important, again, because we want to claim cognitive value for the Christian form of a theistic seeing-as, namely that "God exists" is true from within a physicalist ontology.' The problem appears because if these particular cases of theistic seeing-as are merely appropriate for the expression of these values, theology is in danger of losing its cognitive value. Where does normativity come from then? The answer is that 'the normative account arises, rather, from the description of the human condition.'[96] In other words, the theistic language is appropriate because it is able to pick out, to name those values which are normative for the human beings. In other words, this is a normativity which works backwards rather than forwards. *Inasmuch as these values are correctly identified, then using such theistic talk is normatively justified, although not normatively necessary.*

This loosening up of normativity, as Hardwick calls it, is moreover consistent with the Gospel:

> This loosening of the normative requirement for a theistic seeing-as is imposed by the content of the gospel itself (including its critique of idolatry). When Christians have best understood themselves, they have wanted to say that the love of God is shed abroad upon all humankind, not merely upon those who use Christian (i.e., in Post's sense, "theistic") language or adopt a specifically Christian form of life. The emphasis in the gospel is upon the *reality* of God with which human beings have to do, not upon their special languages.[97]

In order to see what is wrong with Hardwick's revisionism, besides his condescending confidence that 'God' does not refer, his methodology must be carefully observed. The logic behind his position is that first order speech acts – traditionally understood to refer to an ontologically existing being – should rather be understood as being covert references to a valuational complex. Now it is important to notice that for Hardwick, this valuational complex is readily describable in the language of existential philosophy, as openness to the future. This is a point of no small importance, for Hardwick insists on the further necessity, or at the very least a desirable possibility, of using a theistic language, over and above the normal, public language which he has used to render the content of the valuational stance. The point is that Hardwick has not

---

[95] C. Hardwick, *Events of Grace*, p. 187. There are further problems with attempt to make 'the entire theological tradition available again' from within naturalism (*Events of Grace*, p. 70), some of which are aptly pointed out by Charles Milligan, 'The Limits of Conventional Religious Language for Contemporary Meaning,' *American Journal of Theology and Philosophy* 17.3 (1996).

[96] C. Hardwick, *Events of Grace*, p. 188.

[97] C. Hardwick, *Events of Grace*, p. 188.

supplied any extra reasons why we should not feel compelled by Dewey's complaint. If already the valuational complex has been expressed in a language understood by most people, moreover, if those values have been objectively established as being normative, why bother with the language of myth and religious stories?

The only way in which such language might still be justified, is if it is able to express what the language of existentialism, or any other language, is unable to express.[98] That is, if here is a surplus to what that prior language tries to capture, but is unable to. Such a surplus will have to be an *unconceptualised* something. It would be a mistake to call it an unconceptualised experience of *value*, for that would already involve our ability to pigeonhole it somewhere on our conceptual system, which would mean it is not unconceptualised. Moreover, to speak of that something in terms of value would be assume that the language of value is self-explanatory, primary. This is indeed something which we can take Hardwick to be assuming, although it would be hard to demonstrate. At any rate, Hardwick's supposition is that the language of value is prior (if not necessarily basic) to the language of religion.[99]

The upshot of holding a) that a theistic seeing-as is only an *appropriate*, but not *necessary* expression of those values and b) implying that theistic seeing-as is non-redundant, presumably because there is an unconceptualised surplus, is that theistic language must be non-cognitive. And this is precisely what Hardwick does not want. It may be that, inasmuch as theistic language gives expression to those values already captured in the language of existentialism, and insofar as those values are normative for the human condition, theistic language is cognitive. But to the extent that religious language is distinctive, and not some trivial mirroring of another language, then the question has to be put of the cognitive status of that which it uniquely expresses. And, unfortunately, Hardwick doesn't offer us much reason to distinguish his claims from what Lindbeck calls 'experiential-expressivism'.

William Dean

Hardwick's dilemma consists in finding a way between religious non-cognitivism and an archaic illusion that 'God' refers. To his credit, the outcome of his marriage between theology and naturalism is surprisingly rich. While the concept 'God' may not refer to an ontological being, it does serve a function in delivering a very loaded content. William Dean's dilemma is similar: he also wants theology to not shy away from a substantive notion of God, to risk

---

[98] Charles Milligan notes, 'I do not see where language of God's love contributes to the content of the nature of God as presented or to the enrichment of human existence', p. 303.

[99] Here one wonders whether he has really assimilated Lindbeck's claim that it is the stories of the Bible which give content to our values, rather than the other way around.

venturing beyond a neo-pragmatic methodological shyness, yet without falling back upon an 'obsolete transcendental objectivism'[100], which he, together with West and Stout, rejects. Dean comments that neo-pragmatic theologians like Stout, Taylor and Robbins, are too stressed by methodological purity and stop just short of a proper constructive theology. Indeed, as our discussion of Eberhard Herrmann will reveal, this is a chief neopragmatic concern. As Robbins has indicated, neo-pragmatism conceives knowledge as an ability to manipulate sentences in order to achieve certain practical results. Testing that knowledge can therefore only be a matter of pragmatic checks. It is easy to understand why such theologians will stay clear of substantive theologies. *The fear is that a rich notion of God lacks adequate and agreed upon methods of pragmatic verification.* Especially in verificationist versions of epistemology, this is an insurmountable problem, because in the absence of a method of verification, we cannot be confident in the meanings we ascribe.

Dean believes that such a myopic concentration on sentences and pragmatic tests forgets the realities of religious experience. To be sure, what neo-pragmatic philosophy clarifies is that experience cannot be disjuncted from a sense of its cultural relativity. Indeed, empirical and process theologians 'were inclined to trust too simply their capacity to intuit universal truths about God.'[101] Experience does not come naked; not only it stands in need of interpretation, but it is always already interpreted. The fault of the new historicists, however, is just as grave, for they cannot explain 'how it is that the religious person is able to arrive at a theistic hypothesis that has even the remotest chance of pragmatic confirmation.'[102] This is an absolutely crucial and valid point: *religious believers seem to manipulate religious concepts with a confidence which far outruns their knowledge of how the truth of their sentences could be verified.* To this the new historicists might reply that they are simply uttering gibberish. Yet it is difficult to call meaningless a significant number of concepts whose actual use seems to be governed by rules. Moreover, there seems to be authentic disagreement over the meaning of words which lack apparent methods of verification, or truth conditions other than the trivial '*s* is true iff *s*'.

This, then, is *Dean's dilemma: on the one hand, a neo-pragmatic attention to exclusively pragmatic means of sentential testing does little justice to the complexity of the religious phenomenon; on the other, an empirical privileging of experience is too casual in its forgetfulness of culture.* In the first case we have an imagination which seems unbounded by anything resulting from experience, but this disregards a whole range of meaningful phenomena. In the second, there is an openness to the pull of transcendence, the lure of objectivity

[100] W. Dean, *History*, p. 139.
[101] W. Dean, *History*, p. 143.
[102] W. Dean, *History*, p. 142.

– yet in blissful ignorance of its cultural-linguistic condition. Is there a way to navigate these tricky waters?

Dean thinks there is and he turns to the thought of radical empiricists. These believed in an imagination that is both able to construct subjective variations and is derived from and determined by environmental possibilities outside the subject.[103] Whereas the neo-pragmatists 'can see no more in the concept of God that a heritage of lucky and unlucky guesses – lucky when they turned out to have some utility, unlucky when they did not',[104] a "radically empirical epistemology allows [us] to contend that the religious person may have a vague, indistinct, unclear, groping sort of empiricist apprehension of the "whole," to use Dewey's term, of the "more," to use James' term, of the divine "lure," to use Whitehead's term, of the "creative event," to use Wieman's term, or of the "creative advance," to use Meland's term.'[105] What Dean sets his sight on, following the radical empiricists, is something more than simply a human imaginative construct. *Unless theology works with something more than subjective fantasies – whether they are individualistic or even social and practical understandings of, say, the Kingdom of God, it is in danger of losing contact with reality.*

At this stage in Dean's work he seems particularly vulnerable to Robbins' well-aimed attack, as we saw in the first section of this chapter. He struggles *to put much content to these experiences* of the whole, of the divine lure. Whatever it is that Dean considers theology to be pulled by, it still does not have too much content at this earlier stage. In his 1994 study, *The Religious Critic in American Culture*,[106] he seems to be moving in a more neo-pragmatic direction, but not so much as to compromise his initial empirical leanings. The main challenge of his earlier *History Making History* has been to give an account of the 'objective pull' which would not succumb to the myth of the Given. Yet all his efforts of putting much flesh on an admittedly 'vague' cause and determination of the religious experience failed. The reason was that anything which exceeds a human subjective imagination is also bound to exceed the limits of reason and intelligibility. *The Religious Critic* finds a way in which to speak about this excess, that which pulls, fuels and determines a subjective imagination in purely social, historical and linguistic terms. God is not simply a vaguely defined 'whole,' or 'more,' but a 'sacred social convention'.

The problem of value based theologies is that they are subjective. Even if one is able to account for the objectivity of values, the transition from these ethical values to a theistic description is filled with gaps. On the other hand, values are adopted and then relinquished. Different social groups may have

---

[103] W. Dean, *History*, p. 142.
[104] W. Dean, *History*, pp. 142-3.
[105] W. Dean, *History*, p. 142.
[106] (Albany: SUNY Press, 1994)

different values, with no way of reconciling their normative orientations. This subjectivism does not satisfy Dean. Yet the alternative, as we saw, is equally knotty. So how does one account for a pull which comes from beyond the bounds of the human imagination, yet remains human, historical? The solution is provided by a thick description of social conventions.

Dean holds that 'What we believe is an interpretation, a construct; but an interpretation can grow from an empirical intimation of the past and it can become a social fact that affects our future beliefs. Our interpretations and constructs become conventions, where a convention is not a fantasy internal to the subject but a historical reality external to the subject.'[107] This notion of a social convention supplies Dean with the requisite distinction from a merely subjective imagination. A convention, so to speak, takes on a life of its own. Let us listen to Dean again:

> A convention, in short, lives through time as a tradition, but as a tradition that is continually augmented by new criticisms and precedents. A convention is a reality apart from its causes, even though its causes contribute to it. Like any organism, it is more than what caused it, just as a child is more than what its parents and its environment would make it. [...] What a convention is, in itself, is a mystery, just as a person or the sacred is a mystery.[108]

God is a sacred convention. 'The sacred convention is a concrete, evaluative thrust living and operating in a society. It has a life of its own, just as a whole organism has a life that cannot be reduced to the lives of its parts. [...] The sacred provides the deepest normative drive in a society as that society works out of its religious sense of the whole.'[109] The obvious advantage of this model is that it inherits from valuational theologies the sense of the connection between God and his practical effects for humankind, without thereby reducing God to the subjective imagination of the people. At least this is what Dean would intend. God is a function of Israel, of the Church, but it is more than that. How is it more?

God as a sacred convention exceeds its formative conditions and acquires a life of its own. This 'life of its own' is what provides the excess which Dean needed in order to escape sheer subjectivism. Moreover, the excess is rendered in what seem to be purely social, linguistic, historical terms. No mention is made of 'dubious entities', although Dean sometimes still continues to speak in terms of the 'whole'. Only now this 'whole' is rendered symbolically and conventionally. Another obvious advantage of Dean's proposal is that it affords him a highly nuanced and positive notion of God, beyond the initial vagueness to which he seemed destined earlier.[110] Yet the question remains: if God is

---

[107] W. Dean, *Religious Critic*, p. 101.

[108] W. Dean, *Religious Critic*, p. 105.

[109] W. Dean, *Religious Critic*, p. 137.

[110] Precisely such a positivity allows Dean to argue for the public role of theology. Whereas Stout hesitates to work with a hi-definition notion of God, Dean's sacred

more than simply a function of these human constructions, what is the content of this 'more?' Isn't Dean falling back to a content-less vagueness when he should explicate the most interesting bit of his proposal, namely the 'excessive' nature of the convention?

This religious question is based in fact on a non-religious difficulty with Dean's proposal. How exactly is it that a convention takes a life of its own, *independently* of human agency? Does Dean unduly reify conventions? Again, Donald Davidson's attack on conventions as semantic intermediaries will prove instructive in this respect as well. That discussion has to be delayed until the next chapter, but some additional points have to be addressed.

To say that God is more than a human imaginative construction, based upon the notion that a convention lives beyond the controlling powers of its creators, is an empty suggestion unless one is able to specify in cognitive terms in what this excess consists. But it is difficult, we think impossible, to make those specifications independently of describing the 'action' of a convention in terms of the actions of human agents who use it. This argument stems from the very neo-pragmatic stance which seems to inform Dean *at this particular point*. What he wants is a notion of God which is both a human construct and simultaneously exceeding human construction. But that excess has to be given some description, some content, lest it be an empty promise. It may be that the excess *causes* us to think and behave in various ways, independently of how that excess might be *described and intentionally employed by human agents*. But causes are not reasons. Dean seems to have re-encountered the very same problem which he was attempting to escape. In *History Making History*, his notion of the 'whole' as that which determined and constrained experience from outside was an empty one, appearing to employ the Myth of the Given. The linguistic dress in the form of social conventions which he puts on it can only be effective if he holds, as he does, that a convention is more than what human agents control. Dean writes that 'The reality of a convention is found in the fact that, like the American Constitution, *it turns one day and acts in unpredictable ways, it takes initiatives.* In this independent action and in this mystery lies the distinct reality of a convention.' *Yet this independence, this excess, this 'more' remains just as content-less. For it is impossible to fill that 'more' with content without at the same time admitting that a convention is within the control of human agency.* To fill with content – i.e. to give a description which can then play a role in a justification – the notion of the excessive life of a convention – is either a self-refuting exercise (it will show that there is no excess beyond how human agents sustain conventions) or it is impossible.

---

conventions are highly defined and the theologian has the responsibility to analyse the particular religious conventions active in a given society. See Donald A. Crosby's appreciative commentary in 'Construction, Convention, and Conviction', *American Journal of Theology and Philosophy* 16.1 (1995), pp. 21-32.

Let us return now to an earlier point, which will close our discussion of Dean's sacred conventions. He is keen, like Hardwick, to harmonize his proposal with biblical studies, but also with a Chicago tradition of socio-historical criticism of theological ideas. To treat God as a convention, he argues, is consistent with contemporary directions in biblical studies, because now

> it has become increasingly evident that Hebrew biblical writers and rabbis imaginatively constructed their religious world. Through a chain of interpretations, creatively shaping and reshaping their tradition to voice new needs and address new problems, the ancient Hebrews reinterpreted their covenants with their God and/or their God itself. [...] The Hebrew God, like any convention, is altered by an imagined image that becomes socially effective. [...] At the same time it is also true that the God of Israel is, finally, more than the sum of Hebrew interpretations of God.[111]

Besides this being a clear instance of the problem we mentioned earlier, namely 'in what sense is it more?', it reveals a problem with this approach. There are very few scholars and theologians who will object to the claim that biblical understandings of God are socio-historically shaped. The very fact that one uses language means that the conceptual resources for the expression of beliefs and ideas are limited and context relative. It is easy to imagine how this might constitute a problem for crude correspondence theories of truth, whereby a piece of reality has to be clearly mirrored in a stretch of language. Once that stretch of language is shown to contain cultural 'impurities,' the whole act of knowledge and reference appears compromised. *Yet if one construes knowledge not necessarily in terms of piece by piece correspondence to reality, or in terms of a neo-pragmatic ability to manipulate sentences, or yet in terms of Quine's naturalized epistemology, but along critically realist lines, or even internal/pragmatic realist lines, as our ability to stay in touch with reality through the use of language, then the very fact that there are 'cultural impurities' in our expressions is something to be expected rather than dreaded.* But crucially, their presence does not mean that our expressions about God, socio-historically constructed as they are, are at all qualitatively inferior to our expressions about, say, chairs and particles.

Dean achieves something like the opposite effect to what he intended. The notion of God remains not only empty – insofar as it is supposed to exceed human imaginative productions – but also out of cognitive reach. We are left with only our socio-historical idiosyncrasies, rather than actual meaningful communion with the divine. Although Dean holds that the God of the Hebrews is more than the sum of these human compositions, this 'more' remains an empty promise, utterly useless in theology. For all of his criticism of a neo-pragmatic dualism between language and experience, it is hard to escape the

[111] W. Dean, *Religious Critic*, p. 138.

conclusion that he perpetuates the same dichotomy, in which he substitutes history for language.[112]

Eberhard Herrmann

On the European continent, the communication between neo-pragmatism and theology, but especially the philosophy of religion is picking up pace. Among scholars pursuing the dialogue,[113] Eberhard Herrmann has contributed an original proposal that forms the topic of this present section. A professor of theology at Uppsala, Herrmann's philosophy of religion was elaborated under the influence of Putnam's critique of metaphysical realism. A less obvious influence, but just as determinative, is Rudolf Carnap's later philosophical work. Both Putnam and Carnap contribute to a critique of the notion that there is a *perfect description of reality*, a description which does not presuppose any acts of human cognition, or any humanly created conceptual systems. The claim of metaphysical realism is that such a description of reality is true because it corresponds to the very features of the world. These features of the world, its properties, are there whether they are acknowledged and conceptualised or not. For all we know, concludes the metaphysical realist, our best theories of the world, regardless of how well they are entrenched or justified, may not capture the signature of the world. Thus, truth is defined in radically non-epistemic terms, as being independent of human attempts to verify it. There are certain things and properties which exist and their existence is independent of human cognition.

Carnap's criticism on this position is assumed by Herrmann to have been devastating. Questions of existence are either internal – in which case they are trivial and confined to a given framework – or they are external in which case they are pragmatic and amount to questions of whether it is preferable to use one conceptual framework or another. Transported to the field of religion, this discussion entails that, as Peter Byrne notes, 'the question of whether there really is a *theos* will become merely the question of whether it us useful to employ a theistic vocabulary or not.'[114] Rortian reminiscences are not accidental here. The question of the existence of God cannot be dissociated from the religious framework from within which we pose it. But the question of

[112] Robert S. Corrington, 'Beyond Experience: Pragmatism and Nature's God', *American Journal of Theology and Philosophy* 14/2 (1993).

[113] Among these, we should mention Dirk-Martin Grube, 'Realism, Foundationalism, and Constructivism: A Philosopher's Bermuda Triangle?', *Neue Zeitschrift für Systematische Theologie* 40 (1998), pp. 107-126; 'Religious Experience After the Demise of Foundationalism', *Religious Studies* 31 (1995), pp. 37-52; 'Refuting the Evidentialist Challenge to Religion: A Critique Inspired by William James', *Ars Disputandi* [http://www.ArsDisputandi.org] 3 (2003).

[114] Peter Byrne, *God and Realism* (Aldershot: Ashgate, 2003), p. 87.

whether we should be using the framework or not is not to be settled by an independent assessment of whether God exists or not. Such an assessment is an incoherent idea. 'The choice of conceptual framework is determined by its relevance in relation to the activities which are considered necessary or desirable for the task in hand whether it is, for example, survival or the attainment of the good life or quite simply the solution of problems which gives us pleasure to solve.'[115] The pragmatic element is strong here: asking about the existence of something and the choice of scheme which frames that inquiry are always embedded in practical activities.

But Herrmann does not stop here. Theories, whether scientific or religious, contribute to the knowledge of reality. Here knowledge of reality no longer means a representation of a theory-independent reality, but the construction of frameworks which are adequate to the *resistance* offered by reality in our observational experience. By speaking of resistance, Herrmann wishes to make room for the notion that reality always exceeds our conceptualisations. But, as with Rorty and Davidson, the resistance is causal rather than epistemic. So if theories are to count as knowledge, they must be empirically adequate, i.e. they should be able o generate testable hypotheses in order to be able to say what is true about what is observable.[116] However, theistic frameworks do not contribute in any sense to the formation of empirical hypotheses. Thus Herrmann concludes that theism is not comparable to a scientific theory which speaks about the empirical world. Nevertheless, *theistic frameworks remain cognitively meaningful because they relate to another sort of experience, existential experience.* Now Herrmann's project begins to look like the demarcational variety, which in fact flows naturally from Carnap's logic. Science belongs to the empirical realm, whereas religion belongs to the existential. As Herrmann explains, 'On the basis of the pragmatic realism which I argue for, so-called metaphysical theories become part of the conceptualizations of how reality as conceptualized by us offers resistance *in our existential experiences of what it means to be human* i.e. to live with life's inevitabilities.'[117] Thus, while on their face value, religious claims purport to be about extra-conceptual realities, if we want to retain their cognitive meaningfulness we have to construe them in terms of the existential adequacy of their narratives, rituals, practices and so on.

Herrmann makes the same point in a paper read before the European Society for the Philosophy of Religion, in the fall of 2006:

> If conceptions, images and narratives of God are existentially adequate concerning how reality offers resistance in the inevitabilities of life, the question of God is similar to the question of the consumer's priorities with the difference

---

[115] E. Herrmann, *Religion, Reality, and a Good life: A Philosophical Approach to Religion* (Tübingen: Mohr Siebeck, 2005), p. 175.

[116] W. Herrmann, *Religion, reality and the good life*, p. 128.

[117] W. Herrmann, *Religion, reality, and the good life*, pp. 127f. (our emphasis).

> that we in the case of the consumers' priorities have to do with empirically adequate or inadequate theories and in the case of God with existentially adequate or inadequate views of life. There is no point in adding or emphasising that God as such, besides the conceptions, images and narratives of our views of life really exists. If it is rational, i.e. in this connection existentially adequate to talk about God, we cannot help accepting what we have conceptualized as God.[118]

What is taken to follow from this rejection of metaphysical realism is a radical epistemising of God. It is misguided to construe religion as that framework which attempts to capture something out there which might offer human beings a consolation, comfort, generally speaking a theodicy, all the while insisting that our religious narratives (no matter how adequate in meeting this practical task) may nevertheless be utterly mistaken. This is a metaphysically realist incoherence: to 'claim that there is a God's consolation, mercy and justice existing independently of us human beings and irrespective of how we in interaction with reality conceptualize it.'[119] The sceptical conclusion is believed to also follow in religion: 'Analogously, if God's consolation, mercy and justice are independent of how we conceptualize them, we can actually never know either what God's consolation, mercy and justice are nor when it is that we meet them.'[120] What Herrmann finds it hard to countenance is the notion that what divine consolation looks like might be (in principle) utterly different from the palette of human modalities and instruments of consolation. These are some potent arguments and they need to be judiciously evaluated.

Professor Herrmann has brought to our attention a model of a pragmatic-realist philosophy of religion. A driving force behind the argument is an attempt to block scepticism, both philosophically and religiously. It is assumed that 'an external perspective' on truth and knowledge, which presupposes a Perfect Description of Reality, leads to scepticism, inasmuch as it cannot block the possibility of global error, the thought that we might be massively mistaken in our beliefs. But, as Carnap and Putnam show, the notion presupposes an external perspective which does not make sense. In place of such an external perspective, we might do well to recognize that the only questions of existence which make sense are those internal to a 'framework'. The notion of framework is absolutely crucial to this 'epistemic' approach to truth and knowledge. We have seen that the notion of conceptual scheme has suffered somewhat at the hands of Donald Davidson, but also Richard Rorty. Davidson cannot conceive of a conceptual scheme which is not tied to a language. But then the notion that we might have two untranslatable languages is incoherent: *either a language is translatable, or it is not recognizable as a language at all.* This argument itself will not hold water all the time, for there are languages and

---

[118] W. Herrmann, 'Religion without metaphysics', unpublished paper, Tuebingen, September 2006, p. 22.

[119] W. Herrmann, 'Religion without metaphysics', p. 25.

[120] W. Herrmann, 'Religion without metaphysics', p. 25.

cultures for which we have as yet been unable to come up with satisfactory translations. Moreover, Davidson's argument is verificationist. This would be ironic for someone like Peter Byrne who holds that the 'framework approach' to truth and knowledge, relativising these notions to a conceptual framework, is itself 'driven throughout by the crudest verificationism.'[121] It is a conceptual mistake, he holds, to confuse use with a method of verification. Lack of a method of verification was never an impediment to intelligible use. All that was required were shared *rules of use*. Historically speaking, the fact that methods of verification evolve, change and suffer modification beyond recognition is also not an impediment to continued reference. All that is required is a minimal understanding of rules governing use. The fact that ancient Greeks could meaningfully speak about the atom - even while they did not share with us either our knowledge of these entities, or our methods of verification - does not mean that it was the same thing that we were trying to approximate. As Frederick Will points out, himself another 'pragmatic realist',

> There is no little irony in the fact that the possibilities of conceptual variation, viewed synchronically, should be regarded by some philosophers to be a most serious obstacle for determining in any fair, unbiased, undistorted way, the character of objects and features of the world, when, these same possibilities, viewed diachronically in the history of science, have been one of the most productive methodological resources of modern physical theory.[122]

In what follows we will try to disregard the possibly correct objections to the notion of framework and grant Herrmann this common ground.

The reader will forgive us for anticipating a discussion of the two features of Putnam's notion of conceptual frameworks. First, conceptual frameworks are meta-linguistic. To hold otherwise would be to play right into Davidson's verificationist critique: if they are linguistic, then they should also be translatable. But one would be tempted to ask: what is the difference between Putnam's frameworks and, say, Roderick Firth's notion that we can conceptualize reality prior to linguistic training? There is a huge difference between the two. Putnam would not envisage a non-linguistic conceptualization, but only a meta-linguistic one, in the sense that a given natural language puts at our disposal the resources to make conceptual framework discrimination. This is more central to our response to Herrmann than is immediately obvious. *It is simply not the case that all speakers of a common language share a world-view and an ontology*. Having a language is compatible with entertaining different conceptual schemes. That is why Putnam can speak of both numbers and sets, of both chairs and particles in the same language.

---

[121] Peter Byrne, *God and Realism*, p. 91.

[122] Frederick Will, *Pragmatism and Realism* (Boston: Rowman and Littlefield, 1997), p. 38.

The second important feature in Putnam's internal realism is that it is the same reality which we conceptualize differently, not - as Herrmann holds - *different parts of reality are assigned to different conceptual schemes.* Let me quote Putnam here: 'one can describe *the same room* (giving the example of how many objects there are in a given room) using two different vocabularies…'[123] Crucially, this is not a question of first having a 'view' of the room, then deciding which object fits into what conceptual scheme.

A question which now seems unavoidable, is about what exactly individuates a conceptual framework. How is one conceptual framework introduced? Carnap suggests the following procedure: first, a general term is introduced, a predicate of a higher level, for the new kind of entities, permitting us to say for any particular entity that it belongs to this kind; secondly, the introduction of variables of the new type.[124] John Kekes, however, poses the following question to Carnap:[125] how is the new general term introduced? There are two possibilities: either in terms of an ostensive definition, or in terms of another framework. Either way, writes Kekes, the dilemma of external questions should not arise for Carnap. For, if it is by an ostensive definition, it implies that the thing defined exists. If it is in terms of another framework, then what looks like an external question in one framework is an internal question in another framework.

All of this is to say that *Herrmann fails to justify the relegation of 'God' to the existential framework.* This is not to say that 'God' cannot be talked about existentially. Carnap's intention was to construe his talk about conceptual frameworks in such a way as to render 'external' questions meaningless. But this has proved difficult to do, for conceptual frameworks - if there are such things - cannot be interpreted territorially. But this is precisely what Herrmann attempts to do: God belongs to the existential framework, *not* to the empirical one. There are several problems with this: first, it is contrary to Putnam's, as well as Carnap's notion that something might be talked about utilizing a variety of conceptual frameworks: one might describe the same thing in terms of quality, of physical magnitude etc. To come back to the Putnam quote: it is the same room one is describing, not assigning different conceptual schemes to different parts of the room. This would be to assume an external perspective, a *perfect description of reality* which has already *counted* how many objects there are in the room, before it allocates them. *Ironically, then, to say that God belongs to the existential framework, rather than the empirical framework is to assume a perfect description of reality.*

---

[123] Hilary Putnam, 'The Question of Realism', in *Words and Life*, p. 309.

[124] Rudolf Carnap, 'Empiricism, Semantics and Ontology' [http://www.ditext.com/carnap/carnap.html], section 3.

[125] John Kekes, 'Skepticism and External Questions', *Philosophy and Phenomenological Research* 31/3 (Mar. 1971), pp. 325-340, pp. 331ff.

One final point before the argument about consolation. Herrmann assumes that existence questions can only be internal questions and as such must be trivial. Once we have accepted the conceptual scheme of religion, we cannot avoid accepting what we have conceptualized as God. But this is wrong. Carnap certainly does not hold that internal questions are trivial, and neither does Putnam. A conceptual framework gives us a way to answer such questions, not to eliminate them. Once we have decided which conceptual framework to adopt, whether Celsius or Fahrenheit, then the answer to the question 'what is the outside temperature?' is certainly non-trivial. Here we may return to a point made about Putnam: a language allows for a multiplicity of conceptual frameworks. In the same way, a conceptual framework need only be taken as giving rules for use, guidance, rather than settling questions *a priori*. The fact that such questions are not settled *a priori* is shown by the fact that theists and atheists can meaningfully disagree. Herrmann mistakenly objects that such a disagreement assumes a correspondential relation between words and reality. For such meaningful disagreement to take place it is sufficient to have shared rules, shared meanings. This is certainly not asking for too much.

Herrmann's position should be familiar to those accustomed to recent pleas about making reality accessible. Ranging from Putnam and McDowell to Rorty, the claim is that in order for something to be intelligible, it must be connected to use. However, *there is great variety in how 'use' is understood, or what it is taken to imply* (as Putnam himself realized). The story is a little bit complicated in that it involves certain subtle differences between Putnam (and possibly McDowell) on one hand, and Rorty, on the other hand. For Putnam, reality is describable only once a conceptual scheme is in place. Descriptions of such reality are always framework-relative. However, given a conceptual framework, there is piece-meal access to that reality, there is representation although there are no representations. What needs to be stressed here is that the criterion of accessibility for Putnam consists in a conceptual relation - vaguely defined between the object of knowledge and what we already know. This amounts to the quite uncontroversial claim that knowledge is simultaneously appropriation. However, with Rorty the situation is different. For Rorty, reality only makes sense from within a *practical* attempt to cope with it. Rorty goes *beyond a merely conceptual relation* - in the trivial sense that for something to make sense it must be connected with what I already know - towards a *pragmatic and instrumentalist approach*: it must enable me to get the good life that I want. Rorty's recent writings on religion give ample evidence for that, as we saw.

Now it is significant that Herrmann also chooses to speak in terms of the good life.[126] This places Herrmann in the (uneasy, perhaps, given their respective attitudes to even a modest realism) company of Rorty and Dewey!

---

[126] W. Herrmann, 'Religion without Metaphysics', p. 24.

Rorty, echoing Dewey, says: 'even if a nonhuman authority tells you something, the only way to figure out whether what you have been told is true is to see whether it gets you the sort of life you want.'[127] This is very near to what we hear in the paper: in order for us to have an accessible divine consolation, it must be related to the multiple and various ways in which we console each other as human beings. Otherwise, if we conceive of God's consolation as utterly unrelated to the various ways in which *human* consolation figures in *human* life, we run the risk of making it utterly inaccessible.

This is where the 'crudest verificationism' comes to the fore. Putnam's arguments about intelligibility and accessibility - which corroborate his rejection of the external perspective - do not necessarily require this position about divine consolation. All that they require is that divine consolation be intelligibly related to other things we already know. In other words, all that is required is that we have minimal rules for its linguistic employment. Herrmann requires too much of divine consolation: that it be related our human practices of consolation. Of course, there is the ancient theological instrument of analogy - in its various metamorphoses - which ensures that our talk of God must not remain independent of our normal linguistic practice. From the theistic perspective espoused by Byrne, Herrmann runs the risk of losing an appropriate object of theistic belief in the sense that it would make God's action conceptually dependent upon human action, when it is precisely human action which is supposed to be ordered by the divine.[128]

One closing thought: Herrmann debunks a religious metaphysical realism on the grounds that it assumes an external perspective which philosophy has rejected. *But from within a religious worldview, the notion of a divine external perspective is very intelligible, although not everyone agrees on a method for its verification. God can intelligibly be imagined as holding an infinity of right descriptions of reality, because he has created reality*. Interestingly, Herrmann himself finds it difficult to avoid an external perspective. Making a gesture in the direction of realism, he writes that there would still be a world even if there were no human beings. This is not very different from the 'brains in a vat' hypothesis: both lack a method of verification, whilst both are held to be meaningful. Our suggestion, then: *it is precisely theism which makes coherent the notion of an external perspective. It is correct that truth cannot be independent of noetic activity, but it is wrong to restrict this activity to human thought.*

With this discussion of Herrmann, we have reached the point where the philosophy of Donald Davidson can make a significant contribution to the

---

[127] Richard Rorty, 'Pragmatism as Romantic Polytheism', in Stuart Rosenbaum, ed., *Pragmatism and Religion*, p. 121.

[128] Byrne explains that theodicy is central to his definition of religion.

debate about realism, justification and meaning, including the meaning of religious beliefs.

Chapter 3

Donald Davidson's Neo-Pragmatism

Meaning, Truth and Justification in Davidson's Philosophical Project

Davidson's philosophical programme has already been introduced in the first chapter. It's continuity with Quine's sensibilities can hardly be over-estimated. The differences that there are can only be understood on the background of an essential kinship. Nevertheless, they remain essential. Davidson has no hesitation to denounce the lingering empiricism of his mentor, or his residual scientism. Still other consequential differences remain between Davidson an Rorty, despite the latter's claim to carry forward Davidson's convictions on most things, with the notable exception of truth. A major premise of the book has been that some of these divergences can help ground some very different theological projects. The group of theologians we have investigated in the previous chapter all confess to a certain pragmatic allegiance. Their work has not been influenced by the classical pragmatists alone, but also by more recent forms of neo-pragmatism, as we saw. With the exception of J. Wesley Robbins and (of late) Nancy Frankenberry, they owe no debts to Davidson. The exceptions themselves, when they do claim a debt, tend to lump together Davidson's and Rorty's projects. It is to their significant differences that we now turn.

The present chapter provides a closer and more critical analysis of Davidson's project of a) giving a theory of meaning in terms of truth conditions, and b) his coherentist account of knowledge and justification. We shall undertake a discussion of his theory of meaning by, first, looking at the constraints that must be placed on it, then, second, describing the theory *per se*, third, discussing it's consequences for the notion of *a language* and, finally, its implication for ontology, especially the semantics of incommensurability. We then discuss Davidson's coherentist theory of knowledge by starting with a discussion of his divergence from Rorty on the notion of truth and ending with McDowell's critique of 'unconstrained coherentism'. The next chapter builds on this critical presentation in its discussion of theologians that explicitly draw upon Davidson.

Constraints upon a Meaning Theory

An introductory account of Davidson's meaning theory has already been given. It is notoriously difficult, as various commentators have noted, to introduce Davidson's philosophy. Part of the reason for this consists in his style which consists of writing individual articles tackling a huge variety of themes, all of them inter-related and without exception very difficult. One nevertheless must begin somewhere. We have begun with the differences which set him apart from Quine. A fuller account, however, is required and to that we now turn.

What is a theory of meaning? What should a theory of meaning aim to do? This second-order question stands behind most of the essays grouped under his *Inquiries into Truth and Interpretation.* The question of form is not at all trivial, for it is precisely in the assumption that the form of such a theory is clear that previous meaning theories smuggle into their foundation. Let us explain. Before Davidson theorists of meaning simply assumed that what such a theory should elucidate is the concept of meaning. How is it that words acquire the meanings that they do? In virtue of what do they have these meanings? What these theories assumed is that there is such a thing as a *meaning* and this is what we should be giving an analysis of. On a Davidsonian perspective, however, *such theories presuppose that what makes communication work and what makes understanding possible are entities called meanings, whose ontological status can be quite diverse, but which nevertheless play a crucial explanatory role in the theory.* This assumes too much, for, in his opinion, this is precisely what a theory of meaning aims to find out, that is, what is it that enables human communication and understanding. It is circular and hasty to assume that 'meanings' play this role and that a theory of interpretation should be about meaning.

Glock makes a distinction between analytical and constructive theories of meaning.[1] Analytical theories provide an analysis of the concept of meaning. This was done in various ways: by tying meaning to reference, to behaviour, to causes, to verification, use and so on, even to truth conditions. All these notions are supposed to show *in virtue of what* do words or sentences have the meanings that they do. Let us take for example what are sometimes called 'communication-intention' theories such as those of Strawson, Wittgenstein, Grice, Austin etc. The intuition these is that sounds cannot mean anything by themselves. Thus, meaning must come through sounds and something on top of that: normally intentions and the conventions that these instantiate. A language, therefore, contains a set of conventions and it is the intention of a speaker to use words in conventionally recognizable ways in order to deliver the meanings that he intends.[2]

In Davidson's opinion, on the other hand, this type of approach presupposes precisely what it aims to elucidate. One cannot explain meaning by recourse to thought, since thought itself is linguistic and thus stands in need of explanation itself. The communication-intention theory, in Evnine's words,

---

[1] H. -J. Glock, *Quine and Davidson*, p. 142.

[2] See Simon Evnine, *Donald Davidson* (Stanford: Stanford University Press, 1991), p. 72.

> does, therefore, presuppose that the task of saying in virtue of what people's mental states have the propositional contents they do is independent of, and prior to, the task of giving a theory of meaning for a language. It is precisely this that leads Davidson to reject the communication-intention approach. For Davidson the question of how mental states get their contents, and how sentences get their meanings are interdependent.[3] We cannot therefore hope to use thought to explain linguistic meaning.'[4]

Thus, if the aim of the theory is to give an account of meaning which would take the form of 'in virtue of what does a stretch of language have the meaning that it does', it needs to bring in some contents which is able to provide that explanation. But unless we can make sense of a non-linguistic and yet informative notion of content, we cannot hope to provide such an account without the threat of circularity.

Bjørn Ramberg, in what is perhaps the most insightful analysis of Davidson's philosophy of language, introduces the form of Davidson's meaning theory by a discussion of so-called 'classical theories of meaning' which assume a close relationship between meaning and reference: to know the meaning of a word is to know how to pick out its referent.[5] When classical theories ran into difficulties of keeping 'sense and reference sufficiently apart to examine any relationship between them'[6] causal theories stepped in to fulfil that role. The causal theory (Kripke and Donellan) 'attempts to explain the power of words (or other semantic notions) to refer to objects in terms of causal chains involving the objects and our linguistic representations of them.'[7] The problem with this variety of the causal theory was its inability to account for the nomological relation between referents and words. The solution offered by Fodor, Devitt and Field was to turn to the language of thought, which thus escapes 'the troublesome realm of voluntary speech acts.'[8] The idea was to make the language of thought primary in the referential relation, while natural language is derivative of it. So here we are again with the notion that we explain meaning with relating it to a content which must be describable independently of giving a theory of meaning for a natural language.

A further problem compounds this difficulty, as Ramberg comments: 'a causal theory of reference cannot give rise to the sorts of empirical predictions that we want a semantic theory to generate; they are always *ad hoc*

---

[3] See D. Davidson, 'Truth and Meaning', *ITI*, p. 35.

[4] S. Evnine, *Davidson*, p. 74.

[5] Note that theories which rely on the existence of 'meaning' are a variety of these classical theories: words mean what they do in virtue of their *referring* to particular meanings.

[6] Ramberg, *Donald Davidson's Philosophy of Language: An Introduction* (Oxford: Blackwell, 1989), p. 18.

[7] B. Ramberg, *Davidson*, pp. 18f.

[8] B. Ramberg, *Davidson*, p. 20.

explanations of meanings already known.'[9] Thus, if we explain meaning in terms of reference, we shall first have to identify contents and then connect it to words. But this means that we have already interpreted the mental language of a speaker, or of a community of language users. Armed with that knowledge we can only construct a theory of meaning which aims to correlate elements of two known sets: words and mental contents. But if that is so, an important issue will remain unsettled: in virtue of what do we assign these contents to these words? The theory again fails the normativity test: it will fail to generate empirical predictions that a semantic theory has to generate. But why must it generate such predictions? Because of the so-called constraint of *finite axiomatization*. But we have already anticipated somewhat.

To sum up, it appears that both classical theories and more recent causal approaches fail because of the very aim of giving an account of the meaning. Can we find a way around that? Davidson thinks we can. But we have to think outside the box in order to find it. This is where his *constructive* theory of meaning comes in. Rather than explaining in virtue of what a linguistic sign has the meaning it does, it does not explain directly what meaning is. Instead 'it provides, for every sentence s in the language under study, a matching sentence (to replace '*p*') that, in some way yet to be made clear, 'gives the meaning' of *s*.'[10] So the form of a meaning theory is not a direct explanation of meaning, but an *equivalent* description of a set of theorems, knowledge of which would be sufficient (though not necessary) for the understanding of speakers. As Glock points out, 'although Davidson does not reduce philosophical semantics to empirical linguistics, he effects an important change of perspective.'[11] We already saw that, opposing Quine, he does not aim to give a reduction of the concepts of semantics into the concepts of behaviour. But the line which he threads is incredibly fine, as Strawson points out. It is a '"Homeric struggle" between formal semanticists, who treat language as an abstract system of complex rules, and those who regard language primarily as a kind of human activity. He explains natural languages by reference to formal calculi, but he also places it in a larger context of human behaviour and human beliefs.'[12]

Indeed, one of the more complicated aspects of Davidson's meaning theory is his reliance upon a formal semantics. As opposed to communication-intention theories, the intuition behind formal semantics is that sentences are composed out of words in systematic ways.[13] This is the so-called principle of compositionality, which acquires a pivotal role in Davidson's project. The elegance and explanatory power of a formal structure is able to bring out a complex variety of actual aspects of communication. He will attempt to use the

---

[9] B. Ramberg, *Davidson*, p. 27.

[10] D. Davidson, *ITI*, p. 23.

[11] H. -J. Glock, *Quine and Davidson*, p. 143.

[12] H. -J. Glock, *Quine and Davidson*, p. 143.

[13] See S. Evnine, *Davidson*, p. 72.

powerful structure of Tarski's T-sentences in order to explain and illuminate what goes on in communication and understanding. 'The guiding intuition behind my interpretation of Davidson', as Ramberg writes, 'is that all his writings on language can be read as attempts to exorcise the ghosts of reification from our thinking about communication.'[14] A formal semantic structure provides such an instrument. Before we go on to an analysis of the actual deployment of such an instrument, let us break down the constraints placed upon a meaning theory. Some of these have already been hinted at, but it will help to describe them clearly.[15]

The first condition is *extensional adequacy*. 'For each sentence *s* of *L* it generates a theorem that specifies the meaning of *s*. As Glock notes, this derives from his holism. If linguistic meaning and mental contents are knit together, two things follow for a meaning theory: first, it should not postulate *intensional entities*; second, it should be couched in a language which does not avail itself of *intensional constructions or notions*.[16] As we have already seen, this does not eliminate intensions, but gives then what Glock calls an 'approximation'. The second of these consequences means that a theory of meaning cannot make use of the operator 'means that', for it creates an intensional context.[17] This means that the work done by it would have to be done by something else, as we will see below.

Davidson's commitment to extensional adequacy is an important issue that will surface in the critical analysis below. *The preference for extensional languages*, writes Evnine, *is partly ideologically motivated.* Then there is also Davidson's nominalism which rejects the unnecessary postulation of entities for which there is no demonstrable use. It then follows that 'the question whether semantics can get by without meanings is therefore tantamount to the question whether some purely extensional theory, such as Davidson's, can be successful.'[18]

A second requirement for a successful meaning theory is *empirical verifiability*. 'The theory is empirically verifiable without any prior knowledge of what the speakers of *L* mean by their expressions.' The task of this verification famously falls upon 'radical interpretation', an off-shoot from Quine's radical translation, but as opposed to the latter, explicitly semantical.

The rationale for radical interpretation is provided by the third condition, namely *non-circularity*. 'The evidence on which the theory is based should not employ "concepts too closely allied to that of meaning," which it seeks to explain.' Not only must the theorems of the theory not make any use of

[14] B. Ramberg, *Davidson*, p. 2.

[15] We are indebted to Glock's summary here, see p. 144.

[16] H. -J. Glock, *Quine and Davidson*, p. 148.

[17] See S. Evnine, *Davidson*, p. 78.

[18] S. Evnine, *Davidson*, pp. 79-80.

intensional notions or constructs, but neither must the evidence used to test the theory.

Finally, the fourth condition is that of *finite axiomatization*. 'The meaning-giving theorems must be generated by a finite number of axioms and rules of inference.' This is an important requirement and it is based on a further implicit principle: a theory of meaning must account for how it is that speakers can learn a language. Since the sentences which we can understand is potentially infinite, if the theory contained an infinite number of axioms, one for each of the infinite sentences, the theory could not be mastered. Hence knowledge of the theory would be impossible and thus its possession could not conceivable help one understand the language.

Following this presentation of the constraints placed upon a meaning theory, Glock further points out three further principles which have a bearing upon the construction of the theory. The first is the *principle of compositionality*, according to which the meaning of a sentence is determined by the meanings of its constituents. It is to be noted that this principle has been successfully invoked against the classical and causal-based theories of meaning. If the meaning of a sentence is made up of the meaning of its constituents and the meaning of these constituents is given by the objects in the world to which they refer, then it is impossible to understand how the meaning of the sentence is accomplished. What is missing is a rule attaching to the combination of individual words into a sentence.[19] A second *principle of sentential priority* holds that sentences have semantic priority over words. As we will see momentarily, rather that treat words as primary carriers of meaning in virtue of their individual reference, Davidson proposes a shift of perspective which holds that words have meaning in virtue of their role in establishing the truth conditions of a sentence. The relationship between language and world is thus relocated from the referential word-to-reality level to the semantic sentence to truth value level. Finally, the third idea is that the meaning of a sentence *s* is given by specifying its truth conditions. To give truth conditions is an equivalent way of giving meaning.

Now let us turn to the actual deployment of the meaning theory.

Meaning and Truth-Conditions

The chief problem with theorems of the form

(M) *s* means that *p*

is that the logical connective 'means that' creates an intensional context within which co-extensional terms cannot be substituted among themselves while

[19] For more on this see Kirk Ludwig and Ernie LePore, 'Truth and Meaning', in K. Ludwig, ed., *Donald Davidson* (Cambridge: Cambridge University Press, 2003), p. 38.

keeping the truth value. We thus have to find a way of giving the theorems of a meaning theory in a different way than by employing intensional notions. Davidson explains that

> Anxiety that we are enmeshed in the intensional springs from using the words 'means that' as filling between description of sentence and sentence, but it may be that the success of our venture depends not on the filling but on what it fills. The theory will have done its work if it provides, for every sentence s in the language under study, a matching sentence (to replace 'p') that, in some way yet to be made clear, 'gives the meaning' of s. One obvious candidate for matching sentence is just s itself, if the object language is contained in the metalanguage; otherwise a translation of s in the metalanguage. As a final bold step, let us try treating the position occupied by 'p' extensionally: to implement this, sweep away the obscure 'means that', provide the sentence that replaces 'p' with a proper sentential connective, and supply the description that replaces 's' with its own predicate.[20]

The result is another theorem,

(T) *s* is true if and only if *p*

As Glock observes, we are never told why meaning should be a function of truth conditions. Similarly, Evnine speculates on the partly ideological reasons for Davidson's preference for purely extensional languages. Davidson's gamble for the extensional seems to be further motivated by the difficulties associated with the intensional, well documented by Quine. Although he does not share the latter's iconoclasm about intensions, he does think that they can be a liability in that they introduce an element of circularity into a theory of meaning. Thus, if the work of a theory of meaning can be done without such notions, all the better. The point of the theory is not to give an account of intensions, but of the process of understanding and interpretation, of communication in general. There is nothing with forces us *a priori* to provide an explanation in terms of intensions. As Davidson observes elsewhere,

> I did not say speakers or interpreters actually formulate such theories [of truth]. It does seem to me, though, that if we can describe how they *could* we will gain *an important insight into the nature of the intentional* (including, of course, meaning), in particular into how the intentional supervenes on the observable and the non-intentional.[21]

The aim of the theory given by Davidson should be clear by now: not reduction but approximation, or, as Evnine puts it, Davidson does not describe meaning,

---

[20] D. Davidson, 'Truth and Meaning', *ITI*, pp. 22f.

[21] Quoted by Piers Rawling, 'Radical Interpretation', from 'Radical Interpretation Reinterpreted', in K. Ludwig, *Donald Davidson*.

but is charting a way around it. The aim is to explain the intentional behaviour of human beings, our ability to use sounds and marks in order to convey thoughts. This ability, for Davidson, is indelibly connected to our sharing a common world and common inter-personal relationships.

But how do we get beyond the troublesome 'means that'? By replacing it with the sentential connective 'is true if and only if.' The theorems are supposed to give the 'semantic properties' of the sentences of *L*. But it will not be able to do any better than by using the sentence itself or a translation of it. Three things have to be done, in Davidson's opinion. First, remove the problematic 'means that', then provide the replacement of *p* (from (M)) with a proper sentential connective which is truth-functional (or extensional), finally, supply the description that replaces '*s*' with its own predicate. The reason for third step is that a sentential connective must stand between a sentence and another sentence, not between the name of a sentence and a sentence. We thus have to insert a predicate to turn the name into a sentence. Hence

(T) *s* is T if and only if *p*

What remains to be done is to put enough restrictions, without appeal to further semantical notions,[22] on the predicate 'is T' so that it will only yield all the instances of (T) obtained by replacing *s* with a name of a sentence in the object language and *p* with either that sentence itself or a translation of it.[23] But what might such a predicate be except 'is true'? Thus a Davidsonian theory of meaning consists of theorems which give the truth conditions for the sentences of the language. The conditions are specified either by using the same sentences, if the language of the theory is the same as the object language, or translations of the sentence, if the languages are different.

Moreover, the truth conditional theory is able to explicate what goes on in communication by doing justice to the principle of compositionality. Thus, Davidson explains that 'The work of the theory is in relating the known truth conditions of each sentence to those aspects ('words') of the sentence that recur in other sentences, and can be assigned identical roles in other sentences. Empirical power in such a theory depends on success in recovering the structure of a very complicated ability--the ability to speak and understand a language.'[24]

All this has been somewhat overcomplicated. Davidson thinks he has succeeded in finding a way *around meaning* that nevertheless does the job supposed to be done by the concept of 'meaning'. What goes on in communication is explained by the notion of the truth conditions of sentences. As we saw, the basic unit of communication and of meaning is the sentence.

---

[22] D. Davidson, 'Truth and meaning', p. 23.

[23] S. Evnine, *Davidson*, p. 81.

[24] D. Davidson, 'Truth and meaning', p. 25.

Individual words have meaning insofar as they play a role in the establishment of the truth conditions of the sentences of which they are parts. Whereas previously the meaning of words was given in terms of a referential relation to parts of reality, Davidson proposes a theory of meaning that does not rest on any such referential relation, but only on a 'pre-theoretical' notion of the truth value of a sentence. Thus, Davidson's use of the notion of truth in meaning theory is not loaded with any epistemological baggage, as Ramberg insists. It is pre-theoretical in the sense that it does not give a description of how people find out the truth of their sentences. Since the theory of meaning gives a description of a structure, such particular questions are irrelevant to it. What is relevant, though, is a basic human ability to understand the notion of 'is true'. Thus, the semantic conception of truth provides a concept that can be made to serve the function reference was intended to fill.

So much for the theory. It remains to be seen how it can be verified. The task of testing it rests on the shoulders of radical interpretation, as a method of interpretation which restricts itself only to extensional evidence, rather than any prior knowledge of meaning. As Ramberg stresses, 'a semantic theory has empirical content only if there exists an evidential base that can be described independently of the theory, and in relation to which the theory will be more or less adequate.'[25]

The aim of radical interpretation is precisely to demonstrate that communication and understanding are possible if one possesses the sort of truth theory just explained. Should that be the case, it will have done the work of a meaning theory. The radical interpreter will refuse to avail himself of intensional notions like meaning and beliefs. The evidence on which he must rely 'must be of a sort that would be available to someone who does not already know how to interpret utterances the theory is designed to cover: it must be evidence that can be stated without essential use of such linguistic concepts as meaning, interpretation, synonymy, and the like.'[26] What might such possible evidence be? The short answer is, on the one hand, a speaker's publicly available speech behaviour, on the other hand, the circumstances which describe his immediate environment. The aim of the theory is to describe how complex and higher level phenomena such as meaning and thought supervene upon behavioural activity. Our discussion of Davidson in the first chapter contained hints at Davidson's *distal* versus Quine's *proximal* stimulus. For him, all that can be said about meaning, and all the evidence necessary for interpretation (which are basically one and the same thing) must be available to any public observer.

Since a radical interpreter cannot make use of knowledge of the beliefs of a native, the only way in which to break the circle of beliefs, meanings and speech is by way of truth. This is precisely what his theory of meaning makes

---

[25] B. Ramberg, *Davidson*, p. 31.

[26] D. Davidson, 'Radical Interpretation', *ITI*, p. 128.

possible, since it renders meaning in terms of truth conditions. But if we want to break the circle *we will have to hold truth while testing for meaning.* Davidson elaborates,

> A good place to begin is with the attitude of holding a sentence true, of accepting it as true. This is, of course, a belief, but it is a single attitude applicable to all sentences, and so does not ask us to be able to make finely discriminated distinctions among belies. [...] Suppose then, that the evidence available is just that speakers of the language to be interpreted hold various sentences to be true at certain times and under specified circumstances.[27]

The point is precisely what Ramberg solicits: an evidential base which is specifiable independently from the theory. The interpreter will have to use as an evidential base two items: the attitude of holding true a certain sentence, for example 'Es regnet,' and the times and circumstances under which it is uttered. This evidence is describable without appeal to intentions, beliefs, thoughts and other intensional attitudes of the speaker, but purely extensionally. On the other hand, the things and events in the world which *prompt* the speaker to assent to the sentence, things like the fact that it is raining in the vicinity of the speaker, are also publicly available to the interpreter. To hold for truth is to suppose that the speaker is right about the fact that it is raining and this prompts him to utter a true sentence. The meaning of that sentence, which is what we are after, is precisely the meaning of the sentence that we would be prompted to utter given the same circumstances. As Evnine so palpably puts it, 'Davidson goes straight to the world itself to help fix what mental states and sentences are about.'[28]

Thus Davidson has found a way, via truth conditions, to interpret an alien speech without appeal to beliefs and intentions. A crucial element in the procedure is the so-called principle of charity which stipulates that we must treat speakers of a language as being mostly right about most of the things which cause them to have the beliefs they have and utter the words they do. The causal correlation between mental contents and events and things in the world is absolutely crucial for Davidson. It provides the necessary evidential base, shared as between speaker and interpreter, on the basis of which assignments of meanings can be reliably made. Bruce Marshall puts it nicely: 'The thought, then, is that the pattern of a speaker's prompted assents to similar or identical sentences in similar or identical circumstances enables the interpreter, tutored by he principle of charity, to locate the truth conditions of those sentences'.[29] If radical interpretation is possible, that is, if we are able to interpret the speech of an alien people exclusively by making use of their overt behaviour in specific environmental conditions, it follows that Davidson's truth-conditional semantics works.

---

[27] D. Davidson, 'Radical Interpretation', p. 135.

[28] S. Evnine, *Davidson*, p. 145.

[29] B. D. Marshall, *Trinity and Truth*, p. 95.

Ramberg points out that 'the link between sentences and features of circumstances is the core of Davidson's theory of interpretation, because it is the very transaction in which truth is exchanged for empirical content.'[30] In this consists Davidson's change of perspective: meaning is located at the level of sentences held true given specific circumstances. The link between language and the world is located at the sentential level, which are either true or not. Now Ramberg is quite adamant that *Davidson's use of a semantic concept of truth has no epistemological implications*. This remains in doubt, as we will show below. Whether epistemologically creditable or not, the point remains that interpretation is only possible if we take our interlocutors to be responding to and be causally determined by the same features and things of the world that we are. These features are plain for all to see. Unless this were so, it would be impossible to ascribe propositional content, as Davidson urges: 'Though our beliefs, intentions, fears, and other feelings are private and subjective if anything is, they cannot be identified or explained except by tying them from the start to external objects and events.'[31]

Meaning, if we are still to speak in terms of this concept, goes even more public with Davidson than with Quine, due to the former's emphasis on distal evidence. But this does not hold simply for the radical interpreted or another foreign language. Radical interpretation works at home too, 'The problem of interpretation is domestic as well as foreign: it surfaces for speakers of the same language in the form of the question, how can it be determined that the language is the same?' Thus, 'All understanding of the speech of another involves radical interpretation.'[32] This seems to be pushing matters too far. Surely when we interpret other speakers we do not start from scratch, but we already have a knowledge of the meaning of the words of a language, of the conventions that constitute the language and the grammar. Davidson's claim that radical interpretation is domestic as well as foreign will thus surely appear contradictory unless we bear in mind Ramberg's caveat: 'The process of radical interpretation is intended as a theoretical description of linguistic competence, a rationalization of the practice of interpreting speech, not as a description of an actual procedure such as the methods of translators.'[33] In other words, we do not have to apply radical interpretation to speakers of a common language, but we could if we wanted to. Indeed, sometimes we even must, for, as we shall see, a discrepancy sometimes occurs between the conventions employed in a given language and what a certain speaker appears to intend by his words. If interpretation could only be given an intensional theoretical description, it would seem that we have no way of understanding the speech of a deviant

---

[30] B. Ramberg, *Davidson*, p. 72.

[31] D. Davidson, 'Representation and interpretation', in Davidson, *Problems of rationality* (Oxford: Oxford University Press, 2004), p. 96.

[32] D. Davidson, 'Radical Interpretation', p. 125.

[33] B. Ramberg, *Davidson*, p. 66.

linguistic user. But precisely because it can be rendered extensionally, a truth-conditional theory of meaning illuminates the many ways in which we can communicate even without the use of linguistic conventions. We will return to the topic of conventions below.

Conventions and Language

With charity being applied across the board, a recurrent criticism of Davidson is that we are left without the possibility of ascribing error to the natives. This is a point that has generated considerable debate, but it will not occupy us here, since our main interest is with the theory of meaning rather than epistemology. Davidson provided many convincing arguments, which in our opinion go a long way towards countering this objection. In the process of responding to such critics, he has sometimes indicated that what radical interpretation is after is not so much an interpretation of the speech of individual speakers, but of the *language* of a speaking community. Hence, in Evnine's rendering, 'if we are after an interpretation of a language as used by some community, the evidence we want is about which sentences are usually held true by the members of that community.'[34] This creates a logical gap between an individual who may be mistaken in thinking that particular truth-conditions for a sentence obtain when in fact they do not, and a whole community. Defending along these lines is not particularly convincing, but it does show that, early on, Davidson was prepared to allude to the notion of a language of a community as being the object of interpretation.

Later on in life, however, he has begun to shift his theoretical sights to the interpretation of the individual speaker. So radical has been this shift that it has taken even some Davidsonians by surprise, as Ramberg notes. How does one reconcile his earlier labours in semantics with the seemingly sweeping and self-undermining claim that 'there is no such thing as language'? More specifically, however, Davidson claims that 'there is no such thing as a language, not if a language is anything like what many philosophers and linguists have supposed. There is therefore no such thing to be learned, mastered, or born with. We must give up the idea of a clearly defined shared structure which language users acquire and then apply to cases.'[35]

What are we to make of such a claim? Surely Davidson cannot mean that there are no languages. After all his theory of meaning depends, as he himself insists, upon the possibility of applying a Tarski-style truth theory to *natural languages*. Does Davidson recant of his earlier work with natural languages? The most plausible explanation is that Davidson's eventual deconstruction of the notion of language is a result of carrying through some of his earlier explicit ideas and implicit principles. His earlier text, 'Communication and

[34] S. Evnine, *Davidson*, p. 106.

[35] D. Davidson, 'A Nice Derangement of Epitaphs', in Davidson, *TLH*, p. 107.

Convention', contained in the *ITI* collection is three years earlier than 'Nice Derangement'. In philosophical years that is not very much. But for all that it is worth, its critique of conventions is animated by the same spirit which fuelled his critique of the reification of meanings. In that paper we find the same pattern of argumentation: if a given entity or notion serves no explanatory function, i.e. if an alternative theory could be devised which is simpler and more elegant by utilizing a minimum of items, we can dispense with it. Applying radical interpretation, he finds that we can perfectly well interpret without the use of conventions. This is not to say that there are no conventions, but only to clarify their role as abstractions of a much richer process which does not depend upon them.

In showing that conventions are redundant in interpretation, Davidson introduces a space between interpretation, considered as the attempt to formulate a truth theory for speakers of an object language, and the fact that conventions are actually formed and seem to guide communication. *By concentrating the full force of his arguments on the redundancy of conventions, Davidson does in fact leave us without a plausible explanations of why these are formed and what is the semantic significance of their continued and inevitable employment.* As we will argue, he denies himself a rationale for investigating the continued significance and role of the notion of language.

Of course, Davidson admits that in actual practice conventions are formed. But their existence is not needed to account for the regularities of interpretation. Communication succeeds not because of the regularities of convention, i.e. not because both the speaker and the interpreter are armed with the same repertoire of conventions or 'advance theories'. There is understanding because in the actual interpreting situation, the speaker knows how to make himself understood by reliably identifying the same truth conditions that we identify as obtaining.

> Agreement on what a speaker means by what he says can surely be achieved even though speaker and hearer have different advance theories as to how to interpret the speaker. The reason this can be is that the speaker may well provide adequate clues, in what he says, and how and where he says it, to allow a hearer to arrive at a correct interpretation.[36]

So adequate interpretation can proceed without prior knowledge of conventions, or what Davidson will later call 'prior theory'. The experiment of radical interpretation was intended to show precisely this.

The appeal to conventions, moreover, obeys the intuition that one characteristic of meaning is that it is immediately readable, observable. We want to explain the intuition that somehow, in communication, both speaker and interpreter have in mind the same thing. But convention can perform that function only if there are such clearly identifiable meanings which it can tie to

[36] D. Davidson, 'Communication and Convention', p. 278.

linguistic signs. As Ramberg puts it, 'It is only if we see meaning as something to be *captured* in the words we use, and conveyed by them from one speaker to another, that we think there must be something connecting the speakers, something – such as a language – they share, that bears meanings as a vehicle.'[37] Communication, though, can be explained without appeal to such regularities, either shared meanings, or shared conventions. If it can, then there is no need to burden ourselves with inscrutable and idle notions. Conventions are real, but their analysis does not throw light on the nature of meaning. Davidson brings a number of related ideas together in what is an illuminating statement of his understanding of meaning:

> It is easy to misconceive the role of society in language. Language is, to be sure, a social art. But it is an error to suppose we have seen deeply into the heart of linguistic communication when we have noticed how society bends linguistic habits to a public norm. What is conventional about language, if anything is, is that people tend to speak much as their neighbours do. But in indicating this element of the conventional, or of the conditioning process that makes speakers rough linguistic facsimiles of their friends and parents, we explain no ore than the convergence; we throw no light on the essential nature of the skills that are thus made to converge.[38]

Convention cannot explain those 'linguistic habits' because it is dependent upon them, rather than their source. Language plays no part in the theoretical description of meaning because the 'bending into public norm' of those linguistic habits has no effect upon the habits themselves. This is the one thing to which we will forcefully object. Davidson supposes that, even though a language is formed (in whatever way), and even though we are speakers of such a language, we can quite unproblematically dispense with all the information and formation which that language provides us with. It will be argued that, while it is indeed possible to understand other persons without sharing a 'prior theory', such an understanding is only very incipient. In order to acquire what we shall call, following Mark Platts, a semantic depth into what the speaker intends to communicate, we must rely on evidence other than that which is merely extensional. We will have to, so to speak, 'enter the language', indeed, master the language. While Davidson is right to insist that communication is possible without making use of such concepts, there is more than needs to be elucidated and shared than bare truth conditions. But in disagreeing with Davidson we nonetheless wish to affirm a debt to his efforts in radical interpretation. For it rightly shows that there is a gap between interpretation and language. The failure of the model is in supposing that there is no further task for semantics and the philosophy of language to tackle. These critical remarks must await a fuller presentation of Davidson's proposal about language and, then, incommensurability.

---

[37] B. Ramberg, *Davidson*, p. 103.

[38] D. Davidson, 'Communication and Convention', p. 278.

In 'A Nice Derangement of Epitaphs', Davidson introduces a distinction between *prior* and *passing* theories in an attempt to highlight the *dynamic nature of the linguistic situation.* An interpreter approaches the interpretive situation armed with a so-called prior theory, that is, a certain expectation as to what sort of beliefs a speaker might have. By focusing on cases of deviant language use such as *malapropism*, Davidson shows that communication would still be possible even if no conventions were in use. What both speakers must be able to do is to synchronise their passing theories, to adjust them to each other in such a way that a transitory[39] understanding is achieved. There is no further need to regiment that success in a convention. That is why the theories are passing: they achieve momentary success and then they are left behind, in search of better passing theories. They are theories, though, because 'when a word or phrase temporarily or locally takes over the role of some other word or phrase (as treated in a prior theory, perhaps), the entire burden of that role, with all its implications for logical relations to other words, phrases, and sentences, must be carried along by the passing theory.'[40] One may pause to wonder here: what is the difference between speaking about a passing theory which contains words and their logical relations to other words and phrases and speaking of a language? Davidson's reply would be that there is no more to a language than the identification of the truth theory with which it operates. As Ramberg comments,

> once the full import of Davidson's holistic empirical strategy has soaked in, we see that the only possible criterion of identity for languages is the successful application of one and the same theory of truth. For Davidson, there is no way in which a language, as that which a speaker makes use of when successfully communicating, can be given independently of the truth-theory that determines it's structure.[41]

So in testing for the meaning of a speaker, it makes no sense to ask what language he speaks beyond asking what truth theory he operates with. Linguistic mastery is irrelevant to the task of communication and understanding. Now this is a thesis with which Michael Dummett and others have taken serious issue with. We will present Dummett's arguments against Davidson's position before we move on to our own proposal.

It is not our aim to present the general philosophical project of Michael Dummett, though it is closely related to and in conversation with Davidson's own. Dummett's position, for instance, on truth-conditions and his proposal that they be replaced with verification conditions given that we should drop the so-called 'bivalence thesis' is certainly an important contemporary option. But Dummett is more Wittgensteinian than Davidson (or Quine for that matter).

---

[39] D. Davidson, 'Nice Derangement', p. 102.
[40] D. Davidson, 'Nice derangement', p. 103.
[41] B. Ramberg, *Davidson*, pp. 99f.

This shows in an accented willingness to stick as close as possible to a description of what speakers *actually do when they communicate*. It is thus not hard to see why he would object to a Davidsonian semantics as a description of a theory, knowledge of which *would* enable speakers to communicate. We should not strive to give an analysis of a hypothetical procedure that would illuminate meaning, but of the actual practice and linguistic habits of speakers.

In actuality, linguistic practice is very different. In practice, we are bound to patterns of linguistic meaning embedded into language. We hold ourselves responsible to these patterns. This is a variation of Wittgenstein's private language argument: if there are no shared rules for the use of a stretch of language, then it would be impossible to tell the difference between right and wrong use. Dummett thus accuses Davidson of implicitly denying the publicity of language and treating words like Humpty Dumpty.[42] Language is normative. As David Gorman shows,[43] normativity does not imply that deviant uses are impossible, or even un-interpretable. Deviant uses are certainly possible, but they are not the norm. The discrepancies on which Davidson builds must not be blown out of proportion. But it is precisely because there is a background of normative patterns of language use that these can be understood as such. *The undeniable service that Davidson did for the philosophy of language is to have rescued us from a certain self-imposed structuralist prison-house of concepts.* The resigned feeling that we are bound to think in a certain way and believe certain things because of the way in which we have been linguistically trained is not compelling. It is possible to communicate cross-culturally and cross-linguistically because interpretation can go on where there is not much shared. But deviations can only be spotted as such on the backdrop of normative use. Hans-Johann Glock makes a similar point in a discussion of whether mood determines force: Davidson 'rightly stresses that human beings can put words to extra-linguistic work in ways that transcend conventional meaning. But it assumes rather than shows that the illocutionary force of an utterance is among the extra-linguistic features of utterances, that is, that it is determined by the *speaker's intentions* rather than *linguistic conventions*.'[44] Moreover, as he further notes, the counter-examples adduced by Davidson are themselves governed by conventions.

Dummett also objects to the ubiquity ascribed to interpretation by Davidson. An overwhelming explanatory burden is placed on the notions of truth conditions and on stratagems of interpretation. Understanding, not

---

[42] Michael Dummett, '"A Nice Derangement of Epitaphs': Some Comments on Davidson and Hacking', in E. LePore ed., *Truth and Interpretation: Perspectives on the Philosophy of Donald Davidson* (Oxford: Blackwell, 1986), p. 470.

[43] David Gorman, 'Davidson and Dummett on Language and Interpretation', in R. W. Dasenbrock, ed., *Literary Theory After Donald Davidson* (University Park, PA.: Pennsylvania University Press, 1993), p. 220.

[44] H. -J. Glock, *Quine and Davidson*, p. 162.

interpretation, should be the basic category in use. Whereas understanding is typical, interpretation is atypical. There is thus 'a way of understanding a sentence or an utterance that does not consist in putting an interpretation on it.'[45] To put it in our own words, *meaning is not so much hypothetical as it is observable.* We do not infer meanings as much as we perceive and read them, as it were, off the sleeve.[46] The suspicion that this introduces an element of mystery in understanding, making it seem like an unnatural ability, has some force to it. But what is the alternative? To treat the evidence for meaning in terms of features of reality described extensionally. *This alternative makes the transition from the causal to the mental seem tenuous at best, and this will hardly do for a reliable strategy of interpretation.* While Dummett's option may appear *mysterious*, Davidson's is certainly '*awry*,' as Glock captures it:

> While we find it easy to describe human behaviour, even that of a completely alien community, in "rich" mental terms, we are ignorant of the austere physical descriptions that radical interpretation treats as evidence. We can describe a person's features as "sad", "radiant" or "bored", yet do not know how to describe his face in purely physical terms. [...] And even a complex philosophical lecture is easier to understand than to describe in terms of its physical or phonetic features. In other words, we are able to state the conclusions of the alleged inference, without even being able to understand the premises from which they are supposedly derived.[47]

The fact that we are able to perceive such aspects cannot be as easily dissociated from our having a given language than Davidson appears to think. But it remains to be shown that radical interpretation is unable to render the rich contents of people's linguistic practice in purely extensional terms.

Coming back to Dummett's objections, they militate for the fact that a theory of meaning must give an account of the *linguistic ability* of a speaker, and this involves receiving entities like conventions into the body of a theory of understanding.

Although Ramberg dismisses the bulk of Dummett's criticism of Davidson, he does indicate that *Davidson should have left some theoretical function for the concept of a language.* This shows in his more restrained attitude to conventions. The success of the radical interpreter does not show 'that no conventions need be adhered to, only that the field linguist and the subjects of her interpretation need not conform to the *same* conventions.'[48] Thus, each successive truth theory, i.e. the passing theories, are a process of 'spelling out what the set of linguistic conventions of her subjects is on any given occasion. The radical-interpretation model could then be seen as a *rationalization of the*

---

[45] M. Dummett, 'Comments', p. 464.

[46] See Ramberg's accusation that this introduces an element of mystery (108), and Gorman's reply (216).

[47] H. -J. Glock, *Quine and Davidson*, p. 189.

[48] B. Ramberg, *Davidson*, p. 102.

process whereby we come to learn the conventions of a language, rather than a model of what it is we do when we, as masters of a language, makes use of that language.'[49]

But whereas Davidson is unable and unwilling to find a continued role for language, Ramberg is more willing to do so. Moreover, the reason why Davidson is so iconoclastic is his assumption that the only theoretically interesting content of the notion of language can derive from the notion of linguistic ability. That is, only if language is an irreducible part of the process of interpretation, which of course for a Davidsonian isn't the case, can it have a theoretical function. There is no other explanatory task for the concept of language than the process of interpretation. Hence, for Davidson, the issue of interpretability and the issue of what language is being spoken are necessarily connected matters.

Ramberg points out that this conception is actually a common premise to both Davidson and Dummett. It's effect on the former is a categorical rejection of any place for language in semantics, while for the former it means that any explanation of understanding must include an account of linguistic ability. So 'It is *because* he agrees with Dummett on the earlier point [the common premise] that Davidson goes on to infer that there is nothing for a language to be.'[50] Ramberg's solution is elegantly simple: drop the shared premise! Hence we can claim both that interpretation does not require a knowledge of a language *and* that languages are convention-governed social practices.

Because Ramberg has introduced a logical distance between interpretation and linguistic conventionalisation, which renders them 'theoretically independent notions', a place can be found for the former without jeopardising the principal insight of truth-conditional semantics. The establishment of such a place is important because 'in dismissing the body of conventions that constitute a language as a contingent feature of linguistic communication, as nothing more than a complex, and immensely valuable, practical aid, Davidson *obscures the dialectical relation between meaning and what we might call the production of meaning*.'[51]

Language, Ontology and Incommensurability

Why should we make semantic space for languages? Do we not risk bringing back the very dubious notion of conceptual schemes, if we consider language as being semantically relevant? Indeed, one of the reasons for the theological usefulness of Davidson's philosophy was that it provided such an effective rationale against relativism and incommensurability. For example, in our first book, *Postliberal Theological Method* Davidson's arguments about the scheme

[49] B. Ramberg, *Davidson*, p. 102.

[50] B. Ramberg, *Davidson*, p. 107.

[51] B. Ramberg, *Davidson*, p. 110 (italics mine).

content dichotomy were deployed against a postliberal assurance in the internal coherence of Christian language and practice. But, as Ramberg notes, 'The real point of "On the Very Idea of a Conceptual Scheme" is simply that if we are extensionalists about meaning, we cannot imagine what it is for a language to have an "inside", one that remains inaccessible to us even if we have somehow managed to map the "outside" of the language by the pairing off of extensions of sentences in radical interpretation.'[52] The upshot of this is that there is no further step in interpretation beyond the assignment of truth conditions to sentences. Once that is accomplished, we have *ipso facto* understood the language. The postliberal project is possible only on the backdrop of an account of meaning which is independent of an account of truth. Davidson is right that such an account is not possible.

But then why resurrect the notion of a language? Why insist on assigning language a role in the semantics? The reason has to do with a rich account of what goes on in interpersonal communication. Ramberg is simply more aware of the fact that *in actual practice* we experience fractures in our communication, indeed we experience that the words we have at our disposal and which we use to communicate sometimes do not match the linguistic instruments of other people. Even if Davidson himself knows this very well, he does not think it is semantically significant. Ramberg disagrees. Such communication breakdowns must be explained and their relationship to meaning must be shown. *But we can only investigate this relation between meaning and the production of meaning, if we keep the two notions sufficiently apart.* Not only must they be sufficiently apart, but they must also be, as Ramberg notes, dialectically related. What we will show is that Ramberg fails to do justice to this dialectical character of their relation, despite his lip service to it. Consequently, he still hasn't established the semantic function of the concept of language.

A semantics of incommensurability is an important task partly because of the spectre of ideological distortion. The important point made by Ramberg is that precisely *because* meaning can be distinguished from the production of meaning that we can say about the latter that it has departed and that it misconstrues the former. This is a very important point and it is worth allowing it to sink in. Unless we can give a description of meaning without making appeal to conventions, it would be impossible to speak about these conventions as involving any distortion. For to speak about distortion means having a standard by which to measure it. Thus, Ramberg astutely points out that neither Dummett, nor Davidson can do justice to this ideological aspect of communication. Dummett cannot account for it because for him meaning is reduced to linguistic conventions, while Davidson cannot explain it because he does not see any value in continuing to study conventions. But if we keep radical interpretation – which appeals to truth conditions – distinct from an

[52] B. Ramberg, *Davidson*, p. 120.

analysis of conventions, we can make sense of the very notion that our languages are different and that sometimes conventions obstruct what we mean to say (to speak about a common language) or our understanding of foreign speakers (to speak of a heterophonic situation).

Radical interpretation, as we saw in the previous sections, involves a *fluid* notion of meaning, the correlate of an interpretive process where dialogue partners continuously re-adjust their truth theories in order to best accommodate the evidence. The evidence consists in distal stimulations, those 'middle-sized dry objects' which cause us to believe and say much the same things as they cause other people. But with every application of the truth theory, with every use of a word or of a sentence in a language, it becomes applied to varying circumstances. A certain *sedimentation of meaning occurs*, whereby a history of previous applications is more or less deposited into a convention. Thus,

> Conventions, being hammered out over time, are of various viscosity. For this reason, changes in use have a gradual impact on conventions, but an immediate impact on the radical interpreter. In so far as we in practice communicate as speakers of a language, that is, by relying on conventions, and not as radical interpreters, the potential lag between convention-bound use of language and radical interpretation of language represents a possible diffusion of meaning. To speak a language, in other words, is necessarily always to be in danger of misrepresenting what is said.[53]

But to allow for such a gap is to allow for the fact that various historical and social circumstances have particular effects on the shape of the sedimentation, or of the production of meaning. But this is nothing else than the notion of incommensurable paradigms, of which Kuhn and Whorf speak. 'A paradigm in this sense embodies a particular historical narrative, namely the formation, interpretation and specification of those conventions of reasoning and language that are the distinguishing features of the paradigm.'[54] Because they are formed in varied circumstances and are the result of the application of certain values and criteria, paradigms, or traditions, embody within themselves such values, criteria, norms and so on. *This account of the unique ways in which paradigms model their objects is a Kuhnian insight that must be preserved.*

But the crucial point, for Ramberg, is that *this particular sedimentation is something that can be given an account of!* Now it becomes clear why it was important to keep meaning distinct from the production of meaning. Unless conventions can be kept distinct from linguistic meaning (discoverable by radical interpretation), no account of their genesis would be possible. But an account of their genesis is possible precisely because radical interpretation uncovers linguistic meaning, while, say, sociology of knowledge gives a thick

---

[53] B. Ramberg, *Davidson*, p. 112.

[54] B. Ramberg, *Davidson*, p. 127.

account of the practices and norms which have contributed to the particular shape of the sedimentation. The two elements must be available to independent investigations in order to make their relation visible. A historico-sociological account can display the evolution of norms in a given paradigm, it can highlight the break down in communication. Such a theoretical framework also makes possible the critique of ideology:

> a critique of the ideological co-option of language [...] must be a critique that shows how a discrepancy between linguistic conventions and the meaning of what is said serves to disguise certain social facts. It should demonstrate how linguistic conventions have been manipulated, that is, how the production of meaning *via* a language has actually served to obscure linguistic understanding, and how this has served particular interests or social institutions.[55]

It is instructive to relate this account to two philosophers. Gadamer, who is alluded to by Ramberg, is well known for his discussion of the historicity of understanding. But historicity is not something than can be thematised, brought into view, as Ramberg thinks it can be done. Ramberg's notion of radical interpretation amounts to nothing less than a denial of our historicity, from Gadamer's point of view. Tradition is not something that we can critically analyse, but something that analyses and constructs us as the linguistic beings that we are. Much like Gadamer, in a sense, Rorty would argue that it is impossible to leave behind our tradition and assumed a detached position from which to scrutinise ourselves. This would be like stepping outside our own skins, which is impossible and would probably be painful. Rorty actually insists that it is impossible to distinguish ontology from cultural politics. The conventions which we employ are not the sort of things that can be verified by a naked glance at reality. Ramberg seems to be seriously at odds with Rorty here, for indeed Rorty leaves very little room for any critique of ideology.[56] There is no distinction between preference and theory for Rorty. All that we can do is experiment with various configurations of our language and see what works. But even what works is connected to the concepts available to express it. Thus, in a certain sense, our linguisticality encapsulates us.

To some extent, the issues we have been addressing in the last paragraph are epistemological rather than semantic. Ramberg insists on the importance of this distinction for Davidson's programme, which is exclusively semantical: no consequences flow from it for epistemology. This is an issue which we think is not that easily circumvented, and it will be addressed in the next sections. But does Ramberg's strategy succeed? Can he make good on his promise to make room for incommensurability in semantics?

---

[55] B. Ramberg, *Davidson*, p. 133.

[56] See our previous discussion of Cornel West's response to Rorty.

The answer to that hangs on his ability to keep radical interpretation distinct from an account of meaning which uses conventions. Two separate questions need to be addressed:

(1) Can we specify truth conditions in an informative way and without aid from conventions/ intensions?
(2) If, as we think, we cannot, does it mean that this distinction is impossible? Does it therefore mean that a speaker is bound by his conventions and that no critique of ideology is possible?

With regards to the first question, Davidson's and Ramberg's opinion is at the very basis of radical interpretation: namely that we can find out what speakers mean by simply correlating their assent with the circumstances which prompt that assent. The question, therefore, is if such an appeal is sufficient for the individuation of sentence meaning. Glock thinks it isn't. Moreover, he argues that various passages in Davidson 'strongly suggest that Davidson himself succumbs to the myth of the given. Interpretation is the derivation of statements about what a speaker says, thinks and does from descriptions of him "as a physical system."'[57] Davidson relies on the public availability of circumstances, on the basis of which ascriptions of meaning can be made. *This appears to assume that whatever those circumstances are, they somehow magically reveal their self-descriptions to us in epistemically relevant ways, i.e. in ways which we can employ as evidence for ascribing meaning.* But, as Wittgenstein has so persuasively shown, our ability to discern features of reality come together with our having dealings with reality, together with patterns of approaching it, not least of these being a certain linguistic disposition. The Wittgensteinian point is aptly applied by Glock: 'Meaningful speech is not merely a physical phenomenon, in that it is embedded in distinctively human capacities and forms of interaction. Furthermore, within this context, it does have a life of its own, and our understanding of it is not derived from physical facts. The bottom line is not physics but praxis.'[58] In an argument against Dummett's full-blooded approach to an explanation of understanding, McDowell makes a point relevant here: 'we should not conceive the outward aspect that matters as something one presents to just anyone; one shows one's mind, in one's words, only to those who understand one's language.'[59] *Thus, the thesis that a physical description of reality in non-intensional terms is equivalent to a description of meaning assumes that reality has a single preferred self-description.* But this is nothing else than the myth of the Given. If we understand that we cannot draw a sharp line between the

[57] H. –J. Glock, *Quine and Davidson*, pp. 188f.
[58] H. –J. Glock, *Quine and Davidson*, p. 190.
[59] John McDowell, 'In Defence of Modesty', in *Meaning, Knowledge, and Reality* (Cambridge: Harvard University Press, 1998), p. 100.

features of reality and the conventions we use to speak about it, then we will have to drop the hope that we can explain those convention by just accepting reality's self-revelation. It is simply impossible to isolate talk about 'circumstances' from talk involving practices, conventions, etc.

Now all this has been rather theoretical. The literature provides ample evidence that Davidson's extensional semantics is unable to account for the rich variety of linguistic usage. We take that evidence to be conclusive. What this shows is not that meaning has no relation to truth, but only that radical interpretation can only hope to solve the extensionality problem by harking back to the myth of the given and a crude objectivism.

The second issue is whether, in the absence of radical interpretation, a useful distinction between meaning and the production of meaning is still possible. Can we still hope for a critique of ideology and the possibility of an enlightening and possibly liberating genealogy of our concepts? If the possibility we hope to retain involves having the ability to describe the differences between paradigms in such a way that we *understand* a) that they are different and b) in what their difference consists, then we believe it is possible. But what makes it possible is not having an ability to describe meaning in non-intensional terms. Such a description will not be a description of meaning at all. *Indeed, interesting differences between paradigms are not so much related to the middle-sized dry goods that we can unproblematically describe. Rather they relate to more theoretical matters, which no amount of 'circumstantial visibility' can make any clearer.* Lack of 'circumstantial ability' is not an impediment for this kind of understanding. If it were, readers of Kuhn and Whorf would not be able to understand the differences between the paradigms that he is describing. It is precisely from within *content* (as McDowell likes to put it), that such differences make sense. Any perspective from outside content, such as the one envisaged by radical interpretation, would be utterly uninformative. *What makes possible the grasp of differences and incommensurability does not have to come from outside language!* We understand differing paradigms not because we have naked access to truth conditions – indeed we aren't even in the proximity of the distal stimuli.

It appears that Ramberg wants to have his cake and eat it too. He wants an account of meaning change which does not threaten the model of radical interpretation. But the resulting relation between meaning and the production of meaning is not dialectical, as he suggests. He admits that 'Incommensurability is a disruption in the conventional *production* of meaning, not a disintegration of meaning.'[60] What, then, is the cash value of the dialectics? In what sense may we say that meaning itself is affected by the production of meaning? Ramberg's only conceivable reply is to retreat to the level of the practical inescapability of conventions which obscures a meaning which is nonetheless '*theoretically recoverable*'. But in that case, this is no longer an issue of

[60] B. Ramberg, *Davidson*, p. 130.

semantics, but rather of pragmatics. Thus, incommensurability still remains semantically irrelevant, if an independent description of linguistic meaning can be given without recourse to the vagaries of actual usage. But the success of this method rests, as we have seen, with the possibility of giving a description of thick meanings by exclusively appealing to meagre physicalist descriptions.

If meaning is capturable without the tangled detour through historical sediments, the question is not why do we conventionalise it, but rather, why do we conventionalise it so differently? Thus, a semantics of incommensurability will have to explain not only the fact of conventions, but the manner of their formation, the independent trajectories that they take. For it is this trajectory which forces us to speak about different paradigms and worldviews. At a couple of junctures, Ramberg turns to the analogy of the virtues in order to specify the relation between the speaker and conventions. Just like 'a virtue is defined with respect to the hermeneutic circle running through the rational principle or abstract moral precept – the major premise of Aristotle's practical syllogism – and the concrete actions of the *phronimos* – the conclusions of the syllogism', 'every application of a linguistic convention, every instance of conforming to it, is also an interpretation and specification of that convention.'[61] Later, he appeals to the same register to explain how cross-paradigmatic communication is possible, as a matter of practical wisdom, rather than criterial rationality.

But there is more to this analogy than Ramberg reveals. For, if every application is also a specification, an application of a convention, then what the convention is applied to, but also the manner in which it is applied are relevant. This is a process that involves purposes, interests, perspectives and so on. The end result of this process is composed out of two indistinguishable and interpenetrated sides: a factual and a conventional side. The conventional side amounts to a historical trace of linguistic interactions with the real. *Thus, it will not do to appeal to the real as a lynch-pin for the reconstruction of linguistic meaning, for that linguistic meaning always refers to the real under various aspects, and these aspects are themselves the result of an interpenetration.*

One major objection stands in the way of this response, from a Davidsonian perspective: the learnability requirement. Unless the evidence available for learning a given language is completely public (together with the principle of compositionality) we cannot explain how people learn a language. So, for example, a language where people referred only to abstract entities would be a language impossible to be learned. Now, we have already shown that what Davidson and Ramberg consider to be public is actually utterly non-informative, for we would not even now how an exclusively physicalist description would help us in assigning any meanings. Davidson's whole project, in a sense, rests on a minimal anthropology. But the objection still

[61] B. Ramberg, *Davidson*, pp. 111f.

threatens: if the evidence for learning a language has to include intensions, then how can the process get going? What can we reply to this?

First, the apparent circularity spotted here is not necessarily threatening. Even the radical interpreter, as was conclusively shown by many critics, is inescapably circular. Davidson assumes this much in accepting the frankly semantic nature of 'assent'. So circularity in itself should not be a problem, provided that it leads to further insights that we might later use. Second, the blending between convention and fact is precisely such that it precludes the notion of an absolute convention. Interpretation is not forced to rely on concepts which have no relation to the outside world. But the relation is more complicated than Davidson allows. Third, and finally, the conventional side of the matter is not something mysterious, which stands in need of explanation. *Here we have come full circle: only if we accept the notion that intensions are non-desirable (which is itself a dogma) will we feel forced to find naturalist foundations for interpretation.*

That leaves us with an unworkable and extremely thin account of linguistic meaning. On the other hand, the radical interpretation model also works with a deficitary model of learning. It models learning as a process of accumulation, or concatenation of learned sentences, i.e. sentences whose truth conditions have been temporarily fixed. The continuous shifting of passing theories is not determined by a progressive immersion into language, such that with every added learned sentence we also progress in the understanding of previously acquired sentences. What prompts the altering of the passing theories is simply an *accidental* stumbling upon recalcitrant assent (instances of behaviour which do not fit the expectations we have formed on the basis of the passing truth theory). The problem is most obvious, because in such situations we have no idea where to make the appropriate adjustments. If, on the other hand, we extend the range of evidence to include frankly intensional elements, we will have improved the prospects of real understanding, even if we will have narrowed the circle. Because Davidson does not help himself to such intensional notions, the learning process he envisages is nothing but what Hacking has so aptly called a 'parody of a conversation'.

With every new grasped sentence we will not only have covered more ground in the new language, but we will also have acquired a *semantic depth* into the meaning of the previously understood sentences. It is here where difference can play a semantic part without putting a barrier to communication. We will have understood how the meaning of each constituent part of a language is given not only by its relationship to truth conditions, but also by the part it plays in the language. This amounts to an enlargement of Davidson's program without giving up on its central claim that meaning is related to truth.

Beyond Realism and Anti-Realism

Donald Davidson's philosophy opens up novel ways of viewing the classical debate between realists and anti-realists. The critique of the third dogma of empiricism, the dualism of scheme and content, together with the ancillary method of radical interpretation, are taken by Davidsonians as a significant step towards a resolution of the debate. Rorty has been driving this point as early as his *Philosophy and the Mirror of Nature*: 'if we press Quine's and Davidson's criticisms of the language-fact and scheme-content distinctions far enough, we no longer have dialectical room to state an issue concerning "how language hooks onto the world" between the "realist" and the "idealist" (or the 'pragmatist").'[62] The present section discusses whether indeed Davidson does move the philosophical agenda beyond the stale-mate between realists, idealists and pragmatists.

Why does Rorty think that the dissolution of the two distinctions leads to the dissolution of such an old debate? Obviously, because the debate itself presupposed the two distinctions, as in fact they presupposed each other. To give up the analytic-synthetic distinction means that philosophy has renounced the only way possible in which to uphold the unity and identity of a conceptual scheme, i.e. by its 'internal relations', it's truths in virtue of their meanings. If there remains nothing to uphold the consistency of the scheme and if any part of the scheme (including its analytic truths) is revisable, then the notion itself is not worth retaining. Davidson simply abandons the project of grounding knowledge in a system of representations, which map the contents of thought and language piece by piece unto the world. Associated with this representationalism is an understanding of truth as correspondence to reality, an atomistic theory of meaning, and a whole range of theories of reference.

What Davidson proposes is that we simply ditch the project. But what justifies such audacity? After all, there are important intuitions at stake on both sides of the debate. The realists fasten on their intuitions that there is a world independent of our knowing and that it is possible to know it. Moreover, they intuit that truth outruns our abilities to rationally justify our beliefs. On the other hand, non-realists are concerned to make truth accessible again. They fear that realists, by removing truth as correspondence too far from our epistemic practice, make it inaccessible, thus dehumanizing it. This does appear to be a worthwhile debate, with important consequences. Why should we simply drop it?

Part of the reason why we should no longer frame the issue in such terms, i.e. in terms of epistemic intermediaries – either in terms of sense impressions or conceptual systems – is that understanding truth as 'fitting the facts' has no explanatory value. In short, it adds nothing to the simple and basic concept of 'being true' – and that is all the concept we need for purposes of radical

---

[62] R. Rorty, *PMN*, p. 265.

interpretation. But why should the notion of radical interpretation be of importance in the present context? The answer is simple for anyone versed in Davidsonian philosophy and we presented it in our first chapter: to accept the notion of conceptual schemes is to suppose that there may be languages (with which Davidson necessarily associates conceptual schemes) that might be true but untranslatable. This notion simply does not make sense, for if we are unable to radically interpret a language, we have no reason to treat it as a language in the first place. But, as we have showed in this chapter, to radically interpret means to assign truth theories to native speakers. It thus follows that, if we are able to radically interpret, we have managed to also agree with the respective truth theory of a native. But we can radically interpret any speaker of any language (by definition). Since there are no languages that are true but untranslatable, neither can we make sense of the notion that there are conceptual schemes which make truth relative to themselves.

This is a move from representationalism towards semantics and back again in order to show that the simple and basic notion of truth – which bears of no further explanation, other than the disquotational ranges given in a Tarskian apparatus – is just enough for the purposes of radical interpretation. This proposal is nothing short of revolutionary, for it completely alters the perspective on epistemology, ontology, and semantics. Rather than seeking to explain truth in terms of more basic phenomena like correspondence, fitting, coherence and so on, we should just treat truth as basic and explain meaning, for example, in terms of it.

All we have is our beliefs and language. This should not be taken in a solipsistic way. It is simply a consequence of Davidson's rejection of the myth of the given. Its demythologizing entails abandoning the attempt to create theories of meaning and interpretation in terms of reference. According to such theories, we first assign references to words, by way of ostensive reference, then allow other words to build their meaning around this core in the course of being used.[63] The problems associated with such a model have already been pointed out. Changing a gear, Davidson simply proposes that we make sentences the unit of linguistic meaning – in terms of their truth conditions. This leads us into Davidsonian holistic semantics.

It would be a mistake, however, to suppose that this holistic semantics is simply preparatory for a return to ontology! The fact that no epistemological conclusions seem to follow from this holist, disquotational, and truth conditional semantics is emphasised by Rorty as well as Ramberg. Rorty argues that Davidson's program has nothing to do with epistemology and that 'it's "ontological" results are bound to be bland.'[64] But why is this? Davidson would seem to have a way to argue from the fact that (1) we can translate any language, to the fact that (2) this means all languages share a single conceptual

---

[63] *PMN*, p. 304.

[64] *PMN*, p. 261.

scheme, and finally to (3) this conceptual scheme is an adequate mapping of the world. But of course, Davidson refuses such an argument. He refuses the notion that, if there aren't a plurality of conceptual schemes, it means that there is a single conceptual scheme. It's simply a nonsensical notion. More importantly, however, he refuses the ontological induction. Simply because we quantify over, say, chairs and other middle sized dry goods, does not mean that there 'really are' such things in the world as chairs. But why not? For the simply reason that we cannot understand the notion of a confrontation between our beliefs and reality: 'No such confrontation makes sense, for of course we can't get outside our skins to find out what is causing the internal happening of which we are aware.'

What then is the relationship between mind and world, or between language and world? Do we not open the door to scepticism if we refuse to describe this relationship in a piece-meal fashion? Are we still in touch with the world if we cast it in a merely causal role, as impinging from the outside upon our web of beliefs?

Before we tackle some of these concerns, let us ponder for a moment the religious consequences of this holism. In an address to the American Academy of Religion, Kevin Schilbrack, a writer at the forefront of the intersection between Davidson studies and religion, argues that Davidsonian semantics opens the door to religious metaphysics once again.

> The dominant consensus in Religious Studies accepts Kant's view of the bounds of sense – now typically reformulated in terms of language – that religious metaphysics is groundless. It is this epistemological assumption, built into the modern and post-modern study of religions, that Davidson's work challenges. If his account of the relation of mind and world is right, then *there is nothing in principle confused when religious communities talk about the general features of reality* [i.e., metaphysics]. There are no screens that insulate people from the world.[65]

The Kantian ambition for philosophy as the discipline that could tell us what we are able to speak about was abandoned by Davidson. There is no such thing as a conceptual scheme which conditions our access to the world. Schilbrack thus gives Davidson a realist twist and interpretation, one that, as will become apparent, is by no means unanimous. This is only natural, after all, for a thinker who aims to move beyond classic demarcations. Inevitably such a thinker will be claimed by both sides. To return to the point made by Schilbrack, after Davidson 'the difference between perceptual beliefs and metaphysical beliefs is merely a difference of degree.'[66]

A similar conclusion is reached by Rorty. Noting that it does not make sense to speak about the transition between scientific paradigms in terms of gains in

---

[65] Kevin Schilbrack, 'Kicking Rocks with Donald Davidson' [unpublished paper, AAR, 2005], p. 7.

[66] K. Schilbrack, 'Kicking Rocks', p. 7.

knowledge, or better correspondence to reality, but only in terms of better 'coping', he explains, 'For if we once admitted that Newton was better than Aristotle not because his words better corresponded to reality but simply because Newton made us better able to cope, there would be nothing to distinguish science from religion or politics.'[67] We pointed out a similar conclusion reached by Quine. This erasure of the traditional taxonomy between the disciplines, in terms of their access to reality, is a classic feature of neo-pragmatism. If reality stands in a merely causal relationship to our beliefs, if it underdetermines to such a extent our epistemic revisions, we have no basis on which to conclude that some areas of culture are closer to representing reality than others. We simply have no basis to infer, this would seem to be Rorty's argument, from the apparent success of our scientific and other endeavours, that we have progressed in our attempt to map reality. In fact, if we press the logic of this position further, we don't even have much of an idea about what it would mean to 'map' reality, to represent it, to have beliefs that correspond to it.

Agreement seems to mount around the notion that neo-pragmatism is generous towards all cultural discourses. The notion of reality's preferred self-description simply does not make sense. In fact, as again Rorty points out, it is a quasi-theological notion:

> Nature may, for all we know, necessarily grow knowers which represent her, but we do not know what it would mean for Nature to feel that our conventions of representations are becoming more like her own, and thus that she is nowadays being represented more adequately than in the past. Or, rather, we can make sense of this only if we go all the way with the Absolute Idealists, and grant that epistemological realism must be based on personalistic pantheism.[68]

This is an interesting and potent idea, and, as our final chapter will point out, need not serve as a *reductio* against realism.

Having briefly glanced at some of the consequences of this for religious talk, let us return to the more pressing question: how, if no such piece-meal epistemic access to reality exists, can we say that our thought is still in touch with the world? Davidson, no less than any realist, wants to claim that our beliefs are in touch with the world. In fact, when he suggests that his approach to language helps us to 're-establish unmediated touch with the familiar objects whose antics make our sentences and opinions true or false', he appears to lean very close indeed towards realism.

There are two Davidsonian elements which guarantee that thought is after all connected to the world.[69] The first of these is radical interpretation, the upshot

---

[67] R. Rorty, *PMN*, p. 269.

[68] R. Rorty, *PMN*, p. 299

[69] See the discussion in Ernest Sosa, 'Knowledge of Self, Others, and World', in K. Ludwig, ed., *Donald Davidson*.

of which is that 'beliefs are by nature generally true.'[70] Unless we take the speakers to have mostly true beliefs about most of the things he is talking about, we have no way to begin interpreting. As Sosa puts it, 'the meanings that an interpreter attributes to a speaker's utterances are then bound to reside in the commonly shared nodes of the causal trees that prompt the respective attitudes of speaker and interpreter.'[71] Unless we are able to correlate between a speaker's verbal output and his dispositions to assent to various circumstances, as well as our own beliefs about those circumstances, we have no way to interpret. Again, it has to be remembered, that the basic unit across which we distribute meanings are sentences.

Thus the first line of defence against scepticism is an argument from radical interpretation. The second is what can be called Davidson's 'content externalism'. As Davidson puts it, 'in the simples and most basic cases, words and sentences derive their meaning from the objects and circumstances in whose presence they are learned.' There are many sentences and words that aren't learnt this way.

> [B]ut it is those that are than anchor language to the world. The fallout from these considerations for the theory of knowledge is (or ought to be) nothing less than revolutionary. If words and thoughts are, in the most basic cases, necessarily about the sorts of objects and events that cause them, there is no room for Cartesian doubts about the independent existence of such objects and events.[72]

This is in fact Davidson's famous transcendental argument for the truth of most of our beliefs. It holds that since we get the content of these beliefs from causal intercourse with the objects and events of nature, we could not be massively mistaken about them.

To recapitulate, we can be satisfied that our thought is in touch with the world, because without the intercourse between two speakers and a common world (the triangulation argument), there would be no interpretation and no thought. We may put the larger proposal in a sketchy form:

(1) The debate between realism and anti-realism is obsolete because it rests on the assumption of the dubious notion of conceptual scheme and on representationalism.

(2) All the work that needs to be done in semantics and epistemology can be done by the basic notion of truth, without the need to provide further explanations of this notion.

(3) Reality impinges upon our beliefs causally. This ensures that most of our beliefs are true. As a result, scepticism has no grip on us.

---

[70] D. Davidson, 'A Coherence theory of truth and knowledge', p. 153.

[71] E. Sosa, 'Knowledge of Self', p. 168.

[72] Both quotes from 'The Myth of the Subjective', p. 45.

Is this enough to persuade us to leave the battlefield behind? We will argue that it isn't. Neither argument which is supposed to assure us that we are in touch with the world works. Moreover, it will be shown that *such a model that assigns a merely causal role to the world fails to account for the differentiated way in which we actually approach it.*

Barry Stroud distinguishes between two possible readings of Davidson's argument from radical interpretation. On a stronger reading, radical interpretation is taken to imply that 'No believer's set of beliefs could be massively false.' The weaker reading suggests that 'No interpreter could correctly interpret a speaker in such a way that the speaker's beliefs come out massively false in the interpreter's opinion.'[73] Naturally, Davidson claims the second reading, but in fact it does not follow from the weaker, which is the only one that may be supported by radical interpretation. But in order to refute the sceptic, the stronger reading is required, and 'That being the case, [Sosa opines,] we need to go beyond considerations involving radical interpretation if we are to reach the conclusions that we need against the sceptic.'[74]

When Sosa turns his attention to Davidson's content externalism, as another supposed support in the polemic versus the sceptic, he finds it wanting too. First, he distinguishes between (a) dispositions to appropriate verbal behaviour, as in Davidson's '[Two] speakers who "mean the same thing" by an expression need have no more in common that their dispositions to appropriate verbal behaviour; the neural networks may be very different'[75]; and (b) the process or processes which may cause such dispositions in a certain speaker, as in Davidson's 'A sentence which one has been conditioned by the learning process to be caused to hold true by the presence of fires will be true when there is a fire present; a word one has been conditioned to be caused to hold applicable by the presence of snakes will refer to snakes.'[76] A disposition *might have been* put in place by the presence of those causes which gives the content of the word/sentence, but it need not have! This constitutes a 'problem for Davidson's transcendental argument. For there is now no evident impossibility in one's understanding of the concepts of our commonsense objective reality, where this understanding resides, at least in part, in one's complex dispositions to verbal and other relevant behaviour, although one has *not* acquired such dispositions through causal intercourse with exemplars of the concepts possessed.'[77] In other words, we could have acquired those concepts through other means rather than through direct causal contact with the exemplars. In fact this is how most of our concepts get acquired. If we allow for a multitude of ways of acquiring a concept, ways which may include but are not restricted

---

[73] Barry Stroud, quoted in E. Sosa, 'Knowledge of Self', p. 169.

[74] E. Sosa, 'Knowledge of Self', p. 172.

[75] D. Davidson, 'Myth of the Subjective', p. 44.

[76] D. Davidson, 'Myth of the Subjective', pp. 44-5.

[77] E. Sosa, 'Knowledge of Self', p. 176.

to causal interaction with the objects themselves, the sceptical possibility that what we take our terms to be about have nothing in common with any intended externalia is left wide open.

To say that Davidson's transcendental arguments against scepticism misfire is not itself a *reductio* of his own model. Realism itself has frequently been accused of precisely creating a space where scepticism might flourish, i.e. in the epistemically intermediary space between our beliefs and what they are about. Davidson attempts to fill this space with causal, rather than epistemic, intermediaries. His efforts are apparently not enough to block the sceptical moves. But there is also another difficulty associated with this proposal. It is best visible in Putnam's debate with Rorty on the necessity of realism.

In 'The World Well Lost', Rorty sides with Davidson on the nature of the relation between world and language. "[W]e shall *always* be holding mostly true beliefs and, thus, presumably be "in touch with the world" the vast majority of the time.'[78] But this relation of being in touch cannot be described as an individual correspondence between words/sentences and things/circumstances. The search for such ontological foundations for our thought is futile. Moreover, 'the realistic true believer's notion of the world is an obsession rather than an intuition'[79] and it in fact denotes 'those planks in the boat which are at the moment not being moved about.'[80] The inference here appears to be from the premise that we are unable to step outside our own skins and view the world as it is, to the conclusion that it does not make sense to speak of individual, specifiable parts of the world, which can or should be mapped by thought.

Both Rorty and Davidson, as we have seen, think that this is enough. They assure us that, given their epistemic model, we remain in touch with the world, a causal touch, to be sure. Putnam begs to differ, however. He also notices the realistic sounding language used by both philosophers, for example Davidson's talk of reinstating unmediated touch with the familiar objects of the world. But he is convinced that '*to preserve our commonsense realist convictions it is not enough to preserve some set of "realist" sentences.* The interpretation we give those sentences, or, more broadly, your account of what understanding them consists in, is also important.'[81] One may utter all sorts of realist sounding statements, but the intuitions behind realism are not preserved by any interpretations of these statements. In the case in point, they are certainly not preserved by the causal casting of reality.

On a causal arrangement, I have no knowledge of the parts of the world. My postulating certain entities by using certain concepts is only a method that

[78] In Rorty, *Consequences of Pragmatism*, p. 13.

[79] R. Rorty, *Consequences*, p. 13.

[80] R. Rorty, *Consequences*, p. 15.

[81] H. Putnam, 'Richard Rorty on Reality and Justification', in R. Brandom, ed., *Rorty and His Critics* (Oxford: Blackwell, 2000), p. 83 (our italics).

allows me to cope. Insofar as I am describing reality, Putnam explains, the description is the whole system of vocables that I produce. This should give us pause, for if it is considered vacuous to speak about piece-meal descriptions, why should it make more sense at the level of the whole of the language? Are natural languages descriptions of reality? Do we mean the whole system of knowledge? But that system contains a great many diverging theories about reality. To locate the description of reality at the level of the whole 'system of vocables' is only to reproduce the problem at another level.

Leaving that behind, this picture contradicts our best realist intuitions, in their pre-theoretical phase, so to speak, that is, without the whole conceptual baggage of 'correspondence'. For it is hard to think of other people, of my wife and daughter, as simply instruments which help me cope. In another context, Putnam goes on to explain that our everyday linguistic practice is deeply informed by a realist picture. The idea that the statement "Caesar crossed the rubicon" is just something we utter in response to present day assertibility conditions is an idea infinitely remote from our actual form of life.[82]

Rorty's and Davidson's insistence that we are nevertheless in touch with the world does not preserve that picture of an 'enormous human weight', which forces us to treat other people not as simply instruments in the service of a naturalistic epistemological apparatus, but as being themselves those 'joints' of which the world is made. Holding on to talk about 'unmediated touch' merely pays lip service to that picture, while it effectively corrupts it.

Not only is the solution inhuman, but it is also inconsistent, according to Putnam. For, how does the statement "There is a reality (outside ourselves) which we act on" help us cope? On one reading, it seems to be a trivial consequence of Rorty's currently accepted world picture, i.e. those planks in the boat which are momentarily stationary. On another reading, it represents a futile gesture in the direction of an abandoned realism. If the first reading is chosen, it is much too vague, because the currently accepted picture of the world does divide it into discrete parts. Moreover, as our everyday discursive practice shows, we 'cope' with the world in a variety of ways. We approach the study of nature using certain instruments, while we approach the study of the arts, of texts using vastly different methods. It is this differentiated access that Rorty's – and by implication Davidson's – model does not fully account for. Putnam puts it well: 'How, if we deny our relation to these discrete hunks is piecemeal, can we argue that our ability to get in touch with electrons is different from our ability to get in touch with nineteenth century paintings?'[83]

This is an argument of enormous importance and it implies that realism is needed to undergird scientific practice and its success. Let us use an analogy employed by Putnam himself, of a person employing a measurement apparatus.

---

[82] H. Putnam, 'Does the Disquotational Theory of Truth Solve all Philosophical Problems?', in Putnam, *Words and Life*, p. 276.

[83] H. Putnam, 'Richard Rorty on Reality and Justification', p. 83.

Rorty's and Davidson's causal account of the relation between the world and thought holds that the two realms are epistemically remote, yet causally interact with each other. Since we have no way to step outside our skins, abandon our language, or previous beliefs, our concepts in order to grasp reality in its revealing nudity, all that we can do is focus on our linguistic practice. Quine would add: guided by the scientific method. At any rate, the suggestion is that we should focus, analogically speaking, on the measurement apparatus, rather than on the reality measured. The apparatus is all we see. We make certain adjustments, we act upon the world, and we see how the world 'responds' to those actions, but we can only do that via the apparatus. Hence the Davidsonian and Rortian disquotational elaboration of truth: all that can be said about truth is disquotational. It is impossible to further specify in what truth consists, other than to give a Tarski-style recursive definition. We have seen how Davidson uses the notion of truth conditions in his theory of interpretation. The assumption behind this, Putnam explains, is that the use of words can be described in terms of what speakers are allowed to say and do in observable circumstances.[84] Thus, use is a theoretical notion and there are standard ways of describing the use of expressions in an arbitrary language game.

Putnam then asks, but what happens when the measurement apparatus goes wrong? Take for example the electrician. He sometimes learns that he has to distrust the criteria, the tools. But the knowledge of when to distrust these criteria is not itself something which is learned by the rules.[85] Rather, it is something that can only be discovered in the application of those tools to the reality which is studies. Even though our approach to reality is always mediated in some form, it does not follow that present in our experience is not something that cannot be fully anticipated by the theories we use. Putnam describes this cohabitation between elements of thought, our theories and concepts, and elements of reality by his notion of 'interpenetration'.[86]

The argument, then, is that unless our theories and thought connect with reality not simply in a causal way, but *rationally* – in a manner that remains to be elucidated – and in a piecemeal fashion, uttering realist sounding statements is empty talk. Our scientific practice and its success is taken by Putnam as evidence that such piecemeal rational correlation is taking place after all. But in doing so, he insists on maintaining some notion of a conceptual scheme.

In order to explain *convergence*, i.e. the view that new theories in science are better approximations of the reality which old theories attempted to represent, one needs to allow for a distinction between truth and justification, which is what the realist will assume. We need such a distinction so that we can

---

[84] H. Putnam, 'Does the Disquotational Theory of Truth Solve All Philosophical Problems?', p. 269.

[85] H. Putnam, 'Does the Disquotational Theory of Truth Solve All Philosophical Problems?'.

[86] See below.

portray old theories as having been justified, yet false, in light of the new theories which are now justified, but which might well expire and be replaced with even better ones. On the one hand, the fact that new theories contribute to experimental success suggests that the entities which they postulate actually exist, or that in some particular fashion, our concepts are rationally related to them (in a way yet to be explicated). On the other hand, the fact that old theories are sometimes able to predict precisely where new theories might go wrong again can only be accounted for by realism.

In reply, Rorty denies that we are faced with a fact that needs any sort of philosophical explanation. To treat theoretical succession in terms of convergence is an "inevitable artifact of historiography"[87], a decision about how to write history. As such, it does not provide one with an independent vantage point from which to judge this succession, but it is always some sort of narration of success from the perspective of one theory or another. But Putnam takes this convergence not as a historical hypothesis, but as an independent fact about the results of tests of theories.[88] Richard Boyd corroborates Putnam's conclusions: 'Unless, as no empiricist would suggest, the world is molded by our *conventions*, there is no way that the reliability of this principle could merely be a matter of convention.'[89] However, this reliability, Rorty argues, is not the sort that can be established by an independent test. There simply are no theory-independent tests. We can only test a new theory by using criteria from old ones. This is not a special fact which needs explanation.

A further argument deployed by Putnam centres around the notion of reference. If successive theories do not represent better approximations of the same reality, then we are left with the prospect that no theoretical term ever referred. The task of blocking this sceptical meta-induction is assigned to the theory of reference. How exactly is it that various terms from successive and very different theories manage to refer after all to the same reality, contributing to our project of mapping it? This is where the difference in their respective understandings of 'being in touch with the world' is most obvious. For Rorty, 'in one obvious sense we know perfectly well – prior to any theory – that they [scientists from various ages] have been referring to the same things. They were all trying to cope with the same universe and they referred to *it*, although doubtless under unfruitful and foolish descriptions.'[90] This won't do for Putnam, for he does not want a generalized answer, or a transcendental one. But, as Rorty wonders, it is difficult to imagine just what sort of answer might satisfy the sceptic, because 'no discovery about how words relate to the world will [...] assuage [the sceptic's] fear that [e.g.] molecules may not exist.' In other words, Rorty's main argument against Putnam's deployment of a theory

---

[87] *PMN*, p. 282.

[88] *PMN*, p. 283.

[89] Quoted in Rorty, *PMN*, p. 283.

[90] *PMN*, 286.

of reference in response to the sceptic, is that such a theory is actually only a decision about how to write the history of those particular terms. We simply have no way to step outside our own skins and pair concepts and objects. But if this is a question of historiography, it cannot answer the sceptic, because we can write history in more than just one way.

Putnam, as a result of this kind of criticism, recanted his 'metaphysical realism.' He came to realise that our best theory about what we are referring to is simply fallout from our picture of the world. It does not provide any sort of evidence which is independent of the theory we are trying to demonstrate. After abandoning this version of realism, Putnam turns to what he calls internal realism, or pragmatic realism. Internal realism amounts to the view that there is a fixed totality of mind independent things of which the world consists, but this statement itself is true only in the sense of an immanent truth, that is, in the sense that it is part of the total corpus of what one accepts.[91] It is worth reproducing a lengthier quote from Putnam, to illustrate the transition:

> What I am saying is that elements of what we call "language" or "mind" penetrate so deeply into what we call "reality" that the very project of representing ourselves as being "mappers" of something "language independent" is fatally compromised from the very start. Like Relativism, but in a different way, Realism is an impossible attempt to view the world from nowhere. In this situation, it is a temptation to say, "so we make the world" or "our language makes up the world", or "our culture makes up the world"; but this is just another form of the same mistake. If we succumb, once again we view the world – the only world we know – as a product. One kind of philosopher views it as a product from a raw material: unconceptualized Reality. The other views it as a creation ex nihilo. But the world isn't a product. It's just the world.[92]

This appears to be a pretty comprehensive concession to Rorty's points. But points of divergence do remain, since, where Rorty no longer sees any use for the notion of a conceptual scheme, Putnam still does.

The difference between metaphysical realism and internal realism is aptly expressed by Rorty: 'the difference between saying that we are successfully representing according to Nature's own conventions of representation and saying that we are successfully representing according to our own.'[93] What remains in internal realism, however, is the notion of success. Reference remains, but only as internal to a scheme. As Putnam puts it in 'Why is a Philosopher?', "The metaphysical realist insists that a mysterious relation of "correspondence" is what makes reference and truth possible; the internal realist, by contrast, is willing to think of reference as internal to "texts" (or

---

[91] H. Putnam, 'A Defense of Internal Realism', in Putnam, ed. James Conant, *Realism with a Human Face* (Cambridge: Harvard University Press, 1990), p. 32.

[92] Putnam, 'Realism with a Human Face', in *Realism with a Human Face*, p. 28.

[93] *PMN*, p. 298.

theories), *provided* we recognize that there are better and worse "texts."'[94] Clearly legible is here the normative notion of better and worse conceptual schemes, better and worse approaches to reality. But such a success can no longer be defined independently of the scientific narrative itself.

But hasn't Davidson shown that the notion of a conceptual scheme is inherently problematic? In what follows *we would like to show that it is still possible to speak coherently about conceptual schemes, while leaving intact Davidson's criticism of a certain understanding of such epistemic intermediaries*.

Putnam illustrates the phenomenon of conceptual relativity by giving the example of two different conceptual schemes: Carnap's and the Polish logician's.[95] According to Carnap's scheme, the world consists of three objects, x1, x2, x3. Then 'Suppose, for example, like some Polish logicians, I believe that for every two particulars there is an object which is their sum', which is in fact the basic assumption of mereology. If we take this option, the world will contain seven objects: x1, x2, x3, x1+x2, x2+x3, x1+x3, and x1+x2+x3. Thus the number of objects we can count in a world depends on the conceptual scheme which we have adopted. Putnam says that the notion of object is inherently extendable and it does not supply it's own counting principle. Our counting, it follows, will be partly conventional – depending on the conventions in place in a given scheme – but once we commit to a given scheme, our answer is quite definite.

A possible way to avoid the relativism which seems to loom behind conceptual relativity is, to use a metaphor, to understand reality as a dough and our conceptual schemes as the cutters which separate the dough in conventionally chosen shapes. As we have seen, the metaphysically realist Putnam was briefly tempted by this analogy. But ultimately the metaphor fails because it considers the dough to be independent from the cookie cutter, and thus independently available. Putnam writes: 'Unfortunately this metaphor is of no real assistance in understanding the phenomenon of conceptual relativity. Take it seriously, and you are at once forced to answer the question, "What are the various parts of the dough?"'[96] In other words we would be asking for those 'representation-independent particulars that we group together in one way or another'[97] whenever we use a given conceptual scheme. In this case we can only allow that one conceptual scheme is right, the one that 'cuts reality at its

---

[94] In H. Putnam, *Realism with a Human Face*, p. 114.

[95] This example appears both in 'Truth and Convention' (*Realism with a Human Face*, pp. 96-7), as well as in *The Many Faces of Realism* (LaSalle: Open Court, 1987), pp. 32-5.

[96] The Many Faces of Realism, p. 33.

[97] Jennifer Case, 'On the Right Idea of a Conceptual Scheme', *The Southern Journal of Philosophy*, 35 (1997), pp. 1-18, p. 6.

joints,' while the other possible ways of organizing the parts of reality are simple modes of speech.

Needless to say that both Putnam and Davidson reject the dubious cookie cutter metaphor. But Davidson also throws out the very notion of a conceptual scheme together with it. He motivates this by the impossibility of entertaining the notion of incommensurable conceptual schemes, i.e. conceptual schemes which are true but untranslatable.

In Putnam's defence, as Jennifer Case deftly shows, Putnam's description of conceptual schemes does not involve actual incommensurability. There is no real contradiction between the statements in one scheme and those in the other, o genuine inconsistency. If there were, they would not be equivalent in the sense in which it makes for such an interesting case. Secondly, moreover, Case explains that there is an important difference between Davidson's and Putnam's understanding of what a conceptual scheme is, a difference which is sufficient to account for their opposite philosophical trajectories. While Davidson ties the notion of conceptual scheme to the idea of a natural language – which is supposed to be translatable or not a language at all, Putnam's examples fasten on what Case calls 'optional languages'. It is Davidson's own premises which lead to his conclusion. By identifying a conceptual scheme with a language and by defining the identity criteria for languages in terms of translation, he is prevented from reaching any other conclusion about a conceptual scheme. But the interesting thing about conceptual schemes is precisely that they need not be uniquely associated with a natural language. Both Carnap's and the Polish logician's schemes function within the same natural language. They can also function – with some restrictions perhaps – in a multitude of natural languages. Thus, optional languages (Case is aware that this is not a perfect term and she is right: calling these conceptual schemes languages is loose) range independently of natural languages.

But if this is the case, then something important follows for interpretation, for it appears that *an interpreter may have more than a single 'home' conceptual scheme*. Here is Putnam (at length):

> It seems to me that the very assumption that there is such a thing as the radical interpreter's "own" language – *one* language in which he can give the truth conditions for *every* sentence in *every* language he claims to be able to understand – is what forces the conclusion. As long as one operates with this assumption, conceptual relativism will seem unintelligible (as it does to Davidson). But if one recognizes that *the radical interpreter himself may have more than one "home" conceptual scheme, and that "translation practice" may be governed by more than one set of constraints*, then one sees that conceptual relativity does not disappear when we inquire into the "meaning" of the various conceptual alternatives: it simply reproduces itself at a metalinguistic level![98]

[98] H. Putnam, 'Truth and Convention', p. 104.

But this is precisely the point that we have been pressing in our discussion of Davidson's interpretation theory. We find it reproduced at the epistemological level: *the simple and basic notion of truth is simply not sufficient to do the work required of it either in semantics or in epistemology*. This is not to say that the notion of correspondence should be called on to explain it. That is another question. The point is simply that *we have not explained all that bears explanation about the relationship between mind and world if we rely simply on the notion of truth*.

The consequences for interpretation, as we already anticipated, are significant. It will simply not do to treat our interlocutors as having true beliefs, much like our true beliefs. What plays an important part in the fixation of belief and meaning is not simply reality, those objects which cause us to have the beliefs we do, *simpliciter*. In a way that will become clearer further below, it is *the causes as judged* that fix our beliefs. But, as Putnam has so ably shown, there is more than just a single way to judge those causes, those things in the world. Case nicely sums up the similarities and contrasts between these two neo-pragmatists:

> Davidson and Putnam both reject the scheme-content dualism. But Davidson, in rejecting it, throws out the very idea of a conceptual scheme. Davidson uses a theory of interpretation to argue, I think convincingly, that we do not need and cannot use the scheme-content dualism in order to make sense of the notions of language and sameness of meaning across languages. If his theory of interpretation were richer, encompassing not only ordinary translation practice, but also relative interpretation, he might have realized that we do not need and cannot use the scheme-content dualism in order to make sense of the idea of a conceptual scheme either. Putnam amends and extends Davidson's conclusions by introducing richer and more realistic conceptions of language and interpretation, thereby avoiding throwing out the baby with the bath water.[99]

What is this notion of relative interpretation, which is supposed to supplement ordinary translation practice? Putnam argues that it is possible to correlate each sentence in a conceptual scheme with another sentence in another.[100] There is no single way to do this, however, and such a correlation is not one indicative of synonymy. He points out that 'the kind of "translation" just referred to does not provide what we would ordinarily regard as a linguistically synonymous expression. Moreover, these "translations" (the technical name for them is "relative interpretations") are not unique; the mereological sum version can be interpreted in the version without mereological sums in more than one way But the question "which translation scheme, if any, preserves the *meanings* of the sentences being translated?" is a bad question. The ordinary notion of "meaning" was simply not invented for this kind of case.'[101] Putnam seems to

---

[99] J. Case, 'On the Right Idea', p. 13.

[100] H. Putnam, 'Truth and convention', pp. 98-101.

[101] Quote in J. Case, 'On the Right Idea', p. 9.

speak about two different levels of language: a level of the meanings of the words and sentences, to which we might add a meta-linguistic level, of the kinds of things we might do with those meanings. The second level is the level of relative interpretations, while the first is that of translation and meanings. While at the first level, one stabilises meaning pretty much in the way in which Davidson suggests, i.e. by correlating with extensions and the beliefs of other speakers, at the second level more needs to be taken into account.

On this occasion Putnam does not speak about a possible dialectic between the two levels. However, the possibility needs to be taken seriously, or else we cannot understand what the fuss was about. How precisely is interpretation theory enriched, if relative interpretations range independently of translations? This remains an aspect which we feel is insufficiently developed, as in fact it is with Ramberg's own lip service to a similar dialectic between meaning and the production of meaning.

A clue to why Putnam leaves this relation un-analysed is that he does not see the notion of meaning to be appropriate in this context. He argues that one cannot say either that a sentence from a conceptual scheme and its relative interpretation in another conceptual scheme share the same meaning, or have different meanings. We must simply concede that 'the notion of "meaning," and the ordinary practices of translation and paraphrase to which it is linked, crumble when confronted with such cases.'[102] Putnam's suggestion then appears to focus on the meta-linguistic level, on the notion of interpretation rather than translation. Davidson also focuses on interpretation, since for him the notion of translation is so tied to already existing dictionaries and grammar books. But he does not go far enough, in that he does not admit of more than one "home" conceptual scheme.

While the notion of meaning is ill suited for such cases, what is it that distinguishes sentences uttered via a conceptual scheme from those uttered via another conceptual scheme? It is the fact that they are constituted by *different uses of the same words*. Let us take for example the sentence: 'This is an object', as uttered by two speakers of English, one of them employing a Carnapian scheme, the other a Polish logician's scheme. We obviously cannot say that these share the same meaning, because how else are we able to fix meaning except by looking at the causes. But in this case there is no independent cause (the cookie cutter metaphor is bankrupt) according to which we might judge sameness *or* difference of meaning. We can see that in such a case Davidson's radical interpreter will have nothing to start from. But if nothing can be said of the difference in terms of meaning, a lot can be said of it in terms of use.

There is thus a *depth* to sentences uttered in a natural language, a depth which is related to the specific conceptual scheme presupposed by the speaker. Such a depth goes beyond the semantic and grammatological level, while it

[102] Quote in J. Case, 'On the Right Idea', p. 14.

presupposes them.[103] We may call it a semantic depth, to denote the fact that there is something more to be elucidated about what a speaker does when he utters a sentence, beyond ordinary truth conditions. Such a semantic depth is constituted by the relationship between ordinary meaning and a conceptual scheme, itself constituted by internal relations between concepts.[104] There is no need to suppose that the concepts which constitute the conceptual scheme itself are parts of *Mentalese.* They are ordinary linguistic vehicles, whose *use* gives them a certain identity as parts of the web that these relations create. At the level of the conceptual scheme, the use to which the words are being put creates what may be called, importing and paraphrasing from another discussion, an *ontological plausibility structure. It is at that level that our concepts interpenetrate with the facts of the world, but to such an extent that we are not able to disentangle them with epistemological cutters in order to arrive at a splendidly transparent Given that will them guide our quest for knowledge and truth.*

Now it is easier to understand how it is that Putnam is able to evade Davidson's otherwise correct attack on a certain notion of conceptual scheme. None of the inconsistencies which Davidson considers inherent in the notion are reproduced at the level where Putnam places the scheme. Admittedly, it remains under-developed just what sort of level is this, but it is after all a 'relatively recherché phenomenon'[105]. But Putnam's notion of conceptual relativity is meant to affirm both that (1) we have piecemeal access to reality, (2) this access is rational, (3) its rational character does not derive from an epistemic access to the Given, but to the interpenetration between fact and convention; finally (4) our access to features of the world is always conceptually mediated by our being embedded in one conceptual scheme or another.

The obvious question which remains can be phrased in terms similar to Putnam's challenge to the realistic sounding statements: what is the cash value of saying that such an access is rational (i.e. that there are ways to discriminate between texts and better and worse conceptual schemes) if the interpenetration is so ubiquitous? *Is not our perception of the facts so contaminated by the conventions in use and our fallible concepts, that it is simply another empty gesture in the direction of a desired, rather than abandoned, realism?*

It will help to recapitulate in order to understand better why Putnam may be in a similar predicament. Davidson cuts the Gordian knot by simply refusing to countenance the notion of epistemic intermediaries. All our epistemic and semantic work can be done by restricting ourselves to using the basic notion of

---

[103] We grant that the relationship between these remains underdeveloped.

[104] It is instructive in this connection to note that Putnam retains a soft analytic-synthetic distinction. Conceptual truth remains for Putnam a possibility, but only as a matter of degree, not of an ontological necessity.

[105] Quote in Case, 'On the Right Idea', p. 14.

truth. There is no further necessity to explain in what truth consists, by reducing it to simpler concepts. There just aren't any such concepts around. The basic concept of truth does it's work at the linguistic end, in terms of truth conditions, and that is all the end we have. That is all the objectivity we have, i.e. the one than can be expressed in language and the one which is inter-subjectively produced by speakers who learn how to deal with reality and thought only by communing with others who do the same. Where does this leave the relationship between mind and world? This is precisely the relation which Davidson thinks it makes no sense to further explicate beyond saying that the world causes us to hold mostly true beliefs. No rational relation obtains between the 'joints' of the world and our 'stretches' of language. Rorty draws the right sort of morale from this: no qualitative differences remain between cultural discourses. Science, religion, ethics, literature and politics are all in touch with the same reality, neither of them possessing an intrinsic privilege in the sense of being closer to reality's preferred self-presentation.

The problem with this model (and this will be seen more clearly in the next section) is that we have no idea what we can revise in terms of what we take to be recalcitrant experiences. *Since reality maintains a causal and not a rational connection to our webs of belief, we are in danger of losing empirical content.* As Putnam argues, we are in danger of losing thought altogether. This is a vision of 'a human being resembl[ing] an animal producing various cries in response to various natural contingencies, [...] or better, a plant putting forth now a leaf and now a flower. Such a story leaves out that we are *thinkers*. If such a story is right, then not only is representation a myth; the very idea of thinking is a myth.'[106] It seems that our thought is cut off from the world.

But Putnam faces a similar predicament, and this situation forces us to think what, if anything, may count as a solution? For Putnam's internal realism is just as holistic in terms of epistemic justification. Theory is just as underdetermined by the data. It would seem that whether one is a realist or one is an idealist, or whether one has gone beyond the distinction makes no difference in practice, when it comes to justifying our assertions. What difference remains? Why is it still worth retaining a distinction between realism and idealism? We seem to have reached a deadlock. Pure semanticists like Davidson infer from (1) we have no knowledge by acquaintance, no access to the Given, that (2) it makes no sense to speak about reference, for it is always a decision about how to write the history of science, rather than an independent assessment of a confrontation between words and things. On the other hand, internal realists like Putnam hold that reference is still possible because, although there is no rational access to the hard facts, these facts interpenetrate with our theoretical conventions. But, as we have seen, Putnam is at a loss to explain just how – even though interpenetrated or contaminated – these incursions of the Real have a rational bearing upon justification. Putnam can only relativise reference and truth to a

---

[106] Putnam, 'Why is a Philosopher?' in *Realism with a Human Face*, p. 114.

conceptual scheme and then suggest that there remain, after all, better and worse schemes. But the decision on this quality of the scheme remains inescapably holistic for Putnam as well, and precisely because of conceptual relativity. In which case, he too is at a loss to cash out on the notion of a piecemeal access to reality.

Some light may be thrown on this issue by a somewhat neglected philosopher, Frederick Will. The main problem besetting these approaches, Will would suggest,[107] is that both conceive the two domains, of the world and of thought, as being independent from each other and the philosophical task as being that of uniting them. But to start from their autonomy can only result in offering 'crazy solutions'. It is not that Davidson's view does not put thought in contact with reality: the view in question does not hold that things do not determine thought, but that 'the kind of determination just exemplified is taken to be altogether a matter of the *generation* and *conditioning* of thought and not a matter of the character and identity of the thought itself.'[108] We have also granted this much. But the problem, as Putnam also understood, is that it is not enough to speak about any kind of relation between thought and things. Davidson's relation is causal, while Putnam's is rational – via a conceptual scheme. Will finds both wanting.

The reason for their respective deficiencies – and perhaps also for the deadlock we seem to have reached – is that *both build on a common mistaken assumption, which is that, if there is no knowledge by acquaintance, then there are no individual facts to be known.* This assumption lies at the basis of Rorty's *Philosophy and the Mirror of Nature.* It is related to *a further mistaken assumption, that realism needs foundationalism as its basis.* These are both assumptions which Will denies. Both assume the autonomy of the two realms, that of nature from that of the mind. Both are happy to consider thought just as thought, as an episode or even in the theatre of the mind. These thoughts are then considered to be capable of representing something outside the mind just in virtue of their nature as thoughts. This is an consequential mistake:

> The inadequacy is revealed rather in many more subtle and pervasive ways in which the capacity of one thing to serve as a representation of another depends on a multitude of things beyond the vehicle or representation and the represented object. The history of the visual arts seems to testify amply that the mechanisms and conditions of representation are not fixed by eternal laws.[109]

Will therefore grants that there is no knowledge by acquaintance. There goes the myth of the Given. But from this it does not follow that there are no individual facts that can be known. This is a *non sequitur* for it presupposes,

---

[107] Will does not refer explicitly to either Davidson or Putnam, but it the positions he describe have important similarities with their own programmes.

[108] F. Will, *Pragmatism and Realism*, p. 2.

[109] F. Will, *Pragmatism and Realism*, p. 9.

rather than demonstrates that the only knowledge of particulars is by acquaintance. It assumes rather than demonstrates another myth, that 'conceptualisation is an all or nothing affair.[110] Together with the notion of knowledge by acquaintance also goes the notion of semantic atomism, which has also been at the basis of attempts (like Putnam's) to connect a conceptual scheme with the world, by fixing the referents of its observational terms. This attempt is both futile and unnecessary for realism.

This accounts for the insightful notion that the capacity of a thing to represent, or to refer to something else, does not reside simply in its own nature, but in its relation to a variety of practices. The artistic illustration unpacks this notion: 'The possibilities of representation with line and color are not now in the Western world what they were in the years before Matisse and Picasso, just as they were not then what they were for artists in Africa or the Far East. And these differences are not due solely to variations in the media in these cases, to variations in the pigments, the vehicles, the means of application, and the surfaces to which they are applied.' Of course not, there are what may be called styles, preferences, whole philosophies (one might even venture, conceptual schemes, if it would not over-stretch it), these all contribute to the *manner* of the representations. It is no different in the realm of thought, Will explains. Our concepts do not refer in isolation from their participation in a practice.

However, there is a certain feature of these practices which suggests that reality is not at all indifferent to them. The phenomenon has been called the 'open texture' of concepts by Waismann, and it has been called attention to by Wittgenstein and Austin, among others. Here is Will's description:

> The phenomenon in question is a certain looseness or porosity in our concepts that leaves open, in the application of terms conveying these concepts, the possibility of borderline cases of an interesting kind. It is easy to imagine situations in which one would be at a loss to say that some common terms, like "cat" or "man," either did or did not definitely apply. Suppose we encounter one of Waismann's hypothetical creatures, for example, one that in all other respects appears to be a cat but later grows to a gigantic size, or shows some other queer characteristics such as the capacity to be revived after death.[111]

What do we say in such circumstances? It is in situations like these that, as Austin writes, 'We don't know what to say. Words literally fail us.'[112] This feature reveals something about language, Will thinks. It shows that it is logically impossible to complete an empirical description. No matter how comprehensive we make our descriptions, it is always possible to encounter some such thing that fits our description in most aspects, but not in all. In such

[110] F. Will, *Pragmatism and Realism*, p. 31.
[111] F. Will, *Pragmatism and Realism*, p. 10.
[112] Quoted in Will, *Pragmatism and Realism*, p. 11.

cases, it is no longer clear what these words would signify or how they would apply to the things.

> But if this is so, then the fact that these words do not fail us now in this particular way indicates something about the character of that world, at least up to now. Our success in employing linguistic practice involving words of this kind must be due in part to the fact that the world in which this practice goes on is not populated to any great extent, with entities of the kind supposed, that they remain for the most part in the category that Leibniz referred to as "bizarre fictions". Though having the idea of a purple guitar does not require there being an archetype of that idea in the world of things, successful employment of the language of musical instruments – of lutes, violins, horns, organs, and the rest – depends in fundamental and far reaching ways upon the character of the world in which this successful employment takes place. And if it is granted that having a concept of a thing is derivative and hence dependent upon such a practice, then it appears that having a concept of a thing is thus directly dependent upon things.[113]

The point which is being made here is that, even if semantic atomism does not hold, it is still possible to know – in virtue of the general success of our practices – that these practices are adequate to the world around us. We can know this because we are able to identify those instances in which they are simply not adequate and label them as 'bizarre fictions'. To be sure, this is certainly not the sort of independent assessment of the success of our theories. Will is the first to admit that these theories can only be assessed in the process of applying them. But their general success shows that they can be used to discriminate the genuine characteristics of things.

We can only identify (always fallibly) the 'genuine characteristics of things' on the background of our present conceptualisations, provided we admit that conceptualisation is not an all-or-nothing affair. To explain how this discrimination can only be achieved in the process of applying the concepts we have, Will uses the analogy of a map. 'What is explicitly represented, drawn on the map, is a basis, a skeleton of information defining, but not fully defining, the feature of the quadrant, continent or whatever is its object. It is not inconsistent with its character as a map, but rather essential to it, that it leave room for refinement, detail, and even in some cases revision of basic outlines.'[114] We can only find out if the map is correct in the process of using it. *But by using it we do not thereby commit ourselves to its possibly ossified and mistaken 'ontology', but leave room for correction and reform.* But in this case, the realist concern is with 'the question of the aptness in general of ways of speaking and thinking in various domains of life and inquiry, and, with that, the general appropriateness of the complex of practices with which these ways are

---

[113] F. Will, *Pragmatism and Realism*, p. 13.
[114] F. Will, *Pragmatism and Realism*, pp. 31f.

integrally related and which these forms of speech and thought, in their own particular modes, represent.'[115]

The beauty of Will's defence of realism is that it does not standardise reference and representation. Representation is not a relation which unites two otherwise independent realms. On the contrary, it is an exploitation of an already rich variety of existent and possible relationships in order to discriminate the genuine characteristics of reality. Will's pragmatism shows up in his denial that these genuine characteristics of reality are all part of a single, coherent, and axiomatisable ontology, or what Dewey has called 'antecedent reality.' Contrary to mistaken readings which supposed that Dewey was rejecting important realist intuitions about the priority of reality over thought, Will suggests that 'What Dewey wanted to emphasize in saying that antecedent reality is not the object of language is that the features we come to ascribe to reality in the development of knowledge through inquiry are ones the reality of which must be made out, or ascertained in the inquiry', rather than presupposed from the outset. Our conceptual schemes should not turn into 'ossified' Procustean beds, into which we force reality, but rather as flexible, revisable and ultimately dispensable tools which we use in our efforts to know it. Neither, however, should we treat their success as a terminus point.

> [W]e must, if we are not to become victims, as well as beneficiaries, of that success, no permit it to blind us to whatever signs there may be of aspects of misfit, of failure in respect to correspondence. Still less may we permit successful performance of a conceptual scheme in one area to be unthinkingly taken as a guarantee, rather than, at best, a promise, great or little, of performance in any area in which the aspirations and problems of both life and inquiry are prima facie widely different.[116]

With this caution against a tempting scientism we close our discussion about realism and non- or anti-realism. Will seems to have offered a solution to the dilemma into which both Davidson and Putnam have been forced. It resides in a refusal to consider the inference from (1) there is no knowledge by acquaintance to (2) there are no individual facts to be known, to be compelling. If we feel it is compelling, then, if we want to preserve realist intuitions, we will want to find some rational way of linking our thoughts to things. But to the extent that such an attempt presupposes the autonomy of mind from world, it is doomed to failure and can only lead to crazy solutions. Putnam's is one such crazy solution, as Kenneth R. Westphal comments.[117] Indeed, 'Our cognitive predicament is not one of establishing a link between our thoughts and their supposed objects, it is instead one of exploiting the links our thinking does and

---

[115] F. Will, *Pragmatism and Realism*, p. 33.

[116] F. Will, *Pragmatism and Realism*, p. 35.

[117] K. R. Westphal, 'Introduction', in Will, *Pragmatism and Realism*, p. xxv.

must have with things in order to discriminate the genuine characteristics of things.'[118]

John McDowell is just as dissatisfied with Davidson's complete renouncing of empiricism and his distribution of reality in an exclusively causal role. He agrees with Davidson that the idea of the Given, as the notion that the space of reasons extends more widely than the space of concepts[119], is a hopeless and incoherent quest for a foundation of thought that nevertheless lies outside of thought. Such a notion cannot offer a foundation for thought because the deliverances of receptivity, impressions, those emissaries from the world, as Davidson describes them, which are supposed to anchor our thought to reality are precisely outside of the realm of concepts and thus cannot stand in justificatory relationships to our beliefs. All that the best defences of the Given have been able to give us are exculpations, when what we really wanted were justifications.[120] The inability of showing that there are reasons which are not concepts amounts to the recognition that, if there are impingements of nature upon our beliefs in the form of impressions, these are describable wholly in causal and natural terms. They are brute incursions, as it were, generating beliefs we cannot refuse. But this has nothing to do with judgments which properly belong to spontaneity (to continue using the Kantian vocabulary used by McDowell) which is the realm of freedom. This leads Davidson to hold that only beliefs justify beliefs. Hence his coherentism.

Of course, as our discussion revealed, Davidson hopes that this is enough to secure a relationship between thought and reality. To ensure that, he appeals to a transcendental argument which purportedly shows that belief, by nature, is generally veridical. The inference which Will castigates can be seen here in action: if there is no knowledge by acquaintance (no Given), then there are no individual facts to be known (abandon all traces of an empiricism). The relationship between mind and world can therefore be regulated from the isolated position of the mind. The gap will be bridged by transcendentally arguing for the truth of most of our beliefs. But for McDowell, to abandon empiricism is to throw the baby out with the bath water.

The idea of the Given was the one response offered to the intuition that we need to have some sort of rational 'friction' between our beliefs and reality. Of course, it has been a deeply flawed solution. *But to propose abandoning the very question to which it was supposed to serve as an answer is to naively suppose that the question itself is gratuitous*, when it is not.[121] McDowell correctly points out that the quest for friction, the craving for objectivity is not just a fancy that can easily be left behind, forgotten, as we move on to other things. Davidson's mistake is to have mis-understood the very *force* of the

---

[118] K. R. Westphal, 'Introduction', p. xxiii.
[119] J. McDowell, *MW*, p. 7.
[120] J. McDowell, *MW*, p. 8.
[121] J. McDowell, *MW*, p. 15.

question. Simply refusing to ask the question does not mean that it will go away. *In fact it will return in the form of anxieties which are generated precisely by Davidson's own coherentism, for the picture it paints is that of a whole body of beliefs which are rationally unconstrained by anything outside them.* But that is precisely the type of fear that the myth of the Given hoped to provide a solution for. To just change the discussion, as Davidson does, 'does nothing to explain away the plausibility of the empiricist picture, according to which we can make sense of the world-directedness of empirical thinking only by conceiving it as answerable to the empirical world for its correctness, and we can understand answerability to the empirical world only as mediated by answerability to the tribunal of experience, conceived in terms of the world's direct impacts on possessors of perceptual capacities.'[122] The problem, therefore, is to suppose that since we have been unable to make sense of those impacts which take place in experience, the whole project should be dropped as meaningless. But the picture is plausible precisely because the world-directedness of empirical thinking (which Davidson also wants to have) is conceivable only in terms of answerability, whether we are able to mediate this answerability in terms of the Given or not.

Thus, McDowell's argument also takes a transcendental form. Unless our empirical beliefs stand in appropriate justificatory relations with the world, we cannot say that these beliefs are about the world. It will simply not do to explain this *aboutness*, this directedness in terms of brute causal impacts, as Davidson does. Empirical content is inextricable from relations of justification which help us say whether this particular belief is correct or incorrect about the world. Outside such justificatory relations, McDowell holds, there is no aboutness, no directedness. Empirical content simply cannot be in the picture if we 'carefully stipulate that the world's impacts on our senses have nothing to do with justification.'[123] Unfortunately McDowell does not argue very much for this notion of aboutness in terms of justification beyond resorting to Kant's own argument that 'Thoughts without intuitions are empty, and the point is not met by crediting intuitions with a causal impact on our thoughts; we can have empirical content in our picture only if we can acknowledge that thoughts and intuitions are rationally connected.'[124] On the other hand, neither does Davidson's hope that thought is nevertheless in touch with the world mean very much, given that he denies any piecemeal approach to reality. But it is precisely this piecemeal approach to reality which is necessary, according to McDowell, in order to make sense of the very idea of belief. If we cannot know what a belief is about, i.e. if we are not able to discriminate between beliefs in terms of their being correctly or incorrectly held about this or that state of affairs, then the very notion of belief goes by the board.

---

[122] J. McDowell, *MW*, p. xvii.
[123] J. McDowell, *MW*, p. 15.
[124] J. McDowell, *MW*, pp. 17f.

Thus, if McDowell is right, not only does Davidson's picture fail to take seriously the anxiety behind the myth of the Given, an anxiety which is again given an opportunity to arise, but his transcendental argument also fails. He can argue that belief is on the whole veridical only by helping himself to the idea of belief, but that is precisely what he ends up denying himself.

But to say that we can only have aboutness in terms of relations of justification in which experience plays a part is not enough, for after all, there remain serious problems about the notion of extra-conceptual impacts on the senses as having justificatory value. On the one hand, if we conceive these impacts as belonging to the non-conceptual, they are not in rational relations to our beliefs. On the other hand, if we take them as being conceptual, then they are already *inside* our web of beliefs, and thus cannot provide the required friction with a reality external to it.

This is the image which Sellars first depicted, of a distinction between the space of causes and the space of reasons. If we conceive those impacts upon our nerve endings as properly belonging to the space of concepts, then their impact within our web of beliefs, the space of reasons, can only take the shape of an uncontrolled holistic ripple effect. But that is surely not reassuring to McDowell, for it is precisely that picture which cannot accommodate empirical content. On the other hand, the space of reasons is *sui generis*, it is a realm of freedom, rather than one determined by outside forces. We could, of course, abandon that notion of freedom and adopt what McDowell calls a 'bland naturalism', but that creates more problems than it solves. Thus, McDowell's predicament is that if we conceive of these spaces in such a different fashion, it appears very difficult to see how any rational transfers can take place from one to the other.

The only two imaginable alternatives seem to be Davidson's complete departure from empiricism, or, on the other hand, a complete naturalising of mind. What makes it very difficult to conceive of an alternative is 'a deep-rooted mental block.'[125] This veil on our thought originates in a dualism between the space of causes and the space of reasons. The space of causes is the space in which we place something by describing it in terms appropriate to what is natural, i.e. in causal terms. This space has been identified with the *natural*, mistakenly, as McDowell argues. On the other hand, the space of reasons is the space in which we place something by describing it as standing in rational relations to other items in that same space, relations of inference, justification, contradiction and so on. However, this understanding of the realm of causes, or of nature, has been deeply impacted by modern science which created a certain image of that space.

> The image marks a contrast between two kinds of intelligibility: the kind that is sought by (as we call it) natural science, an the kind we find in something when

---

[125] J. McDowell, *MW*, p. 69.

> we place it in relation to other occupants of the "logical space of reasons", to repeat a suggestive phrase from Wilfrid Sellars. If we identify nature with what natural science aims to make comprehensible, we threaten, at least, to empty it of meaning. By way of compensation, so to speak, we see it as the home of a perhaps inexhaustible supply of intelligibility of the other kind, the kind we find in a phenomenon when we see it as governed by natural law.[...] Now if we conceive the natural as the realm of law, demarcating it by the way its proper mode of intelligibility contrasts with the intelligibility that belongs to inhabitants of the space of reasons, we put at risk the very idea that spontaneity might characterize the workings of our sensibility as such. The faculty of spontaneity is the understanding, our capacity to recognize and bring into being the kind of intelligibility that is proper to meaning. We disclose this kind of intelligibility by placing things in a logical space that is *sui generis*, by comparison with the realm of law. But sensibility, as I said, is part of our nature, part of what we share with mere animals.[126]

We have indulged this lengthier quote because it so adequately describes how the dualism between nature and spirit has been applied into epistemology. According to this deeply engrained picture, the workings of our sensibility are, just like the workings of animal sensibility, describable in merely causal terms. On the other hand, if spontaneity is *sui generis*, that puts at risk its very connection to what there is, the empirical content of our beliefs. As we saw, neither the Given, nor Davidson's unconstrained coherentism is satisfactory. Defenders of the Given are unable to provide us with reasons, while Davidsonians lose empirical content altogether. Is there a way out of the deadlock? The comparison with animals, with whom we share perception, would seem to compel us to separate spontaneity from receptivity. The image would thus be reinforced of our animal nature co-habiting with our rational or spiritual one, with no obvious ways to see any sort of cooperation between the two, given their radically diverging character.

There is a way out of the deadlock, if we are willing to imagine a possibility that Davidson does not even countenance. 'We can dismount from the seesaw if we can achieve a firm grip on this thought: receptivity does not make an even notionally separable contribution to the co-operation [between sensibility and understanding, or receptivity and spontaneity]. The relevant conceptual capacities are drawn on *in* receptivity.'[127] The proposal is thus to imagine a co-operation between our senses and our conceptual capacities in such a way that there is no logical gap between the deliverances of the senses and some activity that our conceptual abilities might perform *on* those deliverances. Rather, these conceptual abilities are already in operation in receptivity: 'in experience, one takes in, for instance sees, that things are thus and so.'[128] If there is no logical gap between impression and judgment, it follows that there is no attempt to

[126] J. McDowell, *MW*, pp. 70-72.
[127] J. McDowell, *MW*, p. 9.
[128] J. McDowell, *MW*, p. 9.

isolate a conceptually uncontaminated piece of the Given that might ground belief.

But if those deliverances are still conceptually 'contaminated', then how is it that we have friction? It is because experience remains passive. 'In experience one finds oneself saddled with content.'[129] But now the pendulum seems to swing the other way. Indeed, McDowell's argument can be taken as an attempt to stabilise the anxiety generative movement of the pendulum between the Given and Coherentism, by compensating, now here now there, with corrections to misperceptions. He compensates for his talk about what we called 'conceptual contamination' with talk about the passivity of experience. The problem this creates is that it may look like a piece of sophistry: saying that conceptual capacities extend all the way to the content of experience, then calling them passive. In what sense are they still conceptual then, one may be justified in asking? They are conceptual, McDowell replies, because they are the very same capacities which are drawn on, this time actively, in spontaneity.[130]

Imagining this possibility is so difficult precisely because of the grip that the dualism of causes and reasons, of nature and reason, has on us. Speaking of spontaneity extending all the way to the very content of experience threatens to make the powers of the mind mysterious and supernatural. But this fear should only seem compelling if we construe nature as to exclude second nature.[131] We will return to the notion of second nature in our final chapter. For now it suffices to point out that second nature, as an actualisation of potentialities that belong to human nature, cannot float free of these. We are no less natural beings because we actualise our human nature by drawing on spontaneity. We are forced into thinking that unless we understand that 'what became available at the time of the modern scientific revolution is a clear-cut understanding of the realm of law, and [if] we refuse to equate that with a new clarity *about nature*. This makes room for us to insist that spontaneity is *sui generis*, in comparison with the realm of law, without falling into the supernaturalism of rampant Platonism.'[132] What modern science revealed was, in other words, a clearer understanding of the relation between causes and effects, and there is no need to generalise this into an exhaustive description of what is natural. We need not suppose that there is something un-natural or supernatural about the idea of our spontaneity cooperating with our receptivity, with the result of 'having one's eyes opened to reasons a large by acquiring a second nature.'[133]

McDowell refuses the dualism between the two spaces of intelligibility, while continuing to accept their distinction. It is possible to accept their

---

[129] J. McDowell, *MW*, p. 10.
[130] J. McDowell, *MW*, p. 11.
[131] J. McDowell, *MW*, pp. 84ff.
[132] J. McDowell, *MW*, p. 78.
[133] J. McDowell, *MW*, p. 84.

distinction without turning it into a standoff if we warm to the possibility that the (causally determined) impingements on our senses draw on the conceptual abilities that properly belong to the second 'sphere'. In drawing upon them, we are presented – in experience – with the fact that things are thus and so. Does this mean that in perception we actually take in the world? It is pointless to rehearse the classical problems associate with this view. What exactly do we take in? What kind of thing is the fact that things are thus and so? If we want to keep the distinction between the two spaces, we must neither allow our concepts to properly belong to the realm of causes, nor allow what belongs to the space of causes enter that of freedom. The trick, then, is to imagine aboutness and intentionality, i.e. the fact that our thought are nevertheless about the bits of the world, without collapsing the two into one another. We seem to have stumbled on another perennial problem of philosophy. How do we solve it?

McDowell's solution is brilliant, but unfortunately it overstretches one's optimism. He writes, 'To see exercises of spontaneity as natural, we do not need to integrate spontaneity-related concepts into the structure of the realm of law; we need to stress *their role in capturing patterns in a way of living*.'[134] In other words, what these actualisations of our spontaneity which are passively drawn on in experience present us with are aspects, patterns, of reality. But this brings us back to pragmatism. In fact, McDowell has no problem tagging himself a pragmatist, on an understanding of pragmatism as a rejection of dualisms: 'What I recommend in the lectures could be represented as a pragmatism in Rorty's sense, even though, in trying to give expression to it, I borrow from thinkers such as Kant, whom Rorty finds utterly suspect. And I am claiming that Rorty's own pragmatism is half-baked, according to standards set by his own account of what pragmatism is.'[135] It is a pragmatism because it refuses a dualism between a reality which has its own perfect description and a language and thought that might never accurately 'get it'. 'In the context of a full-blown pragmatism, impressions can come into their own as precisely a mode of openness to the world.'[136] Rather than being those mysterious emissaries from the world, they are precisely windows on the world.

Not that we could not be wrong in our beliefs. There is a certain *optimism* which pervades through this argument. It is a generalised trust that the conceptual schemes we use, or rather the conceptual apparatus that we have developed and which is part of our traditions, languages, and cultures, is adequate to the nature of reality. That is, it reliably allows the self-presentation of aspects of reality, of patterns of living. Whether the conceptual scheme of Carnap or that of the Polish logician, their descriptions allow reality to shine

[134] J. McDowell, *MW*, p. 78.
[135] J. McDowell, *MW*, pp. 154-5.
[136] J. McDowell, *MW*, p. 155.

forth through them. Both Putnam and McDowell hold that in giving such descriptions of reality we have given all the description that could be given.

This does not mean that our languages, cultures and traditions are intangible. The fallibility of both or our traditions as well as even the most basic of our observation statements is beautifully brought out by the logic of McDowell's position. We can revise any belief, even observational ones, because even in observation, we drawn on conceptual resources that properly belong to a *sui generis* context, and can thus be mistaken or otherwise inadequate.

> And part of the point of the idea that the understanding is a faculty of spontaneity – that conceptual capacities are capacities whose exercise is in the domain of responsible freedom – is that the network, as an individual thinker finds it governing her thinking, is not sacrosanct. Active empirical thinking takes place under a standing obligation to reflect about the credentials of the putatively rational linkages that govern it.[137]

But there remains something unsettling about this programmatic suggestion. That is, what are these aspects of reality? What are those reasons at large? If we accept that there are important qualitative differences between the two realms, between the world and mind, then even if we grant that in sensibility our conceptual apparatus is passively drawn on, what guarantees that the deliverances of sensibility have anything to do *with* the world? What sense, if any, does it make to speak of 'real' *aspects* of the world? The suggestion that will be part of the argument of the final chapter, is that *it only makes sense to speak of aspects of an otherwise causal world if one is also prepared to speak about an intelligent mind who created it.* Unless we are willing to imagine such a possibility, it makes no difference to distinguish between real and illusory aspects of the world. Unless there is something to which these aspects might correspond, something like a divine intention, or a *plenitude* of divine intentions, we cannot say that some aspects are real, while others aren't. Ironically, this is an argument that resembles McDowell's own argument for 'aboutness'. We can only make sense of a thought about something if we are willing to place that thought in inferential relationships with that which it is about. Similarly, it might be argued, one can only hold on to normativity in respect of aspects, if there is something to which they correspond.

[137] J. McDowell, *MW*, p. 12; see also p. 40.

Chapter 4

Theology After Davidson

Religious Studies and Radical Interpretation

We have arrived at the point where Davidson's philosophical venture begins to pay dividends in theology and religious studies as well. The rejection of representationalism entails the rejection of the scheme content dichotomy. If there are no epistemic intermediaries between the world and the mind, the relationship between these should not be construed in either realist or non-realist terms. Now Davidson's confident affirmation of a way beyond the traditional realist/non-realist debate has its critics, as we saw. But the fact remains that he goes to great lengths in helping us imagine what epistemology without representation might look like.

The next chapter (5) will explain where we think Davidson needs a theological supplement. While his programme, especially the rejection of the third dogma, his analysis of the relationship between truth and meaning, but also his attack on the epistemic significance of the notion of language, promises to lead theology out of some of the traps of modernity, there are misgivings which can prove legitimate. Our appropriation of Davidson has not been uncritical, however enthusiastic we are about certain features. In fact, the present chapter introduces a group of scholars within the field of religious studies (current section) and theology, whose Davidsonian outlook led to fresh and important contributions. Let me recapitulate the general argument of the book in order to place their contribution in its sequence.

We have noted that there are two possible directions that might be taken by theological and religious appropriations of neo-pragmatism. The split between these mirrors an internal tension within the movement itself, between drifts in realist-or non-realist-sounding directions. Admittedly this over-simplifies matters. The point could be put more carefully though: *on the one hand, there are neo-pragmatists who lean more in the direction of an austere linguistic methodologism*, while putting as little weight as possible on the contribution of the 'world' or 'experience', however one might conceive them. These would be thinkers who more often than not tend to read a lot of Rorty into Davidson. *On the other hand, another neo-pragmatic strand finds it very hard to abandon certain empirical propensity.* These scholars tend to underscore the strong alethic element in Davidson's work, when they do draw on Davidson, they create updated versions of radical empiricism, or in general insist on the importance of experience, this time holistically constrained. To this inherent tension corresponds *a theological parting of the ways, between, to put it crudely again, language-oriented or world-oriented theorists*. Thus far we have concentrated on the former group with some exceptions. Now it is time to introduce the latter. We hope to show how their work bears critically upon what is in our eyes an unfortunate theological application of neo-pragmatism, but also to point out the significant limitations of a Davidsonian approach to religious studies and theology.

This chapter is divided into two sections which deal respectively with religious studies and theology. In fact we are primarily interested in the contribution made by two scholars who draw heavily on Donald Davidson: Terry F. Godlove and Bruce. D. Marshall, but we shall also engage with other important contributors such as Nancy Frankenberry and others.

Davidson in Religious Studies

The field of religious studies, but also theology, has been under the influence of social patterns of analysis ever since Durkheim's *Elementary Forms.* More recently the work of Clifford Geertz was decisive for the understanding of religions as cultural systems. It has become common place to talk about the radical or partial incommensurability of religious forms of life and about the way in which religion constructs perception. Adopting a religious perspective means inhabiting a kind of world, *seeing* in a certain way. This seemed to receive further support from the pioneering work of Thomas Kuhn in the philosophy of science, but also Paul Feyerabend and Nelson Goodman. The semantic pivotal point has shifted from the level of the words and sentences to the level of whole systems of belief. Agency has shifted from the individual believer to the level of the cultural system itself, which now begun to be endowed with the power to signify, to construct objects, to condition adherents, to legislate justifications. In short, a religion acquired the status of an epistemic framework which 'licenses seeing'.

We have noticed the main elements of such a view in Charley Hardwick's description of a religious statement as involving two elements: a valuational complex and an attendant 'seeing as'. Now the agent is no longer the *locus* of meaning and reference. We have suggested that on such a model alone can such large scale revisions of the meaning of belief be attempted. If meaning and reference are located at the level of the scheme, that is, if in virtue of its composition and internal logic and grammar the scheme constructs reality, and if quite naturally no single agent is in the possession of the whole, then understandably she might be oblivious to important aspects which pertain to meaning and reference. She might refer to and mean something while she believes to refer and mean something else.

Terry Godlove identifies two components of what he calls the 'framework model'. First, it operates a distinction between a *neutral, un-interpreted* reality which impinges on our senses and a reality that our concepts have *organized.* Second, it assumes that this second, conceptualised reality might be utterly different from the real reality, which is unknowable by us. Quite clearly, the framework model presupposes the distinction between an interpreting scheme and a neutral content and this is a distinction whose untenable character is demonstrated by Davidson. But Rorty and Jeffrey Stout, following a long tradition of interpretation, it is true, trace the origins of the scheme-content dichotomy to Kant. Stout, for instance, writes that 'Hegel and his fellow nineteenth-century historicists joined their opponents in accepting Kant's distinction between conceptual scheme and un-interpreted content... Hegel, like Kant, thought he needed to distinguish scheme from content in order to make his case against immediate cognition.'[1]

But Godlove argues persuasively[2] that in fact the distinction can only be traced back to Kant if a certain 'subjective-necessity' reading of the first *Critique* is appropriate.[3] Such a reading, however, is inappropriate, for had the forms of receptivity and the categories of judgment a mere subjective necessity, then inquiry into their origin should not have been precluded so categorically by Kant. For Kant, the very reason why we should not undertake empirical enquiry into the origins of the conditions of thought (the precursor of the framework model) is because these conditions would have to be presupposed by any such empirical enquiry. These categories cannot be either implanted into the human mind, for in such a case they would not yield human knowledge but a mere reflection of the inner constitution of the mind; nor can they be derived from experience, for the same reason. The categories must be *self-thought*, that is, they arise together with our modes of affection in the course of experience.[4] Godlove believes that *this undercuts the very possibility of setting up a distinction between scheme and content, for we can never even imagine the notion of a reality which would not at the same time be perceived with the help of the categories.* Indeed, even speaking about the 'help' of the categories is misleading, 'But because our categories and forms of receptivity arise spontaneously in the course of our ongoing experience we misrepresent ourselves in implicating an objective world that is either indifferent to them, or waits to be relativized to them.'[5]

To think about the empirical origin of these categories, or to engage in empirical study of their causes, is what Durkheim insisted on doing. He could not accept Kant's prohibition against doing this, for he did not perceive the true nature of Kant's perspective. Durkheim shifted the inquiry undertaken by Kant

---

[1] Quoted in Terry F. Godlove, *Religion, Interpretation and Diversity of Belief: The Framework Model from Kant to Durkheim to Davidson* (Cambridge: Cambridge University Press, 1989), p. 153.

[2] See Stephen Palmquist's positive review: [http://www.hkbu.edu.hk/~ppp/srp/arts/RIDB.html].

[3] T. Godlove, *Framework Model*, pp. 9-16.

[4] T. Godlove, *Framework Model*, pp 28-32.

[5] T. Godlove, *Framework Model*, p. 36.

from the first person perspective to the third person perspective. Kant's inquiry was a transcendental one, while Durkheim's becomes an empirical one. For Kant that would be an illegitimate move, for the categories whose genesis it aims to elucidate must be presupposed from the very beginning in such an inquiry.

> Kant writes from the first-person point of view, adopting the stance of one who reflects on the character of his or her own experience. From the first-person point of view, we are confronted not by neutral content – whatever that may come to – but by the familiar objects of empirical experience which, we can come to appreciate, not only do but must represent themselves in conformity with those forms under which we can encounter them.[6]

Durkheim complains that the transcendental approach lacks 'all experimental control; thus it does not satisfy the conditions demanded of a scientific hypothesis.'[7] Hence, 'he refused to draw what he saw as an arbitrary curtain of inexplicability around the origin of our a priori rules of experience.'[8] To cut a long story short, Durkheim proposed that the categories of understanding derive from society. It is interesting to note the similarities to William Dean's turn to the notion of social convention for an explanation of the idea of God. Durkheim fully recognized that 'we cannot construct for ourselves what in fact constrains any act of construction whatever.'[9] What was needed, therefore, is something which goes beyond the bounds of a merely subjective imagination, something timeless, but also something which remains humanly accessible, i.e. empirically investigable. Godlove makes an instructive hermeneutical point: 'In order to account for the necessity and universality of the categories, we are forced to admit society – an ideal entity capable of imposing its requirements upon its members – into our ontology.'[10] *Just as William Dean had to postulate, and thus reify, the notion of a social convention as something which is both dependent but also exceeds the conditions of its genesis, in order to account for its efficacy, so Durkheim has to postulate society as something both human, and exceeding the bounds of mere humanity.*

Thus, for Durkheim, the conditions of objectivity are themselves objects in the world, yet somehow universal and necessary. Kant's way of constructing the conditions of objectivity is entirely different, however. From the Kantian point of view, to speak of objectivity in terms of a neutral world impacting the stimuli is impossible. Thus, the distinction between scheme and content cannot even get going for Kant. For Durkheim, on the other hand, by taking the categories into a third-person analysis, is to be captive to a transcendental illusion. The upshot of all this, is that if Kant does think in terms of frameworks

---

[6] T. Godlove, *Framework Model*, p. 21.
[7] E. Durkheim, *The Elementary Forms of Religious Life*, quoted in Godlove, p. 42.
[8] T. Godlove, *Framework Model*, p. 43.
[9] T. Godlove, *Framework Model*, p. 62.
[10] T. Godlove, *Framework Model*, p. 45.

(and Godlove does believe there is value in talk of frameworks, as *interpretive* rather than epistemic), then these do not organise formless sensations, but an objectivity which is *already given*. For Godlove's Kant, objectivity precedes the notion of a framework. This is a crucial point to which we shall return.

Durkheim's frameworks are epistemologically interesting because the conditions which originate in society are the sources of objectivity. They construct a world. It is not difficult to see how this model degenerated into the radical constructivism which characterises so much of contemporary religious studies and theology. While Durkheim believed that all these schemes had a common core, an insight which Godlove thinks brings him in the vicinity of Davidson, this assumption is easily abandoned to the point where inter-scheme communication is something which calls for 'extraordinary measures'.[11] Religions have radically different ways of constructing the world. The relationship between the language games of religion and those of science is a precarious one, but absolutely discontinuous. Thinkers like those whom we discussed in earlier chapters are all assuming these dichotomies. Hardwick, for instance, is very much aware that religious talk is not salvageable except by sacrificing its continuity with scientific talk. If we are to continue holding the truth of 'God exists', we must re-interpret it so as to find it true. This revisionism, as we hinted, raises serious questions about the theory of interpretation which it employs. If such a theory rests on the dubious distinction between scheme and content, it must fail.

Godlove proceeds to show that the framework model is false. He has so far shown that it cannot be traced back to Kant. Next, with Davidson's help, he aims to show that its relativistic implications are incoherent. We will not rehearse here Davidson's already familiar arguments against the scheme content dichotomy. The point of Davidson's argument is that we cannot even begin to imagine disagreement without presupposing a vast background of agreement. If two speakers are to disagree over a single sentence, they must agree about many other sentences which must be presupposed by the understanding of that single sentence. The more sentences depend upon one sentence, the harder it will be to disagree over that sentence. *Thus there are regions of our web of beliefs which are more prone to eliciting disagreement than are others.* These are the theoretical levels of our web, or what may be called the higher reaches of the web. These are the beliefs disagreement over which is least obstructive to further understanding. If, however, we disagree about matters of empirical purport, it will be much more difficult to continue the process of interpretation, but not impossible.

Now Godlove's point is that religious traditions cannot even introduce preponderant disagreement. This flatly contradicts the constructivist hypothesis. Yet Godlove, to his credit, does not wish to deny the reality of divergence and difference. In fact this is one criticism which has been

[11] T. Godlove, *Framework Model*, p. 81.

repeatedly and rightly levelled against Davidson. So Godlove squarely admits that disagreement and difference are significant. But they are located at another level, the theoretical level. But in order to meaningfully disagree about theoretical matters, enough common beliefs must be presupposed about empirical and observational realities. In order to interpret the speech of others, charity is forced, strictly speaking, only over observational subject matters. The higher up we go, the less agreement are we forced to admit.

The crucial aspect here is that the difference is not something which belongs to the conceptuality while the sameness belongs to that which is causally impinging upon our senses. This would get the scheme content distinction going again. The notions which operate at the higher levels of theory are conceptually dependent upon the notions which operate at the lower levels of observation. This is the absolutely critical point, because it presupposes a conceptual continuity between the empirical and the theoretical. If we view religions are theoretical systems, then we can and should also assert the conceptual dependency of religious notions upon mundane notions. Godlove stresses that this dependency is conceptual, though the question of a causal dependency is also interesting.

Thus, *if we want to understand religious discourse, we cannot dualistically separate it from discourse about other more mundane things, including the discourse of science.* Granted, religious discourse is relatively independent of observable change.[12] This shows in at least three areas: a) religious discourse makes little use of ostension; b) it deals in a high level of abstractions, at least at the level of doctrines and dogmas; finally c) it is about how things are and less about how they appear. These characteristics suggest the theoreticity of this particular cultural area. But the 'point is that the intelligibility of religious belief, as largely theoretical, depends upon the prior intelligibility of more concrete, shared, extrareligious beliefs and subject matters. The direction of *this* dependence is irreversible.'[13]

In other words, the world is already rendered before the religious narratives or frameworks do their interpretive work. The interpretation stands in a *conceptual/rational* and not merely *causal* relationship to that which is interpreted. What is interpreted is something which is already meaningful. Thus, it might be said that religions *illuminate* the world, a world which is already *inhabited.* They provide orientation, but among familiar things, things which already stand in rational relations to other things, religious of profane. 'Competing or complementary religious narratives are intelligible *as* competing or complementary against this background of objective validity.'[14] All this is to

[12] T. Godlove, *Framework Model*, p. 106.
[13] T. Godlove, *Framework Model*, p. 109.
[14] T. Godlove, *Framework Model*, p. 133.

say that *transcendental* coherence makes possible the *interpretive* coherence which a religious viewpoint brings.[15]

Godlove succeeds in bringing Kant and Davidson together again. The transcendental unity which is provided by the *selbstgedachte* forms and categories describes precisely the agreement which Davidson holds must precede any disagreement.

Agreement is absolutely crucial for Godlove, for it provides the necessary (though not sufficient) condition for the discovery of error. Let us return to Durkheim for a moment. There is an element of what Godlove calls *pure* charity in Durkheim. He is not compelled by any transcendental argument to find religious adherents true, yet he nevertheless considers that all religions have a common core of truth. For him a conceptual framework constructs reality. Religions are conceptual frameworks which thus construct reality and provide objectivity. It follows that the disagreement which may appear between religions does not only 'infect' the higher, theoretical echelons, but also the lower reaches of the system. Disagreement may extend all the way down to the roots. Yet Durkheim also holds that for all their differences, the conceptual schemes presuppose a 'latent set of organising categories.'[16] But in order to cash out that unity and commonality, it had to be dug from underneath the (vastly differentiated) symbolic husk. In Durkheim's own words: 'one must know how to go underneath the symbol to the reality which it represents and gives it meaning.'[17] Thus, the unity can only be discovered via the tortuous path of reinterpretation. Hence, 'By interpreting apparently deviant and egregiously false beliefs as accepted truths symbolically expressed, Durkheim avoided the ascription of serious conceptual diversity.'[18] This symbolic reconstruction apparently went hand in hand with the spirit of sociology, which held that a human institution cannot rest upon an error. This means that there are no religions which are false, all religions have a way in which they are true.

There is a key difficulty associated with this view. It is also endemic to Hardwick's reconstruction: it leaves us unable to identify real error. Godlove has made this point earlier in the book, invoking Putnam and Wittgenstein. It is impossible to relativise truth to a set of assumptions or beliefs, for it will leave one unable to distinguish between being right and thinking that one is right, in turn leaving no difference between asserting or thinking, on the one hand, and making noises on the other. There is a similar situation in this case: what is the normative background which allows for the discussion of error, if a) all religions are true in their own way and b) the divergence between religions extends all the way down? In Godlove's terms, the transcendental coherence which alone could provide such a normative context, has been overthrown by a

---

[15] T. Godlove, *Framework Model*, pp. 137-8.
[16] T. Godlove, *Framework Model*, p. 111.
[17] Quote, T. Godlove, *Framework Model*, p. 111.
[18] T. Godlove, *Framework Model*, p. 111.

religious coherence. Moreover, this religious coherence varies from context to context, yet it somehow still employs latent universal and necessary categories. These categories have to be dug out, but one wonders: if all we have is a local religious coherence and if these frameworks are symbolically related to one another, what is the final framework, from the perspective of which such reinterpretation makes sense? Or, from which normative perspective are we to judge that this or that religious statement is a patent falsity which has to be reinterpreted? Durkheim, it seems, has no way of justifying his insistence on both social constructionism *and* on the underlying unity of the schemes. He has no way of telling apart statements which must be judged false from statements which need to be analysed for symbolic meaning.

But Davidson has. 'Whereas 'Durkheim turns to charity to refine his understanding of an already identified religious "tissue of errors", Davidsonian charity makes possible the identification of belief, true or false.'[19] Applying Davidson to the work of religious interpretation does not ensure, as some critics think, that we will be unable to find religious adherents wrong. *But does the imperative of finding them right on the whole, an imperative that we saw is shared by Durkheim, reasonably lead to revisionism?* We take up this question in the rest of this section.

We have argued that the deconstruction of the framework model is one aspect of radical interpretation which counts against revisionism as an interpretive thesis, rather than as a normative thesis. As a matter of interpretation, revisionism holds that important and classic religious statements have been *wrongly* understood to be about one thing, usually something transcendent, when in fact thy have been about something else. Interpretive revisionism, we have argued, presupposes the framework model, because it depends on meaning and reference being located at some less accessible semantic level. As is well known, this triggers a depth semantics. Durkheim himself was willing to claim that each religion works its truth in its own fashion. By undercutting the root metaphor of a religious framework, we also thereby remove one explanation of interpretive holism.

However, it is possible, as Godlove himself exemplifies, to engage in revisionism without the scheme-content distinction, moreover being motivated by radical interpretation itself. Granted, this will be a completely different approach, for the radical interpreter of religious discourse does not seek to *re*-interpret an already identified religious 'tissue of errors' – as with Durkheim – but, starting from scratch, wants to attribute meaning and beliefs to the 'native'. Given such a strategy of *radical* interpretation, it is perhaps unsurprising, that the results to which the interpreter arrives may contradict what the native takes himself or herself to mean and believe.

Some will say that coming to realise the lack of fit between the results of radical interpretation and what the speaker actually holds (we will not consider

---

[19] T. Godlove, *Framework Model*, p. 114.

here how this might be possible from within radical interpretation) is reason enough to falsify the results of the analysis. Godlove concurs with Wayne Proudfoot, for example, that 'no acceptable theory can deliver interpretations of utterances or impute beliefs that the subject consistently disavows.'[20] But there is a sequence of two assumptions which should prevent the immediate drawing of falsifying consequences. First, since radical interpretation is holistic, our ascription of truth and falsity is not piecemeal, but is distributed across networks of utterances. Whether we should take this as a problematic aspect of holism is another issue altogether. The fact remains that according to radical interpretation, we cannot attribute a single belief without simultaneously attributing a number of other beliefs. If we suspect error, it becomes hard to pinpoint it.[21] Thus, on the first count, when we have reason to suspect that the 'subject consistently disavows' a belief which we have ascribed to him, we have a choice as to where to make the appropriate adjustments. The second factor is also crucial: radical interpretation tends to work with a truth-conditional theory of reference. If reference is a by-product of truth, then our terms refer to those objects in the world which satisfy them. Since there may be cases where we mistakenly think our utterance to be satisfied by something, when in fact they are satisfied by something else, *and* if, as Davidson's truth-conditional theory of meaning holds, meaning is given by truth conditions, we might not always be aware of the very meaning of our utterances. *Thus, a revisionist interpretation which ascribes to us meanings that we are not intending can get off the ground even without the help of the framework model.* This is not to say that *with respect to Christianity* and its metaphysical assertions, for example, radical interpretation guarantees revisionism. As Godlove will show, it remains an empirical question whether in fact revisionist reading strategies are appropriate, but we cannot simply dismiss the possibility from the armchair. Let us look more closely at Godlove's rationale.

The adopted standpoint of radical interpretation constrains the sorts of evidence that can be brought to bear on interpretation. As it should be familiar by now, radical interpretation aims to break the cycle of belief and meaning. Since it cannot simply help itself to beliefs, knowledge of which presupposes a prior grasp of meaning, it must find a way to enter into the web of belief and meaning. The only way we can identify beliefs is by checking for assent on the part of the speaker with respect to changes in the environment. Davidson's entire theory of interpretation depends on the claim that 'all thought and

---

[20] T. Godlove, 'Interpretation, reductionism, and belief in God', *The Journal of Religion* 69/2 (1989). pp. 184-198, p. 186.

[21] Thus, Hans Penner holds that there is no such thing as the meaning of *a* religious belief. ('Holistic Analysis: Conjenctures and Refutations', *Journal of the American Academy of Religion* 62/4 (1994), pp. 977-996, p. 990. Frankenberry makes a similar point in 'On the very idea of symbolic meaning', in J. Harley Chapman and Nancy K. Frankenberry, eds., *Interpreting Neville* (Albany: SUNY, 1999), p. 102.

language must have a foundation in such direct historical connections, and these connections constrain the interpretation of thought and speech.'[22] As we have argued in a previous section, Davidson works with a distal notion of causes, as opposed to Quine's proximal causes. This is inherent in his dissolution of the scheme-content dichotomy. Our language derives its meaning from direct causal connections between people and world. This means that when we interpret the speech of other people, 'we must in the plainest and methodologically most basic cases, take the objects of a belief to be the causes of that belief. ... Communication begins where causes converge: your utterance means what mine does if belief in its truth is systematically caused by the same events and objects.'[23] As interpreters we have to look for *causality* between the world and the utterances of speakers, because 'the causality serves the interpreter as a point of entry into how the speaker perceives her place in her surroundings and, so, into the content of he beliefs and the meaning of her words.'[24] *But we have no way of telling how a speaker perceives her surroundings except by assuming that it perceives it very much in the same way we do.*

This point is of no minor importance, as we will see later on. Davidson, and Godlove following him, assumes that once the scheme-content dualism has been thrown off, all that remains to be said is that people relate to their environment in much the same way. To be sure, Davidson does not hold that we all have one interpretive scheme. Rather, he urges that all talk of interpretive scheming is besides the point. Ontology for Davidson seems rather unproblematic. It is macroscopic objects that seem to be reliable causes of our beliefs and hence utterances. If, however, it were possible that we perceive our surroundings and our place in these surroundings differently, it would be more difficult to rely so heavily on charity, on the assumption that the native perceives the world in the same way we do. Now it could be said that, even if her beliefs are systematically caused by the same macroscopic objects that cause our beliefs, she perceives these objects in ways which might be different from ours. In such a case, the *content* of her beliefs, is only partly determined by the macroscopic objects themselves. Tracing the causal connections will in that case not be enough, for the content of the beliefs might vary with respect to the objects in the world.

Davidson rules out this very possibility because he is unwilling to countenance a third option between his rejection of the scheme-content dualism and the framework model. If indeed the dualism goes, we can reliably just look at objects in the world and, by tracing their causal connection to speakers, establish the content of their beliefs. *But if a case could be made for a continued significance of conceptual frameworks which does not involve the*

---

[22] D. Davidson, 'Belief and the basis of meaning'.

[23] D. Davidson, 'A coherence theory of truth and knowledge'.

[24] T. Godlove, 'Interpretation, reductionism', p. 191.

undesirable consequences of the older third dogma, then it would be hard to avoid the conclusion that such metaphysically unpretentious scheming will have to play a part in the very content of our beliefs. It suits Davidson's position very well to argue that it is the macroscopic world which fixes the content of our beliefs, because the other alternative is self-contradictory. As we will argue in the next chapter, the case for a continued significance of the notion of conceptual framework can and should be made, along the lines suggested by Putnam and McDowell. But let us return to Godlove.

Although our only way into understanding is by tracing causal connections, Godlove admits that '*by itself* even the strongest correlation between utterance and world is inconclusive, even if we happen to know on independent grounds that the speaker's words and beliefs are uniformly true of their cause.'[25] Not only must we trace the causal connection, but we must also assume that the speaker is himself aware of the causal connection. The example Godlove gives is illuminating:

> Suppose that someone is struck by a baseball and is thereby caused to say and believe that she has been struck by a baseball, but suppose that, from what we can tell, she had no *reason* to so believe (it hit her from behind). We would be reluctant to make the offending baseball part of the subject matter of her belief, and our reluctance would be due to her apparent lack of appreciation for the causal connection between herself and the ball. Without this appreciation the close fit between the cause and the object of belief is mere coincidence.[26]

We must remember that we approach this situation as radical interpreters who do not know what 'A ball hit me' means. We make the appropriate causal correlations, yet we cannot ascribe to the speaker what we mean by our belief that 'a ball hit me' because we appreciate that she could not have been aware of what actually hit her. Now she may infer, guess, surmise that a ball hit her, and on the basis of this utter the appropriate sentence. But as radical interpreters we have no access to those mental processes, real enough as they are, but equally inaccessible to an observer. If we do interpret her utterance as our 'a ball hit me' this would correctly capture her belief, but entirely accidentally.

Now let us turn to religion. Since religious beliefs are highly theoretical, correlating them with aspects of the environment is a very complex affair. This is not to say that there is no relation, but only that the ties are tenuous and not straightforward. At such a theoretical level, Davidson's interpretive strategy can yield both naturalistic and more charitable results.

> If [...] religious discourse is typically highly theoretical – if its ties with observable change in the world are, at best, "complex and intricate," and perhaps undetectable – we will, on that account, be pushed toward a naturalistic

[25] T. Godlove, 'Interpretation, reductionism', p. 191.

[26] T. Godlove, 'Interpretation, reductionism', p. 191.

> interpretive strategy. That is, we will be pushed toward an interpretive strategy that fixes the meaning of an utterance in ignorance of what a speaker may take to determine its meaning. And so we may find it necessary to interpret an utterance by connecting it with an event (a cause) of which the speaker seems unaware.[27]

This is precisely Durkheim's strategy. We can see why Godlove can entertain this possibility, but it is hard to understand why it could give the *content* of the speaker's beliefs. Yet Godlove goes on to say, 'But on the other hand, we can make out, for each, reasons supporting a very different kind of interpretive strategy. After all we are trying to understand *persons*, who (typically) claim that their religious actions and utterances are continuous with the rest of their meaningful activity, activity that, from the interpreter's point of view, can be more readily understood along observational lines.'[28] While both interpretive strategies are plausible, Godlove sees no reason why not to privilege the latter, even if it has to 'persevere in the face of, respectively, thoroughgoing natural necessity and extreme theoreticity'.[29] On the former model, interpretation will have to rely on the general rationality of the religious adherent. Let us quote him at length again:

> From the Davidsonian point of view, we want to know whether an appreciation of a speaker's rationality can guide our interpretation of his or her religious discourse – discourse which cannot be easily correlated, directly or indirectly, with detectable environmental change. We can return a positive answer only if we can view that person's utterances as springing from the (mostly true) picture that the speaker holds *of* his or her environment. For it the only (direct or indirect) correlation we can draw between utterance and world appeals, on the worldly end, to something of which the speaker is apparently *unaware* (an oppressive economic order, a repressed desire), then clearly our interpretation cannot be driven by our knowledge that he or she is a rational animal.[30]

The question is whether such a strategy is not *descriptively reductionist*? By fixing the secret mundane causes of the faithful person's beliefs, have we also fixed their content? For Godlove, this is an empirical question and it will have to be discussed in particular contexts. Let us take Durkheim's equation of 'God' with 'society'. The argument is that 'Durkheim does – or, anyway, could very well – say, *without falling into descriptive reductionism*, that belief in God is just belief in society.'[31] This may strike one as odd, for did Godlove not support Proudfoot's view that we should not ascribe beliefs which agents reject? But Godlove clarifies that what he is after here is a theoretical possibility, a limit case. Whether in fact such a limit case actually obtains is a matter of empirical discovery. For example, should 'we know beforehand that

---

[27] T. Godlove, *Framework Model*, p. 155.
[28] T. Godlove, *Framework Model*, 156.
[29] T. Godlove, *Framework Model*, 156.
[30] T. Godlove, *Framework Model*, pp. 156f.
[31] T. Godlove, 'Interpretation, reductionism', p. 186.

someone takes God and society to answer to very different descriptions',[32] then to conflate the two beliefs would be a mistake. But it is at least theoretically possible to have a notion of society which fits the notion of God.

Now let us remember that a 'powerful incentive'[33] of the radical interpretive strategy is to 'make as straightforward as possible the self-conscious causal tie between affirmation and world.' Hence,

> if the local society fits the local description of God, and/or if the speaker seems to count herself as standing in its causal presence when she speaks of "God," the very directness of the causal relation encourages us to take her to be talking and thinking about society. It may even be a powerful enough consideration to license the overriding of certain incompatibilities between the nature of society and the conception of God.[34]

Several conditions must therefore obtain in order to defuse the charge of reductionism: a clear causal connection must be established between 'society' and utterances involving 'God'; the local description of God must closely fit the local description of society.

The reason why Godlove's interpretive strategy generates such ambiguous results derives from the tenuous ties between religion and the environment. Unless we are able to establish some sort of relationship to observable things, we will have a hard time getting inside the web of meaning and belief. Over time, however, it might look – with respect to some religious discourse – that the only observable reality to which it might be correlated is society, i.e. believers uttering 'God is great' invariably after, during, prior to, generally in the proximity of some social gathering. If that is the only empirical tie we have, we have to balance our ascriptions of belief around it. Although it may be that not all of the beliefs held about "God" are true of the society, those which do not fit will have to be sacrificed as false in order to preserve an already tenuous link. The options open to the interpreter are numerous and there is no instruction manual for this task. This ambiguity is due to the holism of meaning and belief:

> In short, the holistic interpreter must weigh the applicability of some religious beliefs and doctrines to society more heavily than others. For example, the Durkheimian thesis may be incompatible with the ancient Christian dogma that God is impassible and immutable. If so, then (I am inclined to say) so much worse for the dogma. On the other hand, if there is no good sense in which the community is creative and salvific, then we cannot reasonably take the belief in question to be *about* the Hebrew-Christian God.[35]

---

[32] T. Godlove, 'Interpretation, reductionism', 186.

[33] T. Godlove, 'Interpretation, reductionism', 192.

[34] T. Godlove, 'Interpretation, reductionism', 192.

[35] T. Godlove, 'Interpretation, reductionism', p. 194.

It seems that matters are not as straightforward as one might like them to be. Interpretation involves evaluating which beliefs are more determinant of a given notion than others. As a matter of fact, Godlove identifies one major obstacle in the way of identifying the Christian belief in God with belief in society. That is, by ascribing agency to communities, the sociological reduction will end up in polytheism: multiple communities, multiple Gods. This is hardly comforting, for we might easily imagine an ideal community or society, perhaps humanity as such, which would not lead into polytheism, while it would surely lead to something equally problematic from a Christian point of view.

What underlies such a strategy is a certain theory of reference according to which a term refers to whatever in the world *satisfies* its description.[36] As opposed to an understanding of linguistic reference according to which it is more directly determined by the standards and practices of particular linguistic communities,[37] 'reference is a semantical by-product of truth and, so, is not strictly determined by the standards in force in a speaker's linguistic community.' Thus, what on the former model of reference appears reductionist because 'society' and 'God' do not play similar roles in the language games, on the latter model appears demonstrable, because they may be substituted *salve veritate*. 'We learn to what object a term refers by discovering of what the containing sentence is true, a task which involves placing the sentence within a yet broader context of sentences.'[38] Thus, it is possible to identify belief in God with belief if society if the former beliefs expressed many literal truths about society. But an additional consideration must be adduced:

> The idea is that, if a sufficient number and kind of religious beliefs happen to be true of society *and* if the subject seems to be aware of the causal connection between society and those beliefs, we then have some grounds to take society as their object.'[39] Again, 'To take seriously Durkheim's approach to religious belief is to ask to what extent the nature of a given community' fits the conception of deity to which it has given rise *and* whether its holders are aware of their conceptions provenance.[40]

Let us summarize: Godlove simply wanted to show that Durkheim's strategy is not *inherently* reductionist because we simply cannot take for granted notions of either 'God' or 'society', but must discover what the speakers mean by these. We go about this task by triangulating between our beliefs, the speaker's beliefs and, finally, the environment. If the connection to the world is as tenuous as it is in the case of religion, the interpretation itself is less determinate and its fine-tuning requires adjustments of different kinds, with no

---

[36] T. Godlove, 'Interpretation, reductionism', p. 193.
[37] T. Godlove, 'Interpretation, reductionism', p. 192.
[38] T. Godlove, 'Interpretation, reductionism', p. 193.
[39] T. Godlove, 'Interpretation, reductionism', p. 195 (emphasis mine).
[40] T. Godlove, 'Interpretation, reductionism', p. 198 (emphasis mine).

rules available. This is the down-side to holism. But since we are historical beings, this is what we are stuck with.

What we would like to ask is whether in fact we would not understand more and better if we would be less austere with respect to what we might use in interpretation? Notice first that Godlove himself sometimes appears to switch from the austere perspective of the radical interpreter to the one of the explanatory theorist. That is, he sometimes assumes that he knows full well what, say, belief in immortality and impassibility involves – although he implies that this is one of those beliefs which can be sacrificed in order to preserve those which can be made sense of in terms of their empirical link. But, one might ask, how in the absence of such an observational connection, has Goldlove been able to identify the content of those beliefs? To take another example: society. How, if a) the only way to identify the content of beliefs is by correlating with the environment and b) the only plausible observational connection is society, is it possible to identify two beliefs: about society *and* about God? Given the above restrictions, we should be able to identify only one belief, rather than two or more, about which we would later wonder if they are not about the same object. In other words, *this procedure gets the radical interpretive strategy upside down: it starts with beliefs and then wonders whether they are about the same entity. But the radical interpretative procedure makes it impossible to even identify beliefs without already triangulating with the environment.*[41]

There is a further problem here: Davidson stipulates quite clearly that we triangulate with empirical, observable objects and actions in the world. Society, on the other hand, is a theoretical notion itself. Thus it can hardly be cast in the role in which Godlove places it, since it assumes that what the interpreter means by society must be the very same thing which the speaker means by it, or else no triangulation would be possible. The speaker must have already conceptualised 'society' in much the same way we have. This is not impossible, but it will turn society into one of those pivotal beliefs, disagreement over which is seriously destructive for further interpretation. This introduces an unnecessary constraint. More importantly, it reverses the order of conceptual dependency stipulated by Godlove. Remember that he argued decisively that the theoretical reaches of the web of beliefs are conceptually dependent upon the lower, more observational reaches and not the other way around. Similarly, if we are to be good Davidsonians, we have to pick our foundational building blocks from among occasion sentences which are as unproblematic as possible.

Further criticism must be delayed until we have had chance to show the limitations of Davidson's theory of interpretation in the next chapter. It will

---

[41] We will argue that this constitutes a *reductio* of the strategy of austere radical interpretation itself, in that it cannot account for the numerous notions of which we have a grasp even though we haven't the faintest idea about how to correlate them with the environment.

then emerge that interpretive austerity which refuses to make use of intensions, but relies exclusively upon extensions is unable to successfully discriminate between meanings. To the extent that it leads to interpretive results which end up ascribing beliefs to agents who actually believe quite the opposite, this demonstrates that the strategy itself, *as a theory of interpretation* is fundamentally flawed. This is not to say that it can do no work in understanding, but only that some of its pretensions have to be tempered.

Symbol, Metaphor and Literal Meaning

Our initial bet that drawing on Davidson would lead to a wholesale critique of revisionist programmes has proved somewhat exaggerated. It is still possible to draw revisionist conclusions, along naturalist lines, from a radical interpretivist point of view. It must however be granted, we think, that some of the motivation for such a strategy has been removed by the abandonment of the scheme-content distinction. If religions are not coded systems of language, they do wear their meanings on their sleeves, so to speak. It remains a question of empirical interpretation whether naturalist readings are advisable, but they have certainly been included in the menu.

If one critique of revisionism stems from the disbanding of the framework model, another possible line of attack comes from the direction of the semantics of metaphor. Nancy K. Frankenberry has done theology a great service in bringing Davidson's reflections on metaphor to bear on what she has called the 'theology of symbolic forms', which is precisely what has been identified here as interpretive revisionism. We will summarise from the outset her argument: endorsing a Rortyan variation on Davidson's theory of metaphors, she contends that the specific nature of symbols does not lie in a special coded meaning that they have. There is no symbolic meaning over and above the literal meaning. Rather, the special nature of the symbol consists in what it *does*, not what it *means*. Thus, the theology of symbolic forms is misguided in looking after depth-meanings, beyond the literal meaning of the words and sentences.

Recall our criticism of Hardwick's surplus meaning. If there is such a meaning which cannot be put into the, say, primary language of values, what is its connection to the theistic translation? If, on the other hand, it can be paraphrased, why should one continue to use it? Davidson makes a similar point in his seminal paper, 'What Metaphors Mean': 'If a metaphor has a special cognitive content, why should it be so difficult or impossible to set it out? If, as Owen Barfield claims, a metaphor "says one thing and means another", why should it be that when we try to get explicit about what it means, the effect is so much weaker.' He speaks about 'a tension in the usual view of metaphor. For on the one hand, the usual view wants to hold that a metaphor does something no plain prose can possibly do and, on the other hand, it wants to explain what a metaphor does by appealing to a cognitive content – just the sort of thing a plain prose is designed to express.'[42] In other words, the usual attempt is to explain the uniqueness of metaphor by appeal to semantics, i.e., by invoking a special kind of meaning in virtue of which a metaphor does what it does best.

It is undeniable that metaphorical (and symbolic) talk is of a special nature. But it remains a question, how can we explain this specificity? Frankenberry identifies

> two main paths [that] diverge in the interpretive road and one cannot travel both. Either the interpreter attempts to naturalize or rationalize the meaning of beliefs about superhuman agents in conformity with conditions in the actual world (the path of liberal theology), or the interpreter takes the religious utterances at face value and accord literal meaning to language about superhuman agents. The first method saves the appearances, but flouts the actor's point of view. The second method, more common in historical or anthropological studies of religion, saves the actor's point of view, but flaunts the "patent falsity" of religious language.[43]

This brings another perspective on Godlove's first, naturalistic, strategy of interpretation. To go the naturalist path is to do what Robin Norton considers to be 'the cardinal sin of flouting the actor's point of view.' One may come up with interpretations, but it is doubtful that these would be interpretations of the speech-acts of a person. One possible way to read Davidson, in fact a reading which we strongly urge in this book, sees his attempt to render meaning in terms of truth conditions as part of his attempt to explain the linguistic behaviour of human persons. Davidson is not simply interested in understanding stretches of language *simpliciter*, but other human beings. Jay Allman puts it well: 'So I think it is fair to describe a Davidsonian inquiry into the conditions of communication and understanding as an inquiry into the nature of one who can communicate and understand others. Davidson displaces interpretation as the understanding of *language* with interpretation as the understanding of people who speak'.[44]

If the understanding of human beings and their beliefs and intentions are the issue, then, even at the cost of flouting the liberal maxim that primitive societies must not be treated as ignorant, we will have to impute error precisely in order to preserve the content of their beliefs. Anthropologist Robin Horton puts it like this:

> Surely all the evidence from fieldwork in religious cultures is that, when men talk about the gods, they are talking about beings that are as real to them as men and women, sticks and stones, rivers and mountains. Surely all the evidence is that

[42] D. Davidson, 'What Metaphors Mean' *ITI*, p. 261.

[43] Frankenberry, 'Religion as a Mobile Army of Metaphors', in Frankenberry, ed., *Radical Interpretation in Religion* (Cambridge: Cambridge University Press, 2002), p. 176.

[44] Jay Allman, 'Metaphor and Davidson's Theory of Interpretation', *The Southern Journal of Philosopy* 39 (2001), pp. 16f.

> when people say their crops have been destroyed by the anger of the gods or prospered by their approval, they are talking literally.[45]

Now it is important to remember that, although Frankenberry speaks from the perspective of radical interpretation, she does in fact assume that translation has already been given. The question is now whether the adherents mean those things symbolically or literally. The case for the symbolic interpretation is difficult to make for at least three reasons, gleaned from the work of another anthropologist, Dan Sperber: first, symbols are so multivalent that it is impossible to pair them with interpretations. This point is rather obvious. Take for example Bultmann's confidence in rendering 'resurrection' as a belief in a rejuvenated life, a drive for authentic existence. There are countless other candidates for rendering the 'meaning' of revelation, without any way of discriminating between them. Second, symbols never wear their meaning on their sleeves and symbolic systems do not provide algorithms for the interpretation of particular symbols except a (perhaps endless) referral to other symbols. Finally, there are religious actors like the Dorze of Ethiopia, who engage in symbolic rituals and forms of life without at all caring about any interpretation for those symbols.[46]

All the evidence seems to point to the fact that, if symbols do have such a coded meaning, beyond the literal meaning that they do wear on their sleeves, there isn't any reliable way to get to it. It is an idle notion that does not turn any wheels. But the very point of speaking about a coded meaning was to explain what is special about metaphors. All the evidence indicates another important thing: when religious people speak about the gods, this is precisely what they are talking about. To the extent that such talk uses symbols, its symbolic character need not be explained by reference to any other layer of (surplus) meaning. How, then, can it be explained?

Davidson's solution is that the special character of metaphor lies not in what it means: it means what its words mean literally and nothing else; but in what it *does*. Thus, Davidson turns from semantics to pragmatics in order to explain metaphor. Jay Allman defends him against a number of critics who hold that this is against the very programme of radical interpretation. He points out, against Frank Farrell, that

> By appealing to metaphorical meanings, Farrell seems to give semantics a monopoly on interpretation; linguistic behaviour can only be explained by appeal to semantic entities. But as I have just sketched it, this is something Davidsonian theory expressly denies. To interpret an utterance is to explain an act, and grasp of semantics is only one of the elements that goes into, and is by itself insufficient for, successful interpretation.[47]

---

[45] Quoted in Frankenberry, 'Religion as a Mobile Army', pp. 173f.

[46] See N. Frankenberry, 'Mobile army', p. 175.

[47] J. Allman, 'Metaphor', p. 11.

By broadening the context in which metaphor is to be analyzed, Davidson leaves the domain of the cognitive and enters that of the non-cognitive. This, as we shall see, is extremely significant. A metaphor, or rather the metaphorical element of the graphic form, does not assert anything, but it inspires, it prompts an insight. The words of the metaphorical construction do assert something. But what they assert is patently false, which is precisely the signal that alerts people that they are faced with a metaphor.[48] Just like I may be able to transmit something non-verbal to a friend who would understand why I blink, a 'patent falsity' alerts people to look for something other than a literal meaning. The blink does not have any meaning. But it prompts a series of actions on the part of my friend.

For Davidson, 'No theory of metaphorical meaning or metaphorical truth can help explain how metaphor works. Metaphor runs on the same familiar linguistic tracks that the plainest sentences do; [...] What distinguishes the metaphor is not meaning but use.'[49] We use metaphors because they help us do something, they evoke a certain 'seeing as' in the hearer and in ourselves. They help us see the world in a different way. But the crucial thing is that they do not do this by way of delivering a cognitive content. Rather, they non-cognitively *prompt* the new seeing-as. 'Metaphor makes us see one thing as another by making some literal statement that inspires or prompts the insight.'[50] The trouble with the usual theories of metaphor is that they have fastened on this *effect* of the metaphor and read it back into its very *meaning*. But we have a perfectly transparent way of understanding how such effects are possible without having to *postulate* anything as dubious as metaphorical meaning.[51]

The non-cognitive character of the prompting must be stressed according to Davidson. Frankenberry even goes as far as to say that the likeness between different parts of reality which the metaphor prompts us to see is not antecedent to the metaphor, but it is something which the metaphor produces. Metaphorical utterances are mere stimulations, evocations. They are sometimes 'tossed' by geniuses like Jesus and they succeed in changing the whole problematic and ways of looking at the world, ways of talking. Frankenberry thinks that Davidson's account of metaphor (semantic and pragmatic) needs to be supplemented by a Rortyan socio-cultural approach which registers the role of metaphors in effecting cultural change: 'Richard Rorty has sketched an original theory of cultural change in which strong poets, revolutionary scientists, and edifying philosophers toss off new metaphors that catch on, alter the environment, and, when successful, survive as literalizations.'

---

[48] D. Davidson, 'What Metaphors Mean', p. 258.

[49] D. Davidson, 'What Metaphors Mean', p. 259.

[50] D. Davidson, 'What Metaphors Mean', p. 263.

[51] Frankenberry finds that of principal interest in the Davidson-Rorty theory of metaphor is its parsimony in not proliferating orders of truth and meaning.

But how can the new metaphors catch on, given that they bear no cognitive relation to previous language? Moreover, how is it that they evoke *this* new seeing-as and not another one? Is it merely accidental? *Switching to the non-cognitive, Frankenberry, Rorty, perhaps even Davidson, leave themselves no rational way of adjudicating between competing metaphors.*[52] Rorty sees metaphors as prompting switches of vocabularies and these vocabularies have no rational way of adjudicating competing claims. One must simply indwell them and judge their felicity from within, as it were. Now is not the time to discuss how consonant this view is with Davidson's discarding of the third dogma. At any rate, Rorty's notion of vocabularies and stages of cultural development intercalates non-cognitive gaps between cultures. This utterly non-teleological model refuses to put cultural change in terms of successes or failures, in terms of better or worse understanding of reality, humanity or culture. 'Nietzschean history of culture, and Davidsonian philosophy of language, see language as we now see evolution, as new forms of life constantly killing off old forms – not to accomplish a higher purpose, but blindly.'[53]

Our argument has been – and chapter 5 will cap it off, that Davidson, by insisting to treat the world as being in a mere causal and not rational relation to reason, leaves himself without a possibility of evaluating knowledge. In this case Rorty does draw the inherent consequences of their holism: knowledge is not better or worse, it is a human project judged only from the perspective of what statements and theories *happen* to prevail and evolve.

But if such a cultural change is non-rational, if new religious metaphors do not count as developments, as explanations of older religious discourse, *then revisionism is back in*! 'This approach offers one way of allowing for the fact that the repertoire of religious texts and presuppositional attitudes over time gets creatively rewritten, either added to or abandoned, according to a process of natural selection from one historical epoch to the next.'[54] Closer yet to the theme of our book,

> It explains the reconstructive efforts of pragmatist and historicist theologians in taking the living metaphors of their traditions and killing them off so that, dying as metaphors, they might rise again as familiar and common uses. It could also explain the work of contemporary philosophers of religion who, in the tradition of Dewey try to revamp a vocabulary about "natural piety" and "an attitude of adjustment to the whole" as metaphors intended to get us to think of "the religious" in new ways. These efforts would not then be dismissed by critics

---

[52] We leave aside the question of whether metaphors can compete among themselves. The fact is that people do take some metaphors to be in competition with others. Take for example patriarchal versus matriarchal metaphors for deity.

[53] Rorty, quoted in Frankenberry, 'Mobile army', p. 182.

[54] N. Frankenberry, 'Mobile army', p. 183.

> simply as "changing the subject" from religion because they happen to omit the distinguishing feature of superhuman agents.[55]

One cannot help thinking that Frankenberry wants to have her cake and eat it too. On the one hand, she insists on the utterly non-cognitive relation between the metaphors and new vocabularies, while on the other hand, she does not want these revisionist strategies to be considered as having changed the subject. To take another example, she speaks of the new uses evoked by the new metaphors as 'arresting, abnormal speech [that] can deliver sharp critiques *of* selected literal meanings in the history of religion.'[56] But in order to make sharp critiques *of* something, those critiques must at least stand in cognitive relation to that something, which is denied on this view of metaphor. *Prima facie* it may be granted that the revisionism she has in mind is neither explanatory, nor interpretative. It is not explanatory because she does not claim that the new vocabulary explains why our forerunners in the faith believed in the sorts of things they believed in. Neither is it interpretive because the meaning of their words must be taken at face value, according to Davidsonian interpretation theory. In what sense, then, is it revisionist? It is revisionist with respect to what the meaning of religion should be today. It revises the assumption that in order for a discourse to be religious, it must be about superhuman agents.

We have no stake in this claim, for we are not interested in the religious nature of a discourse as such. Let us recapitulate our argument in this present section. Frankenberry's model of metaphorical talk has the obvious advantage of keeping the literal interpretation of the speech of religious believers. *It is better, from an interpretive point of view, to simply ascribe patent falsity to what they say, rather than to engage in massive and dubious reinterpretation.* While revisionism as an interpretive thesis is ruled out on this approach, her drawing on Rorty brings revisionism back into the picture on account of a metaphor's non-cognitive relation to the new vocabulary that it prompts.

Despite all these errors and setbacks, *a Davidsonian theory of interpretation, we believe, tends to give more – if not enough – attention to the self-understanding of the religious believer. Secondly, it simplifies our understanding of symbolic speech and action, by refusing to postulate unnecessary meanings and truths. Third, it asserts a basic continuity between religious talk and mundane talk.* To paraphrase, religious notions run along the same familiar tracks as more mundane notions. But the fact remains that its austerity with intensional notions forces it to account for complex meanings by a rudimentary coordination with observable behaviour.

[55] N. Frankenberry, 'Mobile army', p. 184.

[56] N. Frankenberry, 'Mobile army', p. 185 (emphasis mine).

Bruce D. Marshall and Realism

Our analysis of the dialogue between Davidson and religious scholars had ambiguous results. While we had hoped to show that Davidsonian semantics encourages a privileging of the intentions of religious believers, the work of Godlove and Frankenberry casts some doubt on the immediate conscriptability of a truth conditional semantics against theological revisionism. The next three sections of this chapter further investigate the usefulness of Davidson's work for theology by engaging with the work of Bruce D. Marshall. Each section discusses one of the three thematic areas that are framing this conversation: ontology, justification and meaning.

The present section critically discusses the proposal of Marshall's book, *Trinity and Truth,* with respect to a theory of truth and how this correlates with the traditional demands of realism. In particular, we are interested in the theological modification of a theory of truth.

Beyond Realism and Anti-realism

Marshall is not interested in realism for its own sake. He shares a common concern with a number of contemporary philosophical theologians, namely to use philosophy, including ontology, epistemology and other branches, as disciplines ancillary to theology. The latter is to carry a critical dialogue with these discourses without, however, treating them as epistemically primary[57]. This means that should a philosophical account of truth, of morality, of meaning, be in contradiction with Christian belief, these would be "annihilated", in the words of Donald MacKinnon.[58] The basic idea is that philosophical theories should be used as instruments for bringing out the meaning of the Christian Gospel.[59] There should be no interest in these alien theories except insofar as they function as enhancers of the Christian truth.

It should therefore come as no surprise that Marshall has no particular investment in a realist theory of truth. Inasmuch as realism can fruitfully be brought to bear on the question of Christian teachings, it is worth discussing.

---

[57] These theologians usually regard Hans Frei as giving the best description of this *ad hoc* relationship between theology and philosophy. See Hans Frei, *Types of Christian Theology* (New Haven: Yale, 1992), pp. 70-91.

[58] Bruce Marshall, *Trinity and Truth* (Cambridge: Cambridge University Press, 2000), p. 242.

[59] See for example Hans Frei's use of formal literary devices as instruments that reveal the identity of Jesus Christ in the Gospels, in *The Identity of Jesus Christ: The Hermeneutical Bases of Dogmatic Theology* (Philadelphia: Fortress, 1975), pp. x-xiv, 1-12, 86-154.

Should it get in the way of extracting a specifically Christian account of truth and knowledge, it will be abandoned without hesitation.[60]

As it happens, Marshall is not very convinced that realism as a philosophical theory about truth, at least in the version which employs a correspondence theory, fares very well on the contemporary scene. There are purely philosophical reasons for which he is suspicious of correspondence realism as a good theory about truth. It might be useful to remember that there are a variety of realisms and a correspondence theory of truth need not figure in all of them. In fact, as Peter Byrne points out,[61] correspondence is assumed by otherwise idealist theories of truth and knowledge. In such theories, the right side of the correspondence relation describes the facts about sense perception, rather than facts about the world. Precisely for reasons such as these it is necessary to discuss not really whether theology entails realism, but precisely what kind of theory of truth, or what kind of realism or non-realism it entails.

Marshall's approach to the dispute over correspondence theories of truth betrays his holist approach to epistemology. One important issue has to do with the notion of mental intermediaries between beliefs and the world. He finds this problem exemplified in Thomas Aquinas. Although Aquinas cannot be accused of introducing third parties between human mind and world, his idea of correspondence understood as isomorphism between mind and reality still presupposes the notion of forms. This largely Aristotelian notion, Marshall fears, has outrun its usefulness and rather than helping Aquinas in his project, it more than often gets in the way. Upon clarifying his take on Aquinas, following criticism by Fergus Kerr, Marshall points out that it is not a question of whether Aquinas is a direct realist or not. He is. The question, rather, is whether his own way of doing without intermediaries is part of a workable theory of truth.

The notion of an ontological gap existing between mind and world may tempt us into thinking that we need epistemic intermediaries to bridge it. This 'craving for objectivity' only invites the sceptical threat, which is why we have to reinstate mind in an unmediated contact with the world. Rorty, Davidson and, following the latter, Marshall see this unmediated touch with the world as a causal relation between reality, or experience, and our beliefs about it. We shall come back to this crucial notion of a causal relation between belief and world.

The notion of form is an unworkable one since it only makes sense in a physical realm, Marshall points out. It is not clear what this notion is supposed

---

[60] It should be pointed out that this 'ancillary' approach to realism is also shared by McGrath. Although he lacks the biblical elaboration of the concept of truth present in Marshall, he shares with the latter an emphasis on preventing 'realism' from setting the agenda for theology. He is, however, more optimistic about the promise realism still has as a scientific theory.

[61] Peter Byrne, *God and Realism*, pp. 8-9.

to do when applied to the immaterial realm of mind. However, if we drop form, not much content is left to the idea of correspondence, as iso-*morph*-ism between reality and thought.

This is both a debate over the best interpretation of Aquinas, as well as about whether one *should* be a Thomist with respect to correspondence realism. Marshall thinks that in order to follow the spirit of Thomas's work on truth, one has to depart from the letter of his correspondence talk. However, Fergus Kerr thinks the letter is still important, and for a reason most relevant to our debate. He suggests, without much elaboration unfortunately, that "a certain ontological mind/reality isomorphism may after all be implied in the Christian doctrine of creation."[62] Kerr reminds Marshall that one should take account of Thomas's participationist metaphysics which involves another sense of true, more fundamental than the other senses: truth as borne by forms and by sentences. Things are true, according to Kerr's reading of Aquinas, according to their *adequatio* with the divine intellect, insofar as they fulfil what was ordained for them by the divine intellect. What Kerr brings to the fore here is a sense in which, for the Christian, truth as a notion is incomprehensible apart from the being of God. This reveals the possibility of another kind of isomorphism, between the mind of God, or the divine intellect (which is also the being of God) and humans and their own minds. The possibility of such an isomorphism, about which more will be said on another occasion, involves the possibility of a non-mysterious correspondence. Marshall is quite right to denounce the incoherence of the notion of an isomorphism between reality and mind. Yet the notion of an correspondence between two minds is less threatening. As Kerr comments on Aquinas:

> He does not picture knowing as the subject's projecting value and intelligibility upon raw data. Rather, we exist at all only by participation in being (the doctrine of creation), and, since minds are what we are, we participate by exercising our intellectual capacities, and of course to a very limited extent, in God's own knowledge of the world.[63]

Marshall connects correspondence to the notion of form, as it is implied in the idea of an isomorphism between mind and world. Even aside from the arguments above, he has another reason to abandon correspondence: the notion is arguably vacuous. The objection may be summarised as follows: if a true sentence can be said to correspond to anything, it corresponds to the whole of reality. Correspondence as a notion does not tell us how to match pieces of our language with parts of the world. It follows that it is not so much false, as it is empty, or useless.

---

[62] Fergus Kerr, "Book Symposium: Bruce D. Marshall, *Trinity and Truth*", *Modern Theology* 16/4 (October 2000), p. 504.

[63] Kerr, "Symposium", pp. 507f.

Not only is correspondence useless, but it also threatens to make truth inaccessible. This fear of inaccessibility prompted non-realists such as Dummett, but also realists like Putnam to epistemise truth. Truth becomes warranted assertibility, sometimes prefixed by 'idealised'. The problem is, of course, that

> "Idealized warranted assertability" seems at least as remote and inaccessible a measure of truth as the "correspondence to reality" which, on account of inaccessibility, it was supposed to replace. Easing this problem by tying truth to current rather than ideal epistemic practices brings out the difference rather than the identity of truth and justification, since justification admits of degrees and can be lost, while truth, as anti-realists themselves generally concede, does neither [...][64]

Marshall is just as unsatisfied by realist as he is by anti-realist attempts to distil the essence of truth. Both end up reducing truth to some other putatively more basic concept.

> Realists and anti-realists alike appear to assume that "truth" is an especially obscure and elusive notion, for which conceptual equivalents need to be found which we can more readily grasp. But Davidson in particular has suggested that this assumption has the matter backwards, as the problems had by both realists and anti-realists in coming up with an informative and plausible substitute for "true" in part attest. Far from being a daunting puzzle, truth is about as basic and obvious a concept as we have. The notion of truth is much more clear to us – we have a much firmer grip on it – than any concept we might use to analyze or explain it.[65]

In effect we are being asked to move beyond realism or anti-realism with respect to truth. The basicality of the notion of truth must be assumed. It is not entirely clear what this is supposed to mean for Marshall. The clearest scenario is that we should refrain as much as possible from giving conceptual substitutes for truth. But the problem was not that of finding such substitutes anyway, but of analysing the content of the notion, which means breaking it into distinctive analysable parts. Marshall seems to be suggesting that the notion of truth is simple, i.e., it is not composite. There is nothing to be said about truth to illuminate and indeed to further our already firm grasp of the notion. Which is not to say that there is nothing to be said about truth at all. But we should give up the hope of coming up with anything like an explanatory account. On the contrary, any such account already presupposes our existing notion. All other such accounts are already truth-functional, which makes them explanatorily useless.

---

[64] B. D. Marshall, *Trinity*, p. 225.

[65] B. D. Marshall, *Trinity*, p. 233.

What Marshall and Davidson are doing here may be best described in terms of a Rortyan change of vocabulary. All we need to know about truth is given by Tarski's T-sentences of the form:

'Grass is green' if and only if grass is green.

Sentences of this type show how 'is true' works for particular sentences of a given language. Taken together, all T-sentences that may be constructed for a given language extensionally define truth for that language. Deflationists, however, will say that T-sentences tell us everything there is to know about truth.[66] This implies that truth is not simply a basic notion, but a redundant or trivial one. While deflationism rightly stresses that T-sentences capture something quite basic of the essence of truth, it has trouble accounting for the unity of truth. It follows that Davidson has to account for both the unity of truth while neither trivialising nor giving conceptual definitions for truth. He does that by giving two broad generalisations concerning truth.

On the one hand, there are ties which bind truth to meaning and belief which are partly constitutive of the concept of truth. Truth as captured by T-sentences is not an epistemic notion[67]: whether the sentence on the left is true depends on both its meaning and its truth conditions actually obtaining, regardless of whether anyone is justified in asserting it. The constitutive relation between truth and belief shows in the fact that belief has to be on the whole veridical, given its relation to truth and meaning. This is Davidson's famous transcendental argument against scepticism. Furthermore, the notion of belief presupposes that of objective truth. Marshall concludes that

> The ties of truth to meaning and belief help display the unity of truth, and so tell us more about truth than Tarski's schema by itself. [...] What unifies truth is the role it plays in enabling us to *interpret* other speakers, no matter what language they speak. A concept that plays this role must be the same concept for the speaker and the interpreter, and must therefore be a single concept for whatever languages they speak.[68]

It appears that Davidson and Marshall give disquotationalism an interpretation which while making truth accessible to belief nonetheless refuses to epistemise it. This seems to go in a realist direction inasmuch as the second condition for a sentence being true has to do with the truth conditions specified on the right branch of a T-sentence actually obtaining.

This brings up the second generalisation made by Davidson. He sometimes refers to the function of the sentence figuring on the right branch of a T-sentence as specifying an arrangement of the world. The temptation to offer such *informative generalisations* stems from the fact that on a holist reading the

---

[66] B. D. Marshall, *Trinity*, p. 235.

[67] This is where Rorty massively dissents from Davidson.

[68] B. D. Marshall, *Trinity*, p. 238.

right branch simply gives truth conditions. But this tells us little about truth itself. To shed more light on truth itself, it may be said that truth depends on what sentences mean and on how the world is arranged. Davidson does indeed risk upsetting sympathetic critics such as Rorty when he says that "What Convention T, and the trite sentences it declares true … reveal is that the truth of an utterance depends unjust two things: what the words as spoken mean, and how the world is arranged."[69] Marshall rightly points out that such a description of the sentences on the right branch involves truth-functional operatives and therefore does not say more, but actually less about the notion of truth. We do not need to draft in description in order to explain truth. It is truth which explains description, not conversely.

This tells against hanging too many explanatory hopes on these sorts of generalisations. They are helpful in telling us more about the concept of truth by illuminating some of the connections it has with meaning and belief. As Marshall puts it,

> The problem with such notions lies in our readiness to ignore their explanatory limitations, not in the thought that language is tied to the world. It is truth that ties language to the world, in the fashion displayed by each T-sentence. The difficulty we have in finding notions which allow us to generalize effectively about this tie need not suggest that the tie is puzzling or mysterious, still less that it is absent. Our conceptual frustration attests rather to the utterly basic way in which the concept of truth captures this tie.[70]

Marshall proposes to follow Davidson and Rorty (to a lesser extent) beyond the distinction between realism and anti-realism. What all these thinkers find so repugnant is the idea of an intermediary set up between mind and world. Such epistemic intermediaries do more harm than they do good. Their very existence is dubious in the first place; how best to describe them is also unclear. Perhaps more importantly, their epistemic utility is hard to see, since they merely shift the debate to another, more obscure and less accessible domain. It follows that we ought to give up the notion of correspondence, except when it is taken rather metaphorically as suggesting no more than that truth is non-epistemic, and that our best justifications still do not ensure truth.[71] However, such an employment of correspondence is only the expression of the hope that our thought brushes against the world and that our beliefs stand under its judgment. It, however, does nothing to say how we might best justify our beliefs. Correspondence does not figure in the order of justification anymore than coherence does in the order of truth.

---

[69] D. Davidson, "A Coherence Theory of Truth and Knowledge", in *Truth and Interpretation: Perspectives on the Philosophy of Donald Davidson*, ed. Ernest LePore (Oxford: Blackwell, 1986), p. 309, also quoted in Marshall, *Trinity*, p. 239.

[70] B. D. Marshall, *Trinity*, p. 241.

[71] D. Davidson, 'Truth Rehabilitated", in R. Brandom, *Rorty and His Critics*, p. 66.

Despite these severe restrictions on correspondence, it is still strongly suggested that thought is in touch with the world. However, that relationship is causal. Our contention, which we hope to make persuasive later on, is that such a causal relation, given that it is not itself accessible to reason, being as it were outside logical space, is just as mysterious as old correspondence, inviting yet another variety of scepticisms. A merely causal linkage between experience and one's body of beliefs is not enough to ensure friction, of the important, epistemic type, between mind and world.

More on that will follow. Marshall does not leave a Davidsonian account of truth theologically unmodified. He does consider such an account to be "the most plausible outcome currently available of the long philosophical debate about what truth is."[72] How does the Davidson-Tarski account of truth fare under theological scrutiny?

The first observation to be made is that for the Christians, Jesus Christ is the truth (John 14.6) and so is the Holy Spirit (1 John 5.6). It appears that truth attaches not only to sentences, and possibly forms, but also to a person. Starting from this observation flows the entire theological modification of the concept of truth. It soon becomes apparent that the shift in the content of the concept of truth which Marshall outlines also reflects negatively against realism, as traditionally conceived. Although Marshall lost all interest in realism for philosophical reasons, it is apparent that his theological reasons would have lead him in the same direction.

At first blush the Tarski-Davidson account of truth for sentences should have no trouble accounting for the truth of

(1) "Jesus is risen" is true if and only if Jesus is risen.

Surely, Marshall argues, Christians would have no trouble assenting to such a sentence. The person who assents to such a sentence would be having a true belief, while the one who doesn't would be holding a false one. However, he goes on to say, we do not learn anything from this sentence about how truth might be borne by a person. In other words, using T-sentences for the purposes of theological assertions only exemplifies how 'is true' works when truth is born by sentences, not when truth is borne by a person. Unless we are prepared to employ two very different notions of truth, one for a theological context, one for a mundane, common-sense one, we should be able to find a coherent way to state that the two accounts are not "utterly disparate"[73] At stake here is the very unity of truth, which as we already saw, is an intuition that must be preserved at all costs.

Why is a Tarski-Davidson characterisation of the *content of the concept of truth* incomplete and "how may it be expanded theologically without losing an intelligible tie to the characterization Tarski and Davidson give"?

---

[72] B. D. Marshall, *Trinity*, p. 241.

[73] B. D. Marshall, *Trinity*, p. 245.

The main problem has to do with the fact that the truth of "Jesus is risen" is, as Marshall perhaps misleadingly calls it, automatic.[74] In that case, the sufficient conditions for the truth of the sentence "Jesus is risen" are what a person means by those words and whether in fact Jesus was risen. The truth of the belief, like the truth of the sentence, would be automatic. There are two considerations which, when taken together, suggest that the truth of that sentence or belief cannot be automatic.

First, Marshall rightly points out that having a relationship to Jesus depends on having true beliefs about him, beliefs which correctly identify him. He is quite right to emphasise this aspect especially considering the current anti-cognitive trend in thinking about theological method. Secondly, "Any relations which created reality has to Jesus depend as a whole on Jesus himself."[75]

> This comes out perhaps most clearly in the way the New Testament characterizes Jesus' resurrection. The Father raises Jesus by his own free and sovereign action, which is to bestow his spirit upon the slain Jesus. This gift to the crucified Jesus fully enacts the Spirit's mission, begun at Jesus' baptism, to abide in and on the Son. The Spirit gives the dead Jesus the divine freedom to rise from the dead, by including Jesus once again in an ordered but mutual bond of being, knowledge and love with the Father. Jesus rises, therefore, in the utterly sovereign, self-determining freedom of God. […] *The risen Jesus is not passive or inert, and therefore not at the disposal of human beings, or of anything created – except, of course, insofar as he freely gives himself to them Jesus' being at their disposal, one could say, is not itself at their disposal, but only at his own. Upon his own action, therefore, depends any relation to him which creatures may come to have.*[76]

Marshall is expressing here a classic Christian conviction in the purely gratuitous and loving nature of the relationship between God and mankind. There is nothing which forces God into being at our disposal. This relationship is entirely at his own disposal.

There is nothing problematic, at least from our point of view, about these two considerations, when taken separately. But Marshall suggests that when taken together, they suggest that the truth of the belief cannot be automatic. The very content of the belief entails that any relationship which we have with Jesus depends as a whole on his own free will and action. So far so good. But since our relationship to Jesus depends on our having true beliefs about him, it means that the very truth of those beliefs themselves cannot be automatic, but is itself at the disposal of Jesus. Our reading of Marshall, which is indeed not the only possible construal of his argument, is as follows.

---

[74] B. D. Marshall, *Trinity*, p. 245.

[75] B. D. Marshall, *Trinity*, p. 246.

[76] B. D. Marshall, *Trinity*, p. 246.

(2) All relations of created reality, including human minds, to Jesus depend as a whole on the action of Jesus himself.

From which it follows that:

(3) Any element necessary for such a relation to obtain must depend in some way upon Jesus' action.[77]

But

(4) It is necessary that a person hold true beliefs (which identify Jesus) in order to have a relationship to Jesus

Hence

(5) The truth of the beliefs which identify Jesus are caused by Jesus himself.

It follows that for the truth of "Jesus is risen" it is necessary that Jesus acts upon the mind, which means for Marshall that he must bring it about that the sentence they hold is true. This is the specifically Christian theological modification of (at least a theological account of) truth. In at least this specific respect, writes Marshall, Jesus is the truth.

If these are the requirements of an account of truth applicable to sentences involving divine persons and their actions, it would appear that the unity of truth is in peril. Unless we are prepared to abandon this intuitive notion, we "should expect the truth-bestowing act of the triune God to unify all true beliefs."[78] The biggest obstacle in the face of such unification is that, unlike sentences about God whose truth is evidently at the disposal of God, the truth of "Grass is green" is not at the disposal of grass itself. It seems that another way has to be found of unifying these two types of truths. Marshall's suggestion is that once we recognize that all things have their origin in God the Father, then "In all creatures there lies at least a trace, a *vestigium*, of the Trinity, such that they both resemble and desire the Father."[79] In contrast to Jesus the Son, who is the truth in that he perfectly bears the image of God the Father, created things resemble the Father in a more remote and partial way. But they still do. This is what licenses Marshall to propose that all truth conditions are wholly at the disposal of the Trinity. This is more obvious in Jesus' case, since he is both the presenter of God (and therefore truth) and the presented (as divine revelation).

> Yet that grass is green is as much presented to the world by the triune God as that Jesus is risen. The Father as much sees to it that the truth conditions for "grass is green" are met as that those for "Jesus is risen" are met. As Jesus Christ presents

---

[77] B. D. Marshall, *Trinity*, p. 247.
[78] B. D. Marshall, *Trinity*, p. 272.
[79] B. D. Marshall, *Trinity*, p. 273.

> the truth conditions for the belief that he is risen to the world, in order that this belief may actually be true, so also he presents to the world all the truth conditions which the triune God wants to see met, and in this way brings about the truth of every true belief. And as the Spirit creates the conviction that "Jesus is risen" is true, so the Spirit may also be credited with creating the conviction that grass is green; any holding true of a sentence he brings about.[80]

Thus the concept of truth is unified for all statements, regardless of what realities, divine or human, they are about. Or so it would seem. There is one exception to this overarching truth-bestowing act of the Trinity. It concerns sentences which, like "Florensky was murdered in the Gulag", are true, yet whose truth is not willed by God. Marshall's explanation for this apparent deviation from the norm is that

> Because there is evil in the world traceable to the doings of created free agents, there will be some actual states of affairs which correspond to nothing in God, arrangements of the world for which there is nothing in God of which they are the likeness, even remotely.[81]

In the following section we shall discuss the coherence and felicity of Marshall's arguments, in the light of both analytic discussions of truth and Christian convictions regarding creation, reality and indeed revelation.

Critique

There is no doubt in our mind that Marshall's vigorous defence of Christian theology is a most welcome presence on the theological scene of today. A not inessential explanation for his thoughtful arguments, precise reasoning and careful hermeneutics is his engagement with analytic philosophy. He has done this in such a way that few theologians would dare. His familiarity with Davidson and Quine might well have been that of a philosopher of mind, rather than a theologian who also has time to read Barth and Aquinas. The critique that we will offer here does not wish to take anything away from the courage of his project. Quite the contrary, we wish to recommend that such an encounter with analytic philosophy be given a more central space in discussions of theological method and epistemology. There are, however, several bones of contention. Dissatisfaction is caused partly by philosophical reasons and partly by theological ones.

There are two focal points of dispute, in our opinion. The first relates to what we shall call his *automaticity argument*. This is the argument that the truth of sentences like "Jesus is risen" cannot depend simply on what the sentence means and whether in fact he was also risen. There must be a further truth

---

[80] B. D. Marshall, *Trinity*, p. 273.
[81] B. D. Marshall, *Trinity*, p. 274.

condition involved and that is that the Trinity must *cause* that belief to be true. The second point is one about the epistemic value of causality.

First, the automaticity argument. Premise (2) of his argument is correct, in the sense that in order for human beings to have relations to God, it is necessary that God first act and make Himself available to our gaze. However, (3) is a logical *non sequitur*. It does not follow that any element necessary for such a relation to obtain must depend in some way on Jesus' action. The only thing which results from (2) is

> (3') At least one of the necessary conditions for such a relation must depend in some way on Jesus' action.

To understand why this is the case it must be remembered that Marshall intends to block the notion of creatures having relationships to their creator which are not dependent on the action of the creator. This is how Marshall translates disposability. God is not at the disposal of creatures, hence all relations we have to him must depend on his own free action. We have accepted this much. What has to be safeguarded is therefore the dependence of a given relationship to God. It is quite clear, however, that for such a dependence to obtain it is only *necessary* that *one* necessary condition of the relationship depend on God, not that *all* conditions depend on God. Dependence upon Jesus is sufficiently real if it characterises *at least one necessary* element of that relationship. Now one may imagine a relationship whose entire necessary constituents depended on the action of God. But such a relationship would not be any more dependent on God than one described by (3'). Dependence as a logical attribute does not allow of gradation.

If things stand like this, it is not necessary that the truth of our identifying beliefs depend upon Jesus. It is, of course, possible, but it is not required by Marshall's argument so far. Let us imagine a set of necessary conditions for a relationship between human beings and God. First, a necessary condition of such a relationship might be that human beings correctly identify God.[82] Secondly, it is necessary that God be personally available to human beings, in some accessible form. Christians hold that he has revealed himself in the Scriptures and throughout history, but supremely in the person of Jesus, his Son. A third necessary condition is that human beings be capable of relationship to a divine being. The list could be plausibly extended, but this is enough to show that if at least one of these conditions is entirely at the disposal of God, then the whole relation would be utterly dependent upon God.

---

[82] There is, of course, a sense in which such a condition need not obtain. We might as well have challenged this part of Marshall's argument. For example, the disciples on the way to Emmaus had a relationship to the resurrected Jesus without being able to correctly identify him. Moses at the burning bush has a relationship to God, although he is not at first aware of it.

Marshall does have what he thinks is a stronger argument for his claim and it is a specifically Trinitarian one. After offering what is a very weak philosophical argument[83] against the claim that it is only the holding of the belief which may need to be caused by the Trinity and not the truth of the belief, he turns to the distinctive roles of the Trinitarian persons in each divine action. He points out that

> Were responsibility for creating the *attitude* of believing sufficient to characterize Jesus' own action in bringing about the true belief that he is risen, there would be no distinction between Jesus' role in the one divine action of bringing about this true belief and the role of the Spirit in that action.[84]

While Marshall is right to insist on the distinctiveness of each divine person's involvement with creation, it is not conclusive that "*Opera trinitatis ad extra indivisibila sunt*" entails that in each particular action, each divine person must have a clearly recognisable role. This would appear to throw us into an infinite circularity whereby each divine person is involved in each other's actions. Marshall is right to insist that the work of the Son must be distinguished from that of the Spirit. But if we were to apply his reasoning here, we would have to say that, if the Spirit creates the attitude of belief, and if all the economical activity of the Trinity is one, than both Jesus and the Father need to be involved in that *specific* action too. That is, if one reads *divine unity in action* like that. Some schematisation might better help us understand the difficulty. Say the Holy Spirit is engaged in action A. According to this interpretation, each divine person must have a clearly distinguishable part in that action. Let us call those separate 'sub-actions' A1, A2 and A3. But then if A1 is an action of he Father, it must also be the case that all the other persons must have a clearly isolatable part in A1 too. We might call these A11, A12, and A13. We could go on like this up to the point where it becomes very difficult to speak about distinguishable roles, to say nothing about an appropriate basis upon which one could differentiate between the respective actions. This would seem to throw us into an ineffable vortex of divine entanglements. Some may rightly point out that this is but the divine mystery of *perichoresis*. But if that is so, then we are not sure much epistemic use can be made of it. The reality of divine perichoresis is an important insight, but precisely because it is such a mystery, it cannot have a pivotal role in any argument which tries to isolate economic roles for the divine persons. We might then say that divine perichoresis is true but vacuous, or, more 'optimistically', true without being terribly helpful. It functions as a rule, stating that whenever one speaks about one divine person, one also speaks, by perichoretic implication, about the whole of the Godhead.

So far we have attempted to cast doubt on Marshall's argument that the truth of sentences like (1) cannot be automatic. His suggestion initially appeared to

---

[83] B. D. Marshall, *Trinity*, p. 248

[84] B. D. Marshall, *Trinity*, p. 249.

grant religious truth a qualitatively different status compared to what truth is in what Pickstock calls "the busy commerce of everyday where disquotationalism exerts its minimalist rule".[85] Such a distinction would have cast in doubt the very unity of truth, an intuition which Marshall is keen to preserve. But we have seen how Marshall extends this theological modification of the content of the concept of truth[86] to cover truth as applied to everyday life sentences like "Grass is green". The effect of this move has been to remove the sting from his theological modification of truth. It is not simply the truth of theological sentences which cannot be automatic, but the truth of all sentences depends on God's action in some way.

Two points need bearing out. First, applying the theological modification of truth across the board risks ascribing evil to God. Marshall is aware of this problem, but minimalises its falsifying potential. He thinks that sentences like "Florensky was murdered in the Gulag" are true, but God is not willing to meet their truth conditions, he does not want to cause them to be true. It follows that there is, after all, a domain where the Tarski-Davidson account of sentential truth is sufficient and where in fact no theological supplement of the concept is possible.[87] For Marshall it is because of the existence of free agents and their entirely voluntary actions that there are such sentences. Here we seem to be presented with the problem of evil transferred to the issue of who makes sentences about evil true. The problem is acknowledged, but for some reason Marshall elects to retain it as an exception. We are not sure, however, that there is room for such exceptions. At stake is the very unity of truth. Besides, the number of such sentences is unfortunately not insignificant.

Marshall seems to be caught between the two extreme options. He can deny the unity of truth and risk elevating theological truth over and above mundane truth. But then, he need not have attempted to apply the theological correction even to "Grass is green". If the damage has already been done, in the form of sentences about evil, why bother with the rest? On the other hand, he has the option of a sort of divine determinism, which we suspect has been subterraneously present throughout the argument of *Trinity and Truth*, and which has surfaced at places like: 'all created things bear the image of God to some extent' and 'God makes true every true sentence'.

The problem can be solved by changing the criterion which applies the theological modification of truth to mundane things. Too much is hinged on vestigiality, such that God is made the author of evil. The solution is akin to Vico's notion of the convertibility of the true with the made.[88] God makes

---

[85] John Milbank and Catherine Pickstock, *Truth in Aquinas* (London and New York: Routledge, 2001), p. 2.

[86] B. D. Marshall, *Trinity*, p. 245.

[87] B. D. Marshall, *Trinity*, p. 274.

[88] For an illuminating account, see John Milbank, *The Religious Dimension in the Thought of Giambattista Vico 1668-1744* (Lewiston/ Queenston/ Lampeter: The Edwin

certain sentences true because he creates events described by them, because he makes them. Vico would say that God has true *scientia* of a thing. In the same way, human knowledge is most accurate about those things in whose creation human beings played a large part, like literature, art, even history. This would then be the principle: an author, a creator, a maker, generally, knows *and makes* the truth of her own creations. Inasmuch as we have created certain things we ourselves are creating the truth conditions for sentences relating to those things. It follows that the truth of "Grass is green" is given by God, not because grass is a trace of God, however remote and imperfect, but because it is God who created grass and because it is God who made it to be green. But the truth of "Florensky was murdered in the Gulag" is not created by God, but by whoever murdered Florensky in the Gulag. There will be no need to look for traces of God in true statements. There is still something to be said about the "truth of things" inasmuch as they conform to the being of God, that is to what God has ordained for them, but that is a separate, albeit important issue.

So much for the automaticity argument. We hope to have shown that it is an unnecessary modification of the concept of truth. The second main thrust of our critique concerns the notion of causality. Marshall inherits certain strictures about causality from Quinean and Davidsonian holism. It is helpful briefly to rehearse them.

Davidson's famous critique of the third dogma of empiricism is directed at what he diagnoses as Quine's inability to have it both ways: to still speak of a tribunal of experience which judges our beliefs and at the same time conceive experience as being outside the space of reasons. One cannot coherently speak of content as something *given* in sensorial experience awaiting organisation by a conceptual scheme. The reason for this, Davidson suggests, is that Quine has not fully developed the implications flowing from the distinction between the two logical spaces, a space of causality and one of reason, or freedom. This distinction is part of a venerable tradition in analytic philosophy, stemming from Sellars, but it can also be traced as far back as Hegel. It turns on the qualitative distinction between nature, as a realm of causality and brute force, and mind, as the space of freedom and choice. It is the old problem of a gap between mind and world. Platonism tries to bridge the gap by imagining the presence in the mind of certain forms which somehow mysteriously originate in nature. Naturalism, on the other hand, imagines a complete reduction of the mental to the physical.

Mellen Press, 1992), pp. 78, 81, 84 (vol. 1), 9-11 (vol. 2); Robert Miner, *Vico: Genealogist of Modernity* (Notre Dame: University of Notre Dame Press, 2002), esp. pp. 26ff. Reflecting upon the relationship between truth (*verum*) and making (*facere*) leads one to the appropriate conclusion that realism makes no sense apart from the thought of some Maker knowing truths about reality. For this point, see A. Plantinga, "How to be an Anti-Realist?", *Proceedings and Addresses of the American Philosophical Association* (September 1982), pp. 67ff.

Davidson rightly points out that Quine, although being aware of the distinction, attempts to bridge the gap in an inefficient, some might say even irresponsible manner, by way of intermediaries. Speaking of sense data as intermediaries between mind and world, however, has the effect of pushing the two further apart. Since for Quine sense data translates the impact upon our nerve endings of whatever goes on outside our skins, they are in the causal realm. But as causes, they cannot deliver reasons. If we are to speak in terms of the Kantian theory of perception, such sense data are parts of receptivity, rather than spontaneity. But this is precisely what makes the Myth of the Given attractive, as Davidson realises: hoping that we can find a point at which to anchor our spontaneity and make it responsible before the world. The problem is that in Davidson's opinion, we cannot swear intermediaries to truth. We cannot know whether they are misleading us or not. Furthermore, it is not these putative intermediaries which do the job of justifying, but our beliefs about them. It is not the fact that I *see* that grass is green which justifies my belief that it is, but my belief that grass is green. Davidson's solution is therefore a coherentism whose maxim is that only beliefs justify beliefs. Something which is not in the space of reasons cannot justify any belief.

But this creates a problem for holism. It is in fact one of the defining marks of holism, and it is surprising to see that Marshall does not consider it that problematic. If it is only beliefs which justify beliefs, and if experience impacts our web of beliefs only indirectly, then we cannot possibly know which *particular* beliefs are true and which aren't. How then can we say that we have bridged the gap between mind and world, if we are not able to do so for particular sentences? The typical Davidsonian answer invokes a transcendental argument in saying that we can only know that *most* of our beliefs are true. But we can never say with certainty *which* are. The upshot of holism, therefore, is that it has created the conditions for another type of globalised scepticism. So what if we are in unmediated touch with the world if we are not able to tell at which particular point this touch has any epistemic value? Pickstock's comment on Davidson gives voice to the fear of relativism enshrined here:

> He remains, therefore, with an unsustainable dualism which must collapse either into a thoroughgoing physicalism, which would hand the determination of truth entirely over to natural science, or else into a species-relativism in such a way that the one 'coherence' we are locked into, perhaps discloses nothing whatsoever concerning the world and is itself radically inexplicable.[89]

If this creates a problem for the philosophical quest about truth, it will certainly create a problem for a theological reconstruction of this quest, like that attempted by Marshall. To get straight to the point: what is the cash value of saying that Jesus causes certain sentences to be true, if one has already

---

[89] C. Pickstock, *Truth in Aquinas*, pp. 2f.

excluded 'causes' from the space of reasons? Can Jesus' action be anything other than a barely visible trace, perhaps not even this much? More puzzles follow: how are we to know which are those beliefs *caused* by him, if we censor causality like this? The only point at which Marshall mentions he is aware of the problem is in the final pages of the volume:

> But we need not always be able to tell which beliefs God makes true; it suffices that we can tell for the most part, and especially with regard to those beliefs which are epistemically primary. There need be no guarantee that a justified belief is true (there hardly could be, since in some cases people are justified in holding incompatible beliefs), only that justified beliefs are true on the whole.[90]

It is hard to see why Marshall is so optimistic with regards to those epistemically central beliefs. If it is the community which decides which beliefs are epistemically central, there is no reason why we could not expect our community to revise those beliefs. It cannot be the case, according to Marshall's coherentism, that the community has recognised those central beliefs as originating in the teachings of Jesus, or in the Scriptural narratives, or in divine revelation, or what have you. That would merely cast us back into the Myth of the Given, which is something we should of course be afraid of. This very much looks like blind faith, in the sense that we can only hope that our best and most cherished beliefs are true.

Even the accessibility of truth to belief, which Marshall beautifully ties to the work of the Spirit, is compromised here. What he gives with one hand, in speaking theologically about the Spirit's leading us into all truth, he takes with the other, in imposing restrictions upon causality. There is no way of knowing which beliefs are those which the Spirit *causes* us to have, since this very work of the Spirit is inaccessible to our reason. Pickstock's pessimistic forecast seems warranted: either Davidson allows some epistemic value to causality, or he risks naturalism, on the one hand, and relativism, on the other.

Marshall closely follows Davidsonian holism. But while he does modify it to fit a theological account of truth, he does not reform the latter's conservatism with respect to causality. Perhaps this much is also required by a theological account of truth.[91]

We will linger on some related issues, before concluding this section. Marshall follows Rorty in thinking that philosophy has been obsessively preoccupied with finding bits of the given on which to build philosophical

---

[90] B. D. Marshall, *Trinity*, p. 278.

[91] This is not the place for such an analysis, but a conceivable argument might start from both the biblical notion that 'Jesus is the truth' and the notion that 'the Spirit will lead you into all truth'. While the first one forces a modification of the Tarski-Davidson account of truth conditions, the latter challenges Davidsonian holism, or at least aspects of it.

arguments. All holist thinkers agree that this has proven a dead end. What is not already in the space of reasons cannot give any sort of justification to anything. Worse, philosophy has only managed, in feeding this craving for objectivity, to further remove itself from the world. The task now appears to be that of reinstating an unmediated link with the world. While there is a lot of promise in the Davidsonian project, the issues outlined above suggest that some serious critique is also called for before one could put it to fruitful theological use. One of the reasons for this is that the world remains decidedly out of epistemic touch and that it only approximates what Rorty describes as "those planks in the boat which are at the moment not being moved about."[92]

In Marshall's opinion, Thomas' way of speaking of truth is unsatisfactory. He sometimes speaks about truth as being borne by sentences, sometimes as being brought about by forms – "when they come to exist in the intellect by passing through different media which link the intellect to the world."[93] This latter view is the problem for Marshall. While it appears that Thomas invokes intermediaries, this is not really the case, for he is a direct realist. Yet it is his own way of doing without intermediaries which upsets Marshall.[94] The notion of form is suspicious, for it presupposes so much of the defunct aspects of Aristotelian metaphysics, that it is no longer comprehensible today. 'The problem with calling on substantial and accidental forms in an account of truth is that there is no need, and no convincing evidence, to believe there are such things.'[95]

If not much sense can be made of the notion, than neither can much sense be made of the notion of correspondence of mind to reality, which rests on that of form.

> The thought of the mind corresponding to reality draws much of its intelligibility from a use of "form" which is, in itself, entirely lucid: one physical object impresses its shape upon another, thus making the other correspond to it (the ring and the wax). Intelligibility tends to fade as we extend this idea into the realm of the immaterial: for Thomas neither the mind nor the intelligible species, being without matter, can have a shape, yet the one is "formed" by the other. If, as it seems we must, we drop Aristotelian forms altogether (and with that the attempted extension), not much seems left of the idea of one thing corresponding to another. How can we have isomorphism with no *morphe*?[96]

We have already pointed out that Marshall does away with correspondence as a workable theory of truth. It fails to provide us with two things we can

---

[92] R. Rorty, 'The World Well Lost', in *Consequences of Pragmatism* (Minneapolis: University of Minnesota Press, 1982), p. 15.

[93] B. D. Marshall, *Trinity*, p. 218.

[94] Bruce D. Marshall, "Theology after Cana", part of "Book Symposium: Bruce D. Marshall, *Trinity and Truth*", p. 521.

[95] B. D. Marshall, "Cana", p. 522.

[96] B. D. Marshall, "Cana", pp. 522f.

compare to one another.[97] But the main point of the critique is that we actually understand truth better than we understand correspondence, or any other explanatory notion for that matter. How then, is the link between mind and world (re)established? Davidson argues that it is truth that ties mind to the world. However, if Pickstock is right, it is possible that all we are left with is a coherent system of beliefs, with no particular links, not even causal, to reality. That is an entirely logical possibility. John McDowell castigates Davidson's unconstrained coherentism, echoing a thought similar to Pickstock's: if there is nothing from experience that might rationally figure in our system of beliefs as sources of justification, then we have not really reinstated any link with the world. Hilary Putnam voices a similar concern, this time pertaining to realism: it is not enough to make realist-sounding statements.[98] Both Rorty (of all people!) and Davidson make them. Both speak in terms of being in touch with the world. But all that talk simply translates into an expression of *hope* that it is the world which generates most of our beliefs. Yet it is precisely this fear which made the myth of the given attractive in the first place. Davidson's solution does not alleviate the fear, but only transfers it to another level. Like it or not, a dualism is being reinstated between the mind – as the logical space of reasons – and the world – as the natural realm of causality. Davidson's position is the typically modern strategy of crossing a divide: firmly setting camp on one side of the gap, gathering all the resources available on that side of the gap, and finally bridging it from one side.[99] This inevitably involves a revisionism, a reconstruction of the world which hardly resembles what is normally considered to fit the description. Rorty's metaphor of currently stationary planks seems to capture well the implications of holism.

Davidson thinks his position is saved by invoking the transcendental argument which holds that the ties which hold between meaning, belief and truth ensure that most of our beliefs are true most of the time. Yet McDowell's criticism is straight to the point: if experience does not even figure in the space of reasons, than our beliefs will have no empirical content. Nothing will be left of the notion of a body of beliefs,[100] if such beliefs have no content. The same point is astutely made by Putnam: if we drop intentionality, we have to drop thought as well.[101] The route by which McDowell arrives at his conclusion is a long and complex one and we cannot rehearse it here. It rests on a possibility that Davidson does not even consider, which is that there can be a cooperation of receptivity and spontaneity, such that the latter is always already passively

[97] See Marshall's 'slingshot argument', *Trinity and Truth*, pp. 227-233.

[98] H. Putnam, "Meaning holism", in *Realism with a Human Face* (Cambridge: Harvard University Press, 1990); H. Putnam, "Richard Rorty on reality and justification" in R. Brandom, ed., *Rorty and His Critics*, p. 83.

[99] John McDowell, *MW*, p. 94.

[100] J. McDowell, *MW*, pp. 17, 18, 68.

[101] H. Putnam, "Why is a philosopher?", *Realism With a Human Face*, p. 114.

draw into operations of the former. It then follows that experience can serve as a tribunal for our beliefs, because it is already conceptual. This cooperation results in the fact that "the structure of elements that constitutes a thought, and the structure of elements that constitutes something that is the case, can be the very same thing."[102] However, as John Haldane has observed, this is "as close as makes no substantial difference to the old orthodoxy of Thomist metaphysical realism".[103]

Unless Marshall offers a better alternative to Thomas' understanding of truth, he might as well be less dismissive of the latter's employment of the notion of forms. Kerr and Pickstock helpfully underscore that Thomas should not be pressed into an epistemological, post-Fregean mould, but one should keep in mind that for him epistemology (knowledge) belongs together with ontology (being), but more importantly with theology (God). Thus, the 'theory' of correspondence was never intended to stand independently of the doctrine of God who creates out of nothing and in whose being humans creatively participate. Thus, Pickstock speaks of knowledge as "God's perpetual return to himself."[104] Marshall's suspicion of the given, of intermediaries, causes him to revolt against Thomas' notion of form itself. Unfortunately, the holist alternative only perpetuates the dualism between nature and reason.

What may we conclude about Marshall's relationship to realism? If he has no particular investment in the debate between realists and non-realists, he is more interested in truth and our connection to the world. However, *the theological modification of the concept of truth is in fact unconvincing and forces him into either breaking the unity of truth, or attributing evil to God.* We have suggested that a much more viable solution, if indeed one must modify the notion of truth, is in a Vichian *verum-factum* principle. At the same time, Marshall's holism is too entrenched to be modified by his excellent theological insights like the fact that the role of the Holy Spirit is to lead us into all truth. This 'leading' role of the Spirit is too much in the causal realm to be of any epistemic significance. Conversely, more promising resources are present in philosophers like Putnam and McDowell, but also Alston, who are less restrictive about what *can* inhabit the space of reasons. And if realism necessarily contains a principle of 'friction,' then there still seems to be a point to the debate between realism and anti-realism.

---

[102] J. McDowell, *MW*, p. 27.

[103] Quoted by Kerr, "Symposium", p. 506. Cf. John Haldane, "A return to form in the philosophy of mind", *Mind (new series)* 11/3 (1998), pp. 253-277; F. Kerr, "Aquinas and analytic philosophy: natural allies?", *Modern Theology* 20:1 (2004): 123-139.

[104] Milbank and Pickstock, *Truth in Aquinas*, p. 12.

Marshall and Davidson on Epistemic Justification

With *Trinity and Truth* Bruce Marshall has produced one of the most stimulating recent discussions of theological prolegomena. His effort comes on the backdrop of post-liberal musings about grammatical theology and of a resulting mistrust of notions like truth, ontology and rationality. By drawing on the resources of the analytic philosophical tradition he succeeds in bringing much clarity to the debate, and, even if this may not be a clincher, its fresh perspective is most laudable.

Marshall draws on the analytic tradition that stems from Quine's attack on empiricist philosophy and issues in the development of Davidson's holism. As it will be shown, Marshall takes this current of thought, which Hans-Johann Glock has called 'logical pragmatism,' to license a particularly unapologetic theological method. Although he finds much useful material in Davidson, Marshall believes that a theological supplement of the Davidson-Tarski account of truth is required. The focus of this discussion is his understanding of theological justification.

We shall explore the coherence of Marshall's and Davidson's respective accounts of justification. While remaining critical of Davidson, we will show that some notions used by Marshall, like that of epistemic priority, do not sit well with a holist epistemology. We will conclude that both fail in significant respects in their accounts of justification.

Austerity and the Rejection of Analyticity

Quine's critique of the distinction between the analytic and the synthetic has acquired the status of orthodoxy in most analytical circles. Together with the epistemic holism by which it is supported, it has even began to capture the imagination of theologians. Whether this translates into a metaphysical contingentism, or into a crypto-fideist theological rationality, theologians hope it helps them preserve God's prevenience by denying the priority of any intellectual discourse over his actuality. The trouble is, of course, that it is very difficult to use philosophy against itself in its conflict with theology and hope to get away with it too. The present section discusses the connection between Quine's rejection of analyticity and Marshall's rejection of the so-called epistemic dependence thesis of foundationalism.

Both Quine and Marshall reject specific brands of foundationalism. The former exhibits a somewhat ambivalent relation to the Vienna circle of logical positivism, a relation which is ultimately critical in his rejection of empiricism. Quine objects to the so-called two dogmas of empiricism: the distinction between the analytic and the synthetic and reductionism. Since we have already this aspect of Quine's thought, we will rehearse some of his arguments only insofar as they will resurface in later discussion.

Hans-Johann Glock distinguishes between two of Quine's arguments. In 'Two Dogmas of Empiricism' he argues that analyticity fails because it rests on other intensional notions such as synonymy, definition, necessity and so on. These concepts can only be explained by making appeal to other members of the family. Yet, none of these concepts can be explained in a purely extensional idiom. Quine's extensionality requirement sets his philosophy apart as an austere distrust of intensional concepts. Therefore, since intensional concepts cannot be explained, the dichotomy between the analytic and the synthetic is vacuous.[105]

This first attack, based on the charge of circularity, is itself circular, as Glock demonstrates.[106] Quine wants to discredit intensional notions by requiring an extensional reduction which presupposes that such intensions have already been discarded. Perhaps realising this, Quine had abandoned this line of argument by 1953, preferring instead one which argues from the fact that our empirical statements do not stand the test of experience alone, but only as a corporate body. We may call this *epistemological holism*. If that is the case, and if the meaning of a statement is its method of verification, it follows that a statement does not acquire its meaning by being directly correlated with experience, but only as being part of a web of statements which as a whole faces the whole of experience. This compromises the effort to distinguish for each statement a factual and a conceptual component, which lay at the basis of the positivist analytic-synthetic distinction. Since it is impossible to so distinguish between a factual and a conceptual content *at the level of individual statements*, one cannot define analytic truths as those without factual content. Analytic statements themselves are empirical derivations from the data of the whole of science. It follows that they are themselves revisable, just as empirical statements are.

If there are no such distinctions between truths in virtue of experience and truths in virtue of meaning, it follows that the whole foundationalist attempt to ground knowledge in necessary truth is doomed. Quine has, in other words, pointed out that intensional notions are empty unless they are correlated with experience and with extensional concepts such as reference or truth. We have moved from a rejection of mysterious mental entities (which made up the myth of the museum) to an imposition of an extensional austerity on theories of meaning.

Although Davidson is less of an eliminativist about intensional notions than Quine, the former's semantics remains austere. All an interpreter is allowed to go on are patterns of behaviour. This requirement results from the holist dogma that meaning must be public, a deeply held assumption exemplified in

---

[105] W. v. O. Quine, *From a Logical Point of View* (Cambridge, Mass. and London: Harvard University Press, 1980, 1st ed. 1953), pp. 37, 46, 56-7.

[106] H. –J. Glock, *Quine and Davidson*, p. 75.

Wittgenstein's private language argument.[107] It is instructive to point out that invoking the public character of meaning does not settle the debate since there is more than one possible interpretation of what 'public' means. Quine takes it to mean that the factors which fix the meaning of a sentence for the interpreter are the same ones that fix it for the speaker. That is, the speaker has no control over the meaning of his sentences. It is therefore useless for an interpreter to query an author about his meanings, since all the available evidence is in a public space anyway without anybody having privileged access to it.

This radical reading of publicness is an overzealous and actually erroneous reading of Wittgenstein. Rather than preserving what is special about meaning, it throws the baby out with the bath water. The cumulative argument of this chapter and book will clear the ground for a recovery of some notions believed to be discredited by holism, without reviving mentalistic assumptions. At any rate, what Wittgenstein intended to convey by his private language argument is simply that an author cannot think thoughts that are not already *statable* in public language. The requirement, therefore, applies less to what interpreters *actually* have at their disposal, but to the fact that all the available and sufficient information for meaning is *in principle* statable in public language. We find in Wittgenstein no such distrust of first person authority that is questioned in variants of semantic holism.[108] This reading of the private language argument is enough to guard against the pernicious mentalism most of us have come to distrust.

In Davidson's opinion, Quine was actually not austere enough about meaning since he introduces a notion of stimulus meaning.[109] In fact Davidson keeps faulting Quine for not completely abandoning empiricism and for not assuming a radical third person view of language.[110] This may have to do with Quine's shifting perceptions of holism, which Glock ably points out. While initially Quine had a monolythical understanding of the holistic web, this soon gave way to a more refined picture. It did not make sense to say that in the face of recalcitrant experience any part of the web could be revised as easily as any other part. For example, if I had the recalcitrant experience of discovering Hitler's remains in Japan, it would make no sense to alter my beliefs about the law of gravity just as easily as my belief that he committed suicide in Berlin. The revised picture is of a web anchored at its edges by the so called observation statements. These do stand the test of experience on their own,

---

[107] Ludwig Wittgenstein, *Philosophical Investigations*, trans. G. E. M. Anscombe (Oxford: Blackwell, 1974, 2nd ed. 1958), paras. 243, 246, esp. 256.

[108] For a clear analysis of Davidson's attempted reconciliation of first person authority with externalism, see Glock, *Quine and Davidson*, pp. 262-7.

[109] D. Davidson, 'Radical Interpretation', in *ITI*, p. 136; 'Afterthoughts', in *SIO*, p. 151.

[110] D. Davidson, 'Epistemology Externalised', in *SIO*, p. 194.

while the inside of the web faces the tribunal of experience as a whole, which means that revision is made according to pragmatic criteria.

This means that for Quine meaning is still tied to experience at an important point. This is where Davidson launches his attack against the so-called third dogma of empiricism, the distinction between scheme and content. Quine leaves a space through which experience in the form of sensations creeps back into the web. This opens the door to scepticism, argues Davidson, for we have no way of telling that sensations do not mislead us. He thus rejects any form of epistemic intermediaries between thought and world.[111] Experience, argues Davidson, is not within the space of reasons and for that reason it can play no part in the justification process. All that we have to go on, he argues, are other beliefs.

What happens to meaning, then? The short answer is that we tie meaning to truth and hold belief to be veridical on the whole. The first element is a translation of the extensionality requirement, while the second is a transcendental argument intended to block scepticism. Davidson's project of turning a Tarski-style theory of truth conditions into a theory of meaning is an attack against the idea that meaning is fixed prior to practical activities which settle the truth of the sentences. This notion helped establish the dualism between scheme and content, with the meaning of the scheme already in place and something like language intervening between critical agent and reality. The trouble is that such intensional notions need clarification and this must take the form of a non-circular explanation of what is involved in meaning. If we want to avoid circularity then we must avoid convention too, which is another intensional notion. Davidson suggests that we replace 'means that' with 'is true if and only if', thus fulfilling the extensionality constraint. Put simply, in order to tell another's meaning we have to check his behaviour for assent to simple observational sentences. The upshot of all this is that we cannot fix the meaning of alien sentences separately from investigating their truth. Secondly it means that justification and truth have a bearing on meaning.

For Marshall this debate has direct consequences for the dispute between revisionists and post-liberals. The dissolution of the analytic-synthetic distinction, the austerity requirement and the link between truth and meaning play beautifully in his argument against both revisionist and conservative foundationalism.

The previous argument had at its basis a manifest suspicion of intensional notions. This resulted, through a less than apodictic argument, in a deconstruction of the analytic-synthetic distinction and into the Davidsonian marriage of meaning and truth. Being convinced that meaning cannot be fixed independently of and through different procedures than those used in justification, Marshall makes a compelling case against modern methods of theological justification. He distinguishes three theses that characterise modern

[111] D. Davidson, *ITI*, ch. 13, *SIO*, ch. 10, p. 144.

justification. An *interiority thesis* holds that Christian beliefs are justified to the extent that they adequately express certain inner experiences. The *foundationalist thesis* argues that justified belief must be either tied in virtue of their meaning to self-evident or incorrigible data, or logically grounded in beliefs which are. Finally, the *epistemic dependence thesis* holds that the primary criteria for deciding about the truth of Christian beliefs must not themselves be distinctively Christian. The three theses are intimately related and so are their respective critiques.

In regards to the interiority thesis, Marshall appeals to holist arguments against the notion of the Given,[112] whether empirical or subjective. Experience is dependant on belief, on having certain propositional attitude states. Quine has shown that the relation between beliefs and experiences is less straightforward than is assumed by standard versions of foundationalism. There is a natural affinity between the interiority thesis and the foundationalist thesis. Giving up the former results in at least seriously weakening the latter.

Marshall approves of Davidson's critique of Quine. The scheme-content distinction actually underwrites both the interiority and the foundationalist theses. If our belief system confronts reality from a mediated distance, then the correspondential representation of such reality becomes primordial for knowledge. By treating the system of beliefs as a web, rather than as an architectonic structure, Quine weakens its foundations. However, as we pointed out, Quine retains the possibility of a direct access, thus holding on to a notion of the Given. He thus fails to reject the third dogma entirely. While his critique of analyticity left a number of candidates to the position of epistemic foundations without employment, there is still a hope left for foundationalism, if only we could make the notions of 'surface irritations' or 'sensations' epistemically relevant. Marshall and Davidson believe we cannot. We should be suspicious of any evidence which purports not to come in the form of another belief.

The epistemic dependence thesis is a very original reading of modern strategies of theological justification and revisionist accommodation. Desiring to make Christian theology credible in an intellectual milieu increasingly hostile to Christianity, theologians like Schleiermacher defended the truth of Christian beliefs by attempting to harmonise them with modern secular *Wissenschaft*. If this was to be done without confusing the two and losing Christian specificity, ways had to be found of establishing what is properly Christian. Schleiermacher's concept of the so-called 'regions of belief' fulfilled this function. Once beliefs were safely placed in their proper semantic context and their meaning made transparent, theologians could get on with the business of justifying them. Crucially, however, the procedures used in fixing their

---

[112] 'Empiricism and the Philosophy of Mind' in H. Feigl and M. Scriven (eds.), *Minnesota Studies in the Philosophy of Science* (Minneapolis: University of Minnesota Press, 1956).

specifically Christian meaning differed from those used in elucidating possible truth. The fact that the epistemic dependence thesis required that in adjudicating their truth appeal must only be made to non-Christian beliefs resulted in a dichotomy between the meaning of the beliefs, which was discovered by appeal to other Christian beliefs, and their truth. Not realising that truth is endemic to meaning, modern theology unwittingly departed from specific Christian meanings in its attempt to legitimise Christian faith before a secular world. However, for Marshall this could only be done by assuming that meaning is an unproblematic concept, one that is easily fixed and stable. Just what is involved in the dependence of meaning on truth will be shown in the next section. It suffices to point out at this time that Marshall fears that such strategies lose a distinctively Christian meaning precisely by allowing methods of justification which presuppose the dependence thesis.

Charity and Assimilative Power

The loss of analyticity entails the departure of experience from the order of justification. Since we cannot distinguish between a linguistic and a factual component of statements, it is futile to look for those experiences which are the epistemic origin of certain beliefs. Davidson and Marshall do not deny that experience figures in the causal chain, but both deny that it belongs to the 'space of reasons' which could turn it into a justification for a belief. But if all we have at our disposal for justification are other beliefs and if we cannot find any secure footholds for epistemology, it may seem that we are left with what McDowell calls an unconstrained coherentism.[113] Indeed, the rationale for finding such foundations for knowledge was to break the epistemic circle which unites beliefs among themselves. The idea was to find a direct link between a few of these beliefs, or a class of beliefs, and something extra-epistemic. Holist thinkers like Quine, Putnam,[114] Davidson and others believe that this is only enforcing scepticism. The way to fight scepticism, Davidson argues, is to only retain that which is within the space of reasons for purposes of justification.

Bruce Marshall takes to heart this holist requirement. It serves as an opportunity to consider certain Christian beliefs as epistemically primary.[115] Yet the fear remains in the form of a simple question: what if all of our coherent beliefs eventually turn out to be false? What licenses us to pick out certain beliefs and award them epistemic primacy?

---

[113] John McDowell, *MW*, pp. 26, 96, 139, 143, 144.

[114] Putnam's coherentism, to be sure, is less 'unconstrained' than either Davidson's or Rorty's. See Rorty, *Truth and Progress: Philosophical Papers III* (Cambridge: Cambridge University Press, 1998), ch. 1; Hilary Putnam, *Realism With a Human Face*.

[115] B. D. Marshall, *Trinity and Truth*, p. 82.

Davidson fights off scepticism by way of a transcendental argument which claims that by and large our beliefs must turn out to be true.[116] This argument flows directly from his requirement of charity for radical interpretation. If we want to interpret an alien individual and if all that we have to go on are his behavioural dispositions then we have to ascribe truth to most of his sentences in order to discover their meaning. In other words we have to hold for truth while testing for meaning.[117] The argument was already presented and we shall assume familiarity with it. Radical interpretation is an example of the sort of constraints austerity puts on understanding. This self-imposed constraint has important consequences for the nature of belief and its truth. Unless belief was in general veridical, writes Davidson, we would have no way of understanding each other. The reason is precisely because understanding requires that we treat others as holding mostly true beliefs about most things most of the time. To be more specific, since knowledge of self, knowledge of other's minds and knowledge of the world are deeply intertwined it cannot turn out that our beliefs about any of these domains of knowledge were massively mistaken.

With this argument Davidson thinks he has blocked off scepticism. We shall argue that this is not the case. Marshall employs the charity maxim to refute the charge of fideism. The criticism is serious enough and unlike some of his post-liberal colleagues, Marshall does not simply 'retreat to commitment', not even to a sophisticated so-called Wittgensteinian fideism, or to a vague *ad hoc* apologetic. Although the charge loses some force together with the collapse of the foundationalist position from which it was most potent, it still cannot seem reasonable to consider epistemically primary anything we may like. A way had to be devised to offer reasons for our central beliefs which does not create epistemic dependence. With this Marshall is trying to walk a very thin line between, on the one hand, holding on to the positivity and particularity of the Christian beliefs which form Christian epistemic priorities, and justifying these beliefs, thus making them depend on something logically prior. Following the Barthian insight that to offer reasons why we consider something to be the revelation of God is identical to erecting a superior and more fundamental ground than revelation,[118] post-liberals have always struggled with the twin demands of faith and rationality.

Marshall claims to have found a way to justify epistemically primary beliefs through the notion of *assimilative power*. The assimilative drive has two acknowledged sources. First, it stems from the very content of the Christian claims, central to which is the narrative rendering of the identity of Jesus Christ together with the command to subject everything to him.[119] This places upon

---

[116] D. Davidson, 'Three Varieties of Knowledge', *SIO*, *passim*, but esp. p. 213.

[117] D. Davidson, *ITI*, pp. 135, 137.

[118] Karl Barth, *Church Dogmatics* 1/1, trans. G. W. Bromiley (Edinburgh: T&T Clark, 2nd. ed. 1975), p. 305.

[119] B. D. Marshall, *Trinity and Truth*, pp. 108-115, 118.

the Christian the burden of actively seeking out domains of the world and of knowledge in order to harmonise them with the Christian gospel. This 'making of every thought captive to Christ' by which we establish the 'epistemic status' of 'alien' beliefs naturally presupposes that we must first understand them. This brings us back to a context of radical interpretation, where charity is required of us.

Indeed, charity is the second source of the assimilative requirement.[120] The links between meaning, truth and belief make it impossible to have a belief system whose central beliefs and epistemic priorities would make us find others mistaken on the whole. The interplay between finding others right, discovering what they mean and knowledge of the content of our own beliefs suggests that if we find others to hold mostly false beliefs, one of two things must happen. We can either reassign truth values to their statements, thus revising the initial understanding of their words, or, we can revise some of our own beliefs which made us ascribe exaggerated falsity to the other speakers. Marshall thinks that these two options mutually limit each other.[121]

The upshot of all this and indeed the beauty and elegance of Marshall's proposal is that in order to ascribe primacy to the Christian belief system we must at the same time be willing to revise some of its central statements if necessary. It turns out that Marshall's epistemic primacy does not issue in a blind fideism, but is actually a self-critical position. Such a willingness is commendable and this seems to return theology to a more public space of discourse. Indeed, as Marshall points out, to assimilate means to find a way of holding alien and novel beliefs true, in a way at least consistent with the Church's central beliefs.[122] Furthermore, the question of whether they can be assimilated is finally a question of whether 'the church can share a particular stretch of belief with at least some of those who are not its members'.[123] Rowan Williams[124] has put this beautifully in terms of each tradition having to occupy a contested space, where the 'poverty' of concepts forbids any community to claim monopoly over any portion of knowledge. In light of the current celebration of incommensurability and difference, this is quite an old-fashioned position to hold, but a timely one nevertheless.

It is not entirely clear if Marshall manages to preserve the epistemic priority of the central beliefs. In fact it turns out that our especially central beliefs have a right to epistemic primacy proportionate to their assimilative power. It is true that Marshall intended to find a way to hold such beliefs in an epistemically responsible way without creating epistemic dependence. Yet it looks like the

---

[120] B. D. Marshall, *Trinity and Truth*, pp. 153-158.

[121] B. D. Marshall, *Trinity and Truth*, p. 155.

[122] B. D. Marshall, *Trinity and Truth*, p. 148.

[123] B. D. Marshall, *Trinity and Truth*, p. 149.

[124] Rowan Williams, 'Between Politics and Metaphysics: Reflections in the Wake of Gillian Rose', *Modern Theology* 11 (1), 1995, pp. 3-22, p. 4.

epistemic priorities themselves are dependent upon agreement with *most of the beliefs* other people hold true. In reply to this problem, Marshall distinguishes between the epistemic role played in the admission of new beliefs by the majority of beliefs people hold true from that played by the epistemically primordial beliefs.[125] While the need to optimise agreement results in a large number of beliefs being accepted into our belief system, we have no other way of distinguishing between rival beliefs which passed through 'the net' except by appealing to those epistemic priorities. We will thus have to disagree with particular beliefs other people hold precisely in order to find them true on most other matters. Yet the fact remains that we cannot disagree with them on most things. Should our priorities require us to do so, then those that do would have to be relinquished, or our ascription of meaning revised.

Marshall in fact does not reply to the really pressing objection. His reply only explains why we need both epistemic priorities and the charitable maximising of agreement. But one can imagine a situation where what was given unrestricted epistemic primacy has to be relinquished precisely because it causes such generalised disagreement. It seems that Marshall has misused the term 'unrestricted', when he should have said unrestricted 'in principle'. Indeed, the very notion of epistemic status raises plenty of questions. He explains the notion: 'roughly put, the more persistently we try to uphold the truth of a belief, the wider the range of beliefs over which it has epistemic primacy, and thus the higher (or more deeply rooted) the epistemic status it has for us'.[126] The right to this epistemic power (not its actual exercise) depends on a belief's ability to accommodate the widest possible range of alien beliefs. It appears that there is not such a huge qualitative difference between Marshall and epistemic dependence supporters, except for the former's confidence that we do not have serious reason to worry about the truth of our central beliefs. The point at which this dependence intervenes is different too.

To state the diagnosis at the outset, the fact that Marshall unintentionally slips back to a version of the dependence thesis has a lot to do with the austerity he inherits from Davidson and Quine. He misreads charity as applying across the board, even to theoretical beliefs which – on a holist reading – face experience only derivatively and thus do not require to have charity applied to them. Charity is only useful in order to get a head start in interpretation by applying it to observational beliefs. This is the only situation in which it makes sense to apply it. We will try to show that austerity is very hard to achieve and that in fact both Davidson and Marshall cheat on it in various ways. Some sort of 'internal relations' must still be allowed in order to know how warrant is transferred, or which beliefs may need to be revised in light of given recalcitrant experience.

---

[125] B. D. Marshall, *Trinity and Truth*, p. 156ff.
[126] B. D. Marshall, *Trinity and Truth*, p. 127.

The Problem

The pair of thinkers under discussion poses formidable challenges to a number of recent philosophical and theological proposals. We interpret Marshall's critique to apply equally well to the modern pair of conservatives and liberals as well as to their post-modern alternative, post-liberals. A distinction between meaning and truth is operative in all of these systems. While the former group tends to concentrate on the content side of the third dogma of empiricism, focusing either on reality or on the data of experience, the latter group misconstrues the analogy between religion and language. The post-liberal tendency is to assert a specifically Christian meaning and immediately divorce it from a secular legitimising discourse. It is confident of the meaning of the religious scheme, which is then taken to determine reference *a la* Frege. If we grant the validity of Marshall's arguments, such a position is untenable because it works with a defective notion of meaning. Following Davidson, Marshall asks: what does meaning mean? Clarifying the notion of meaning leads Davidson to formulate what he hopes to be an extensionally adequate theory of meaning. Questions of meaning can be illuminated by deploying them in the form of theorems of a truth theory. A verificationist theory of meaning unites with an epistemic holism and the under-determination of theory by evidence, to generate a form of semantic holism.[127] Accordingly, what a statement, sentence, belief or thought means at a particular time is contingent upon a host of facts, not all of which being necessarily transparent to everyone. Davidson wants meaning returned to the world, which includes human sign making, from the obscure space of the mental. Although not as radical as Quine, the latter's discrediting of intensionality plays right into Davidson's concerns.

Meaning turns public, where by public is meant a democratic availability of evidence relevant to meaning, such that what is meant by the author/ speaker is identical with what is grasped by the interpreter. There is no authority left to guide us in the ascription of meaning other than publicly observable behaviour. This imposes an austerity demand on the interpreter. All interpretation is radical interpretation and radical interpretation begins at home.

Given this austerity and the suspicion of intensions, it is no wonder that analyticity gets such a rough treatment in holism, and together with it the so-called internal relations. Something very important results from this suspicion: if intensional elements are discredited, or at least have to be extensionally translated and, furthermore, if what they mean or what makes them true is not particularly obvious for anyone (given the fact that a belief can be held true in virtue of many considerations), it follows that the logical links between beliefs, thoughts, and sentences are extremely tenuous. *How can we tell whether a belief has a direct bearing on another belief if their meaning depends on such an inscrutable and volatile multitude of facts? The upshot is that if we follow*

---

[127] H. –J. Glock, *Quine and Davidson*, p. 77.

holism to its ends, there is no way to tell whether a belief a is in the logical or epistemic proximity of a belief b. It should be obvious that this has devastating consequences for the project of justifying individual beliefs. Warrant cannot be transferred in holism, as Plantinga observes in relation to coherentism, either from an experience to a belief, or from a belief to another belief. The first variety of transfer is not particularly interesting to holist thinkers,[128] while the second poses more of a problem.

For Marshall only a belief can justify another belief. But are we being good holists when we assert that? If we go by the theory, we are not. Consider the Duhem-Quine hypothesis. In the justificatory process it is not simply the premise which leads to a conclusion, but also a number of other factors which vector in, facts about logic, about mathematics, other beliefs and so on. Holist justification, then, is not a matter of individual beliefs, but of whole systems. This conclusion is consistent with Davidson's scattered and indirect discussions of justification. A belief is justified if it coheres with the rest of what we believe. But we can only *hope* – if we have understood Davidson's transcendental argument – that most of our beliefs are true. This is supposed to prevent scepticism, but it is doubtful whether it can be translated into anything more epistemologically interesting than 'I really hope I am right on this one'.

We are anticipating too much of the later argument already. In what follows we shall argue that *a modest analyticity can and should be retained together with a number of other intensional concepts.* This makes transfer of warrant possible and it also opens the way to bring experience back to the 'space of reasons'. If austerity goes, charity and radical interpretation are not necessary conditions but important methodological aids. This affects the scope of Marshall's assimilative power.

Rethinking Austerity and Analyticity

We want to suggest that preserving a moderate notion of analyticity is necessary in order to safeguard the particularity and identity of belief and the transparency of warrant transfer in the process of epistemic justification. Quine's critique of the analytic-synthetic distinction appeals to a number of theologians who see this as a method of preserving divine freedom.[129] *While we grant that the attack on linguistic necessity (the notion of truth in virtue of meaning) is correct, this should not be taken to suggest that no significant difference remains between analytical and synthetic propositions.* We will hold that it is imperative to retain a distinction between a factual and a conceptual

---

[128] Alvin Plantinga, *Warrant: The Current Debate* (Oxford: Oxford University Press, 1993), p. 79.

[129] For a helpful summary of theological appropriations of Quine, see Randal Rauser, 'Can There Be Theology Without Necessity?', *Heythrop Journal* XLIV/2 (2003), pp. 131-146.

content at the level of individual statements and not simply at the level of the whole science.

Let us start with Quine's critique of analyticity, where two stages may be distinguished. The first stage of the attack involves the criticism that analyticity cannot be properly explained without regressing to a vicious circularity. Quine rightly notes that the concept is dependent for its meaningfulness upon a number of other intensional concepts like self-contradiction, synonymy, convention and others. However, none of these notions can be explained without appealing to other members of the intensional family. It seems that the rejection of analyticity is but a consequence of a prior suspicion of intensional notions in general. We may note an initial incoherence here, together with Glock: Quine demands that the 'meaning' of analytic be defined, not simply its extension. But it is precisely 'meanings' that we are supposed to be weary of.[130] Glock concludes convincingly that the requirement that intensional notions be translated into an extensional idiom presupposes that intensional notions have already been discredited, which is what the circularity charge set out to do. As a result of such responses, the most notable of which being that of Grice's and Strawson's 'In Defense of a Dogma',[131] Quine drops the circularity charge by 1953 when he concentrates on another, more plausible, approach. The original attack, however, betrays his prejudice against the notion of meaning.

Quine's second line of attack presupposes epistemic holism. Since individual statements do not face experience by themselves, but only as part of a whole web of knowledge, it proves impossible to isolate for each individual statement an empirical and a conceptual content. Indeed, the very notion of content is made redundant by this particular holism, a position which Davidson will soon radicalise. But imagine for a moment the implausible picture of scientific work envisaged here. It would leave scientists without any real clue as to what statements to modify in light of a particular empirical occurrence. There is nothing in the experience itself that would allow us to feel confident about the empirical content of protocol sentences. Furthermore, the transfer of warrant from protocol sentences to theoretical statements allows of plenty variation. Just about any modification is warranted, given a recalcitrant experience.

Quine was eventually forced to abandon this scenario and conceded that empirical or observation statements did face the tribunal of experience on their own.[132] Epistemic holism still showed, of course, at the supra-structural level of the transition from protocol sentences, which anchor the web at the edges, to the theoretical sentences closer to the centre.

---

[130] H. –J. Glock, *Quine and Davidson*, p. 74.

[131] *Philosophical Review* 65 (1956).

[132] W. v. O. Quine, *From a Logical Point of View*, viii; Quine and J. S. Ullian, *The Web of Belief* (New York: Random House, 1970), p. 13.

It is hard to imagine that this revision of the initial holism could leave the position on analyticity unchanged. Glock's judgment is spot on: 'if individual observation sentences have a special status because of their connection to experience, why shouldn't individual sentences like ['Brutus killed Caesar or Brutus did not kill Caesar'] have a special status because they lack any such connection?'[133] Since Quine modified his position on the empirical content of protocol sentences, it only seems natural to conclude that the holist objection to analyticity loses its bite.

Davidson, of course, would be little impressed by the preceding argument. He did not approve of Quine's creation of a space for experience at the periphery of the holistic web. He fears that this introduces another dualism, that between scheme and content. His reluctance is understandable, given Quine's perhaps unhappy choice of a proximal stimulus in the shape of sensorial stimulations. Davidson believes that this introduces a third notion between knowledge and world, which adds nothing epistemically interesting to the concept of belief. But this is another matter. The fact remains that although Davidson does not inherit his teacher's behaviourist austerity, he nonetheless remains austere – with respect to semantic notions. Intensions must not be eliminated, as with Quine, but rather clarified.

Although Davidson does not consider the Quinean rejection of analyticity to be of a piece with rejecting intensional notions *tout court*, he considers that Quine has not applied it consistently enough.[134] What fixes meaning (or Quine's behaviourist equivalent) is not the proximal stimulation of nerve endings, which creates an irruption of the factual in at least a portion of science and for some individual statements. Meaning is fixed by what we can discover as truth conditions of speakers when we take them as reacting – in mostly the same way we do – to distal objects in the world. Since experience and the world only retain a causal and not an epistemic role for Davidson, there is even less room for the analytic-synthetic distinction in his work.

But how do statements manage to get their content? Are truth conditions enough to fix meaning? Establishing this is essential for an answer to the question of whether a semantically austere and presuppositionless interpretation theory is possible. Davidson believes we can fill in the content of statements by way of radical interpretation, which is supposed to begin at home.[135] We have argued that extensionality is not enough to yield meaning, or explain what meaning is. We may illustrate this with Lindbeck's crusader example, as extended by Marshall. To begin with, as Glock rightly notes[136] the whole

---

[133] H. -J. Glock, p. 78.

[134] He still leaves room for qualitative distinctions between types of belief. See Davidson, 'A Coherence Theory', *SIO*, pp. 143, and esp. 145.

[135] D. Davidson, *SIO* , pp. 12-13; *ITI*, pp. 125, 235. Quine, *Ontological Relativity and Other Essays* (New York: Columbia University Press, 1969), p.47.

[136] H. -J. Glock, *Quine and Davidson*, p. 176.

radical interpretation procedure is rather experimental, with the interpreter as the scientist and the native as the experiment. Suppose we face the crusader – as the procedure demands – with a repeated occurrence of an event to which we expect his prompted assent or dissent. Whatever this event may be, for the procedure to work we have to assume that the subject divides the world in largely the same way we do, i.e., that he shares a conceptual scheme with us. Putnam's distinction between a mereological sum and a Polish logical sum is a case in point. What is the subject taking our questions to mean? It appears that radical interpretation has to run both ways. The interpreter, as much as the interpreted, is examined. But this requires some minimal hermeneutic anthropology, which goes beyond Davidsonian charity. Furthermore, it is not clear whether truth conditions can individuate sentence meaning finely enough for natural languages.[137] The standard grammatical structure of such languages is not perfectly matched by the logical apparatus used in truth-conditional semantics. Secondly, the non-declarative sentences such as imperatives, interrogatives and optatives pose a real problem as well. Such sentences do not express something that is either true or false, in other words they do not have truth conditions. Aspects of linguistic use such as illocutionary and perlocutionary force cannot simply be reduced to truth conditions.[138]

Davidson does suspect that there is an individuation problem. If we end up with a system which ascribes increasing falsity to the native, it means that certain of our interpretations have been wrong. But the problem with this type of holism is that we do not really know which. Marshall's suggestion that we revise those beliefs which determine us to ascribe massive error is naïve in its simplicity. If we would be able to track the logical dependence of a bad translation to a wrong assumption we would no longer be operating in a holist fashion. This would involve that I already know the factual component or the conceptual component of an individual statement and I know where it derives from. The whole point of holism is that verification of such matters is never straightforward, but contingent upon a series of pragmatic factors which cannot be named at the beginning of the inquiry. A consequence of holism is the fact that we cannot be sure which particular belief is false, as Davidson himself admits.[139]

We take this last admission to be essential to the matter in discussion. It deprives us of the methodological possibility to revise wrong ascriptions. We may indeed make guesses (which is what such pragmatic choices are really euphemisms for), but this is not satisfactory. If the empirical and logical content of individual beliefs remains fluid like this, dependent on behavioural factors, it seems that we have lost the particularity of belief. Strawson, Grice

---

[137] H. –J. Glock, *Quine and Davidson*, p. 156; also see p. 175 on Quine's use of intensional notions he officially disowns.

[138] For Davidson's efforts, see 'Moods and Performances' in *ITI*.

[139] D. Davidson, 'Epistemology Externalised', *SIO*, p. 195.

and some defenders of the analytic-synthetic distinction hold that we need to maintain such distinctions as between revising a definition (the conceptual part) and changing a postulate (factual component) in order to keep track of what a theory is about at a given time. If logical propositions are nothing more than *contingent* extrapolations from experience we run the danger of losing not simply the mind, but the reality of propositional states themselves.[140]

The preceding argument suggests that we run into serious difficulties if we do not take meanings seriously. Their variance according to truth conditions is real, which is not to say that they are reducible to the latter. The loss of the analytic-synthetic distinction involved a loss of confidence with respect to what theories and statements are really about, with the result that warrant transfer becomes difficult. *The question that needs to be asked is whether a variant of the analytic-synthetic distinction can be retained, without returning to the 'pernicious mentalism' we rightly distrust.*

In order to preserve a notion of analyticity, we must reject what is truly problematic about it, namely the notion of truth in virtue of meaning. Davidson's description of the links between meaning, truth and belief suggests that it is anachronic to suppose that something bears meaning in and of itself, apart from the sustaining activity of critical agents. Meaning is an emerging property, not some mental entity. However, he has not been able to give a coherent account of how meaning is fixed by appealing exclusively to truth conditions. Something besides truth conditions is necessary and Davidson seems aware of this lack.[141]

Both Davidson and Marshall feel the need to break the truth-conditional circle, since both are intuitively aware that there is such a thing as one's deviation from a normative meaning. Thus the former speaks about the autonomy of meaning, while Marshall countenances the notion of a normative practice which itself fixes the meaning of words and sentences. They thus both imply that some variation must be allowed between what a speaker considers to be the truth conditions of a sentence and what it's 'real' truth conditions are. But in such a behaviourist context it is incoherent to speak about a 'real' meaning, or even a literal meaning. If all we can go on are dispositions towards behaviour, then there is nothing qualitatively different on offer which could help us isolate such a normative meaning. We might, as Marshall probes, see the native as part of a larger community where a distinctive practice fixes an inner-social meaning. But then there is the question of the borders of such a community. At which point does one community end and another one begin, where the practices which purportedly fix meaning may lead to a different normative meaning? Furthermore, even within a community or a tradition practices differ and so do notions of what is or what isn't normative for

[140] Piers Rawling, 'Radical Interpretation' in Kirk Ludwig (ed.), *Donald Davidson* (Cambridge: Cambridge University Press, 2003), pp. 105-109.

[141] D. Davidson, *ITI*, p. 131.

meaning. Should this not be the case, then Marshall would not have felt the need to write such a book about epistemic justification. The way he solves the issue should sound strange to a thoroughgoing holist. One cannot simply say, as he does, that the Holy Spirit inculcates such practices and virtues in the saints which contribute to a normative meaning. How does one discern the meaning of the Holy Spirit's action within the community in the first place? Is it self evident? What is also required is a specifically theological critique of Marshall's proposal, which must be the task of another essay, since he consciously departs from Davidsonian semantics. However, he does not affirm his departure at this point in his argument.

We can begin to answer the question about what fixes meaning by rediscovering *a pragmatic-linguistic notion of analyticity*.

Quine's circularity objection to analyticity claimed that the notion is suspicious since it relies on other intensional notions, neither of which could be explained without appeal to its intensional relatives. It must be granted that the concept of analyticity relies heavily on that of convention and synonymy. But since we have already given up trying to secure a notion of truth in virtue of meaning, having some circularity is not detrimental. We are not trying to 'discover' those notions knowledge of whose meaning involves accepting their truth. What we are after is a way of isolating the conceptual content of sentences and a way of separating, for each language those statements which have a special conceptual component from those who also have empirical content.

Several thinkers have recently suggested a refurbishment of the analytic-synthetic distinction. Glock and Michael Hymers propose that we rethink analyticity as something involved with learning a language. Glock points out that Quine also believes that there is a difference between analytic and synthetic statements, although it lacks any epistemic explanatory value.[142] Both believe that necessary propositions do not follow from the meaning of words, they rather determine it. Such propositions form what we may call a 'semantic context' to which words belong and which determines the meaning of those words. There is thus a special conceptual link between certain words and sentences. Such conceptual links are learned together with language and in fact some are stronger while others are weaker or less sedimented, less salient. Quine might say less agreed upon. Part of our argument has been that *we have to retain a space of limited conceptual sovereignty, above the hustle and bustle of empirical exchanges*. However, there is nothing mysterious about this special conceptuality, it does not have any necessary link with truth. Such sovereignty is limited in the sense that it can be contested. But to change its axioms is to

---

[142] W. v. O. Quine, *Ways of Paradox and Other Essays* (Cambridge, Mass. and London: Harvard University Press, 1976), p. 113; cf. Gibson, *Enlightened Empiricism: An Examination of W. v. Quine's Theory of Knowledge* (Tampa: University Presses of Florida, 1988), pp. 93-6.

change the language. What is important is that at any given time we need to be able to distinguish the contribution of this conceptuality from that of the world, precisely in order to make better sense of both. Such conceptual links determine the grammar of a language or linguistic practice.

Wittgenstein stipulated that such 'internal relations' obtain only between instruments of language,[143] by which he means words, gestures, behaviour expressions and so on, and not between words and objects in the world, or as Putnam has it, between words and their reference. Hymers builds on Wittgenstein's disparate meditations upon internal relations which actually make an interesting lesson.

In his transition from the *Tractatus* to the *Logical Investigations*, Wittgenstein made several attempts to clarify the notion of internal relations. Initially he gives it an epistemic twist, in the *Tractatus*: a relation is internal if it is unthinkable that its *relata* should not be so related. Internal relations are thus links that are patient of discovery. This view sits well with his analysis of logical form and the picture theory of meaning. By the *Philosophical Grammar*, however, he became increasingly dissatisfied with this interpretation since it transforms linguistic and mental signs into something mysterious. The very existence of such an isomorphism is hard to establish, let alone explain. His later work, starting with the *Philosophical Grammar* attempts to remove the aura of mystery by integrating words in a larger system of language, where they function as signs in a calculus. The reason why a sign means what it does owes a lot to its being part of a grammar. The difference from the earlier view also involves the claim that only instruments of language can be internally related. The initial epistemic criterion is further revised so that two concepts are internally related if in order to understand one I must understand the other. By this stage it is clear that an internal relation is not *contained* in the 'meaning' of individual terms, but it is *constitutive* of those meanings. Hymers notes that a sharp distinction between the analytic and the synthetic is lingering here, or between the tautologies of logic (the rules of the calculus) and empirical propositions.[144] The *Philosophical Investigations* introduces a further qualification of this view in the sense that languages are only analogically similar to a calculus. The rules of a calculus do not apply with the same precision in language. People have a habit of breaking such rules. Indeed, this is precisely one of Davidson's objections to linguistic rules. Wittgenstein, however, does not feel compelled to drop the whole metaphor, but merely to advise caution. To understand a word is still to be able to use it correctly, but correctness amounts to accord with public criteria that vary in precision from word to word. This variation results from their being embedded in complex human practices.

---

[143] L. Wittgenstein, *Philosophical Investigations*, paras. 569, 16.

[144] Michael Hymers, *Philosophy and Its Epistemic Neuroses* (Boulder: Westview Press, 2000), p. 41.

It looks as if Wittgenstein is more accommodating than Davidson with respect to language. Analyticity is not an epistemic property. Discovering analyticity is not to discover something which has, so to speak, an independent ontological existence. It is a linguistic-pragmatic rule of language, which constitutes the meaning of some words and sentences. By creating a semantic context, it gives the rules for how some instruments of language are to be used. However, as Wittgenstein notes, some linguistic rules are followed more closely than others. Abandoning some of these rules may mean changing the language, but that really depends on how stable we expect that language to be in the first place. Crucially, however, there are certain such rules which operate in a language and which are learnt together with it. Such rules are transparent and are not contingent upon experience in the same way empirical sentences are. To change them is to change the language, although this will rarely happen. The point is that at any given time these rules are transparent for most people who master a language.[145]

What does this mean for our argument? We hope to have shown that there are 'semantic and logical contexts' which are learned together with language – through linguistic rules and practices such as analyticity. These *semantic contexts* rule what is meaningful to do with certain instruments of language.[146] A level of *normativity* is thus introduced in the process of justification, inference and scientific explanation. Such normativity is temporary and local, but it is nonetheless real. We are not left clueless about which statements to modify in light of new beliefs. Such new beliefs, through the concepts they employ, project a semantic context which illuminates our epistemic decisions. Yet such semantic contexts are neither exclusively, nor primarily deduced from experience.

Charity and Epistemic Dependence

If there is no such restriction on the use of intensional notions, we no longer need to rely so heavily on the principle of charity for the ascription of meaning. In fact, it can be shown that the principle itself is problematic. It follows that Marshall's use of 'assimilative power' as a justification device is redundant in this particular shape. While his application of the principle results in an unintentional return to a type of epistemic dependence, a revised principle of charity is less threatening to theology.

For Donald Davidson, the principle of charity is our only hope of interpreting the speech of others, given the interdependence of meaning, truth and belief. Interpreters should thus hold for truth while testing for meaning.

---

[145] See Davidson's critique of rule following in 'Communication and Convention', *ITI*, *passim*.

[146] See H. –J. Glock, p. 95: *some* connections must be internal rather than external and some propositions conceptual rather than factual.

This can be accomplished by maximising agreement with natives. Davidson's talk about maximising agreement is part of his initial espousal of charity. This maximisation sets it apart from Quine's own principle of charity, which only applies to the translation of logical constants and to empirical observation sentences. But, since for Davidson the line between theoretical statements and empirical ones is harder to draw, he insists on applying charity across the board.

Later on Davidson began to connect charity with his transcendental argument against the sceptic.[147] If we only held for truth for interpretative reasons it could turn out that our interpretation has been wrong if the interpretees are wrong. The transcendental argument holds that this cannot actually be the case for most of the native's beliefs, or ours for that matter. Davidson has thus supplemented an initial heuristic principle with an *a priori* assumption about human beings.

The problem with the argument, as Sosa and Glock point out, is that it has not managed to defuse the sceptical threat.[148] For Sosa, Davidson fails to distinguish between (a) dispositions to appropriate verbal behaviour and (b) the process or processes that have caused such dispositions in a certain speaker.[149] He takes it for granted that such dispositions have been acquired in the presence of the objects of belief themselves. But it is entirely contingent that such dispositions have been acquired in this way. It may be, Sosa writes, that the disposition may have been there innately, or, it might be added, that it has been taught by description or some other way. This poses a problem for the transcendental argument such that the only conclusion one might draw is that 'the relevant requirement for possession of a concept – say, a recognitional concept – is only one's hosting a disposition that makes for differential sensitivity to the presence or absence of exemplars. And such a disposition *need not* have been acquired through causal interaction with actual exemplars'.[150]

It may be pointed out that Davidson could not have suggested the transcendental argument were it not for his union between meaning and truth conditions. But some people meaningfully hold beliefs and concepts without being able to precisely give truth conditions for them. Examples such as religious beliefs, scientific theories, ethical propositions come to mind.

In all events, *it seems underestablished that we have to treat believers as having mostly true beliefs*. Davidson seems to have realised this and has consequently modified charity into an argument about the general plausibility,

---

[147] D. Davidson, 'Three Varieties of Knowledge', *SIO*, p. 210.

[148] Ernest Sosa, 'Knowledge of Self, Others, and World', in Kirk Ludwig, (ed.), *Donald Davidson*, pp. 172-3; 176-9.

[149] E. Sosa, 'Knowledge of Self, Others, and World', p. 176.

[150] E. Sosa, 'Knowledge of Self, Others, and World', p. 176.

or veridicity of belief.[151] Interpretation does not require that others are mostly right, but only that they are mostly justified in their beliefs. We thus no longer have to *maximise* agreement, but rather to *optimise* it.

Glock notes that even after Davidson reverted to an 'optimal charity', he still insisted on applying it across the board.[152] However, such an insistence is unwarranted – *in terms of his transcendental argument at least.* The whole point about charity is that we can associate the behaviour of speakers with events or objects in the world that are accessible to both speaker and interpreter and thus treat these as the causes of common beliefs. However, for quite a large part of our beliefs such causes are not available, since the beliefs in question might more theoretical than empirical. Its empirical content is, in other words, derived through a long process of inference which makes it difficult to isolate in a context of radical interpretation. The difference in the degree of empirical content[153] that a given sentence may have is thus essential for radical interpretation and charity. Such a taxonomy belongs to the rules of a language. No intrinsic factual content must be assumed other than the fact that it must be transparent for the speakers of a given language at a given time that a certain sentence is more or less theoretical or more or less empirical. No mysterious referential link is presupposed.

Despite Davidson's proclaimed holism, he still thinks there is a difference between our simplest, plainest empirical beliefs and the more theoretical ones. He takes the difference to be one of degree rather than one of kind.[154] But this should be enough for our purposes: charity need only be applied, according to the transcendental argument, in the simplest *perceptual* cases.[155] It follows that even if the transcendental argument is right, we do not have to treat all of the alien beliefs as true in order to make progress in interpreting them, but only the 'simplest perceptual beliefs'. It is wrong to apply charity across the board since the whole point is to hold for truth, but this is possible only for certain types of belief.

The modification of the argument is both a great deal more plausible, as well as less original. The question is no longer one of 'assimilating' theoretical beliefs, or finding ways to hold them true, but one of *perceiving the inferential chain which leads the alien to hold them on the basis of simpler observational*

---

[151] D. Davidson, 'A Coherence Theory', p. 153; 'Afterthoughts', p. 155.

[152] H. –J. Glock, *Quine and Davidson*, p. 196.

[153] There is nothing mysterious about this degree and it is in fact compatible with both Quine's notion of statements which seem particularly germane to experience ('Two Dogmas of Empiricism', *The Philosophical Review* 60 (1951), p. 43, reprinted in *From a Logical Point of View*) and Davidson's (see next note).

[154] D. Davidson, 'A Coherence Theory', *SIO*, p. 152, admits of 'degrees of observationality on internal grounds.'

[155] D. Davidson, 'A Coherence Theory', 151; 'Three Varieties of Knowledge', *SIO*, p. 213; 'Epistemology Externalised', *SIO*, p. 196.

beliefs. The closer we are to the centre, the less agreement should be expected. Alasdair MacIntyre suggests a similar argument about the need to narrate the successes and failures of an alien tradition.[156] This is not necessarily having to agree with it, but simply to credit it for trying.[157]

Returning to Marshall, he is wrong to consider disagreement with theoretical beliefs such as the belief in evolution detrimental to our willingness to hold certain beliefs as epistemically primary. It was this overzealousness to apply charity to all types of belief which forced him back to epistemic dependence. On the other hand, this reading of Davidson would only require him to maximise agreement with the empirical beliefs lying at the foundation of theoretical propositions. At this basic level agreement can be maximised (although there is plenty of room for disagreement here too) while leaving space for differences about the sorts of theoretical conclusions that might be drawn from it.

Interpretation has to recognise a basic level of human characteristics. Among these is the notion of meaning. Even if intensional notions like meaning would be discredited (as Quine would want) and there would be an extensionality requirement on interpretation, still charity would need only to optimise agreement with empirical beliefs. As for the theoretical statements, the type of agreement cannot be specified by charity. We can certainly treat it as a methodological *aid* in interpretation, although by no means as a necessary and sufficient *constraint* upon it.

We conclude that although there is significant promise in Marshall's employment of a truth-conditional theory of meaning, there are also important reasons of concern with respect to the ability of such a theory to account for justification. While the deconstruction of a reified notion of language is most welcome, more room must be made for intensional notions such as meaning and analyticity, for in their absence it becomes increasingly difficult to isolate the content of a belief and to make warrant transfer transparent. Marshall has done theology another service in disentangling post-liberal theology from fideism, although he may have unwittingly re-created epistemic dependence. Furthermore, judged from the perspective of the same post-liberal thought, he has contributed to our disenchantment with the linguistic metaphor which has captured the imagination of theology for the past couple of decades. However, there is still a positive role for language, meanings, conventions and analyticity in theology and in this respect both Marshall and Davidson are more austere than is actually warranted. Keeping such notions on board reveals a normative component of justification, although it is important to remember that this normativity is relative to a linguistic community.

---

[156] Alasdair MacIntyre, *Whose Justice? Which Rationality?* (Notre Dame: University of Notre Dame Press, 1988), chapters XVII and XVIII, esp. p. 362.

[157] The type of justification involved here is clearly deontological.

Publicity and Spirit-Wrought Practices: Meaning as Use

Marshall's careful engagement with recent neo-pragmatism, especially with Donald Davidson, revealed certain problematic features of both foundationalism as well as post-liberalism. To understand that meaning is conceptually dependent on truth (or at least verification) is to be suspicious both of foundationalist attempts to justify Christian theological claims by reference to 'alien' epistemic priorities, and of textualist confidence in the intra-narrative generation of meaning, quite apart from an investigation of truth.

Marshall also helps put to rest a certain garden variety of the latter position, which takes religious beliefs to be pragmatically justified by their results. This is the so-called 'pragmatic thesis', which holds that 'successful practice on the part of the Christian community and its members helps to *justify* the community's central beliefs.' It follows that the epistemic bearing of practice is not to be found at the level of the justification of beliefs. Where practice does indeed have an epistemic bearing, for Marshall, is in fixing the meaning of religious language. The meaning of Christian theological beliefs is fixed by those practices, created and sustained by the Holy Spirit, which are constitutive of the community that calls itself Church.

This section critically discusses this aspect of Marshall's theological proposal. Does Marshall succeed in making coherent his account of how meaning is fixed? This is a rather particular instance of a broader question: in what sense must meaning be public? Engaging with Marshall's proposal will illuminate what possible avenues there are towards answering the broader question.

Here is an outline of the argument. We will first present Marshall's proposal that while meanings depend in large measure on how we use sentences in practical contexts, there is a certain *normative meaning* which is autonomous and remains fixed across practical differences. What fixes that meaning are the Spirit-wrought practices. However, we argue that this does not sufficiently establish normativity. It will be shown that Marshall has pushed himself into a semantic corner by a certain interpretation of the 'publicity of meaning' and what this requires of a meaning theory, namely extensional adequacy. We suggest that 'modesty' should characterise a theory of meaning and that the Bible, together with the Spirit-wrought practices forms an intensional context where religious meanings are fixed.

Meaning and Normativity

Marshall follows Davidson and Dummett in requiring a 'non question-begging' theory of interpretation. Briefly put, this means that a theory of interpretation (as well as one of meaning, although they are not the same) should not make illicit appeal to the intentions and beliefs of the speaker, for these are themselves possessed of semantic content. It was Wittgenstein's private language argument which underscored the difficulty of tying meaning to private mental states. If these epistemically private items cannot form the basis for a theory of meaning, the only knowledge to which a theory of meaning can appeal to must be fully manifested in practice. Hence the notion that meaning is public.

As we shall see, there are differences between the way in which Davidson and Dummett construe this requirement of extensionality. If an interpretation theory is to be non-circular in this way, its only hope of interpreting the speech of others is to pay attention to the practical contexts in which sentences are used. One should, if one is a follower of Davidson, correlate practical situations to which a speaker may be interpreted as assenting to, with his words. If we apply the principle of charity we can suppose that the speaker is reacting to the same aspects of the environment that we are reacting to. Since Davidson believes that a theory of truth can be pressed in the service of a theory of meaning, having the truth conditions is equivalent to having the meaning.

The only way in which to get at meaning is to hold for truth when paying close attention to the speaker's actions. The obvious problem with such an account is its holism. If meaning is given by the use to which we put our words, there is no way in which two people mean the same, or even similarly, by the same words and sentences. This would imply an ironic return to semantic privacy, but it might equally well be interpreted as sheer semantic indeterminacy. There must be a sense in which meaning is invariant across practice. Marshall is well aware of this problem and it precludes a certain interpretation of Wittgenstein's famous dictum that 'meaning is use'.

There is an important sense in which meaning does not depend on practice, writes Marshall. He calls this principle the 'autonomy of meaning'. Using Frege's distinction between sense, force and point, he shows that point cannot fix the sense, for knowledge of point partly depends on knowledge of sense.[158] So, we can identify a speaker's purposes and intentions, but also the point of what he is saying, only after we have identified the sense of his words. The surprising conclusion follows: 'Thus in a non-question-begging theory of meaning it is not so much the use of sentences – the extra-linguistic purposes for which they are uttered – which gives the interpreter their meaning, but the meaning which gives their use.'[159] Marshall seems to have completely inverted the priorities. Is he returning to a psychologism which mistakes meanings for private mental acts which are distinguishable apart from their being manifested in practice? Not quite.

While 'the meaning of sentences and the purposes for which they are uttered vary independently of one another',[160] Marshall still ponders 'how the practices

[158] B. D. Marshall, *Trinity and Truth*, p. 195.
[159] B. D. Marshall, *Trinity and Truth*, p. 196.
[160] B. D. Marshall, *Trinity and Truth*, p. 197.

of speakers as different as the crusader and St. Francis might fix the meaning of "Christus est Dominus" as uttered by each, without surreptitious or premature appeals to their intentions and purposes.'[161] It is not difficult to spot an ambiguity here. While a few pages back Marshall uses 'practice' interchangeably with 'intentions' and 'purposes', here he clearly distinguishes between them. What is the difference? Marshall does not make this explicit, yet grasping the distinction is vital for understanding what he is up to here. In the first instance, we conjecture, practice means an activity that I intentionally engage in with a certain purpose that I am well aware of. In the second instance, on the other hand, a practice is something that people might engage in without being fully aware of all that is involved in it, e.g. an institutional practice. Whilst they might have their own intentions and purposes, there is an overarching rationality attaching to that practice, of which they might be ignorant.

This may be what Marshall has in mind when he speaks of total practice.[162] We can only interpret the sentences of people like the crusader and St. Francis, with their hugely different practical manifestations, on the backdrop of a 'total practice'. Such a total practice will give the meaning of their sentences in the language, in this case Latin. Once we have established this it is easy to see their divergence as being moral rather than semantic.[163]

The question of what 'Christus est Dominus' means depends on the question of what is the total practical context which fixes its meaning. Divergent practices apparently point to different meanings, but the principle of the autonomy of meaning requires that what a sentence means remains fixed across practical variations. Marshall is forced to call upon the notion of a *normative* practical context, for in the absence of such a context it would be impossible to hold on to the objectivity and publicity of meaning.

It is at this point that Marshall thinks we have 'a first take on the epistemic role of the Spirit'. 'The Spirit creates a community – the church – structured by specific practices, and primarily these practices have to guide any effort to fix the meaning of this community's most central beliefs.'[164] The Spirit creates 'a community of speakers on whose lips these sentences have the meanings they must in order to identify [the Father and the Son].'[165] In order for such practices to be normative, they have to be fully controlled by the Spirit:

[161] B. D. Marshall, *Trinity and Truth*, p. 198. In what follows we shall use the notorious example of the utterance 'Chritus est Dominus' as hypothetically used by a crusader when killing a muslim cleric, first mentioned by Lindbeck, *The Nature of Doctrine*, p. 64.

[162] B. D. Marshall, *Trinity and Truth*, pp. 198ff.

[163] B. D. Marshall, *Trinity and Truth*, p. 201.

[164] B. D. Marshall, *Trinity and Truth*, p. 202.

[165] B. D. Marshall, *Trinity and Truth*, p. 203.

> The Spirit instructs the church – and thereby also the world – in the meanings of its own beliefs by his total mastery of the practical situations in which the community and its members (and indeed all human beings) speak. Since the Spirit creates and rules the total situation in which the relevant utterances are made, the meaning of those utterances depends primarily on the action of the Spirit himself, and only secondarily on that of the free human agents who make them.[166]

The significance of this epistemic and theological move cannot be overestimated, not only because it arguably established a normative context, but the manner in which such a context is deemed authoritative, namely by the action of the Holy Spirit. However, there are several reasons why Marshall's solution is inadequate on its own grounds.

Has Normativity Been Sufficiently Established?

The intention behind the above argument has been to establish a normative context for meaning. But since an interpretation theory must be non-circular, i.e. it must not presuppose the knowledge of other intensional notions (for those too have to be interpreted), it must come up with an extensional context. Marshall builds on Davidson's notion of 'prompted assent'[167] of a speaker in a given practical situation. It is essential for Marshall's and Davidson's argument that this prompted assent is itself patient of extensional description. In order for practice to give us a way into meaning, we must be able to characterise that practice in non-semantic terms. Marshall thinks this means that practice has to be characterisable without appeal to intentions and purposes. This is the reason for his apparently mixed feelings about it: on the one hand practice does not give meaning, on the other hand there is a total practice which fixes meaning. *The logical conclusion should be that the total practice – as opposed to local and intentional practices – possesses a quality which suits it for the task of radical interpretation. That quality is that it can be characterised in purely extensional terms.*

Marshall does not put the issue in quite these terms. He does not feel forced to because he does not make explicit the implicit ambiguity in his use of 'practice'. This ambiguity is not merely incidental to his project and in these terms the question should now be: can total practice be characterised purely extensionally? Marshall describes this desired non-question-begging constraint in terms of a prohibition to appeal to intentions and purposes. Yet when he switches to 'total practice', there is no explanation of what non-circularity means here. For the very nature of total practice is that it somehow transcends the intentions and purposes of particular people. Indeed, that is precisely what partly makes it suitable for establishing a *normative* context.

---

[166] B. D. Marshall, *Trinity and Truth*, p. 203.
[167] B. D. Marshall, *Trinity and Truth*, p. 95.

Austerity with regard to intentions and purposes is only a consequence of a methodological austerity with regard to intensions generally. However, intensional items are not exhausted by intentions and purposes. Finding a 'total practice' which is characterisable without the help of intentions does not mean that such a practice is characterisable without the help of other notions which are themselves intensional. Such notions as the *rationality* of a given practice, the worldview it presupposes, its logic etc. are indispensable to the description of a practice. This is precisely what distinguishes a practice from a mere action, on the one hand, or from a simple bodily movement, on the other. Although this is an important argument in the philosophy of practice, there is not enough space here to defend it. What should be enough to establish our case is to show that, *given the extensional limitation which he adopts, Marshall cannot adequately characterise 'total practice' without appealing to these other intensional items*. This would show that his account is circular, even if it does not employ intentions and purposes.

The question, briefly put, is *how do we sort practices into normative and non-normative if we deny ourselves the notion of content (which is intensional)?* How, in other words, should we be able to speak about Spirit-wrought practices without invoking a whole ontology and world-view? Marshall is briefly aware of the difficulty of sorting out practices when he writes:

> We cannot found our ascription of meanings, beliefs and intentions to speakers only on those practices which seem to have a moral bearing, anymore than we can weed out morally charged practices in the hope of showing that what a person's words mean floats free of the moral context in which he speaks. Such efforts are alike bootless because we can only discriminate between morally significant and insignificant practices, and between good and evil practices, *by* deciding what speakers mean.[168]

Given this realisation it is difficult to understand on what basis we *can* discriminate between Spirit-wrought practices and, say, ideologically distorted ones (to invoke a favourite beating-horse).

Marshall's argument is that deciding what the crusader and St. Francis mean depends on finding the most plausible interpretation of speakers of Latin on the whole. This might throw some light on why Marshall does not think it is problematic to distinguish between Spirit-ual practices and the rest in that such practices constitute a community with its own beliefs, practices, and indeed language. In other words it would not be problematic to distinguish between such practices if their difference would be the result of difference between geographically distinct communities. But this is itself question-begging. How can we distinguish, within a common natural language, between different communities save by appealing to their beliefs? How might the difference

[168] B. D. Marshall, *Trinity and Truth*, p. 202.

between their practices be thickly described other than by invoking the very rationality of those practices?

It is impossible to make even a quantitative distinction between practices without invoking some intensional context. Marshall's *implied* analogy between Spirit-wrought practices and the practices associated with a natural language obscure the fact that the (at least moral) difference between practices is not readily visible, thus extensionally available. He was ready to accept this when rejecting the bearing on practice on epistemic justification: 'virtue is distributed in roughly equal measure among the world's religions.'[169] However, if we are able to distinguish between religions, languages and communities, we have a 'total' context which primarily fixes the meaning.

Even granted that this analogy would hold (which is indeed problematic), it would still not establish that normative context. Marshall optimistically assumes that we are readily able to tell Latin speakers apart from speakers of, say, German. How do I know when two people whose language I have never heard before speak the same language? It is surely not enough to watch out for similarities between their vocal output. There is always the possibility that differences would show up. When that happens, do I treat these as evidence that they speak different languages, or as divergence in assignment of truth, or indeed as simply different ways of saying the same thing? It is not possible to infer that two speakers speak the same language merely from their vocal and behavioural propensities.

Let us turn now to the very concept of Spirit-wrought practices. Our argument has been that we cannot distinguish between practices in this way, i.e. without using intensional notions. Had these practices been easily identifiable (which is why the linguistic analogy was implied), there might have been some hope for Marshall's Davidsonian project. However, it is very difficult to decide which are those practices, and decide we must if we want to have a normative context. A further complication arises when one considers what appears to be a 'reification' of practice in Marshall. The notion that practices are available quite independently of how they are instantiated by particular people is dubious. A thick description of such practices is only possible by paying attention to all their use. Otherwise we run the risk of returning to the notion of meanings floating free of the actions of people. This is precisely what Marshall resists. However, it might be objected, a thick description of practice is precisely what we do *not* need. For such a description brings intensional notions with it. What we should be after, some argue, is a *parallel* description of practice which, if it could be accomplished, would give the meaning of the sentences employed. This is a parallel description because its result is *equivalent* to the sort of thick description that employs meanings/ intensions/ rationality/ ontology and so on. Its equivalency comes down to the fact that

---

[169] B. D. Marshall, *Trinity and Truth*, p. 188.

were such a practice learnt by someone, such a person would *ipso facto* know the meanings of the sentences.

This type of argument will be explored in a later section. It has been put forward by Michael Dummett and it's the best chance of making coherent Marshall's proposal. Yet it derives from a certain understanding of the publicity of meaning. The following two sections will therefore ask: what does it mean that meaning is public and what should this entail for a theory of interpretation?

The Publicity of Meaning

The success of Marshall's argument, we have proposed, rests on making plausible a description of practice which – because it is extensionally adequate – illuminates meaning and also gives us a head start in interpretation. It was suggested that his particular attempt to provide such a description fails. The distinction between practices created by the Holy Spirit and other, more mundane human behaviour depends on intensional categories. This is not to say that all such descriptions should fail. The next section will scrutinise Michael Dummett's attempt to give an extensional description of practice which is relevant for meaning. However, both Dummett and Marshall understand the requirement of extensionality as a consequence of their understanding of how meaning is public.

An examination of what the public nature of meaning involves is therefore essential to our thesis. This inquiry also has a broader interest for theology. The complexity of the issue of 'publicity' will discourage theologians from too easily jumping on certain bandwagons. It is misleading to speak of trends in theology, especially today when the field looks to be in such disarray. However, ever since the so-called 'demise' of epistemology, emphasis has shifted from mental states and inwardness to outward linguistic behaviour and practices. The debate around naturalised epistemology is well known. Although theology has been rather hesitant with regard to naturalism (not without reason), it has nonetheless cheerfully embraced certain aspects of pragmatism. A main impetus of this drive has been Wittgenstein's argument against private language.

While it is easy to see what Wittgenstein was polemicising against, it is much more difficult to understand the positive side of his arguments that meaning is use and that it is public. It is one thing to insist that meanings cannot be said to depend on private mental items, or sensations, or private reference. It is quite another to say in what it *does consist*. It is one thing to insist that meanings cannot be taken as hypotheses that we reconstruct through a 'precarious adventure of inference from [people's] outward demeanor.'[170] On this there seems to be widespread agreement, at least among followers and interpreters of Wittgenstein.

[170] F. Kerr, *Theology After Wittgenstein*, p. 85.

What is not readily accepted are the positive entailments of these denials, which Marshall and Dummett propose. *The relevance of this inquiry for the present project is that how we understand the public character of meaning determines what an interpreter has at her disposition to interpret the speech of others.*

Marshall's understanding of the publicity of meaning comes out in the following: 'if linguistic meaning is to be public – if, that is, a speaker means just what an interpreter can correctly make out – then what fixes the meaning of sentences for the speaker has to be just the same as what fixes it for the interpreter.'[171] Meaning, it is argued, is not fixed differently for the speaker than how it is fixed for the interpreters. A speaker does not have privileged access to private contents which would fix the meaning of his words in a different way than his interpreters. As we shall see, Davidson does not share Marshall's restrictions. This construal of publicity is in fact dependant on that of verifiability. If we were to draw a parallel to the discussion of truth, where some argue that truth has to be epistemic, Marshall (and Dummett) argues that meaning has to be epistemic. If meaning is public, then by this definition of publicity, *we cannot know meaning without knowing that we know it.* Our ability to know meaning depends on our ability to verify that we have correctly ascertained it. This is the upshot of Marshall's explanation of publicity: 'a speaker means just what an interpreter can *correctly* make out.' It is difficult to understand the role of 'correctly' here if we were to interpret it in a non-epistemic way. Its force derives from the fact that what fixes the speaker's meaning cannot transcend the epistemic abilities of an interpreter.

Marshall does not make the verificationist connection explicit here. He is in fact suspicious of Dummett's anti-realism. However, for the former, the fault in Dummett's anti-realism does not lie with his notion of publicity (where we think it lies), but in the transition from the manifestability of meaning to the modification of the notion of truth in truth-conditions. Furthermore, Marshall underestimates the difference between Dummett and Davidson on the theory of interpretation.[172]

Witness this approving comment: 'like Davidson, [Dummett] agrees with Wittgenstein that meaning is use in at least one important sense which can be assigned to that multivalent dictum: meaning is public in that "the knowledge in which a speaker's understanding of a sentence consists must be capable of being fully manifested by his linguistic practice."'[173] The question Marshall still has to answer and which the above statement clarifies is this: what is that which has to be readily available in order to be used in understanding others?

---

[171] B. D. Marshall, *Trinity and Truth*, p. 197.

[172] On this topic, see Dummett's appendix to 'What Is a Theory of Meaning? (I)'; McDowell, *Meaning, Knowledge, and Reality* (Cambridge: Harvard University Press, 2001), pp.103ff, 122ff.

[173] B. D. Marshall, *Trinity and Truth*, p. 103.

Now, from the starting point – widely accepted – that meaning cannot be fixed by private mental states, to this 'manifestation argument', we have taken two huge steps. A critique of publicity can help itself to any of these steps, and indeed there might be others, as yet undetected. It is one thing to say that meaning cannot be private. It is quite another to say that its publicity consists in the fact that what a speaker means is nothing more than what interpreters can correctly ascribe to him. And it is still another thing to say that meaning is public *if and only if* the knowledge in which a speaker's understanding consists in must be *fully* manifested in his practice. The attentive reader might have spotted the 'mistake' in the last sentence. Only a few lines back we quoted Dummett as saying that the knowledge in which a speaker's understanding of a sentence consists 'must be *capable of being fully manifested*.' This intended omission highlights an ambiguity in Dummett's writings on the topic. Commentators like McDowell often point out how Dummett's views seem to change from paper to paper, from volume to volume. This pattern is also obvious on this subject, when Dummett writes on occasion that such knowledge must be fully manifested in practice, not simply capable of being fully manifested. Earlier, in his *Origins of Analytical Philosophy*, Dummett reads Wittgenstein's argument against private languages thus: it does not hold that all thoughts are expressed in language, but that they must be *capable of being expressed* thus. This is absolutely crucial, for it makes possible a distinction between speaker's meaning and literary/ normative meaning, a distinction of great importance.[174] This is also a distinction which Davidson retains, whereas Marshall fails to make explicit.

It seems that the step from the private language argument down to Marshall's and Dummett's understanding of publicity is complicated. The next section follows the implications of this notion of publicity for a theory of interpretation. If meaning is public in this way, what form must an interpretation theory have? Dummett argues that an interpretation theory has to be full-blooded, i.e., it must not presuppose knowledge of the concepts expressed by words. It follows that an interpretation theory must proceed without intentions, or without availing itself of what McDowell calls 'content'. Such a theory must describe linguistic behaviour as a practical ability in terms of the implicit knowledge that is fully manifested therein. Here we return to Dummett's attempt to give an analysis of practice which is entirely extensional.

---

[174] For reasons of space we will not elaborate on our views, which hold that we must distinguish between speaker's meaning and literary meaning. Davidson's programme, not least through his retention of first person authority, makes this possible. See Davidson, 'First Person Authority', in D. Davidson, *SIO*; for a critique, see P. M. S. Hacker, 'Davidson on First Peson Authority", *The Philosophical Quarterly*, 47/188 (July 1997), pp. 285-304; for a view sympathetic to Davidson's, see Glock, *Quine and Davidson*, pp. 263-267.

We shall show where his analysis fails and what this means for the topic of publicity.

Modesty and Meaning

Dummett combines the Fregean and Wittgensteinian insights that 'meaning is given by truth conditions' and that 'meaning is use' under his notion of understanding.[175] Linguistic ability is a practical ability and a proper description of it must account for both elements: an implicit knowledge of the truth conditions and the practical manifestation of that knowledge. The notion of implicit knowledge[176] is supposed to protect Dummett's programme from the risk of behaviourism.[177] Linguistic ability is content involving, it is intensional. Neither Dummett nor Davidson wish to naturalise language in the way in which Quine attempted. But in a theory of interpretation, argues Dummett, we cannot simply help ourselves to the idea of content[178], for that should be the result of the theory.

If a theory of meaning must give an account of this double aspect, the question is whether a description of the knowledge of sense will take a different form than a description of the practical ability. Dummett thinks it should take a different form, because the implicit knowledge which a speaker has must be fully manifested in his linguistic behaviour. If there is such a full manifestation, then a description of the practical ability will be *equivalent* to a description of meaning.[179] Does this amount to a reduction of meaning to the practical ability? After a few rejoinders, Dummett clarifies the function such a description would play. It is not that knowledge of the theory should give the meaning, but that, should the theory be correct, mastering the practical ability described in it would amount to having a knowledge of the meaning of the sentences.

It is immediately apparent that Dummett's path is extremely risky. On the one hand he does not want to collapse the theory of meaning into behaviourism. On the other, he wants to avoid psychologism. Yet by insisting that the description of the practical ability should take a different form, 'as from outside content', he makes himself vulnerable to behaviourism yet again. It all depends on whether Dummett can make intelligible a description of a practical ability

---

175 M. Dummett, 'What Is a Theory of Meaning? (I)', p. 3.

176 M. Dummett, 'What Is a Theory of Meaning? (II)', pp. 36ff., 'What Do I Know when I Know a Language?', *passim.*

177 M. Dummett, *Seas of Language* (Oxford: Oxford University Press, 1993), pp. 94-97.

178 M. Dummett, *The Logical Basis of Metaphysics* (Cambridge, MA: Harvard University Press, 1993), p. 13.

179 See M. Dummett's discussion of the 'equivalency principle', 'What is a Theory of Meaning? (I)', p. 42.

which, if it were mastered, would be equivalent to one knowing the meanings of the concepts.

Some differences from Marshall's own project should be clarified at this time, before we delve deeper into Dummett's arguments. Marshall does not share Dummett's so-called 'full-bloodedness'. His analysis of practice does not purport to explain the concepts presupposed by the practice to someone who doesn't possess them. His interpretive exercise aims to *assign* concepts, implicitly assuming that such concepts are known. This is evidence that Marshall's project is modest, at least in McDowell's sense. His non-circularity and non-question-begging constraints function as entries into a web which unites sentences with beliefs and intentions. We have to assign beliefs, concepts and meanings. Dummett, on the other hand, insists that a theory of meaning must not take concepts as being something which do not tolerate further analysis. We must not take concepts as being the *end result* of a theory of interpretation. Rather, we have to explain in what a grasp of these concepts consists! This is Dummett's full-blooded emphasis that a description of practice should not help itself to the notion of 'expresses the thought that'. Quite clearly, this is an important difference between their aims. However, while their aims are different, the method by which they hope to achieve them is the same. The question we have set in this section is whether this method of giving a description of practice, without help from intensional notions, works. For Marshall it is supposed to work for the purpose of identifying, assigning, ascribing intensional properties; for Dummett it is supposed to explain in what their grasp consists.

What is deplorable about semantic modesty, according to Dummett, is that it treats language as a code[180] and meanings as hypotheses. A semantic theory should explain in what consists the grasp of a concept by a speaker of a language and not be content with merely assigning meanings. We have to resist this persistent mentalism, or what Putnam has called 'sophisticated mentalism'.[181] 'To be a speaker of language is to be capable of putting one's thoughts into one's words, where others can hear and see them.' This manifestation imperative is what supposedly helps Dummett to fend off psychologism.

The seemingly forced separation of a theory of sense from a theory of a practical ability has lead philosophers like McDowell to suspect that Dummett fails not only in avoiding behaviourism, but also in avoiding psychologism. McDowell argues that it is impossible to have a semantics which attempts to explain the grasp of *all* concepts in terms of practical abilities. Some such concepts would have to be presupposed which means that modesty should not be everywhere deplored. Naturally, Dummett's reply is that what is difficult is

---

[180] M. Dummett, 'What Do I Know when I Know a Language?', pp. 97-99.

[181] Hilary Putnam, 'Meaning Holism', in Lewis E. Hahn, W. V. Quine, Paul A. Schilpp, *The Philosophy of W. v. Quine*, (LaSalle: Open Court, 1986), p. 409.

not also necessarily impossible. He views McDowell's reservations as being defeatist. Therefore McDowell has had to produce more than simply an empirical argument against full-bloodedness, but a quasi-transcendental one, or rather a conceptual one.

Two strands of this critique stand out. One must bear in mind that what Dummett tries to accomplish is a non-semantic description of a practical ability which does not avail itself of the notion of 'expresses the thought that', or of any other intensional notions for that matter. However, the description has to be able to lead one to that implicit knowledge which a speaker has when he uses language. Crucially, however, the description of the practice must not presuppose any aspect of that implicit knowledge. The first strand[182] of McDowell's critique is that such a description of practice cannot represent it as a rational ability, which is what Dummett himself requires.[183] *It is not possible to represent a practical ability as a rational activity if we deny ourselves access to intensions*: 'the involvement of mind in meaningful speech is explicitly recognised only when we describe utterances in terms of content – in terms of thought expressed.'[184] The second strand,[185] in our view much more interesting, is that the transition from the description of the ability to the implicit knowledge (sense) will always be under-determined by the evidence.

Dummett has to describe the practical ability as exhibiting some sort of pattern. But Wittgenstein has convincingly shown that for any pattern that we have there are also other patterns which a particular behaviour could be taken to exemplify, with no way to decide between them. This constitutes a problem for Dummett, for he does not want to treat meanings as hypotheses, but as being public. When one considers this difficulty one cannot but wonder what are meanings if not precarious inferences from a pattern of behaviour? McDowell agrees with him that meanings should not be turned into hypotheses, but is afraid that this is exactly what will happen if we deny ourselves the notion of content. If we introduce this rift between the form of a theory of sense, on the one hand, and of a theory of practical ability, on the other, we will have a hard time bringing them back together, which is surely what Dummett intends as well. It is precisely because meanings must be fully manifested that he puts so much hope on a description of the practical ability, wherein they are supposed to be fully present (implicitly).

If McDowell is right, a representation of practice cannot provide a lynchpin for semantics. It does not give us a foundational access. Authentic description of practice is always conceptual. Practice without concepts is blind, while concepts without practice are empty. Our argument so far has followed the

---

182 J. McDowell, Meaning, Knowledge, and Reality, pp. 112f.

183 M. Dummett, 'What Do I Know when I Know a Language?', *Seas of Language*, p. 104.

184 J. McDowell, *Meaning, Knowledge, and Reality*, p. 94.

185 J. McDowell, *Meaning, Knowledge, and Reality*, pp. 96-97, 114ff.

consequences of a certain understanding of publicity. If we understand publicity as the thought that what fixes the meaning for the speaker must be the same thing that fixes it for the interpreter (Marshall), or as the notion that the knowledge that a speaker has and in which his meaning consists must be fully manifested in his linguistic practice, we will have to treat practice as being capable of non-conceptual description. But, if we are right, no such description of practice is adequate, either as kick-starting interpretation, or as an authentic description of a rational ability. It follows that there was something wrong with the understanding of publicity which issued in full-bloodedness, or with the procedure of derivation, as it may be seen in the following schematisation.

1. If meaning is public (in the above sense), then a theory of interpretation must be full-blooded.
2. Meaning is public (in the above sense)
3. A theory of interpretation must be full-blooded

However, (3) is false. It follows that, if (1) is true, (2) must be false as well, according to Frege's truth-tables. There is no problem with (1). If meaning is public in Dummett's sense, then indeed, we can only interpret in the sense appropriate to this meaning, namely by giving a non-semantic description of the practical ability in which such meanings are fully manifested. But the sense in which meaning is supposed to be public is peculiar: meaning must be public in specific *verificationist* sense, i.e. in the sense that my knowledge of meaning should be entirely verifiable in terms of my ability to master a practical situation. Its publicity consists in interpreters being able to fully and correctly reconstruct it from material that is available to them (practice).

Dummett's question may be rehearsed thus: if communication is possible, what (if anything) must lie open to view, and where? He is after a necessary condition for communication. But he construes communication as the interpreter being able to verify that what he takes the speaker to say is actually what the speaker does say. Verification enters for Dummett into the very definition of communication. But this strikes us as a conceptual definition of communication which does not take into consideration the many instances in which, as Hans Frei said some time ago, 'we can understand more and communicate better [...] than we'll ever be able to understand *how* we understand, or what the conditions of the possibility of our understanding [...] might be'.[186] *Communication somehow transcends our ability to verify the correctness of our semantic grasp.*

If this is true, there is a sense in which whatever is communicated in conversation is partly non-epistemic, in the sense that it is impossible to give a parallel account of it in non-semantic terms. The knowledge which is supposed to be implicit is sometimes impossible to be made explicit.

[186] Hans Frei, *Types of Christian Theology*, p. 86.

Peter Byrne noted that what is required of communication is not that this implicit knowledge is fully manifested in a practical ability but that we simply know some grammar and some vocabulary.[187] There is an absolute irreducibility of meanings. This irreducibility is both conceptual and interpretative. It is not enough to resist naturalising meanings at the level of their definition. It is also important to resist seeking non-semantic equivalencies to meanings as a method of interpretation. Once one understands that a description of practice which does not use intensional notions such as, for example, 'expresses the thought that' is inadequate for interpretation, one will understand that *modesty is not deplorable but inescapable*. This does not necessarily mean that concepts themselves are in no need of elucidation, as if speakers of different languages must necessarily share the same concepts. Dummett is quite right to emphasise that we must not assume possession of the same concepts. Marshall himself appears to inherit Davidson's conceptualism in this respect. He does not even ask whether speakers of different languages will share concepts. Interpretation must not so much clarify concepts, but assign them, assuming they are not problematic. Yet to understand that we need conceptual analysis does not mean that the only such epistemically interesting analysis should follow Dummett's pattern of non-semantic reduction. There might be cases where we need conceptual clarification, but there is nothing that forces such clarification to be naturalised. Instead, it will happen in a web of concepts where relationships between clear concepts and unclear ones issue in greater understanding.[188]

The upshot of the above is another description of publicity. McDowell concludes one of his arguments for modesty: "we should not conceive the outward aspect that matters as something one presents to anyone; one shows one's mind, in one's words, only to those who understand the language.'[189] Glock is congenial on this point: 'nor is there anything unintelligible about the suggestion that our normal understanding of utterances is based not on tacit derivations, but the result of immediate, unreflective perception, albeit one which is the prerogative of those that are proficient in the language concerned.'[190] The practical ability in which meanings result, if it is described 'as from outside content', is simply not sufficiently public. It allows for a

[187] Peter Byrne, *God and Realism*, p. 100. Byrne thinks that Dummett's position rests heavily on verificationism, which is not a workable hypothesis. His interest being with realism, Byrne argues that Dummett's critique of realism via his critique of truth-conditions does not hurt realists since they are not forced to adopt truth-conditional semantics.

[188] This does not ammount to reinventing language as code. The thesis is not that concepts are knowable apart fro their manifestation in use, but that neither concepts, nor practical abilities make sense independently of one other.

[189] J. McDowell, 'Another Plea for Modesty', p. 100.

[190] H. –J. Glock, *Quine and Davidson*, p. 247.

variety of interpretations and is thus not sufficient to fix meaning. Instead, *the practical aspect which matters only becomes relevant once one has learnt a language, that is, only when it is already conceptually dressed.*

To sum up, Dummett's attempt to find a non-semantic description of practice which is useful for interpretation has failed. Although Marshall's and Dummett's theoretical aims are different, achieving them depends on the possibility of full-bloodedness. We thus see no reason why practice – when stripped of content – should be given such a prominent, even foundational role in theology, neither for purposes of justification, nor for purposes of meaning. In the final section of this chapter, we briefly suggest why Scripture is important for establishing a normative context for the meaning of Christian theological sentences.

Anticipating: Scripture as Normative Context

The above argument may also be put in these terms: Marshall failed to establish a normative context for interpretation because practice – as conceived by him – does not *sufficiently* fix meaning. It fails to establish meaning because there are different competing descriptions of this practice. Marshall isolates himself to a semantic corner by denying himself the very elements that can alone make practice both intelligible and normative. It is dubious that an interpreter working with such restrictions could even identify particular communities, save by their geographical separation. It is also improbable that such an interpreter could isolate the central practices of such a community. For all the evidence he could follow might have absolutely nothing to do with those central practices. In other words, the way in which such practices *manifest* the implicit knowledge that guides them may be completely indistinguishable from how other practices manifest a different knowledge. It is *precisely* problems such as these that gave rise to the positivist discussion of religious language. What is there in the public domain (characterised by the positivists as being the empirical domain) which gives the meaning of the religious claims? The pragmatist comment is this: what is there in the *practice* of religious adherents that fixes their meaning? Yet if we strip practice of meanings it is doubtful that we should ever be able to isolate an element up to the task. *The very way of framing the question is inviting scepticism with regard to the distinctiveness of religious meanings. Yet we have encountered no compelling argument that this is how we should frame the question.* One should simply refuse to allow the fixation of meaning to rest on a 'bare practice'.

The practices of the Christian church are distinctive, central, and identity-constituting when one considers what thoughts they express, what realities and experiences they seek to symbolise. That is, they come loaded with meaning. It is only when one considers them as such that they might be useful for interpretation. There are indeed normative practices. But their normativity is not a sociological consequence. These practices have not simply become normative, they have been *given* as normative. There is an initial moment when such practices were taught. The community was commanded to engage in these and it was also given a particular explanation for the practices. Such explanation is itself normative for the church. The normativity of the practices, we suggest, derives from the normativity of the Scriptures.

However, the Scriptures without these Spirit-wrought practices are empty. Scriptures are authoritative descriptions of what the church was already experiencing when it 'received' them. Yet, before they were given, the church engaged in these practices without having a full knowledge (either explicit or implicit) of what they meant. Precisely because the church regards both these practices as well as the Scriptures as coming from the same Holy Spirit, that they mutually illuminate each other.[191] The practices without the Scriptures are blind. Yet in saying that the Scriptures without the practices are empty, we are simply pointing out that the Scriptures are (partly) an explanation of how God is already at move in the world and especially in the church, as the body of Christ, through the Holy Spirit.

Naturally, this sort of normative context does not work as a foundational resource for interpretation. This is why interpretation will always be modest and precarious. The Spirit-wrought practices and the Spirit-inspired Scriptures mutually illuminate each other. There is no entry into this web from only one side. We never have the Scriptures without the practices, nor the practices without the Scriptures.

---

[191] See Vanhoozer's notion of 'theodramatic triangulation': which 'relates what God does in Christ, the Scriptures that present Christ, and the Word-and-Spirit-guided practices of the church, the body of Christ.' ('On the Very Idea of a Theological System: An Essay in Aid of Triangulating Scripture, Church and World', forthcoming).

Chapter 5

A Theological Supplement to Neo-Pragmatism

Experience and Theology

'Right Religious Adjustment'

The previous criticism of the neo-pragmatic obfuscation of experience does not mean that we counsel in favour of a return to the Given. As John McDowell shows, experience happens within a conceptual matrix. A lot of effort has been invested in the defence of the claim that this does not amount to a return to the scheme-content dualism, which Donald Davidson has so aptly dismounted. Nevertheless, the place of language, of conceptuality and of what has been called 'habituation' as indispensable ingredients of any experience must be adequately addressed. From a theological perspective, the claim is that adequate experience of God is only possible on the condition of a certain disposition, rational as well as volitional and that this disposition is dialectically effected: from the divine side under the form of the *effects* of God's actions upon the self, and from the human side, under the form of *participation* in spiritual and ecclesial practices which form a religious or spiritual *second nature* in the believer. This second nature is not simply an effect of a personal relationship to a personal God, but at the same time the pre-condition for any knowledge of God.

This is not necessarily a novel proposal, but its distinctive character derives from its combination of pragmatist and historicist insights with Paul's conviction that only a spiritually transformed person can know God. Implicit in the New Testament understanding of personal relationship with God is a notion of a *transformed disposition*. However, the pragmatist contribution adds that this connection between knowledge and a certain practical propensity is not unique to religious knowledge, but to all forms of knowledge. As we have seen, neo-pragmatism usually transformed this into a linguistic methodologism bordering on relativism. If John McDowell is right, on the other hand, this amounts to a solipsism in which there is no friction between our beliefs and the world. There are plenty of reasons to be cautious about Davidson's optimism that a merely causal account of the relationship between the world and our beliefs will alleviate our sceptical worries.

Of course, the notion that experience must play a prominent part in theology is not a new one. Schleiermacher-inspired liberal theology considered this to be one of their principal methodological principles. Chicago-style socio-historicism also revolved around this maxim. But in Douglas Clyde Macintosh's opinion, there was something fundamentally flawed about these two theological options. Macintosh was mentioned in an earlier discussion about the place of experience in justification. One of his long-lasting goals was to make theology as scientific as chemistry. This cannot be done if one takes experience at its face value. Macintosh's superiority, from our perspective, over, say, William Dean's radically empiricist theology, is that the former treats experience as a means to speaking objectively about what exists independently of our experience. For Dean, as for James, Dewey, Rorty and many other neo-pragmatists as well, historicism means that historical experience is the end of the story. There is no getting beyond this experience. For Macintosh, on the other hand, this is sheer subjectivism and the purpose of working with religious experience was not to treat experience as the measure of religious value, but to describe the object known through it.[1] The failure of liberal theology, according to Macintosh, was its subjectivism. It constitutes a perfectly valid starting point, but its uncritical acceptance of the data of experience robbed it of the necessary means to becoming a truly scientific knowledge. On the other hand, Chicago theologians erred in their constructivism. Theology should not be content with a socio-historical analysis of the development of an idea, for this risks trading in illusions. Such explanations are religiously anaemic and subjective and amounted to a misconstrual of what it means to make theology empirical.[2]

The grand social horizon of Chicago theology was religiously anaemic in the sense that it did not attend to the individual believer's religious experiences. However, such experiences must be verified empirically. Not the entire content of such experiences could be verified empirically, but one must strive as much as possible to establish a relation between *repeated* experiences and their possible real causes. The scientific status of theology hangs on the possibility of establishing *laws* by which the religious object responds to a certain *disposition* of the religious subject.

The idea of 'right religious adjustment' is one of Macintosh's trademark concepts. Just like in the hard sciences, which he unproblematically assumes to be a good model for empirical theology, a serious analysis of experiences reveals that the objects under analysis respond under certain constraints and not others. The theologian, like the scientist, who must learn to discern the *effects* of the object on the measurement apparatus, must learn to discern the proper religious effects on the life of the believer.[3] One of the criticisms addressed to Schleiermacher and to liberal theology was that it had no way to discriminate between rival claims to truth. The concept of a *right* religious adjustment amounts to the claim that there are normative ways to discriminate between

---

[1] G. Dorrien, *The Making of American Liberal Theology*, vol. II, p. 247.

[2] G. Dorrien, *The Making*, vol. II, p. 238.

[3] Macintosh's relation to the revivalist theology and tradition stemming from Jonathan Edwards is illuminating at this point.

experiences, by paying attention to the effects of these experiences on people. Of course, the question is, what s the source of these norms? How do we justify them except by circular appeal to other religious experiences, themselves in need of validation? Here Macintosh seemed to rely strongly on his own (morally optimistic) intuitions about what such proper religious effects should be.

Despite his caution against liberal subjectivism and Chicago-style constructivism, his reliance on his intuitions about values and norms was itself subjective and culturally constructed. As Gary Dorrien notes, for all his realism, his moral optimism seemed incongruous with the Depression era generation of his students and eventually led to the waning of his influence.[4]

But let's return to his realism, for that is precisely the supplement that he thought was required by a proper empirical theology. Not value, but reality must centre theology, proclaimed Macintosh. Unless there really exists a God, independently of our minds and experience, and unless we have revelatory traces of this God, theology is impossible as a scientific discourse. Yet Macintosh was not free from pragmatist influences, from the time of his studies in Chicago. In fact, for the rest of his life he struggled to reconstruct Ritschlian value theory as a theory of reality.[5] He thus accepts the correspondence view of truth, but combines it with a pragmatic criterion for truth: the difference between distinguishing true and false representations consists in their sufficiency for practical purposes. Moreover, realism is taken to be compatible with a pragmatic criterion of intelligibility.[6] So, it is safe to say, that his pragmatism is circumscribed by his realism, in that the latter sets the definition of truth, while the former, if it comes sufficiently close to science, as Macintosh thought it could, provides the instruments.

Macintosh's realism accepts a personal theism in which God exists independently but also in which he responds to a specific human disposition according to laws.

> The positive results of applying the methods of objective empirical science in connection with religious experience will be, primarily, what we may call the laws of revelation, or of salvation. That is, they will be generalized statements of what Reality, or some Factor in reality, can be depended upon to effect in the individual human soul and through its activity, on condition of the maintaining of

[4] G. Dorrien, *The Making*, vol. II, p. 52. Dorrien further observes (253) that by the end of the 30's very few optimists have remained. Interestingly, this coincides with the mass migration to the United States of those European intellectuals fleeing the mounting Nazi storm on the continent, among whom are those logical positivists which played such an important part in the formation of neo-pragmatism.

[5] G. Dorrien, *The Making*, vol. II, p. 241.

[6] V. Anderson, *Pragmatic Theology* (Albany: SUNY, 1998), p. 74.

> that dependably effective attitude which we have called the scientific or right religious adjustment[7]

Several observations are in order: first, revelation is not limited to sacred texts or traditions. Such textual items are important instruments from the past, insofar as they have recorded and preserved the *experiences* of religious people. In this he is obviously a follower of the Chicago anti-essentialist programme: there is no essence of Christianity in the past. Revelation is that effect of the divine which is present in religious experience. Secondly, the catchwords for his scientific methodology are verifiability, dependability and laws. God is fully identifiable as an 'object' of reflection upon experience. As an object he must be depended upon to have certain effects in relation to certain dispositions. Earlier he has said that a 'scientifically minded religious faith' must posit a 'dependable religious factor'.[8]

For Macintosh God is present on the same 'chain of being' with us humans. That is what is presupposed by a scientific theology. Moreover, his realism assumes that there is a single right description of reality. He speaks of 'the realistic apperception, or cognition of the religious Object as a real Being' who is 'causally active within the field of religious experience'[9]. The relationship between human beings and God is not qualitatively different from the relationship between human beings and sense objects: 'There is no more reason, from the point of view of religious experience, to adopt an agnostic or subjectivist interpretation of the Object of religious experience, than there is, from the point of view of sense-experience, to adopt an agnostic or subjectivist interpretation of the objects of sense-perception.'[10]

Before we move on, let us conclude this brief discussion of Macintosh by pointing out our affinities and disagreements: First, his criticism of Schleiermacherian and Chicago subjectivism, respectively constructivism is useful. While we need to have our beliefs in friction with experience, we also need to realise that experience is not a measure of religious value. Experience itself can be illusory, induced, perverted and so on. It would be a mistake to flee from the 'unconstrained coherentism' of a Davidson only to be satisfied with an un-examined anything-goes experientialism. There may be some mileage in the claim that it is precisely his critique of pragmatism and his rejection of James' view of truth, which bring out the consequences of this philosophical ideology.

Secondly, Macintosh's desire for some sort of normativity in the legitimation of experience, regardless of its weak elaboration and misplaced

---

7 D. C. Macintosh, *The Pilgrimage of Faith in the World of Modern Thought* (Calcutta: University of Calcutta, 1931), p. 227.

8 D. C. Macintosh, *Pilgrimage*, 226.

9 D. C. Macintosh, *Theology as an Empirical Science* (New York: Macmillan, 1919), p. 32.

10 D. C. Macintosh, *Theology as an Empirical Science*, p. 32.

reliance on moral intuitionism, is commendable. Moreover, whilst his description of the notion fails to draw sufficiently on other religious traditions, its concentration on aspects of religious conversion is an important contribution to a specifically Christian epistemology of religion.

A third aspect which we haven't done sufficient justice to pertains to his revivalist background. The Edwardsian stress on experience takes the form of a claim about the intelligibility of theological claims, which is also indebted to pragmatism:[11] the meaning of Christian theological claims is related to specific Christian experiences. These experiences are an unavoidable means of describing God.

Despite striking in the right direction, Macintosh's theology is ultimately crippled and, for our purposes, needs to be surpassed for several reasons. It is difficult to miss the fact that he models his scientific methodology on the model of the natural sciences. This is a rather narrow view of the scientific endeavour and – although the sharp post-Diltheyan distinction between *Natur-* and *Geisteswissenschaften* is overworked and has itself been overcome – it is characteristically ignorant of the perspectival and constructive nature of the natural sciences itself.

Second, due to importing this scientific model, God is all too easily transformed into a more or less passive object of knowledge, in the sense that he must be depended upon to *re*-act to a right adjustment. There is not much room for dialectics, in the sense that God may be experienced as absent precisely when we most expect to experience his presence. Ironically, his moral optimism fails to do justice to those experiences of loss, of doubt, of faltering faith – which are experiences of precisely religious people. Even more profoundly, it is sometimes precisely those religious people which experience God's absence that nevertheless refuse to lose faith. In this consists the very paradoxical nature of human existence in relation to the divine. It is just this obstinate clinging on to God *despite all evidences to the contrary* which gives the very shape of faith. Macintosh's use of conversion, sanctification, confidence, is sometimes counter-intuitive, for it is precisely such religious experiences which alter the way in which we perceive God's dependability, presence and his causal effects in our world. Macintosh views dependability, causality etc. as having the same description, inside as well as outside faith. But, we shall argue, it is precisely the presence of faith, conversion, with the second nature that these experiences bring, that effects a decisive change of perspective on how the world is arranged. Macintosh's realism forces him where we need not go (if he wants to preserve those important insights and intuitions), into the notion of a single right description of reality. *What we hope to argue is that there is no fixed horizon on the backdrop of which everything else is stable. Rather, we are in the middle of a flux of relations: a transformative relationship to an infinite, eternal, personal God; a relationship*

[11] We will see this theme taken up more methodically by John E. Smith below.

to a world, which bears of a plenitude of descriptions because it was created by God; and many other relations. Macintosh assumes the stable horizon of a static realist theory of knowledge and then plots God's being and our relationship to him on that horizon. For us this constitutes a failure of nerve.

Revelation's Threshold

Another theologian who has charted a distinct contemporary position which takes into account the role of religious experiences such as conversion is William J. Abraham. We have argued that experience must play a role in the justification of beliefs, but without going back to a myth of the Given. Macintosh's approach to experience leads in the right direction, by discriminating between religious experiences and requiring a 'right religious adjustment'. Ultimately, however, his indebtedness to a natural-scientific model compromises his effort. Religious experience provides no distinct perspective of the mundane order, but it is rather continuous with it.

Abraham is less indebted to a particular epistemology, much less the general type of realist epistemological theory which Macintosh uses as a foundation for theological knowledge. Quite the contrary, he believes that theology has taken a wrong turn in its choice to canonize specific epistemologies, besides its quite correct insistence on the normativity of specific material claims. In his *Canon and Criterion in Christian Theology* Abraham argues that the primary context of theology is soteriological and ontological, rather than epistemological and that the canonization of particular methods of deriving the material claims of what he calls canonical theism is ultimately detrimental. We will discuss some aspects of this earlier work in the next section, as we deal with the role of Scripture as a semantic context. His more recent work, *Crossing the Threshold of Divine Revelation*[12] builds follows up on his negative approach to epistemology and attempts to come clean on his own epistemological assumptions. Central to those assumptions is the claim that the acceptance of revelation which takes place as a result of conversion is a 'world-constituting event': 'once revelation is accepted, one enters a whole new world where everything is liable to be seen in a new light.'[13]

Whereas for Macintosh we are dealing with essentially the same perspective, Abraham is more attentive to the important role of faith as participating in a 'world constituting experience.' But can such an experience lead to beliefs which might adequately constitute knowledge? This question receives an affirmative answer which has strong affinities to reformed epistemology. It would be simply wrong to dismiss the religious experience and intuition of literally billions of believers who are convinced that God is at work in the world and who thus *perceive* or *see* his presence. Since God is a personal

[12] (Grand Rapids: Eerdmans, 2006).

[13] W. J. Abraham, *Crossing the Threshold*, pp. 85-6.

agent,[14] like all personal agents, he is know through his work, actions and speech. Just like we perceive a personality beyond bodily movements and speech acts, it is legitimate to perceive a divine personality through its activity in history. It is interesting to note that both Macintosh and Abraham accept personal theism, albeit with different nuances. But this seems to have different consequences in their epistemologies of religious faith. Regardless of the notions of freedom normally associated with personal and moral agency, Macintosh necessarily ties the legitimacy of experience-derived religious beliefs to laws and a certain repeatability. He leaves no room for a divine action which contradicts human expectations of what such action should be. Abraham, on the other hand, refuses to tie the legitimacy of experience-derived religious beliefs to any notion of repeatability, laws, and testable hypotheses.

In fact, he presents an alternative between what he calls the *ocullus contemplationis* theory, according to which we are entitled to our beliefs about God based on the sheer fact that we *perceive* him to act in history, and the *explanatory hypothesis theory*, according to which religious beliefs are formed as a result of a complex inferential process. The latter intellectualises faith to a very high extent, forgetting the fact that not all believers are individuals capable of such imaginative hypotheses. Moreover, intellectualising the process of faith obscures the *pull* felt by those who are *drawn*[15] to faith, which cannot be reduced to the cognitive act of making inferences. Our knowledge of God is therefore not inferential, but perceptual: 'we experience God, as it were, straight off, as we perceive the world around us.' We either trust such perceptions or we do not. There is no independent way of discriminating between them. This means, for Abraham, that 'we have spiritual as well as physical sensory capacities that are not reducible to other acts of cognition.'[16] This is a natural, basic, bedrock capacity. 'Believers see God at work in creation and in their own lives; they do not initially argue themselves into believing that this is the case.'[17] Moreover, they are entitled to the beliefs they form in such a way, without having to justify them intellectually. This is not to say that intellectual justification is of no value[18], but crucially if the legitimacy of our religious beliefs does not rest on intellectual arguments, then the failure of these arguments (e.g. natural theology) does not reflect on the truth of our faith.

Having argued that 'we come equipped with an original, native capacity to perceive God's general and special revelation in the world'[19], Abraham then

---

[14] W. J. Abraham, *Crossing the Threshold*, pp. 58, 79.

[15] W. J. Abraham, *Crossing the Threshold*, p. 73.

[16] W. J. Abraham, *Crossing the Threshold*, . 69.

[17] W. J. Abraham, *Crossing the Threshold*, p. 71.

[18] Abraham suggests in fact that explanations may reinforce the initial knowledge provided by the perception: pp. 71-2.

[19] W. J. Abraham, *Crossing the Threshold*, p. 80.

argues that revelation is a 'threshold concept'. He readily acknowledges the metaphorical nature of the concept, with its geographical and spatial connotations. The point is that we may choose to ignore revelation, or we may choose to 'enter it'. When we recognised something as revelation we have thereby crossed the threshold. This recognition itself is not something based upon rational argument, but again it is best characterised in terms of a *gravitational pull.* 'Coming to accept a divine revelation is not simply a matter of adding one more item to one's stock of beliefs. Once one steps inside the revelation, one has to rework one's identity and be open to the implications that lie on the other side of the threshold.'[20]

Now we may pause for a moment to reflect upon this territorial cast of imagery. One might be forgiven for suspecting that putting the issue in such clearly demarcational terms would lead back to fideism. Such a thought is also sobering for our own project in this book. Yet Abraham is adamant that this privileged status of revelation should not be used 'as leverage for avoiding the hard questions about the original identity and legitimacy of the divine revelation espoused.'[21] He operates a distinction between challenging the *content* of revelation after one has come to believe that one has revelation, on the one hand, and the challenging of the claim that one possesses a divine revelation. The former challenge is self-contradictory, while the latter is legitimate. It thus appears that all critical inquiry about the *content* or revelation can take place only from a position outside of revelation. Once one has accepted revelation and crossed into the household of faith, doubt seems out of the question, and critical questioning inimical. The claim of revelation is so all-encompassing and 'Once applied, it is applied simply and totally'. Abraham's rhetoric seems to ineluctably lead him into a constructivist talk of 'world-constitution'.

There are several problems with Abraham's general program, but for now we will touch on just a couple of these, leaving the others for the next section. In very many ways, his theological proposal is very similar to ours. His strong emphasis on the canonical heritage of the Christian tradition, the notion that conversion effects a shift of perspective, these are aspects that resonate with the present project. But at the risk of being over scrupulous, there are a couple of minor quibbles which carry come consequences.

The first of these concerns his notion of the *natural ability* to perceive God. The distinction that he makes between a natural perception of God, which is direct, and a explanatory-hypothetical approach, which is inferential is excellent. He is quite right that faith cannot be reduced to other human abilities or capacities. On the other hand, his choice of ocular metaphors is unfortunate. An advantage of the explanatory-hypothetical approach is that it explains why some people come to faith while others don't. On that view, faith is a question

[20] W. J. Abraham, *Crossing the Threshold*, p. 92.

[21] W. J. Abraham, *Crossing the Threshold*, p. 93.

of interpretation and some choose to interpret the world religiously while others don't. This is an important aspect, but one which is not done justice to by Abraham's preferred *ocullus contemplationis* theory. If indeed perceiving God is a natural ability, then all people should unproblematically posses it. But of course, not all people see God at work in the world, even if many indeed do. Also connected to this issue is the ocular analogy. While it accurately conveys the sense in which perceiving God is not an inferential process, it does not render the sense of difference between how one sees and perceives sensible things, middle sized dry goods, and how one sees and perceives God. The disanalogy may be important here, if only for the sheer fact that 'no one has ever seen God', a central canonical belief.

Abraham adds some clauses which he hopes will save the general lines of his argument, while also accounting for these discrepancies. First, he does acknowledge that a whole conceptual repertoire is drawn on in religious experience, including experiencing revelation: 'Of course, in articulating what is at stake I have left aside for the moment the place that communities have in supplying the conceptual repertoire deployed in speaking in this manner about ourselves and about God.'[22] Thus, he is fully aware that a reservoir of conceptual resources is drawn on. However, he does not engage the question of whether the very shape of these conceptual resources has any bearing on the very content of revelation. He simply assumes that these concepts are already in place, and they are presupposed in speaking about divine and human agency. But of course the stake is not simply talk of divine and human agency, but the very question whether this conceptual baggage, what Kant and McDowell call spontaneity, which is always drawn in the operations of experience, or receptivity, may affect the very content of what is experienced? Could it perhaps be that this is just what makes the difference between those that *see* God and those that don't? Abraham might feel that making the content of revelation depend upon such second order conceptual relations might undermine the basic and natural status of the divine-perceiving ability. But that need not be the case. The very fact that a capacity is basic is compatible with the fact that it draws upon other basic capacities in its operation. For example, the fact that a human being cannot speak without having vocal chords does not mean that his linguistic ability is reducible to a physical description of his vocal apparatus, or that his vocal apparatus is in turn reducible to his speech abilities. Both are natural, endowed capacities even while both require each other for their proper operation.

There is also a second proviso: the reality of sin. Although perceiving the divine in history is a natural ability, it is a

> sense [that] can be impaired and healed. Just as our capacity to discern what other human agents are doing can be clogged by our fat, relentless egos; by our corrupt

[22] W. J. Abraham, *Crossing the Threshold*, p. 68

> and cynical modes of thinking; by our despair and lack of confidence; by the burden of victimhood and oppression; and by our own narrow agendas, so can our capacity to discern rightly what God is doing in the universe and in history.[23]

This is all right, but there are also points where the analogy is weaker, if not altogether equivocating. Correct discernment of what other human agents are doing is surely dependant on having the right attitudes, but the knowledge *that* there are other human agents whose actions we want to decipher is not dependent (except perhaps in fringe cases) on any such attunement. When we receive a letter from someone we don't know we have no problem assuming that someone wrote it. But when it comes to perceiving a divine hand at work in our lives, the assumption is not all that unchallenged. Now it should be understood that we are not objecting to the main points of Abraham's arguments. He is a fellow traveller with us. But his particular construction of the perception of the divine as a natural ability and particularly his failure to reflect more deeply on the essential relationship between the content of the perceiving and one's disposition (conceptual, linguistic, practical, affective) tend to emphasize the continuity rather than the discontinuity between seeing God and seeing other sensory objects. Reflection upon such disanalogies might in fact reflect negatively upon our entitlement to see God at work in the world. If what we see is partly conditioned to something in us, or about us, then it might be that we construct what we see. In which case, why should we be entitled to this 'seeing'? It seems to us that, if we want to continue to speak about entitlement to a way of seeing, we have to further reflect on the relationship between disposition and the content of seeing. If the two are inherently related, do we still have a way to discern right perceptions from wrong ones? Abraham is an excellent guide for us, up to a point. But he does not press these epistemic questions further. As a result, his own project is incomplete, inasmuch as he cannot claim entitlement.

So, in making the *ocullus contemplationis* a natural ability, the temptation is that one may speak about perceiving God without reflecting on the other human operations which are required for this operation.

The second issue which needs some clarification is the spatial and geographical set of metaphors for the 'domain' of faith. One feature of the theologies of both Macintosh and Abraham is that they both seek to be empirically adequate to the religious experience of believers. So it is rather important for their project that all authentic religious experiences are accounted for. But modelling the dialectic between faith and doubt on the pair of inside/outside a threshold is perhaps somewhat simplistic. If revelation has such a world-constituting effect, how is it possible that people of faith also suffer from doubt? Does it mean that in such moments we have dropped out of faith? What sense does it make to speak about dropping out of faith, were it not

---

[23] W. J. Abraham, *Crossing the Threshold*, p. 76.

for these very spatial metaphors? Yet the ordinary experience of religious believers shows that moments of faith co-exist many times with moments of doubt. Thus, unless we are prepared to imagine one's life of faith as involving jumping back and forth over the threshold, we should perhaps drop these unhelpful images. As we will try to articulate in what follows, coming to faith, as a transformation of perspective, is not adequately illuminated as a shifting of places. This obscures the ways in which doubt sometimes feeds faith. Rather, the life of faith could be described as an intentional and focused discipline of discerning a divine pattern in a world which lends itself to multiple patterns. Sometimes we lose focus, we become distracted, the pattern seems to vanish and as we struggle to regain visual grip, we are instead overcome by other, more striking aspects. Having doubts may not be so much dropping from faith as a failure of nerve. More on this in the next few paragraphs.

The Religious Dimension of Experience

As we reflect upon the place of experience in theology, the work of John E. Smith is a source of many rich insights. A pragmatist philosopher as well as a Christian theologian, Smith's life work revolved around his defence of the importance of the religious dimension of experience and its place in theology. He provides us with a fallible, yet immensely stimulating model for making sense of the manifold relationships between God, experience, science, values, the church and so on. Smith's pragmatism, moreover, makes him an ideal discussion partner, for his theology exhibits a profound pragmatic sensibility, especially as it pertains to the totality of human experience as something which is not merely subjective. The pragmatic philosophers which impress him most are Peirce, James, Dewey and Royce, while the neo-pragmatic philosophy of a Rorty is viewed with suspicion:

> Like the Prodigal Son, Rorty, who has repented of his former views and discovered pragmatism, is rewarded with the fatted calf while those of us who stayed within the fold and upheld the insights of the pragmatists when it was not popular to do so are treated only to an opportunity to hear Rorty tell us what we already know. I say all this for but one reason, namely, that Rorty has an authority on the current scene which is the result of these special circumstances and which he does not always exercise responsibly.[24]

The reasons for this unfriendly attitude perhaps have to do with Rorty's overt linguistic methodologism, which might be taken to stem from an skewed reading of an American tradition through the lens of continental deconstruction. But we do not want to dwell on this matter. Yet it was important to alert the

[24] John E. Smith, 'Experience, God, and Classical American Philosophy', *American Journal of Theology and Philosophy*, 14/2 (1993), p. 135.

reader to Smith's own self-understanding in relation to Rorty's neo-pragmatism, which we have also critiqued.

It is a mistake, says Smith, to confuse experience with a tissue of subjectivity. A great part of his work in pragmatic philosophy is dedicated to the recovery of a concept of experience which is different from the one found in empiricism or logical positivism. Experience is not a set of mental phenomena, but a 'valid medium of disclosure through which we come to know what there is.'[25] Giving a description of experience along very similar lines to McDowell's position, which we also endorse, he distinguishes between his view of experience and the notion that it consists in bits of primitive and un-interpreted data of sensation. Rather, 'thought is present in experience from the beginning'[26] and 'The total nature of the being who experiences enters into the transaction, which means that the being is not simply a theoretical knower, but one who lives in and through experience, who puts questions both to the world and to himself, and who has an interest in experience as the source of life and understanding.'[27] Far from being a subjective domain, experience is 'an objective result of man's transactions with the total environment, including himself.'[28]

Yet, because there are two ingredients which go together in experience, 'the material of the encounter and the one who encounters'[29] there is in experience a certain *orientation*, which has to do with the one who experiences. 'Experience is not merely disclosure of the world's content, but it also reflects the many ways in which reality can be approached. The being who experiences not only has purposes of his own in approaching the world and himself, but he is capable of seeing both in many different *contexts*.'[30] What a crucial insight this is: *the world lends itself to interpretation and apprehension from a multiplicity of perspectives. There is thus no single ontology that we can apply to the world, but a multiplicity of ontological perspectives*. As we have seen with McDowell, such perspectives bring out aspects which truly belong to the world, the experience of such aspects always involves thought patterns. It is fallacious to drive a wedge between these and suggest that there is a gap between the world and our experience. Smith also relentlessly drives home this point: the fact that something is present in experience does not reduce it to experience. Through the medium of experience we encounter something which is genuinely transcendent of this experience, yet present within it. Macintosh's critical

---

[25] J. E. Smith, *Religion and Empiricism* (Milwaukee: Marquette University Press, 1967), p. 44.

[26] J. E. Smith, *Religion and Empiricism*, p. 46.

[27] J. E. Smith, *Experience and God* (New York: Oxford University Press, 1968), p. 25.

[28] J. E. Smith, *Religion and Empiricism*, p. 52.

[29] J. E. Smith, *Experience and God*, p. 32.

[30] J. E. Smith, *Religion and Empiricism*, p. 47.

monism preserved the insight that what is present in experience is numerically identical with what exists in reality, yet he was not able to reconcile the linguistic and conceptual nature of experience with this monism.

We suggest that the notion of aspects brings out precisely this fact about experience and reason. Smith's work is the best explanation to date of how this comes about. William J. Abraham also hinted in the right direction, but he failed to question how an existential disposition can alter one's perception to such an extent and what bearing such an orientation has on the very content of experience. Smith provides an answer in his notion that experience has a multiplicity of dimensions. Reality can be approached in many ways. There are *dimensions of meaning* to experience: 'experience includes frameworks for interpreting as well as that which is to be interpreted.'[31]

It is hard to overestimate the importance of this insight. In fact, through our combination of this insight with Davidson's dissolution of the scheme-content dichotomy, plus the theological supplement provided by this chapter, we are carving out an alternative vision for theological methodology that will hopefully suggest solutions to some present issues. *Reality is not something which has a preferred self-description.* This is Rorty's as well as Smith's insight. The difference consists in the latter's claim that the deliverances of experience are genuine components of reality and that there is a fact of the matter about what exists in reality. *Moreover, this minimal realism is compatible with the claim that we always have reality under a description opened up by a practical disposition.* Cultural politics is not the end of the story. Further discussion will hopefully reinforce that conclusion, but for now we have to stay with Smith.

If experience comes under a multiplicity of dimensions, then it is wrong to isolate science as the privileged modality of approaching reality.[32] But if that is the case, then Macintosh's procedure of securing objective theological knowledge is a case of applying mistaken categories. Smith insists again and again, anticipating similar contemporary voices, that God is not an object among other objects on the registry of being. The way in which we approach God should as a result be fundamentally different. Because God is not an object like any other, our experience of God is unlike our experience of sensible things. Herein lies another significant difference to Abraham's project. It would be a mistake to think that Abraham treats God like any other object. But he does tend to describe our apprehension of God in ways similar to our perceiving 'middle sized dry goods'. We do not want to overplay the

---

[31] In the section on the Scriptures we will argue that they are the basic framework for the interpretation of revelation, not as something externally added upon the event, but internally tied to it by virtue of its participation in the economy of salvation.

[32] J. E. Smith, *Experience and God*, p. 40.

differences between the two[33] and neither do we want to take Smith's side in this so-called debate. The point is simply that Smith understands the relationship between the *what* and the *how* of experience much more critically and dialectically. The result of this sensibility is that Smith is more aware of the multiple perspectives which might be taken in experience. Thus an experience may have the same sensory qualities, but it can afford a multiplicity of takes, depending on the purpose, orientation, disposition, interests and categories of understanding which are applied. Abraham simply does not consider the issue from this point of view.

As a consequence of this approach, Smith refuses to return to 'religious experience'. He is interested in 'the disclosure of what [he] would call the "religious dimension" of experience'[34]. To speak about religious experience as such is to mistakenly think that God is an ingredient in that sort of experience[35], to think that a positive answer to the question of the existence of God would simply add another being on our ontological registry. On the other hand, to speak about the religious *dimension* of experience is to understand that the question of God concerns the very depths and purposes of our existence. It cannot be asked, as it were, from a position which is fixed, for to ask the question of God is at the same time to ask the question about our own existence in the world. In terminology by now made familiar by Carnap, Rorty, Herrmann, to ask the question of God is to ask a meta-linguistic question, about the whole point of our discourse about ourselves. This is not simply a theoretical question which presupposes the existence of a well-established framework, which can be a background for theoretical endeavours like the arguments for the existence of God, which are 'a field for the display of logical ingenuity in which the term "God' means nothing more than a concept, or at most another thing that may or may not be real.'[36] Quite the contrary, the question of God is a framework- and disposition-altering question. This is the profound insight contained in Smith's pragmatically-experiential theology: the God problem cannot be talked about separately from the human problem, that is, from asking about the purpose and point of our existence. 'The religious dimension comes into view when we encounter in our own selves a peculiar

---

33 In fact, it could be argued that both employ a concept of analogy, Smith more explicitly than Abraham. Thus, Abraham's perception of the divine is analogically related to perception of sensible *things*, whereas Smith's perception of the divine is (more explicitly) analogically related to the perception of other *selves* in communication. But even at this level it is instructive that Abraham tends to analogize with perception of sensible *things*, whereas Smith tends to analogize with perception of other *selves*.

34 J. E. Smith, *Religion and Empiricism*, p. 51.

35 J. E. Smith, *Religion and Empiricism*, p. 51; *Experience and God*, p. 55.

36 J. E. Smith, *Experience and God*, p. 56.

question and concern, the question and concern for the quality of life and our world *taken as a whole*.'[37]

It is important to note that this is not simply a shift of vocabulary, unconnected to anything in the world. The question of the very possibility of a religious dimension is not gratuitously invented, as a sort of experimentation and imagination without any basis in reality. That is what Rorty would have us believe. There is no further ontological question of existence to follow a question of cultural politics, of whether we experiment with this or that vocabulary. Smith's religious question springs from within a non-religious dimension, as it were.

> In encountering ourselves, however, and in reflecting on the fact of our being in the world at all, we come to realize that our total life is problematic in the sense that we stand in need of a purpose for being, a self-integrating power that makes self-realization possible in a situation constantly threatening us both from without and from within. The problem of the self-integrating power is the problem of God cast in experiential form. In experience we discover not only that there are problems in life, but that there is a problem of life – the problem finding an ultimate object of devotion integrating and unifying the many power and potentialities of our personal being.[38]

Again, the importance of what such a claim entails is huge: *the religious dimension is not unconnected to a more mundane, or scientific dimension.* Admittedly, Smith does not give much thought to the question of how these multiple perspectives are related, but he does stress that we must be engaged in continually relating them.

To speak about perspectives is nothing new. But the particular way in which Smith does it circumvents fideism and incommensurability. Reality is indeed available only under a given description and this is dependant upon a prior conceptual framework, practical purposes, habits of the mind and of the heart. *But a human person can entertain more than just one such perspective.* Smith correctly points out that it is the task of critical knowledge to see to it that these various perspectives communicate with each other. In fact, as we shall see presently, the religious perspective or dimension has to be correlated with the more mundane perspective of everyday experience. Unless such correlations are made, religious concepts risk being vacuous.

This is the truly remarkable aspect of this particular construal of perspectives. Whatever else it might be, this is not a 'territorial' understanding of perspectives. There is reason to hope, therefore, that fideism – with its army of territorial metaphors – is definitively circumvented by refusing to accept a set of linguistic images for the description of what is involved in having a perspective. Being perspectival need not be described in the spatial terms of

---

[37] J. E. Smith, *Religion and Empiricism*, p. 60.

[38] John E. Smith, *The Analogy of Experience: An Approach to Understanding Religious Truth* (New York: Harper and Row, 1973), pp. 60f.

belonging to a group, of inhabiting one particular epistemic region. Allowing oneself to be dominated by such metaphors makes it hard to understand how it is that one person can entertain a multiplicity of perspectives, sometimes even contrary to each other, or at least in competition.

For Smith, understanding this is ingredient in understanding the kind of human beings that we are. The territorialism of the metaphors too easily dismisses the human contradiction, the struggle which takes place in a single individual. Thinking spatially may have to involve the concept of 'world sliding', to recall a science fiction TV series, to make sense of these shifting identities. But it will do so at the risk of debasing the very notion of identity forming space (communities), for if one can 'slide' between communities, if one can 'surf' with such ease between epistemic spaces, the very notion that our identity is constructed by such spaces becomes unconvincing.[39]

Perhaps nowhere is the struggle between perspectives and the temptation to resolve it territorially more intense than in the case of the relation between faith and doubt. In Smith's reading, the temptation to mark a territory of faith as distinct from a territory of doubt begins with Anselm as is continued by Thomas Aquinas.[40] We thus begin to talk about two classes of epistemic agents: the believers and the unbelievers. This misrepresents the human condition: 'The human situation is distorted when a tension which belongs essentially to the structure of existence is resolved by distributing the elements in tension over two distinct classes of individuals. [...] The truth is that there is only one man, one existence, one experience embracing many dimensions and it falls to each individual to participate in these dimensions and relate them to each other in his own life.'[41] This is a very realistic perspective on the nature of the human situation, as it pertains to the relation between the sacred and the profane. The struggle with doubt is not something that can or should be avoided by faith. Rather, faith feeds off doubt, it is a dialectical engagement with doubt, rather than an arrogant dismissal of it. The rather lengthy quote that follows is an apt indication of the subtlety of Smith's position:

> Wherever there is living faith possessed by a person who lives in the world and is aware of its many dimensions, that faith is not shielded from doubt and uncertainty in advance but actually derives its life and dynamic force from a continual overcoming of doubt. When confronted with an item of faith, we want

[39] This is the grunt of Milbank's argument against MacIntyre's notion of tradition constituted enquiry (John Milbank, *Theology and Social Theory: Beyond Secular Reason* (Oxford: Blackwell, 1993), pp. 339-347): if one can learn a second first language with the ease presupposed by MacIntyre, it is questionable whether one's identity is indeed constructed by one's home tradition to the extent that MacIntyre assumes. In our previous work we suggested dropping the notion of tradition as a 'space' of construction and using the notion of 'habitus' to do the same work.

[40] J. E. Smith, *The Analogy of Experience*, pp. 15-6.

[41] J. E. Smith, *The Analogy of Experience*, pp. 16-7.

> first to know what it means; and second, we want to know to what extent it is exhibited in and intelligibly related to our experience. To fail to ask these questions posed by the precariousness of our existence and the undeniable challenge to faith presented by the thought patterns of our secular world is to fall back on some form of authoritarianism. It is to suppose that the content of faith, which indeed we have only and always in earthen vessels, is to be preserved by bare repetition (i.e. by reciting a creed or citing biblical passages in response to questions) without criticism and without reinterpretation. The quest for analogues of faith is at the same time a quest initiated by living faith for the means of overcoming doubt by attaining a sense that our faith is grounded in the structure of what there is, and is therefore more than self-indulgence or wishful thinking.[42]

It takes some pondering to absorb the rich content in the above quote. Doubt is not a necessary exercise, which nevertheless remains external to the interpretation of faith. But in order to *understand* what is at stake in faith, such a correlation with other dimensions of human experience (science, morality etc) is required, for 'in every act of comprehension we are led inevitably to consult that experience in order to understand what the truth claim means and whether it is verified by what has happened in our own case.'[43] We can expect nothing less from a thinker versed in the pragmatist criteria of intelligibility. In order to understand an idea, we have to understand what it means for us, what is its cash value for us, how it can be expected to figure in our own experience. Throughout the pages of this book we have engaged with pragmatist but especially neo-pragmatist conceptions of meaning, including Davidson's notion that the meaning of a concept is given by what makes it true. Smith's version of meaning theory is significantly less truth-oriented and more experience-oriented. Thus the task of correlation with experience is of paramount importance.

But will this turn to experience not eventually lead to verificationism and the ultimate denial of the truth or intelligibility of religious beliefs? This worry has some force, for as we have seen in the case of Davidson, the verificationist temptation is always strong in a movement so indebted to 'logical empiricism'. At least in Smith's case, such worries need not detain us. He rejects the logical positivist conception of experience. But more to the point, although in order to interpret faith one must correlate its contents with human experience, one must not look for repeated instances of revelation in that human experience, *but for analogues*. Observe for a moment the difference from Macintosh's stress on repeatability. Correlation with human experience does not mean that the content of faith will or can be reduced to something which is found in general human experience. No less than Abraham, Smith is a firm believer in revelation. But what prevents him from becoming a fideist, even in the very softened sense in which Abraham is one, is his belief that revelation needs to be

---

[42] J. E. Smith, *The Analogy of Experience*, p. 31.

[43] J. E. Smith, *The Analogy of Experience*, p. 18.

interpreted. Here we come back to the long quote of a few paragraphs above. Belief in revelation does not necessarily entail authoritarianism and dogmatism. Faith is best preserved not by mere repetition. That would be like trying to make oneself understood to a foreigner by speaking louder and slower. We make our faith intelligible by looking for analogues of religious beliefs in human existence generally. This involves stretching oneself across dimensions. It does not involve leaving one's 'world',[44] or abandoning belief in the truth of his religious vision, but actively seeking to show how that vision cashes out in life's other's aspects. Unless correlated with other dimensions of experience, other contexts of meaning, faith risks becoming meaningless. Smith's opinion here is not verificationist. He insists that not all faith contents can be correlated in such a fashion. But where we can we must correlate. We have this treasure from God, revelation, in earthly vessels. This biblical insight alone should remind us that we cannot leave our humanity behind as dogmatic theologians. A certain historicism should be ingredient in evangelical theology in the form of a humble fallibilism. The benefits of experiential analogizing and correlation are simply too large to be ignored: cross-dimensional analogizing ensures that our faith is grounded in what there is rather than a mere self indulgence or wishful thinking.

Smith's philosophy of religion provides us with a systematisation of the two emphases which must be preserved: on the one hand the notion that theology requires both a conative and a cognitive transformation, without leading, on the other hand, to fideism and authoritarianism. Before we suggest some points where his proposal needs adjustment, there is one last worry that needs to be assuaged and which in fact provides a transition to the next section.

Dogmatic theologians have been rightly suspicious about experience based theologies for fear that they end up reducing the content of faith to what is given in experience. In the worst case, they even end up denying God. This is where the analogical nature of the correlation becomes important, as already observed. What theology can do is to elucidate a faith content, by means of experiential analogies. However, that faith content cannot be deducted from the experiences alone, or arrived independently of revelation. As Smith puts it in *The Analogy of Experience*, 'The content of faith is misconceived if it is regarded as a set of truths with no essential relation to the historical medium and the peculiar constellation of historical persona and events through which the biblical communities first apprehended them.' We will not enter deeper into this aspect of Smith's proposal, for it will be analysed in the next section on the normativity of Scriptures. It should be enough to point out that the content of

---

[44] Admitedly, a weak point of our anti-territorial metaphors can be intuited here. It does make sense to imagine oneself being within one space and communicating with others from other spaces, yet it does not make sense to say that one can notice two aspects at the same time. One either sees the duck or the rabbit, but cannot see both at the same time.

faith is considered to be given in the revelation of God. This revelation is constituted by God's self-expression in the person of Jesus Christ, and it has been preserved in the testimony of Scripture to this revelation. Again, an important difference from Macintosh can be observed: *revelation has a normative description and it is not simply what is conveyed in experience.* For Smith this is to refuse to make experience the measure. Revelation remains the measure, but the early Christian community and its Scriptures also play a prominent role in interpretation. We will turn to those aspects after some minor adjustments are suggested.

The Role of Scripture

In beginning this discussion about the role of Scripture it needs to be remembered that the topic of the Bible is not central to any of the neo-pragmatic philosophers that we have discussed. Neither are pragmatic and neo-pragmatic theologians particularly interested in it. Part of the reason for this is that they usually tend to fashion the Christian identity in future rather than past tense terms. This vantage point does have its benefits, to be sure. It better captures the fluid nature of Christianity, though it can and it has overstated this fluidity more often than not. It also has a tendency to legitimise the uses of imagination and creativity, as it moulds Christianity according to new contexts and cultural periods. While these are welcome benefits, they must be taken with moderation. Especially when such a futurist orientation goes hand in hand with a loss of confidence in truth and justification, it tends to promote an unconstrained creativity and an uprooted imagination. It is not judicious to simply assume, as we have argued in an earlier section, that the essence, or, to use a less 'modernist' word, identity if Christianity is preserved after all. Yet, as was also suggested, it is hard to discuss this issue in terms of Christian identity, as a sociological body. Sociological bodies change all the time. Moreover, social bodies like nations and peoples change their governing constitutions all the time. What gives one's identity as a Romanian? Or an American? There do not seem to be any enduring traits uniquely possessed by a Romanian, on which to safely draw in describing her identity. Similarly, with respect to Christianity, we have found persuasive the argument of e.g. Delwin Brown and Davaney, that Christianity is simply different today that it was a hundred years ago. It is perhaps simply best to drop the discussion in terms of Christian identity altogether, for it is much too ripe with sociological variables. Rather, we should concentrate on another question: are we being good followers of Christ? Are we interpreting his gospel correctly?

This change of interrogation is consonant with our emphasis that ultimately being a Christian is not a matter of belonging to a sociological community, or, that it cannot be restricted to one's becoming a part of a divine-human body of Christ. That is surely what is also involved, but it presupposes an *ontological transformation of the individual.* By this we mean one's being included in

Christ, being born of Christ. It is a good question whether this individual transformation can happen apart from a corporate and ecclesial context. We think it can, though this is the exception. The reason we insist on this is that being a Christian (notice our giving up on defending what the identity of *Christianity* means) involves a certain relationship to Jesus Christ. The centrality of Jesus Christ for a life of discipleship is undoubted and unnegociable. But how does one experience Christ? How does one have a relationship with Christ? Are we to degenerate in crude forms of mysticism and naive experientialism?

This is where neo-pragmatism (but also pragmatism) have a direct bearing. The whole conversation up to this point had everything to do with notions of meaning, of experience and justification. Throughout this exchange we have insisted on maintaining a pivotal role for experience in the practice of justification, but also for the notion of meaning. Language, it was suggested, is also important for meaning, besides experience and truth. We felt that Davidson had to be supplemented on those points. The reason why language was so important was that meaning cannot be externalised into truth relations. There are multiple ways of approaching reality. Unless we are prepared to restrict the application of truth to only one of these, we have to understand that truth cannot be discussed apart from one's orientation towards reality. *The notion that one's disposition, orientation and purpose play a part in any discussion of truth and knowledge is a lesson that theology should do well to learn from pragmatism.* This is a part of our creative proposal and it puts a twist on the usual ways of framing the issues. Rather than speak in terms of incommensurable conceptual schemes and frameworks, we have to consider languages as *perspectival instruments*. A language constitutes a way of seeing. But it is possible to have multiple ways of seeing even from within a single natural language.[45]

The significance of this for religious studies and theology is hard to miss, as we saw in the last section on experience. But there remains a question about religious experience, or rather about the religious dimension of experience as it pertains to Christianity. If experience does not wear its meaning on its sleeve and if such a meaning is dependent on having a 'right religious adjustment', how does one know which is that adjustment and how to dispose oneself accordingly? The answer given by this section is that Scripture is a paradigmatic and normative instance of such an adjustment. Its nature is misunderstood if removed from a purposeful and ultimately soteriological context. This is not to deny that Scripture is propositionally true but that its truth is ruled by the divinely ordained intention and purpose.

Put differently, we will attempt to show that *Scripture provides an irreducible intensional context, which, as God's word, gives the meaning of the*

[45] See our discussion of the notion of 'optional languages'.

historical events of revelation and, by being a performance at the same time as it is a script, disposes us rightly for Christian experience.

To speak of Scripture as being of such bedrock significance is not without detractors. William J. Abraham's *Canon and Criterion in Christian Theology* is a repudiation of the claim that Scripture can function as a criterion in theology. The identity of the Christian community is not given by its adherence to the canon as a criterion, by it's considering the Scriptures to be the norming norm for faith. To think like this is allegedly to make a confusion of monumental proportions between soteriology and epistemology, between treating the 'canonical heritage' of the church as a means of grace and making it a norm of truth. Abraham considers the notion that a collection of texts could serve as a bedrock foundation for certainty as absurd. These were simply not designed to be treated like this. Importing them into an epistemological context, with its technical apparatus is awkward and anachronistic.[46] Instead the suggestion is to understand what these texts were really meant to be and how they were meant to be used.

In the process, Abraham expands canon, usually restricted to Scripture, to what he calls canonical heritage, or 'ecclesial canons [which] comprise materials, persons, and practices officially or semi-officially identified and set apart as a means of grace and salvation by the Christian community.'[47] The end result is to 'relocate the whole idea of canon within the arena of means of grace within the church.'[48] In light of our argument so far, this is precisely what we should be doing. However, broadening the canonical scope to include materials, persons and practices, officially or semi-officially identified, amounts to a relativisation of what canon means thus playing straight into the hands of theologians like Delwin Brown, with their own list of canons, themselves considered a means of grace in their own terms.

Moreover, as Vanhoozer notes, levelling the qualitative differences between Scripture and other means of grace does not do justice to the patristic ascription of a differentiated authority to the Bible in relation to other documents and practices of the church.[49] As we shall note, Vanhoozer and Telford Work provide an important corrective to Abraham, while remaining within the same soteriological and practical-performative orientation, through their emphasis on God's use of the Scriptures, as opposed to the church's use of them.

There is something worth salvaging from Abraham's project, however, and that is the idea that any theology of Scripture should be aware of its own tendency to impose upon it alien categories and epistemologies. To be sure, Abraham does not reject any epistemology of theology. As we have seen in the previous section, his *Crossing the Threshold of Divine Revelation* attempts to

[46] W. J. Abraham, *Canon*, p. 12.

[47] W. J. Abraham, *Canon*, p. 1.

[48] W. J. Abraham, *Canon*, p. 21.

[49] K. Vanhoozer, *Drama of Doctrine*, p. 145.

provide just such an analysis. Yet overall he too works with spent dichotomies. The rift he introduces between canonicity and criteria of knowledge, forces us into thinking that either Scripture is a means of grace, or it is an epistemology. But why must we accept such an exclusive choice? Is it not possible to say, like Vanhoozer, whom will be discussed in a moment, that Scripture is more than a criterion of theology but not less? Telford Work notes, as an aside, that precisely because Abraham starts with the church rather than Jesus that he can distinguish between canon and criterion.[50] Moreover, Vanhoozer also points out that Abraham fails to notice the distinction between Scripture as criterion, which provides sure foundations, and Scripture as a norm, which does not mean that debates are already settled, but only that a normative context for the disputation of claims is provided in it.

From the perspective of the argument pressed so far it also emerges that it is unrealistic to sharply distinguish theory from practice, epistemology from soteriology. But this principle applies in the reverse direction: neither can we distinguish soteriology from epistemology. Abraham does realise that the transition from soteriology to authority was a natural one, yet he insists that it was unnecessary and unwarranted, besides being detrimental.[51] But this is precisely where our argument can help: changing the perspective from soteriology to epistemology is *not necessarily* incorrect, precisely because any thing can be seen from a multitude of equally valid perspectives. To chart the historical transition from canon to criterion does not close the discussion. The fact that the original context of the formation and functioning of the canon was indeed a soteriological one does not mean that an epistemic perspective on it can be dismissed out of hand. Of course, neither does this mean that anything goes. But in order for Abraham to clinch the argument he has to show that the epistemic perspective is *inimical*, or detrimental to the canon itself. A thing can have many different uses. Granted, not all of them are equally valid or true, but their falsity resides not in their difference but in their incompatibility with the thing itself.[52]

To sum up, Abraham's dismissal of criterion on the basis of its historically derivative status fails to establish his case. It also fails to consider the variety of ways in which Scripture may be considered a criterion, some of which being indeed compatible with a practical-purposive understanding of knowledge and truth. This is at least one insight worth preserving.

Telford Work has written a brilliant 'bibliology' in his *Living and Active: Scripture in the Economy of Salvation*. Aiming at a 'Trinitarian ontology of Scripture', Work firmly sets the nature and function of Scripture in the context

---

[50] T. Work, *Living and Active: Scripture in the Economy of Salvation* (Grand Rapids: Eerdmans, 2001), p. 86. n. 77

[51] W. J. Abraham, *Canon*, p. 8.

[52] No return to a naive realism is intended by this. The reader should be patient until we elaborate on the normative perspective(s) as given in the Scriptures.

of the divine plan of salvation. By making the Trinitarian God the primary agent of Scripture, Work shifts the tables on Abraham, who takes the church to be the primary agent. His work is important for our project because he also sets Scripture in a *purposive context*. Rather than just viewing it as an inert text, dependent on us readers for its meaningfulness[53], Work argues that the Scriptures are a perspicuous text. They are alive and wield a salvific force through the work of the Holy Spirit, 'pneumatologically empowered and effective'. Scripture's nature cannot be examined apart from its place in a divine action, which is its primary and normative context.

Work concurs with Abraham that no alien epistemology, alethology or historiography should be imposed upon the Scriptures. If one is committed in faith to the notion that God authored this Script, then their truth cannot be detached from their soteriological purpose. But this is precisely what we have been claiming so far, namely that descriptions of reality are always bound to the interests we bring to reality. Unless there are normative interests and purposes, a normative movement within which a text, a thing, a sign is inscribed, there is no way in which to distinguish between good and bad approaches. McDowell's notion that through our being disposed in certain ways we become sensitive to reasons *out there* only makes sense if there is an overarching purpose, a movement which sustains things, artefacts, and signs. The next section argues that McDowell's philosophy requires the theological supplement of creation in order to make sense.

The fact that reality is scripted is for us a reason to hope that our reason does indeed pick out real aspects of reality, not just manufactured illusions. Because God is the author of Scripture, a heavy emphasis of Work's book, 'The *telos* to which God has appointed the texts in the service of salvation is the ultimate criterion of exegetical validity, not the reading techniques used to retrieve it.'[54] Work is aware of the fact that in the absence of such a guiding direction the meaning of the Scriptures is simply dissipated and irredeemably lost to the multitude of interests of the readers. It is for this precise reason that our claim about the relation between truth and purpose must be supplemented by the notion that there are normative, originally intended purposes. As we shall see, these need not be unique, or single, but can extend indefinitely, as God's wisdom extends indefinitely. But where such purposes can be established as ordained by God, they do constrain interpretation in a certain fashion.

Such an original purposive context, for instance, controls the functioning of the notions of truth in the Scripture. Starting from the Augustinian claim that God is the rhetor of Scripture, Work claims that 'To say that God is literally invested in Scripture is to say that its character is his character. [...] this ethical

[53] T. Work, *Living and Active*, p. 187.
[54] T. Work, *Living and Active*, p. 204.

investment *transcends categories of propositional truth.*'[55] This is illustrated by the story of Jonah. His prophecy from God, 'Another forty days, and Nineveh shall be overthrown' (Jonah 3:4) turned out to be false, by epistemological standards. The forty days elapsed without the city being destroyed. However, argues Work, 'the word of prophecy is tied so closely into God's own character that it shares in his grace, mercy, and steadfast love – even up to the point where it can become propositionally false.'[56] If we interpret Scripture according to a so-called neutral epistemology, this prophecy would be a blatant falsity. However, if we read the text according to the purposes and interests of God, rather than according to the disposition of the readers, God's word remains true. But the instructive point is that its truthfulness is tied to its being intended and applied in a certain way by the divine agent himself. Work reminds us of Lindbeck's discussion of *Christus Dominus est.* According to Lindbeck, what determines truthfulness is the disposition of the agent. But, as we also saw, we need a normative disposition, a normative orientation or set of dispositions towards the texts, towards the canon and the beliefs of the church. Lindbeck, but also Marshall, are at a loss to cater to this normativity. Work's emphasis on the presence and importance of the divine intention in the words of Scripture supplies this normativity. Vanhoozer nicely sums up Work's position, and his own: 'What becomes paramount is *God's* use of the biblical texts. [...] Lindbeck rightly sees that language is a means of navigating the social world, yet he fails to see that *God, too, is a member of the linguistic community.*'[57]

Kevin Vanhoozer's *The Drama of Doctrine* also contributes to our argument about the purposeful setting of the Scriptures, as instruments in the ongoing divine drama of redemption. Although he makes but one approving reference to Work's *Living and Active*, it is clear that their projects are very similar, although Vanhoozer's scope is more widely theological and dogmatic, as opposed to the more restricted 'bibliological' aim of Work. As noted, Vanhoozer also objects to Abraham's disjunction between the soteriological and epistemic, judging that Scripture is more, not less than a criterion of theology. But he does not go to much length in uncovering the deeper co-inherence of soteriology (as a practical disposition) and epistemology (as a theoretical stance). We have argued throughout the last couple of chapters that knowledge is indissolubly related to a disposition and purpose. A description is always embedded in a purpose and interest. Thus, it will simply not do to place soteriology next to theological epistemology, for they are not simply autonomous members of a pair. Rather, one cannot be conceived without the other. It appears that Telford Work was more aware of this co-inherence, even if he only discusses it in terms of biblical truthfulness. As we saw, this mutual dependence represents all human knowledge.

---

[55] T. Work, *Living and Active*, p. 61.

[56] T. Work, *Living and Active*, p. 62.

[57] K. Vanhoozer, *Drama of Doctrine*, p. 177 (original emphasis).

While Vanhoozer does not approach the issue from a pragmatist perspective, he makes a crucial contribution to a pragmatic reconstruction of theology. His whole project falls in line with our argument so far, but we can only capture a fraction of its direct import.

Scripture is a 'covenant document', a constitution of the church. Needless to say that this is very different from Abraham's concentration on 'canonical heritage'. Precisely because Scripture is such a 'divinely initiated covenant document',[58] it is different from human constitutions, its normative status is unlike the normative status of other human documents and constitutions. Were it a merely human document, it would make sense to conceive of the identity of Christianity along the lines suggested by Cady's extensionalist model: a creative reworking of the past, yet without much concern for the 'positivity' of the past, for the concrete form of past beliefs enshrined in Scripture. The divine nature of the document invites rather than prohibits creative interpretations and applications. 'Rote memorization' simply won't do.[59] But these creative interpretations and imaginative performances are normatively bound to adhere to the performance enshrined in Scripture itself. This is a point of huge importance to which we shall return: *Scripture is not simply a set of instructions about what to believe and how to live, but is itself a real performance, an example to be followed creatively, yet faithfully.* But more on this later.

The interpretation of this document is canonically ruled. This relates back to Work's point about the divine intention in using the canonical texts. It is not enough to simply read the text just like one would read any other text. But like with any other text, the reader has to aim for the author's intention. In other words, we as readers have to attune ourselves to the way in which God intends this text to be read and to function. One such example was already given by Work: the story of Jonah. In that case, a 'normal' reading strategy will result in the ascription of a blatant falsity to God. That was a case where simply propositional truth was transcended. Another such case is the use of typological reading and figuration. The canonical and apostolic strategy of reading, which Work argues has as its foundation Jesus' own way of reading the Scriptures, brings a *perspective* on the text which some say the original author could not have meant. Such a reading is blatantly false, according to a certain scientific (and not only) exegesis. Yet the church inscribed this as a valid mode of reading, in view of the fact that Jesus himself used it. Thus, it might be said that a canonical reading represents a reading of the text according to a certain disposition. Adopting a canonical perspective means adopting *a ruled way of seeing.*

This is an important insight which Vanhoozer gifts to our project: to inhabit the world of Scripture means to become disposed to see reality in the light of

---

[58] K. Vanhoozer, *Drama of Doctrine*, p. 134.

[59] K. Vanhoozer, *Drama of Doctrine*, p. 128.

Scripture.[60] It means to see reality and Scripture itself in light of their role in God's drama of salvation. Now it might be asked, which perspective is the correct one? Which reading is the exegetically valid one? Is it the literary-grammatical approach or the figural approach? Both are! These are simply different valid perspectives from which the canonical text can be approached. It is, however, important that they do not cancel each other out.[61]

Thus, Scripture is a guide, an initiation into a new way of seeing. But this is precisely what we have been looking for! Our aim was to find a normative constraint on dispositions. If reality and experience always come under a disposition, does this mean that any disposition and any reading which follows is appropriate? We think not. There are constraints upon appropriate dispositions. It falls to the next section to establish the case for such a normativity in light of the doctrine of creation. But for now it seems that we have found a link between a normative canonical source and a practical disposition. The canon serves as a criterion, but only from within this practical attunement, while this attunement is ingredient in the very nature of Scripture. By providing a paradigmatic orientation, the Scripture also serves as what Harry Y. Gamble has called a 'locus of meaning', or what we have called an *intensional context*. How is this possible?

The Drama of Doctrine supplies the beginning of an answer to this question. 'Scripture not only calls for subsequent performance but is itself a *divine* performance, a mode of divine communicative action whereby the triune God furthers his mission and creates a new covenant people.'[62] This means that in interpreting the meaning of Scripture we must not look for a dispositional setting outside of the Scriptures themselves. Because Scripture is itself part of the divine action, *it* is a disposition, besides being a report of facts. This self-involved quality of the Scriptures is an absolutely crucial factor. Not simply an inert text, the canon is perspicuous, it is living and active, and we are drawn into its performance. There are two distinct levels of this triune performance. First, there is a material level of the actual history of salvation, about which the Scripture testifies. But there is also the 'formal principle'[63] of the drama of redemption, its 'normative specification'. Thus, '*the canon is at once a divine/human performance that calls for further performances (faith seeking practical understanding) in the church.*'[64]

In seeking to perform Scripture, and to imaginatively transpose it into new life situations, we are not working with a script, but rather we have a *primary*

---

[60] K. Vanhoozer, *Drama of Doctrine*, p. 148.

[61] See John David Dawson's wonderful *Christian Figural Reading and the Fashioning of Identity* (Berkeley: University of California Press, 2002), for an account of why figural reading depends on the literal reading, rather than canceling it out.

[62] K. Vanhoozer, *Drama of Doctrine*, p. 176.

[63] K. Vanhoozer, *Drama of Doctrine*, p. 177.

[64] K. Vanhoozer, *Drama of Doctrine*, p. 180.

and normative performance which serves as our script. This point will acquire significance immediately. The normativity of this initial performance resides in the fact that it plays a part in the story of salvation. It is not a simple testimony, however involved, about it. 'What gets transmitted is not simply a collection of facts but cognitive, imaginative, and spiritual strategies that serve believers well by providing orientation – direction – for continuing to follow Christ in new situations.'[65]

But this is precisely the orientation we have been aiming at. The drama of salvation as it unfolds from creation to Jesus serves as the basic historical experience that has to be interpreted. In order to adequately interpret that experiential history, one has to be properly disposed towards it. But there are a multitude of available dispositions. How does one choose the right one(s)? Our suggestion is that *by resurrecting the Scripture principle along the lines of Scripture's being both script and performance we can describe the canon as giving a paradigmatic disposition, orientation and interpretation of the historical events in which God dealt with humankind.* Thus, allowing one to be absorbed into the world of the Bible, trusting it, abiding by its direction leads to the formation of a disposition appropriate to understanding its message and the revelation of God, as it takes place in history, through the prophets, in the created world, and ultimately and decisively in the person of Jesus Christ. Following the directions of the text, we as faithful readers will learn to see, to discern those qualities and aspects of experience which constitute God's revelation. Thus, this 'sensibility to revelation' is inherently tied to one's being attuned in a certain manner, according to an original performance and language, as it has been given in Scripture.

Now this interpenetration between disposition and content has some important consequences for theological method. First, we do not have a script in the sense of a neutral description of the events of Jesus' life, or of the history of salvation. Scripture is not simply a testimony about faith, but itself a work of faith. As a performance itself, Scripture gives a description of historical events as faithful interpretations of those events. The appropriate disposition is already on display in Scripture. The canon itself represents a mode of vision, a particular perspective, a description of a particular dimension of reality made possible by a particular orientation towards reality. John E. Smith aptly puts this in terms of a *casting* into language. 'The results [of the encounters between man and God] are there as once deciphered in the biblical record, *which is to say that the record itself represents a casting into language* of the interpreted meaning of the experiences and events which form the substance of the biblical content.'[66] As already cast into language, this content is already performed. We have no detour around the performances of the Scriptures to the real events themselves.

[65] K. Vanhoozer, *Drama of Doctrine*, p. 181.
[66] J. E. Smith, *Analogy of Experience*, p. 98.

The mistake of historical critical exegesis was to think that avoiding the perspective of the biblical writers can lead to a perspective-less discovery of Jesus' identity. But the notion of a perspectiveless approach is incoherent, besides being itself perspectival in how it construes the methods, the aims, the presuppositions of historical work. On the other hand, the mistake of Hans Frei's exegesis was to suppose that we are stuck with the world of the text. It is true that exegesis must pay real attention to the inner grammar of the text, to the specific *fashion* in which its objects are construed. But it forgot the fact that the Scriptural testimony was a presentation of a *real aspect* of the story of a real Palestinian Jew. The uniqueness and particularity of the narrative depiction does not flow from the uniqueness of the reader and his techniques alone. Ultimately it flows from the richness of reality, from the plenitude of unique aspects that it has, and from the God-endowed human ability to sense those aspects by being properly disposed towards them. *The self-enclosed world of post-liberal theology was destroyed by Donald Davidson's argument that meaning cannot be elucidated apart from truth. But Davidson's theory of meaning was itself deficitary in failing to make room for intensions and the real contribution that language makes to how we construct the linguistic world. It is precisely these intensions which cannot be reduced to a simple truth relation to the world, but which are the constituting parts of an aspectival approach. They cannot be externalised, they are internal to a language and a way of seeing. One simply accepts the language and is transformed, disposed and habituated in the process. This is the real contribution that language makes*. But, as we have tried to point out, it is not language alone, but a specifically human ability to discern aspects.

Let us return to our topic. We have argued that in Scripture we have a normative disposition towards revelatory experience. This is not to say that other perspectives are not equally valid, but with one crucial proviso: they must not negate the dimension revealed normatively in the canon. In fact, in this consists the advantage of this *aspectival realism* over other models: it allows for the difference between perspectives. Each way of seeing, with its attendant conceptualisations and languages, practices etc. has a certain *semantic depth*, which can only be probed from *within* that way of seeing. However, aspectival realism also accounts for the fact that these ways of seeing are in rational contact with each other. What we discover in one dimension of experience has bearing on how we interpret other dimensions.[67]

Because of the unavoidability of perspectives, there is a certain circularity attaching to the present argument. To insist on the normativity of the Scriptural performance is only possible once one has taken a certain faith stance which recognises God as the author of this Book. If these perspectives were autonomous from each other this would condemn theology to sheer subjectivism. But while the object is – in a sense – given in the very adoption

[67] Admitedly more work needs to be done in this respect.

of the perspective, critical questions are bound to arise precisely because of our being aware of other perspectives. Such a correlation is required not simply for apologetical purposes, but for the very intelligibility of what we perceive under one disposition. This is another pragmatic insight contributed by Smith. Unless we find the cash value of the content of our religious experience in terms of other dimensions of experience, we fail to grasp its full meaning. To know what it means is precisely to be able to integrate it with the rest of one's life. Even more so in the case of religion who lays claim to an object of ultimate importance, to all life. In switching between dimensions doubt may creep in. Doubt and unbelief are live possibilities. The aspectival realism we have been promoting does not block it off. Neither does it celebrate it.

The Scriptures provide an *irreducible* and *normative* intensional context for understanding Christian experience and divine revelation. It is irreducible because there is no access to an un-interpreted Jesus. Any such experience would itself be perspectival. The Scripture is itself a performance, it is already cast into language. If Davidson were right, then this casting into language would not be the end of the story. We might seek to externalize the content of that performance – the beliefs, the stories, the actors, the stage itself – in terms of truth. But this would be to work with a deficitary notion of meaning as something that could be externalised. Secondly, because we cannot externalise, *and* because we take God to be the ultimate agent of the canon, the performances within the canon are normative. Not only we *cannot* get beyond the descriptions of the text to reach bed-rock revelation, but we *must not*: the Scriptures have been supplied by God as normative interpretations of revelation.

It is instructive to refer back to our discussion of metaphor. A metaphor consists of the adding of two normally unrelated terms. According to Davidson, a metaphor contains a blatant falsity which nevertheless triggers (causally rather than rationally and conceptually) an effect in the reader. From the perspective of pragmatics the interesting thing about metaphors, according to Davidson, Rorty and Frankenberry, is that they allow us to see the world differently. They *trigger* a new aspect seeing. They serve as props in games of imagination, the end result of which is a new way of looking at the world. According to Rorty, metaphors make possible leaps from one vocabulary to another (bear in mind here Rorty's problematic notion of vocabulary). Here comes the interesting bit, according to Frankenberry: 'Richard Rorty has sketched an original theory of cultural change in which strong poets, revolutionary scientists, and edifying philosophers toss off new metaphors that catch on, alter the environment, and, when successful, *survive as literalizations*.'[68] Never mind the problematic restriction of metaphors to a merely causal role in the philosophy of Davidson. Never mind Rorty's subjectivist description of vocabularies and of the relation between cultural

---

[68] N. Frankenberry, 'Religion as a "mobile army of metaphors"', p. 182.

politics and ontology. We have given ample reasons to reject it. But Rorty is on to something when he speaks about metaphors which survive as literalizations. And it also tells us something about how the canonical authors, as well as Jesus himself, by tossing off metaphors usher a new way of seeing. What is typology if not the juxtaposing of two different and unrelated events, a blatant falsity *from one perspective*, yet which provokes a new vision of how events are incorporated into God's plan of salvation? Essential to typology, just as it is essential to the metaphors, is that the component constituents retain their identity. In the case of typology, it is essential that both Joshua and Jesus retain their identities even while one is read in terms of the other, precisely for the effect to be accomplished. Similarly in the case of metaphors.

Metaphor, we suggest, provides one way of understanding how the canon creates an irreducible and normative intensional context. The more habituated we become into this way of seeing, the more literal the metaphors will seem – in relation to this way of seeing. As a normative intensional context, the canonical metaphors, beliefs, and stories function as internal relations within the 'Christian language'. As internal relations, they form the language, they determine its plausibility structure and its scope. A language doe not exist without such analytic truths such like 'All bachelors are unmarried.' Similarly, the Christian language presupposes such analytic truths as 'Jesus was raised from the dead', 'Jesus is the son of God' and so on. *If we understand, as we must, that analytic truths are given within a language (they are not necessary except once a language is presupposed), it is easier to grasp why internal strife about particular previously certain analytical truths (Jesus' resurrection) is at the same time a debate about the very meaning of Christianity, a question of whether one has changed the vocabulary altogether.*

Our position is that precisely because Scripture is a performance which inaugurates a way of seeing and that it does so by its metaphors and truth claims, we trespass on and transcend on those very metaphors at the risk of changing the language and losing the focus of our perspective. The Scripture provides both a conative and a cognitive direction for theological epistemology.

Divine Intellect, Creation, and Knowledge

We have arrived at the third and final theological supplement to neo-pragmatism. Admittedly, the proposals put forward in the last two sections deserve more elaboration, not least in conversation with other historic positions, both in theology and philosophy. The place for continuing the interrogation opened here is in a constructive theology of the aspects of God and the world, as these are normatively inscribed in the faithful *habitus* which is Scripture. That belongs to the future. The more immediate task is to paint in broad and sometimes abrupt strokes the outline of the proposal. What does it mean if we drop the priority of the epistemological and the strictly propositional? We have suggested that it is precisely such an abandonment of the absolute and exclusive priority, though not of the importance and necessity, of the propositional that is assumed by the New Testament and by important strands of the Christian tradition, not least Thomas Aquinas and the Evangelical movement in its more experiential early phase. A convergence between this understanding of knowledge and a pragmatic insistence on the co-inherence of thought and purpose has been noted. A further observation has also been made, of a fit between the neo-pragmatic insistence on the uselessness of the Given and the Christian stress on the fact that proper disposition is necessary for knowledge of the divine.

But, as we also saw, the neo-pragmatic emphasis on the ubiquity of vocabularies, languages and conceptual schemes has tended to lead to a coherentism unconstrained from the outside, where thought has no epistemic friction with objective reality. While in pragmatism this rejection of 'antecedent reality' is more narrowly restricted to Dewey, as opposed to Peirce but also to some extent James, it is far more widespread in neo-pragmatism, where it has taken the form of a dualism between the 'space of reasons' and the 'space of causality or law'. In Rorty's thinking above all the dualism has important epistemic consequences, for justification is no longer understood to be constrained by anything extra-linguistic, but is re-figured as playful experimentations with new vocabularies. Now accenting the importance of the vocabulary for the way in which the subject matter itself gets constructed is something we have also chosen to do, even in opposition to Davidson's hasty dismissal of language and the habituation it produces. But there is no correct logical line that unites the claim that 'all our knowledge is embedded in socially constructed vocabularies which reflect a way of life', to the claim that 'our knowledge is not about objective things out there'.

The work of John McDowell played an important part in an argument to the effect that languages and traditions are immensely significant and, while we must not reify them, we cannot externalise the way in which they negotiate intensions and meanings. While learning does happen in direct contact with the world, the paradigmatic instance of the acquisition of meaning imagined by Davidson, it is also true that particular languages create a habituation, a *Bildung*, which has its influence upon meaning. In the terms of the argument we have deployed, a language makes possible, through its range of intensions and dispositions, a particular sensing of real aspects of the world, aspects and reasons which are out there. McDowell achieves this feat through an ingenious reworking of the relation between receptivity and spontaneity. He accepts the neo-pragmatic critiques of the Given, but will not gag the strong realist intuitions which led to this unfortunate talk. If we can imagine that spontaneity is drawn into the very operations of receptivity, then we can extend the space of reasons to include experience. Experience is for McDowell already conceptual, rather than being the brute facts which confront us, or causally scratch our nerve endings. The attempt is to find a way to hold on to both the *sui generis* nature of spontaneity, as well as to the idea that thought is in rational links with things. Unless we maintain this second idea, argues McDowell, we deny ourselves to talk about thoughts at all, for the very notion of empirical content drops. The merely causal linkage between reality and the world which Davidson develops into a transcendental argument for the truth of the vast majority of our beliefs, will not do, for unless thought is in *rational* contact with experience, it has no content. Davidson's transcendental argument, even if it works, comes too late, for it presupposes that there are such things as beliefs, most of which are true.[69]

The whole argument deployed in *Mind and World* rests on the point that an understanding habituated by a language into a way of seeing, is able to pick out real aspects of the world. These aspects cannot be defined apart from the operations of the spontaneity, but they nevertheless belong to the world. A fundamental optimism pervades McDowell's attempt to make ourselves at home again in the world. The basic hope, not explicitly stated, is that the world as such is amenable to our dispositions and conceptual orientation. Rather than addressing directly this hope and asking himself, what right have we to expect that the 'reasons out there' are not simply human fancies, but real, true descriptions of reality, his concern is that this symbiosis between receptivity and spontaneity should not seem unnatural. In a certain sense, this method is inherent in his general philosophical method. Maximillian de Gaynesford brilliantly explains how McDowell goes about catching his philosophical prey: McDowell aims to defend what may be called 'the Default', which is the common-sense, normal way of understanding the relationship between mind and world, in this case: openness. But the Default now appears deeply problematic. Yet the reasons for which it now seems beyond redemption are themselves the result of entirely contingent historical shifts. If we could imagine life without those shifts, then the Default again would look secure.[70] In this case, McDowell tries to combat the fear that restoring spontaneity in rational contact with receptivity is supernaturalistic, unnatural and rampantly Platonic. He puts it that we do not want 'to reinstate the idea that the movement of planets, or the fall of a sparrow, is rightly approached in the sort of way we approach a text or an utterance or some other kind of action.'[71] The world must not be re-enchanted and read like a text or a book of lessons for us.

How can we show that this is all very natural? By refusing the understanding of the natural as being exclusively defined by causality and law, the sort that is exploited in natural science. We have to imagine that the operations of reasons are at the same time operations of nature and that acts of knowledge are genuinely natural whilst also being genuinely free. In knowledge, our nature is actualised, as it were, in drawing on a habituated spontaneity. Unless we can

---

[69] J. McDowell, *MW*, p. 68.

[70] Maximillian de Gaynesford, *John McDowell* (Cambridge: Polity Press, 2004) pp. 3-9.

[71] J. McDowell, *MW*, p. 72.

imagine that 'the operations of a bit of mere nature be structured by spontaneity, the freedom that empowers us to take charge of our active thinking'[72], then we are left with Davidson's unworkable dualism. But the supposition that 'natural' must be defined exclusively in terms of the causal and nomological is a product of the imagination fuelled by the rise of modern science. This is the shift which makes the mind's openness to the world seem so strange and occult today.

As we saw, McDowell proposes to understand the way in which this can seem natural by reflecting on the Aristotelian notion of second nature. Second nature is no less natural than our animal nature, although it is actualised in the free operation of understanding. If we can imagine the naturalness of this actualisation of second nature, we can also understand why nothing forces us to equate nature with the realm of law[73] and there is no need to see ourselves as bifurcated: a foot in the realm of law, another in the realm of freedom.

McDowell's zeal to keep clear of supernaturalism forces him to hold that the two spheres remain distinct. There is no need to integrate spontaneity-related concepts into the structure of the realm of law, but only stress their role in *capturing patterns in a way of living.*[74] We do this by practical wisdom, the acquisition of which opens our eyes to 'requirements of reason that are there whether we know it or not'.[75] This is where McDowell's optimism is most obvious. For while he refuses to integrate into the world of physics the objects which are instantiated by the concepts of spontaneity, he nevertheless insists that these concepts do help us discern authentic patterns, reasons which are there. He even goes as far as to stress that these reasons are out there whether anybody discovers them or not. Then again, he seems to back-pedal on those claims when he writes that ethical demands bear on us, but not 'independently of the viewer's participation in ethical life and thought, so that they would be available to a sideways-on investigation'.[76] Is there a contradiction here? We think so.

What McDowell wants is demands upon our moral reasoning, demands which have to do with the contingencies of human nature. But those demands are not such that they can be discovered by an independent analysis of human nature. Rather, they emerge from within moral inquiry. Yet they are not the sole product of the inquiry. Rather, the inquiry itself, through its concepts, means, and ends, is an indispensable element of the very discovery of those reasons. The path which McDowell tries to steer is extremely tenuous. On the one hand, he wants to avoid the pitfalls of Davidson's and Rorty's unconstrained coherentism, according to which there is no rational friction and

---

[72] J. McDowell, *MW*, p. 70.

[73] J. McDowell, *MW*, p. 77.

[74] J. McDowell, *MW*, p. 78.

[75] J. McDowell, *MW*, p. 79.

[76] J. McDowell, *MW*, p. 83.

our vocabularies exclusively construct the objects of our knowledge to such an extent that thought is left devoid of empirical content. On the other hand, he also wants to avoid the treacherous cliffs of a foundationalism of the Given, according to which nature unaided by spontaneity writes its own autobiography. This would be the sideways-on picture that he rejects.

But now the hard question must be asked: *why should we suppose that nature is amenable to our thinking?* For that is indeed what is presupposed by McDowell. Admittedly sometimes he speaks as if his only concern would be for what is natural, at the expense of truth. But surely he means more than that. Unless he is prepared to be content with a notion of spontaneity which, however naturally it arises, has no connection to truth, then the hard metaphysical question must be asked: why should we expect that our natural way of approaching the world is also the correct one? Why is this question important? Because *McDowell's notion of actualisation introduces a gap between first and second nature.* Our second nature could well have been otherwise. Is there anything to entitle us to consider this particular actualization, for example our ethical and religious talk, to be worthy of the name 'natural'? Unless we suppose that there is a deeper correlation between our animal nature, which properly belongs to the realm of law and our religious, ethical, aesthetic, rational, technical actualisations, we have no way to answer the sceptic who asks: why bother with morals?

McDowell seeks a natural linkage with something which he is unprepared to re-enchant. His fear of supernaturalism leaves him with two distinct and utterly different domains which, despite claims to the contrary, mysteriously and occultly draw upon each other. He ends up resurrecting dubious notions like truths which are unconnected to the activity of any mind.

We would like to suggest that the Christian doctrine of creation can provide much needed intelligibility to some of McDowell's crucial insights. This will be our third theological supplement to neo-pragmatism, though it is more directly addressed to McDowell. Briefly anticipating, the argument will be that the Scriptures teach that God created the world and as a result of this he alone has perfect *scientia* of it. Reason can be reconciled to nature because God is the origin of both. As intentional creation, there is an element of divine spontaneity within reality itself. There are reasons out there precisely because God is the author of nature, as a book of lessons for us, rather than because nature would have a preferred self-description. One can imagine that there is a huge wealth of significance attached to this theme and we can only begin to tap into it and point its convergence with our pragmatic stance so far.

Reason has not always been separated from nature. John Milbank's and Catherine Pickstock's recent work on Aquinas testify to this. Their exegesis of Aquinas yields a critique of correspondence theories of truth, which mistakenly assume that both the structure of knowledge and the structure of the world are fixed and can be compared. This, they claim, presupposes an epistemological rather than an ontological starting point. But the priority of epistemology would have been strange for Aquinas. But correspondence talk is not eschewed altogether. It gets ontologised. Thus correspondence, or 'adequating is an event which realizes or fulfils the being of things known, just as much as it fulfils truth in the knower's mind.'[77] The being of the things, on the other hand, resides with God, who as creator of everything, including being, holds within himself their *telos*. Thus, truth is primarily in the mind of God, and only secondarily in things, as copying the mind of God.[78] Milbank and Pickstock simply change the frame of reference for the debates around realism. Since nature has no being apart from God, it is futile to speak about a self-description of nature, except only derivatively as a reflection of the truth of God. Truth is not something to be tested in speculative comparison, but it 'sounds itself or shines outwards in beauty.'[79] Knowledge is thus conceptually related to the divine intellect.

Precisely because there is a divine mind can we imagine the possibility of knowledge. McDowell misses this theological dimension in avoiding supernaturalism. As a result, the relation between the two realms seems forced and arbitrary. But if there is a divine mind, which created the world and thus knows it perfectly, it makes sense to speak of stretches of that reality as being amenable to the combined operation of spontaneity and receptivity. A similar argument has been suggested by Alvin Plantinga. In his paper 'How to be an anti-realist',[80] Plantinga acknowledges the strong intuitive support for anti-realism, which is the difficulty of imagining truths which no-one holds. Truths are those sorts of 'things' which are held by someone. It is incoherent to think that truth is somehow independent of mind. But on the other hand we can imagine that true propositions are those which a divine mind holds. This gives added intelligibility to the realist thesis, namely that there are descriptions which are true independently of whether any human mind holds them. McDowell would like to affirm this, but he does so incoherently outside a theistic framework.

We hold that changing the framework of reference from reality to God, as the origin of reality, has momentous consequences. God alone has perfect knowledge of reality, because God alone has created it. While for Aristotle, as Milbank and Pickstock comment, matter is inimical to understanding, for Thomas it is not, proceeding fully from God.[81] Thus, in knowing particulars, there must be in the understanding a 'mysterious point of fusion between sense and intellect.' Imagination plays a role here through the abstractive process which takes place. But the result of this contribution of imagination is not

---

[77] Milbank and Pickstock, *Truth*, p. 5.

[78] Milbank and Pickstock, *Truth*, p. 10.

[79] Milbank and Pickstock, *Truth*, p. 9.

[80] Alvin Plantinga, 'How to be an Anti-Realist', *Proceedings and Addresses of the American Philosophical Association* 56/1 (1982), pp. 47-70.

[81] Milbank and Pickstock, *Truth*, p. 15.

something inferior, because by imagination and creativity, by the fashioning of images, the mind participates in the very creativity of God. Thus, 'imagination can act creatively without fictional betrayal', because truth corresponds not by copying but 'by a new analogical realization of something in the mind in an inscrutable "proportion" to how it is in reality.'[82] There is no mimesis, but 'the expressive registering of the other according to our own creative modality. We correspond to the other only in so far as our expressions approximate to the entire expression of the thing by the mind of God, which is the thing's actual existence over against nothing.'[83]

Creativity is thus elevated to the point where it is no longer a threat to knowledge, in virtue of its participation in divine creativity. Spontaneity contributes images which can participate in the very realization of the *telos* of things, returning them to God. Whereas God has perfect knowledge of particulars, we can have only a partial knowledge, but nonetheless real, through our participating in God's knowledge.

It appears that the focus of an ancient Christian outlook was not a nature which could be described independently of Christian ontology and cosmology, but a divine intellect which holds the ideas of the created things. God creates according to ideas in the divine mind. For Augustine, as Ken Surin notes, these ideas are concepts, whereas for Aquinas they are the *form* of the object created, similar to the plan of an architect. Just like an architect builds a house according to an original design, a blueprint in his mind, so the world is created according to a divine idea. This is a direct consequence of the world's being created as an intelligent act, rather than accidentally: 'As then the world was not made by chance, but by God acting by his intellect [...] there must exist in the divine mind a form to the likeness of which the world was made. And in this the notion of an idea consists.'[84] It is precisely these forms that knowledge must participate in, however distantly and imperfectly. Thus, truth is not a static relation of resemblance between the world as it is and propositional thought, but a relation, which Milbank constructs as dynamic and ontologically significant, between human thought, the things and the mind of God, which contains their *telos*.

Aquinas' Christian ontology of creation, in conclusion, leaves very little room for the emergence of scepticism about the relation between thought and things. These are not independent entities. Reason is not a faculty which has to be artificially and epistemically connected to the world. Rather, what is taken for granted is the origin of both things and mind in God. The final horizon of intelligibility is contoured by the divine intellect, out of which creation springs, and which constitutes the ultimate finality of things. Human mind is already

---

[82] Milbank and Pickstock, *Truth*, p. 15.

[83] Milbank, 'Knowledge', in John Milbank, Catherine Pickstock, Graham Ward, eds., *Radical Orthodoxy: A New Theology* (London: Routledge, 1998), p. 29

[84] Thomas Aquinas, *ST* 1.15.1

part of the process by which reality returns to God. It must not force its way into the essence of things epistemologically. This being the case, it no longer feels the epistemic burden to correspond, but is free to improvise, to imagine and creatively use new vocabularies and concepts. But the reason why imagination *can* play a part in an ontological account in which there nevertheless remains something antecedent, is that human creativity mirrors divine creativity.

This ontological position did not capture the religious imagination for too long. Aquinas' understanding of the possibility of knowledge of singulars as a combination of sense and intellect, with imagination playing a central part, soon gave way before Duns Scotus' new metaphysics. We remain with the notion that the mind can only know forms, but Scotus suggests the idea of *haecceitas*, which is the individual essence of each substance which can be an object of knowledge. Whereas for Thomas only universals could be present in the mind, thus knowledge of a particular thing always involved a combination of universal form and sensible phantasms, Scotus allows that individuals too, in virtue of their *haecceitas* can be objects of the intellect, quite independently of a sensible mediation. But this means, as Anthony Kenny points out, that an individual form may exist in the mind, without actually existing in reality, given that individuals come into and pass out of existence all the time. Hence, the individual present as an object of knowledge to the intellect can only be a *representation* and not identical with the real thing. Thus, 'a window is opened, at the level of the highest intellectual knowledge, a window to permit the entry of the epistemological problems which have been so familiar to us since Descartes.'[85]

It is important to remember this shift, as it marks the beginning of the transition from an ontological to an epistemological outlook. The epistemic distance it supposes between the representation and the real object is absent in Thomas. No such window exists there, notes Kenny, 'because there is nothing in the mind which the mind has not itself created.' The convergence between Aquinas and McDowell is striking at this point if we remember the latter's insistence that even in the operations of receptivity we draw on spontaneity. Yet the ontological horizon assumed by Thomas ensures that the sceptical worries cannot get going because there is no epistemic gap between the things, as creatively constructed by the mind and the things as they are related to the divine forms. Thomas knows full well that the divine forms belong to God and that the forms with which the human mind operates are human creations and abstractions, but which nevertheless participate analogically in the divine intention for the things. Scotus, on the other hand, by supposing that individual substances generate their *haecceitas*, which somehow then enters the human mind introduces a wheel in the mechanism of knowledge which, because it turns mysteriously, creates anxieties about its efficiency. Scotus, and the

[85] Anthony Kenny, *Thomas on Mind* (London: Routledge, 1994), p. 114.

epistemological tradition following him, worries that we have no certitude about knowledge if we are content with the analogical imagination. This is not to say that Aquinas was not aware of epistemic error, as Kenny puts it, 'but the way in which this problem presents itself to him is a question of describing and accounting for the malfunctioning of a faculty (*S* 1, 17, 2). It is not a question of building a bridge between a correctly functioning faculty, or a correctly functioning cognitive apparatus, and an extra-mental reality. But that is what, through Scotus and often in Descartes, the epistemological problem more and more explicitly became.'[86] In other words, there is no knowledge of particulars for Thomas without an active part played by those very particulars in sensibility. Moreover, the creative activity of the human mind is not an obstacle to true knowledge, for it contributes to the analogical realisation of the being of the thing.

But will any imagination do? Is any imagination resonant with the divine intention with respect to creation? The problem is well addressed in an article by Craig Hovey which discusses the work of Milbank, Jeffrey Stout and Charles Pinches on knowledge. Hovey mentions a couple of problems in Milbank's appropriation of Aquinas for the project of Radical Orthodoxy. One of these is also suggested by Christian Bauerschmidt. They suggest that Milbank and Pickstock 'are overwhelmed by a countervailing theological description that catches up those very universalisms [which they claim modernity falsely privileges] in ontology and creation.'[87] Maybe this criticism is a little bit harsh, given their stress on precisely imagination and rhetoric, not usually good sites for universalisms. The second point is much better taken: 'Milbank and Pickstock have developed an account which rightly locates the seat of being and knowledge in God in whom humans participate, but have not suggested how the imagination is shaped by the virtues. If knowledge for the moral life supposedly turns on the role of imagination, then the crucial fashioning of determinative images is accomplished by way of practising the virtues.'[88] Milbank sometimes gives the impression that imagination works automatically. But imagination needs to be trained. Thus, right participation in the divine life cannot simply be a matter of mustering sufficient will and desire. The will does not have the right object unless the intellect is properly attuned to that object.

Similar problems plague Stout's account of moral life as *bricolage.* Stout suggests that 'if Aquinas was not what we usually mean nowadays by a natural-law theorist, and was instead a virtue theorist insisting on the priority of prudence in practical reasoning, then he may have been not only a *bricoleur* but

---

[86] A. Kenny, p. 114.

[87] Craig Hovey, 'Forester, bricoleur and country bumpkin: rethinking knowledge and habit in Aquinas' ethics', *Scottish Journal of Theology* 59/2 (2006), pp. 159-174, p. 166.

[88] Craig Hovey, 'Forester, bricoleur and country bumpkin', p. 166.

an advocate of something called *bricolage.*'[89] This means that Aquinas was not a systematic ethicist, but rather a thinker that made use of the moral resources at his disposal in order to respond to particular ethical problems as they arose in life. We might remember that Stout is a pragmatically oriented philosopher. In this he suggests that there is no access to reality apart from the linguistic resources we have at our disposal. As we already saw, this does not prohibit Stout from being rather optimistic about the possibilities of knowledge. But we must refuse the notion that any single tradition is capable to delivering truth. We must be selective in our approach, utilising resources while simultaneously discarding falsities. But ultimately Stout fails to appreciate that Aquinas did not view the resources at his disposal as equally worthy of his attention. Moreover, these resources are not there, to be drawn on passively, once one has evaluated the ethical challenge. The traditions themselves construct the very perception of the ethical problem as well as the possible solutions. 'Having acquired the virtues, the agent's will does not repeatedly consult the intellect over moral principles, since those principles are largely not articulated or even acknowledged. [...] Habits form a kind of second nature which is more like nature itself than like guiding ethical principles.' [90] Moreover, the relevant virtues are bound up with revelation.

The cluster of points made in the last few paragraphs may be summed up by the conviction that: knowledge of particulars, as well as knowledge of the ethical demands that bear on us is a normative affair. Aquinas was not simply after experimenting with resources. Imagination was not an end in itself. The aim has been knowledge of reality all along. One's disposition towards this sensibility, accomplished through the practising of the virtues, is again normative. *Not all dispositions are right dispositions. In order to discover patterns that are really there, rather than invent phantasms with no real connection to God's intentions and purposes, one must properly become habituated in certain ways and thoughts.* Milbank and Pickstock fail to grasp the importance of this *normativity*, and so does Stout.

Bruce Marshall, on the other hand, doesn't. In a watershed essay, 'Aquinas as Postliberal Theologian', he defends Lindbeck's enlisting of Thomas as supporting the post-liberal notion of a Scriptural absorption of the world. Marshall responds to criticism brought against Lindbeck's exegesis of Aquinas. As a result he puts forward a reading of Aquinas which goes against the received wisdom in the field. He also proposes an understanding of theological justification in a coherentist key. Central in his arguments is the notion of truth as correspondence between the mind and the divine intellect, which holds within itself the ideas of things. The actual use to which the ontological relationship between truth and the mind of God is put leads to a different epistemological target than the one for which Milbank and Pickstock aim.

[89] J. Stout, *Ethics After Babel* (Princeton: Princeton University Press, 2001), p. 338.

[90] C. Hovey, 'Forester, bricoleur and country bumpkin', p. 170.

While the latter place such a stress on the importance of creative human thinking and the use of the imagination in grasping the essence of the particulars, but without reflection on the need for what Hovey calls 'determinative images', Marshall's reading of Aquinas underlines the importance of immersing oneself in the propositional truths of the Scriptures and the creeds.

Only God has perfect knowledge of the truth of things. The reason for that is by now familiar: because he is the origin of everything that exists. Aquinas puts it that 'Divine truth is the standard (*mensura*) of all truth... The truth of a thing is measured (*mensuratur*) by the divine intellect, which is the cause of things.'[91] Hence, for something to be true, it is to be in harmony with God's creative knowledge. As we saw, Aquinas argues that each thing has a form in the divine mind, according to which it has been made. But while God has perfect knowledge of first truth (*prima veritas*), 'only that can be *prima veritas* for us (*ex parte credentis*) which is linguistically embodied. As a result, the formal object of faith takes the shape for us of an assortment of mutually fit propositions, which Thomas calls the articles of faith.'[92] These embrace the Scriptures as well as the creeds. Thus, our knowledge of God is dependent upon the acceptance in faith of these *propositional* articles of faith.

But Marshall further argues, on the basis of his reading of Thomas, that these articles constitute a revealed *web* of beliefs. Being holistically interconnected, it is impossible to accept by faith one of these articles, without accepting all the others. Conversely, one's acceptance of either one of these articles of faith by way of, say, rational persuasion rather than faith is not possible. For, to put it rather abruptly, the conditions under which he or she has arrived at that belief have an effect upon the formal object of that belief. The formal object of a rationally derived belief that 'Jesus has risen' will not be the same as the formal object of the same proposition, accepted in faith. This is purportedly to be explained by the holistic hanging together of all beliefs, whereby what a Christian means by 'Jesus has risen' is dependent on what he means by all the other articles that he has accepted by faith. Thus, *fides* and *scientia* 'differ because they have different formal objects, that is, they hold beliefs by different means.'[93]

Proper knowledge of God depends not simply upon acquiescing to the right propositions, but the *manner* in which one arrives at those propositions is also important. It is helpful to bear this fact in mind: that Marshall insists in the manner of derivation, rather than in the *nature* of what is believed. It is still a *propositional* deposit that knowledge by faith acquires. Since we must rely on the first truths as they are linguistically embodied in the articles of faith, true

---

[91] Quoted from *Summa contra Gentiles* I.62, in Marshall, 'Aquinas as Postliberal Theologian' *The Thomist* 53/3 (1989), pp. 353-402, p. 373 n.40.

[92] B. D. Marshall, 'Aquinas', pp. 374-5.

[93] B. D. Marshall, 'Aquinas', p. 399.

knowledge must start in faith. Now Marshall does not make it crystal clear whether it is just theological knowledge that must rest on faith, or normal science as well. But from his general presuppositions as well as his own insistence on the world-absorbing character of the Scriptures, it seems that he means all knowledge. So what is significant is that he sets up the linguistic embodiment of divine truth, as given in the articles of faith, as a holistically-balanced epistemic criterion for all truth in general. We have already pointed out what Milbank and Pickstock have labelled as the Christological overweightedness of Marshall's account of truth, to the detriment of a creational emphasis. Thus 'for Thomas coherence or agreement with the linguistic paradigms of the religion, especially key ones enunciated in the creeds, is for Christians a *necessary condition* for any sentence about God or creatures in relation to God being a true proposition.'[94]

The central role that faith plays in the Marshall/Aquinas account is certainly worth endorsing. But the undue propositional stress that is placed on it, to an exclusion of, for example, an account of the way it changes disposition, moreover how it itself constitutes a disposition, is something that must be balanced. For example, faith leads the intellect 'to accept a network of propositions which are not evident to the intellect.'[95] An absolute starting point must be assumed in faith: 'faith is the beginning of the journey by which the supreme *correspondentia* is realized'; 'by faith "eternal life is begun in us." If faith is the necessary beginning of the process which ends in complete *scientia*, then there is simply no *scientia Dei*, no correspondence of the mind to God, outside of faith.'[96]

Why should this constitute a problem? The most obvious reason is that it relativises to an unwarranted degree the meaning of beliefs to their interdependence with other beliefs. But no two people hold all the same beliefs without following from this that they do not share any of them. This returns us to a crass incommensurability, not only of whole webs of beliefs, but of individual beliefs among themselves. Marshall is right to insist that there is a connection between the manner of acquiring a belief and the 'formal object' of that belief. But here he falls precisely into the unnecessary dualism between thoughts and things. It is true that people arrive at their beliefs about individual things in different ways. But these beliefs are still beliefs about a common world that we inhabit. This Davidsonian insight is something we considered worth preserving. Marshall accepts its claims too, later, in *Trinity and Truth*. But if we accept that there is a relation between the world and our thoughts and beliefs, we can return some confidence into our claims that our beliefs have the same objects.

---

[94] B. D. Marshall, 'Aquinas', p. 376 (our italics).
[95] B. D. Marshall, 'Aquinas', p. 390.
[96] B. D. Marshall, 'Aquinas', p. 391.

Now, we have placed a certain qualification upon Davidson's semantics. We have argued that it is not simply the causal relation between words and the world which stabilises meaning. In fact we argued that it doesn't. *Rather, we are always at home in the world given the languages we speak, the practices we engage in, given our purposes and interests, which constitute specific dispositions towards the world.* There is no world as such which figures in the content of our beliefs, but always a world under a certain aspect. Not all aspects are real aspects. Some are illusions. Not all patterns are inscribed. Thus, to speak about aspects of the world is not to deny normativity, but to understand that it is always linguistically and pragmatically mediated. But mediation does not mean that our access to reality is blocked. The supposition that it is was made possible by representationalism. And now it seems that Marshall gets hung up on precisely the sort of representationalism that he will later reject.

It is true that different conditions of knowledge produce different formal objects. But unless we understand that these formal objects are *real aspects*, real perspectives, that they afford real glimpses of the same world, albeit from a variety of perspectives, we will be forced to pose the epistemological questions: what if these formal objects do not represent what is out there? Marshall opens himself to precisely this sort of anxiety when he describes the constitution of the formal objects of beliefs as taking place solely under coherentist conditions. What Marshall forgets is that the world itself, the material object itself plays an active part in the process of the construction of the formal object. In McDowell's terms, the human intellect creatively draws upon his spontaneity (which may or may not include the articles of faith) in his experience of reality.

How do we redress this tendency? How do we affirm the importance of faith without denying the autonomy of science? Under Marshall's description, unless science begins in faith, it has no real object. This is blatantly false. But how do we reconcile this blatant falsity with our own claim that the truth of reality resides in God? Can we simply refuse to make this notion epistemically significant? Can we restrict its application to theology? These are all hugely important questions and we will address them in due time. For now we would like to point out that there are resources within Aquinas himself for a different approach.

What needs to be preserved is the notion that reality is created. This removes the pressure to construct truth in terms of an occult correspondence between thought and an autobiographical reality. The focus of the truth relation switches to the divine mind and intellect. But then faith does indeed play a foundational role. This is the conundrum at which we have arrived. Two points plot a way out of it.

First, to construe the importance of faith as leading one to a series of propositions is an oversimplified and one-sided understanding of faith. Thomas himself provides a much more nuanced perspective when he argues that faith is a disposition. To describe this disposition merely in terms of leading one to accept a body of doctrine is to miss the very meaning of a disposition, a *habitus*. Intellectual acceptance can be static, speculative comparing. Faith as a disposition implies a process whereby one's whole being is changed, one's outlook on life, together with one's desire and will. Far more than simply an intellectual acceptance of propositions, it constitutes a change of perspective, a new sensibility to other dimensions of life, in this case the sacred. Marshall actually has this notion of faith, but fails to grasp its implications: 'faith is distinguished from other intellectual dispositions by considering things *under the aspect of their agreement* with the *primas veritas*.'[97] Faith is another take on things. This is precisely that aspect of faith which we emphasised when we rejected the *territorial and spatial* notion of faith as belonging to some new community.

But that is precisely the sort of imagery which is evoked by Marshall's notion of faith which leads to a certain epistemic collection. When, in our discussion of Scripture, we emphasised post-propositionalism, it is the same notion of faith as consisting in a reorientation towards life. *A propositional stance is still assumed as important, but it must not be considered in isolation from the ontological transformation which takes place through conversion and through being the Church, but not least through the work of the Holy Spirit in each individual believer*. In this consists the richness of our concept of aspects: reality can come under many different aspects. But the point we have tried to stress is that *not all of these aspects may be consonant with the divine intention* which lays at the very origin of reality. Not all imaginative constructions are good. To suppose so is to return to either relativism, or to a gullible Platonism which sometimes tempts the proponents of Radical Orthodoxy. Imagination needs determinative images, it needs a normative disposition, or series of dispositions and these are provided in the Scriptures themselves.

But, and this brings us to our second point, whilst the normative imagination captured by the Scriptures is normative for us, but not in a way which may be removed from a soteriological and catechetical context, there is nothing to prevent us from accepting that there are equally valid perspectives, equally real dimensions of the world, as they are apprehended, for example, by science, ethics, art and so on. It is *precisely* because God created the world that *the world is apprehendable under an infinity or a plenitude*[98] *of aspects*. This point can hardly be over-emphasised. This is not to say that these aspects form incommensurable frameworks. On the contrary, though this is a point which cannot be adequately addressed in this work, while these aspects are autonomous, and cannot be unified under a single system, they do communicate. For example, discussions of faith must be related to the world of science and *vice versa*.

We suppose that what drives Thomas and perhaps Marshall to an excessive propositionalism is Thomas' notion of forms. Each individual thing has *a* form

---

[97] B. D. Marshall, 'Aquinas', p. 373.

[98] We owe the use of 'plenitude' to Kevin Vanhoozer.

in the mind of God. But this is an unduly monotonous way of putting the matter. To speak of these forms after the analogy of the blueprints which guide the architect is to lose sight of the very plenitude of the mind of God. Even a human painter or sculptor does not conceive her work to be understandable from a single perspective. But that is precisely what the notion of 'form', or 'ideas' in the mind of God conveys. Perhaps vectoring in the notion of divine simplicity will help matters. Nonetheless, the epistemic value of the origin of things in the mind of God must be conceived more along aesthetic rather than purely propositional lines. Just like textual meaning can be distributed along a variety of dimensions (authorial intention, historical reference, effective history, reader responses etc.),[99] so individual creatures and creation itself need not be imagined as having a single form.

So while Milbank and Pickstock overvalue imagination, Marshall has an overly constrictive understanding of faith, as leading the mind toward that single form. In the process, perfectly valid and autonomous[100] perspectives are unnecessarily subordinated to the articles of faith. This forgets the first point, namely that the articles of faith themselves are constitutive of a perspective which opens up a dimension to the spiritual world. Science is compatible with faith because they both deal in different equally respectable perspectives. It is true that they have different formal objects. Thus, the belief in 'God exists' acquired by way of scientific reasons has a different formal object from the same proposition expressed in a belief acquired by faith. Yet this does not mean that these formal objects do not describe real aspects of the same reality! Mark Platts' notion of *semantic depth* can help illuminate this relation. By science we may arrive at an incipient understanding of the existence of God. But by being immersed in the practices of the Christian or Judaic community, by reading the narratives that describe God's dealings with the world, we acquire a semantic depth of the notion of God. The scientist and the preacher may believe in the same reality, whilst they focus on its different dimensions.

We believe this is how the relation between creation, revelation, and epistemology needs to be portrayed. It doesn't lead to coherentism because we are under no obligation to unify the plethora of perspectives into a single system. The 'system' revealed in the Scriptures is absolutely normative as a habituated orientation on life, as an integral part of God's history of salvation. Science, on the other hand, may be an equally valid perspective.[101] These dimensions would have to be unified if we accepted that each individual

[99] Here we are again indebted to Jeffrey Stout's 'What is the meaning of a text?' *New Literary History* 14/1 (1982), pp. 1-12.

[100] We still believe that whilst these are autonomous from faith in the sense that it is not a necessary condition for their truth, the 'external' perspectives must not contradict, or over-rule normative images of faith in the Scriptures.

[101] The element of restraint derives from the fact that the individual statements and theories of science have to be evaluated before a decision on this is made.

creation has one form. But, as we saw, this is a nearsighted and simplistic understanding of the divine intellect.

The doctrine of creation provides the required intelligibility to McDowell's thesis that there are reasons out 'there'. It also justifies the use of imagination in knowledge, precisely in virtue of its resembling divine creativity. It provides a transcendental horizon on the backdrop of which a workable relation between religion and science can be outlined. Yet, precisely because God is an intelligent and purposive creative agent, it counsels that not all perspectives are justified. Some dimensions are simply invented. Thus, it will simply not do, with Rorty, to simply speak in terms of changing vocabularies and playful experimentation. There are demands which bear upon our linguistic usages and these demands only make sense if the notion of a creator makes sense. The very notion of truth requires the notion of a site where the space of law ontologically connects with the realm of spontaneity. That site is the mind of God and their relation is one of identity. The purpose which some pragmatists and radical empiricists seek to put back into nature is there because reality is a purposive creation. Charles Long observes that the teaching of *creatio ex nihilo* implies among other things that there was a plan of action, an intentionality which applied itself to creation. Since there was no pre-existing matter, God was not bound by anything but himself in the act of creation. Everything that is creation belongs to and derives from God.

Created rationality itself derives from God. The reason why our mind can pick out real aspects of the world is because our mind has been created by the same mind that created that world. Historically, as Alister McGrath points out this has been the energising faith behind the development of science. Creation's ordering by divine intellect entails that there is a structure of the world which allows patterns within nature to be discerned and represented.[102] On the side of the human mind, as Peirce notes in response to the vital question of the possibility of science, 'man's mind must have been attuned to the truth of things in order to discover what he has discovered.'[103] But this ontological adjustment of the human mind to created reality involves a dispositional adjustment in view of the multi-dimensional depth of things. This depth is not something that we have put there, as the mind orders a 'cosmic porridge'. It derives from the infinity and simplicity of God, who creates out of nothing and whose creations swell with meaning. But this depth can be sensed precisely in drawing upon the operations of human spontaneity, as we creatively discern patters which are really there.

This is the pragmatic correction made to theology. The multiple dimensions of reality are really there, but it does not make sense to speak about them

---

[102] McGrath, *A Scientific Theology. Volume I: Nature* (Grand Rapids: Eerdmans, 2001), p. 218.

[103] In J. E. Smith, *Purpose and Thought: The Meaning of Pragmatism* (Chicago: University of Chicago Press, 1984), p. 58.

independently of the creative and autonomous employment of spontaneity. In other words, our vocabularies, our conceptual frameworks, our sets of procedures, interests, and purposes are indispensable components of human experience of the world. But the belief that these do not generate phantasms without any relation to reality presupposes that there are patterns out there and that we are gifted with the tools to bring them to light.

Before we close the chapter, there are a couple of anticipated objections to which we would like to respond.

Perhaps the most immediate reaction to our proposals will be that we are trying to make God epistemically significant and to appeal to a realm of platonic forms which are supposed to anchor knowledge and fuel a new kind of foundationalism. Indeed, the appearance is that by changing the focus to God, by cancelling the futile quest for objective structures in nature (facts), one attempts to touch ultimate epistemic base. However, this adds no new entities to the process of justification. What it does contribute is *a transcendental validation of the necessity of holding oneself responsible before something objective*. But the way in which we actually act responsibly and become aware of the objective demands remains rather old fashioned. The necessity of such a transcendental *horizon* of the intelligibility of demands place on us from the outside, as it were, derives from the Davidsonian unboundedness of the web of beliefs. As we saw, this outlook was possible as the result of a disenchantment of nature and of a sharp dualism between reasons and causes. McDowell's attempt to tame the dualism was ultimately dissatisfactory because of his obstinate refusal to put the supernatural into the natural. We have done that by way of the doctrine of creation. In answer to McDowell's concerns, this does not make us any more (or less) human than we are. The task of justification still involves the same hard work with data, experimentation, validation in a community of inquiry. What we have proposed is a creative and aspectival realism. Under both descriptions this realism serves as a transcendental limit of inquiry, rather than placing any special demands on it. Yet what about faith? Isn't faith supposed to be precisely such an added demand on justification? If Marshall's arguments had their way, yes. But Marshall ties faith almost exclusively to the acceptance of a body of beliefs, resulting in a coherentist account of justification. No one could reasonably accuse Marshall of retuning to foundationalism, because that body of doctrine has the certainty of faith rather than that of *scientia*. At the same time, Marshall's arguments are plausible from the perspective of revelation. The religious dimension is one which is opened up by revelation and the faith it gifts. Under this aspect there are indeed special demands placed upon justification. Yet they do not come in the form of new entities on an ontological registry.

This leads into a second objection: do we, by speaking of dimensions, create a new safe haven for theology? Yes and no. Yes in the sense that, as Marshall notes, faith is an intellectual operation distinct from science. The language of the Christian faith, its normative (yet partly metaphorical) constitution by the

Scriptures, are inherently bound with the dimension that they open up. It is impossible to isolate neutral aspects of reality from the catalogue of human interests and procedures. To the extent that there are parts of this human spontaneity which specifically open up this religious dimension for us (whether these elements, like Thomas' linguistically embodied faith, are gifted from God or not), then it can indeed be said that there is a special site for discourse about God. But there is also a negative answer to the objection. There are at least two elements in our arguments which militate against such a construal. First, together with Davidson, we have rejected the scheme-content dualism. The notion that there are frameworks of knowledge, truth and meaning which do not communicate with each other, but are completely autonomous from each other and construct knowledge, perception, truth, is nonsense. But it is also a mistake to discount the importance of language, *pace* Davidson. Languages initiate a way of seeing. They make possible, though not single handedly, a new take on life and reality. These are the dimensions of experience of which John E. Smith spoke. But we, as individual human beings, hold within ourselves a number of such dimensions. They bear on each other, while remaining distinct. They bear on each other only because at a deeper level they open up windows on a common reality. Part of the task for Christian theology is to create multi-dimensional bridges: to show how a religious faith shines forth in other areas of existence as well. There is no insulation here, but precisely a pro-active and holistic translation of faith into all areas of life. This will lead to doubt, but that will fuel faith, as it overcomes it.

A third objection will most likely come from our own Evangelical tradition: what about the propositional? A complete response would mean, in a certain sense, rereading the book. It can be pointed out that its argument has not been a rejection of the propositional, but *a situating of the propositional within the practical.* The supposition that they are separate is precisely what gave rise to sceptical worries about the relation between words and things. It is not a change of hierarchy here, but the thought that the propositional makes no sense apart from the practical and *vice versa.* Had we not anchored the propositional transcendentally to the mind of God, but left it simply to be battered by the winds of shifting practice, this would have been a legitimate worry. Some might worry that precisely in anchoring the propositional in the divine mind we have replaced something concrete with something vague and ineffable. This is hardly the case. There was nothing concrete about the notion of correspondence to bits of reality. The gigantic effort deployed in this direction amounted to the creation of entities of a dubious and simplistic ontological status: facts. Our perspective is much more well-rounded, in the sense that we can treat reality as a divine work of art. Perhaps this is not the best analogy, connoting too much equivocity. But books, including science textbooks, are works of art too. The point is that to restrict the divinely gifted richness, depth, plenitude of reality is to subordinate God to a simplistic and monotonous ontology. On the contrary, who can put a limit on the unfathomable designs of God? Why do we readily accept the fact that an author can *gift* his texts with variegated meaning, but insist on a unique, boring divine blueprint? The aesthetic polyvalence of good works of art, of what David Tracy would call 'classics' is something taken for granted. But the doctrine of creation teaches us that such peaks of human creativity are but shallow adumbrations of an infinitely rich divine spontaneity.

Bibliography

Abraham, William J., *Canon and Criterion in Christian Theology: From the Fathers to Feminism* (Oxford: Clarendon, 1998).

_____, *Crossing the Threshold of Divine Revelation* (Grand Rapids: Eerdmans, 2006).

Allman, Jay, 'Metaphor and Davidson's Theory of Interpretation', *The Southern Journal of Philosophy* 39 (2001).

Alston, William, "Back to the Theory of Appearing", *Nous* 33 (1999): pp. 181-203

_____, "Sellars and the 'Myth of the Given'", http://www.ditext.com/alston/alston2.html.

_____, *Perceiving God* (Ithaca: Cornell University Press, 1991).

Anderson, Victor, *Pragmatic Theology* (Albany: SUNY, 1998).

Appelros, Erica, *God in the Act of Reference: Debating Religious Realism and Non-Realism* (Aldershot: Ashgate, 2002).

Barth, Karl, *Church Dogmatics* 1/1, trans. G. W. Bromiley (Edinburgh: T&T Clark, 2nd. ed. 1975).

Bartha, Paul and Savitt, Steven F., 'Second-guessing Second Nature', *Analysis* 58/4 (Oct. 1998), pp. 252-263.

Bilgrami, Akeel, 'Is Truth a Goal of Inquiry? Rorty and Davidson on Truth', in Robert Brandom, ed., *Rorty and His Critics* (Oxford: Blackwell, 2000).

Boghossian, Paul, 'Analyticity', in Crispin Wright and Bob Hale, *A Companion to the Philosophy of Language* (Oxford: Blackwell, 1999).

Boulter, Stephen J., 'Could Aquinas Accept Semantic Anti-realism?' *The Philosophical Quarterly* 48/193 (1998), pp. 504-13.

Brint, Michael; Weaver, William, eds., *Pragmatism in Law and Society* (Boulder: Westview, 1991).

Brown, Delwin, *Boundaries of Our Habitations: Tradition and Theological Construction* (Albany: SUNY Press, 1994).

Byrne, Peter, *God and Realism* (Aldershot: Ashgate, 2003).

Cady, Linell E., 'Pragmatism and the Category of Religion: Reflections on William James and Stanley Fish', *American Journal of Theology and Philosophy* 22/1 (2001), pp. 49-67.

_____, *Religion, Theology and American Public Life* (Albany: State University of New York Press, 1993).

Carnap, Rudolf, 'Empiricism, Semantics and Ontology' [http://www.ditext.com/carnap/carnap.html].

_____, *Meaning and Necessity* (Chicago: University of Chicago Press, 1956).

Case, Jennifer, 'On the Right Idea of a Conceptual Scheme', *The Southern Journal of Philosophy*, 35 (1997), pp. 1-18.

Corrington, Robert S., 'Beyond Experience: Pragmatism and Nature's God', *American Journal of Theology and Philosophy* 14/2 (1993), pp. 147-60.

Craig, Edward, 'Meaning and Privacy', in Crispin Wright and Bob Hale, *A Companion to the Philosophy of Language* (Oxford: Blackwell, 1987).

Crosby, Donald A., 'Construction, Convention, and Conviction', *American Journal of Theology and Philosophy* 16.1 (1995), pp. 21-32.

Davaney, Sheila G., 'Theology and the Turn to Cultural Analysis', in Delwin Brown, Sheila G. Davaney and Kathryn Tanner, eds., *Converging on Culture: Theologians in Dialogue with Cultural Analysis and Criticism* (Oxford: Oxford University Press, 2001).

_____, *Pragmatic Historicism: A Theology for the Twenty-First Century* (Albany: State University of New York Press, 2000).

_____, 'Judging Theologies: Truth In An Historicist Perspective', in Charley D. Hardwick and Donald A. Crosby, eds., *Pragmatism, Neo-Pragmatism, and religion: Conversations with Richard Rorty* (New York: Peter Lang, 1997).

_____, *Pragmatic Historicism: A Theology for the Twentieth Century* (Albany: SUNY Press, 2000).

Davidson, Donald, "A Coherence Theory of Truth and Knowledge", in *Truth and Interpretation: Perspectives on the Philosophy of Donald Davidson*, ed. Ernest LePore (Oxford: Blackwell, 1986).

_____, *Inquiries into Truth and Interpretation* (Oxford: Oxford University Press, 1984).

_____, *Subjective, Intersubjective, Objective* (Oxford: Oxford University Press, 2001).

_____, *Truth, Language, and History* (Oxford: Oxford University Press, 2005).

Dawson, John David, *Christian Figural Reading and the Fashioning of Identity* (Berkeley: University of California Press, 2002).

de Gaynesford, Maximillian, *John McDowell* (Cambridge: Polity Press, 2004).

Dean, William, 'Response to Critics', *American Journal of Theology and Philosophy* 25/2 (2004), pp. 163-77.

_____, *History Making History: The New Historicism in American Religious Thought* (Albany: State University of New York Press, 1988).

_____, *The Religious Critic in American Culture* (Albany: SUNY Press, 1994).

Devitt, Michael, *Realism and Truth* (Princeton: Princeton University Press, 1984).

Dickstein, Morris, *The Revival of Pragmatism: New Essays in Social Thought, Law, and Culture* (Durham, NC: Duke University Press, 1998).

Dorrien, Gary J., *The Making of American Liberal Theology: Idealism, Realism, and Modernity: 1900-1950* (Westminster/John Knox Press, 2003).

Dummett, Michael, '"A Nice Derangement of Epitaphs': Some Comments on Davidson and Hacking', in E. LePore ed., *Truth and Interpretation: Perspectives on the Philosophy of Donald Davidson* (Oxford: Blackwell, 1986).

_____, *The Origins of Analytic Philosophy* (Cambridge: Harvard University Press, 1996).

_____, *Seas of Language* (Oxford: Oxford University Press, 1993).

_____, *The Logical Basis of Metaphysics* (Cambridge, MA: Harvard University Press, 1993).

Dworkin, Ronald, 'Objectivity and Truth: You'd Better Believe It', *Philosophy and Public Affairs* 25/2 (Spring, 1996), pp. 87-139.

_____, *A Matter of Principle* (Cambridge, Mass.: Harvard University Press, 1985).

_____, *Law's Empire* (Cambridge, Mass.: Harvard University Press, 1986).

Evnine, Simon, *Donald Davidson* (Stanford: Stanford University Press, 1991).

Firth, Roderick, 'Coherence, Certainty, and Epistemic Priority', *The Journal of Philosophy*, LXI/19 (1964), pp. 545-557.

Fish, Stanley, *Doing What Comes Naturally: Change, Rhetoric and the Practice of Theory in Literary and Legal Studies* (Durham: Duke University Press, 1989).

Flew, Anthony, 'Theology and Falsification,' in Anthony Flew and Alasdair MacIntyre, eds., *New Essays in Philosophical Theology* (New York: Macmillan, 1955).

Fodor, Jerry, *Concepts: Where Cognitive Science Went Wrong* (Oxford: Clarendon, 1998).

Fodor, Jerry; LePore, Ernest, 'Why Meaning (Probably) Isn't Conceptual Role', *Mind and Language* 6 (1991), pp. 328-343.

Fodor, Jerry; LePore, Ernest, *Holism: A Shopper's Guide* (Oxford: Blackwell, 1992).

Føllesdal, D. and Friedman, M., 'American Philosophy in the Twentieth Century', *Daedalus* 135 (2006), pp. 116-126.

Frankenberry, Nancy K., 'On the very idea of symbolic meaning', in J. Harley Chapman and Nancy K. Frankenberry, eds., *Interpreting Neville* (Albany: SUNY, 1999).

_____, 'Religion as a Mobile Army of Metaphors', in Frankenberry, ed., *Radical Interpretation in Religion* (Cambridge: Cambridge University Press, 2002).

_____, ed., *Radical Interpretation in Religion* (Cambridge: Cambridge University Press, 2002).

_____, *Religion and Radical Empiricism* (New York: SUNY Press, 1987).

Frege, Gottlob, 'On Sense and Nominatum', in Jay L. Garfield, Murray Kiteley, eds., *Meaning and Truth: Essential Readings in Modern Semantics* (New York: Paragon, 1991).

Frei, Hans W., *The Identity of Jesus Christ: The Hermeneutical Bases of Dogmatic Theology* (Philadelphia: Fortress, 1975).

_____, *Types of Christian Theology* (New Haven: Yale, 1996).

Gadamer, Hans-Georg, *Truth and Method* (second edition, New York: Continuum, 1994).

Gibson, Roger, *Enlightened Empiricism: An Examination of W. v. Quine's Theory of Knowledge* (Tampa: University Presses of Florida, 1988).

Glock, Hans-Johann, *Quine and Davidson on Language, Thought and Reality* (Cambridge: Cambridge University Press, 2003).

Godlove, Terry F., 'Interpretation, reductionism, and belief in God', *The Journal of Religion* 69/2 (1989), pp. 184-198.

_____, 'Religious Discourse and First Person Authority', *Method and Theory in the Study of Religion* 6 (1994), pp. 147-161.

_____, *Religion, Interpretation and Diversity of Belief: The Framework Model from Kant to Durkheim to Davidson* (Cambridge: Cambridge University Press, 1989).

Gorman, David, 'Davidson and Dummett on Language and Interpretation', in R. W. Dasenbrock, ed., *Literary Theory After Donald Davidson* (University Park, PA.: Pennsylvania University Press, 1993).

Grice, H. P. and Strawson, P. F., 'In Defense of a Dogma', in L. W. Sumner and John Woods, *Necessary Truth: A Book of Readings* (New York: Random House, 1969).

Grube, Dirk-Martin, 'Realism, Foundationalism, and Constructivism: A Philosopher's Bermuda Triangle?', *Neue Zeitschrift für Systematische Theologie* 40 (1998), pp. 107-126.

_____, 'Religious Experience After the Demise of Foundationalism', *Religious Studies* 31 (1995), pp. 37-52.

_____, 'Refuting the Evidentialist Challenge to Religion: A Critique Inspired by William James', *Ars Disputandi* [http://www.ArsDisputandi.org] 3 (2003).

Gunn, Giles, 'Religion and the Recent Revival of Pragmatism', in Dickstein, *The Revival of Pragmatism: New Essays in Social Thought, Law, and Culture* (Durham, NC: Duke University Press, 1998).

Gustafsson, Martin, 'Systematic Meaning and Linguistic Diversity: The Place of Meaning Theories in Davidson's Later Philosophy', *Inquiry* 41 (1998), pp. 435-53.

Haack, Susan, ed., *Pragmatism, Old and New: Selected Writings* (Amherst, NY: Prometheus Books, 2006).

Hacker, P. M. S., 'Davidson on First Person Authority", *The Philosophical Quarterly*, 47/188 (July, 1997), pp. 285-304.

_____, 'On Davidson's Idea of a Conceptual Scheme', *Philosophical Quarterly* 46/ 184 (1996), pp. 289-307.

Hahn, E., Schillp, A., eds., *The Philosophy of W. v. O. Quine* (LaSalle, IL: Open Court, 1986).

Haldane, John, 'Putnam and Intentionality', *Philosophy and Phenomenological Research* 52/3 (Sept. 1992), pp. 671-682.

Haldane, John, 'The Life of Signs', *The Review of Metaphysics* 47 (1994).

Haldane, John, "A return to form in the philosophy of mind", *Mind (new series)* 11/3 (1998), pp. 253-277.

Hampshire, Stuart, *Thought and Action* (New York: Viking, 1960).

Hardwick, Charley D., Crosby, Donald A., *Pragmatism, Neo-Pragmatism, and Religion: Conversations with Richard Rorty* (New York: Peter Lang, 1997).

Hardwick, Charley, *Events of Grace: Naturalism, Existentialism, and Theology* Cambridge: Cambridge University Press, 1996).

Harman, Gilbert, *Reasoning, Meaning, and Mind* (Oxford: Clarendon, 1999).

Harré, Rom, *One Thousand Years of Philosophy* (Oxford: Blackwell, 2000).

Herrmann, Eberhard, 'Religion without Metaphysics', [unpublished paper, Tübingen, September 2006].

_____, *Religion, Reality, and a Good life: A Philosophical Approach to Religion* (Tübingen: Mohr Siebeck, 2005).

Horwich, Paul, *Meaning* (Oxford: Clarendon, 1998).

Hovey, Craig, 'Forester, Bricoleur and Country Bumpkin: Rethinking Knowledge and Habit in Aquinas' Ethics', *Scottish Journal of Theology* 59/2 (2006), pp. 159-174.

Inbody, Tyron, 'Delwin Brown's Constructive Historicism as A Reconstruction of Empirical Theology', *American Journal of Theology and Philosophy*, 18/2 (1997), pp. 147-166.

Janik, Alan and Toulmin, Stephen, *Wittgenstein's Vienna* (New York: Simon and Shuster, 1973).

Kekes, John, 'Skepticism and External Questions', *Philosophy and Phenomenological Research* 31/3 (1971), pp. 325-340.

Kenny, Anthony, *Thomas on Mind* (London: Routledge, 1994).

Kerr, Fergus, "Aquinas and Analytic Philosophy: Natural Allies?", *Modern Theology* 20/1 (2004), pp. 123-139.

_____, *Theology After Wittgenstein* (Oxford: Blackwell, 1986).

Kerr, Fergus; Wood, Charles M.; Marshall, Bruce, 'Book Symposium: Bruce D. Marshall, *Trinity and Truth,*" *Modern Theology* 6/4 (Oct. 2000).

Kim, Jaegwon, 'What is "Naturalized Epistemology"?', *Philosophical Perspectives*, vol. 2: Epistemology (1988), pp. 381-405.

Lindbeck, George, *The Nature of Doctrine* (Philadelphia: Westminster Press, 1984).

Ludwig, Kirk; LePore, Ernie, 'Truth and Meaning', in K. Ludwig, ed., *Donald Davidson* (Cambridge: Cambridge University Press, 2003).

Macintosh, D. C., *Theology as an Empirical Science* (New York: Macmillan, 1919).

_____, *Theology as Empirical Science* (New York: Macmillan, 1919).

_____, *The Pilgrimage of Faith in the World of Modern Thought* (Calcutta: University of Calcutta, 1931).

MacIntyre, Alasdair, *Whose Justice? Which Rationality?* (Notre Dame: University of Notre Dame Press, 1988).

Manning, Richard, 'Interpretation, Reasons, and Facts', *Inquiry* 46 (2003), pp. 346-76.

Margolis, Joseph, 'Pragmatism's Advantage', in *Ars Disputandi* [http://www.ArsDisputandi.org] vol. 3 (2003).

_____, *Reinventing Pragmatism: American Philosophy at the End of the Twentieth Century* (Ithaca: Cornell, 2002).

Marshall, Bruce, 'Aquinas as Postliberal Theologian' *The Thomist* 53/3 (1989), pp. 353-402.

_____, *Trinity and Truth* (Cambridge: Cambridge University Press, 2000).

McDowell, John, 'Having the World in View: Sellars, Kant, and Intentionality. Lecture I: Sellars on Perceptual Experience', *The Journal of Philosophy* 95/9 (Sept. 1998), pp. 431-470.

_____, 'In Defence of Modesty', in *Meaning, Knowledge, and Reality* (Cambridge: Harvard University Press, 1998).

_____, 'Virtue and Reason', in Roger Crisp and Michael Slate, eds., *Virtue Ethics* (Oxford: Oxford University Press, 1997).

_____, *Meaning, Knowledge, and Reality* (Cambridge: Harvard University Press, 2001).

_____, *Mind and World* (Cambridge, MA: Harvard University Press, 1996)

McGrath, Alister, *A Scientific Theology. Volume I: Nature* (Grand Rapids: Eerdmans, 2001).

Milbank, John; Pickstock, Catherine, *Truth in Aquinas* (London and New York: Routledge, 2001).

Milbank, John, 'Knowledge', in John Milbank, Catherine Pickstock, Graham Ward, eds., *Radical Orthodoxy: A New Theology* (London: Routledge, 1998).

_____, *The Religious Dimension in the Thought of Giambattista Vico 1668-1744* (Lewiston/ Queenston/ Lampeter: The Edwin Mellen Press, 1992).

_____, *Theology and Social Theory: Beyond Secular Reason* (Oxford: Blackwell, 1993).

Milligan, Charles, 'The Limits of Conventional Religious Language for Contemporary Meaning,' *American Journal of Theology and Philosophy* 17/3 (1996), pp. 295-316.

Moore, Andrew, *Realism and Christian Faith: God, Grammar and Meaning* (Cambridge: Cambridge University Press, 2003).

Murphy, Murray G., 'American Philosophy', in Luther S. Luedtke, ed., *Making America: The Society and Culture of the United States* (University of North Carolina Press, 1992).

Ochs, Peter, *Peirce, Pragmatism, and the Logic of Scripture* (Cambridge: Cambridge University Press, 1998).

Palmquist, Stephen, 'Review of Terry F. Godlove, *Religion, Interpretation and Diversity of Belief: The Framework Model from Kant to Durkheim to Davidson*', [http://www.hkbu.edu.hk/~ppp/srp/arts/RIDB.html].

Pecknold, Chad, *Transforming Postliberal Theology: George Lindbeck, Pragmatism and Scripture* (New York: T&T Clark, 2005).

Penner, Hans, 'Holistic Analysis: Conjectures and Refutations', *Journal of the American Academy of Religion* 62/4 (1994), pp. 977-996.

_____, 'Rationality and Religion: Problems in the Comparison of Modes of Thought', *Journal of the American Academy of Religion* 54 (1986), pp. 645-671.

Placher, William C., *Unapologetic Theology: A Christian Voice in a Pluralistic Conversation* (Westminster/ John Knnox, 1989).

Plantinga, Alvin, 'How to be an Anti-Realist', *Proceedings and Addresses of the American Philosophical Association* 56/1 (1982).

_____, *Warrant: The Current Debate* (Oxford: Oxford University Press, 1993).

Putnam, Hilary, 'A Defense of Internal Realism', in Putnam, ed. James Conant, *Realism with a Human Face* (Cambridge: Harvard University Press, 1990).

_____, 'Does the Disquotational Theory of Truth Solve All Philosophical Problems?', in Putnam, edited by James Conant, *Words and Life* (Cambride, MA: Harvard University Press, 1994).

_____, 'Meaning Holism', in Lewis E. hahn, W. V. Quine, Paul A. Schilpp, *The Philosophy of W. v. Quine*, (LaSalle: Open Court, 1986).

_____, 'Richard Rorty on Reality and Justification', in R. Brandom, ed., *Rorty and His Critics* (Oxford: Blackwell, 2000).

_____, *The Many Faces of Realism* (LaSalle: Open Court, 1987).

Quine, W. v. O. and Ullian, J. S., *The Web of Belief* (New York: Random House, 1970).

Quine, W. v. O., 'Reply to Critics', in E. Hahn, A. Schillp, eds., *The Philosophy of W. v. O. Quine* (LaSalle, IL: Open Court, 1986).

_____, 'Two Dogmas of Empiricism', in Quine, *From a Logical Point of View* (Camridge, MA: Harvard University Press, 1980).

_____, *From a Logical Point of View* (Cambridge, Mass. and London: Harvard University Press, 1980, 1st ed. 1953).

_____, *Ontological Relativity and Other Essays* (New York: Columbia University Press, 1969).

_____, *The Roots of Reference* (La Salle: Open Court, 1974).

_____, *The Ways of Paradox and Other Essays* (Cambridge, Mass. and London: Harvard University Press, 1976).

_____, *Word and Object* (Cambridge, MA.: Technology Press of the Massachusetts Institute of Technology, 1960).

Ramberg, Bjørn, *Donald Davidson's Philosophy of Language: An Introduction* (Oxford: Blackwell, 1989).

Rauser, Randal, 'Can There Be Theology Without Necessity?' *Heythrop Journal* XLIV/2 (2003): 131-146.

Rawling, Piers, 'Radical Interpretation', in Kirk Ludwig, ed., *Donald Davidson* (Cambridge: Cambridge University Press, 2003).

Reece, Gregory L., 'Religious Faith and Intellectual Responsibility: Richard Rorty and the Public/Private Distinction', *American Journal of Theology and Philosophy*, 22/3 (Sept 2001), pp. 205-219.

Robbins, J. W., 'Donald Davidson and Religious Belief', *American Journal of Theology and Philosophy*17/2 (1996), pp. 141-156.

_____, 'God-less Pragmatism', *American Journal of Theology and Philosophy* 25/2 (2004), pp. 157-162.

_____, 'Neo-pragmatism and the Radical Empiricist Metaphysics of Pure Experience', *American Journal of Theology and Philosophy* 14/1 (1993), pp. 19-34.

Rockmore, Thomas, 'Analytic Philosophy and the Hegelian Turn', *Review of Metaphysics* 55/2 (2001), pp. 39-370.

Rockwell, Teed, 'Rorty, Putnam, and the Pragmatist View of Epistemology and Metaphysics', *Education and Culture: The Journal of the John Dewey Society* (Spring 2003).

Rorty, Richard, 'Cultural Politics and the Question of the Existence of God', in Nancy Frankenberry, ed., *Radical Interpretation in Religion* (Cambridge: Cambridge University Press, 2002).

_____, 'Pragmatism as Romantic Polytheism', in Stuart Rosenbaum, ed., *Pragmatism and Religion* (Urbana: University of Illinois Press, 2003).

_____, 'Pragmatism, Relativism, and Irrationalism', in R. Rorty, *Consequences of Pragmatism* (Minneapolis: University of Minnessotta Press, 1982).

_____, 'Religious Faith, Intellectual Responsibility, and Romance', *American Journal of Theology and Philosophy* 17/2 (1996), pp. 121-140.

_____, 'The Decline of Redemptive Truth and the Rise of a Literary Culture' [http://olincenter.uchicago.edu/pdf/rorty.pdf].

_____, *Objectivity, Relativism and Truth: Philosophical Papers 1* (Cambridge and New York: Cambridge University Press, 1991).

_____, *Philosophy and the Mirror of Nature* (Princeton: Princeton University Press, 1979).

_____, *Truth and Progress: Philosophical Papers III* (Cambridge: Cambridge University Press, 1998).

Rouse, Joseph, 'From Realism or Antirealism to Science as Solidarity', in Charles Guignon, David Hiley, eds., *Richard Rorty* (Cambridge: Cambridge University Press, 2003).

Schilbrack, Kevin, 'Kicking Rocks with Donald Davidson' [unpublished paper, AAR, 2005].

_____, 'The Study of Religious Belief After Donald Davidson', *Method and Theory in the Study of Religion* 14/4 (2002), pp. 334-349.

Schnädelbach, Herbert, 'Two Dogmas of Empiricism: Fifty Year After', in Hans-Johann Glock, Kathrin Gluer, Geert Keil, *Fifty Years of Quine's 'Two Dogmas'* (Amsterdam: Rodopi, 2003).

Sellars, W., 'Givenness and Explanatory Coherence', *The Journal of Philosophy*, 70/18 (1973), pp. 612-624.

_____, *Empiricism and the Philosophy of Mind* [*EPM*], (http://www.ditext.com/sellars/epm.html).

Smith, John E., 'Experience, God, and Classical American Philosophy', *American Journal of Theology and Philosophy* 14/2 (1993), pp. 119-46.

_____, *Experience and God* (New York: Oxford University Press, 1968).

_____, *Purpose and Thought: The Meaning of Pragmatism* (Chicago: University of Chicago Press, 1984).

_____, *Religion and Empiricism* (Milwaukee: Marquette University Press, 1967).

_____, *The Analogy of Experience: An Approach to Understanding Religious Truth* (New York: Harper and Row, 1973).

Smith, N. H., *Reading McDowell: On Mind and World* (London: Routledge, 2002).

_____, 'Rorty on Religion and Hope', *Inquiry* 48/1 (2005), pp. 76-98.

Stalnaker, Robert, *Context and Content: Essays on Intentionality in Speech and Thought* (Oxford: Oxford University Press, 1999).

Stenmark, Mikael, 'Theological Pragmatism', *Heythrop Journal* 41/2 (2000), pp. 187-198.

Stout, Jeffrey, 'Radical Interpretation and Pragmatism: Davidson, Rorty and Brandom on Truth', in Nancy K. Frankenberry, ed., *Radical Interpretation in Religion* (Cambridge: Cambridge University Press, 2002).

_____, 'What Is the Meaning of a Text?' *New Literary History* 14/1 (1982), pp. 1-12.

_____, *Democracy and Tradition* (Princeton: Princeton University Press, 2004).

_____, *Ethics After Babel: The Languages of Morals and their Discontents* (Princeton: Princeton University Press, 1991).

Strawson, P. F., *Entity and Identity* (Oxford: Clarendon, 1997).

Stroud, Barry, *The Significance of Philosophical Scepticism* (Oxford: Clarendon, 1984).

Stubbs, David L., 'Practices, Core Practices, and the Work of the Holy Spirit', *Journal of Christian Theological Research* 9 (2004), pp. 15-28.

Sullivan, Michael and Solove, Daniel J., 'Law, Pragmatism, and Democracy', *Yale Law Journal* 113 (2003), pp. 687-741.

Torrance, Thomas F., *Reality and Evangelical Theology: A Fresh and Challenging Approach to Christian Revelation* (Philadelphia: Westminster, 1982).

Vanhoozer, Kevin, 'On the Very Idea of a Theological System: An Essay in Aid of Triangulating Scripture, Church and World', [forthcoming].

_____, *The Drama of Doctrine: A Canonical Linguistic Approach to Christian Theology* (Louisville: WJK, 2005).

Vidu, Adonis, *Postliberal Theological Method: A Critical Study* (Carlisle: Paternoster, 2005).

Welch, Claude, *Protestant Thought in the Nineteenth Century*, vol. 1 (New Haven & London: Yale University Press, 1972).

West, Cornel, 'Nietzsche's Prefiguration of Postmodern Literature', *Boundary 2: A Journal of Postmodern Literature* 9&10 (Spring/ Fall 1981), pp. 241-270.

_____, 'The Limits of Neopragmatism', in Cornel West, ed., *The Cornel West Reader* (New York: Basic Civitas Books, 2000).

_____, *The American Evasion of Philsophy: A Genealogy of Pragmatism* (Madison: University of Wisconsin Press, 1989).

Wilken, Robert L., 'Who Will Speak for the Religious Traditions?', *Journal of the American Academy of Religion* 57/4 (1989), pp. 699-717.

Will, Frederick, *Pragmatism and Realism* (Boston: Rowman and Littlefield, 1997).

Williams, Michael, 'Rorty on Knowledge and Truth', in Charles Guinon and David R. Hiley, eds., *Richard Rorty* (Cambridge: Cambridge University Press, 2003).

Williams, Rowan, 'Between Politics and Metaphysics: Reflections in the Wake of Gillian Rose', *Modern Theology* 11/1 (1995), pp. 3-22.

Wittgenstein, Ludwig, *Philosophical Investigations*, trans. G. E. M. Anscombe (Oxford: Blackwell, 1974, 2nd ed. 1958).

Work, Telford, *Living and Active: Scripture in the Economy of Salvation* (Grand Rapids: Eerdmans, 2001).

Zaccariason, Ulf, *Forces by Which We Live: Religion and Religious Experience from the Perspective of a Pragmatic Philosophical Anthropology* (Uppsala, 2002).

Index

Paternoster Biblical Monographs

(All titles uniform with this volume)
Dates in bold are of projected publication

Joseph Abraham
Eve: Accused or Acquitted?
A Reconsideration of Feminist Readings of the Creation Narrative Texts in Genesis 1–3

Two contrary views dominate contemporary feminist biblical scholarship. One finds in the Bible an unequivocal equality between the sexes from the very creation of humanity, whilst the other sees the biblical text as irredeemably patriarchal and androcentric. Dr Abraham enters into dialogue with both camps as well as introducing his own method of approach. An invaluable tool for any one who is interested in this contemporary debate.

2002 / 0-85364-971-5 / xxiv + 272pp

Octavian D. Baban
Mimesis and Luke's on the Road Encounters in Luke-Acts
Luke's Theology of the Way and its Literary Representation

The book argues on theological and literary (mimetic) grounds that Luke's on-the-road encounters, especially those belonging to the post-Easter period, are part of his complex theology of the Way. Jesus' teaching and that of the apostles is presented by Luke as a challenging answer to the Hellenistic reader's thirst for adventure, good literature, and existential paradigms.

2005 */ 1-84227-253-5 / approx. 374pp*

Paul Barker
The Triumph of Grace in Deuteronomy

This book is a textual and theological analysis of the interaction between the sin and faithlessness of Israel and the grace of Yahweh in response, looking especially at Deuteronomy chapters 1–3, 8–10 and 29–30. The author argues that the grace of Yahweh is determinative for the ongoing relationship between Yahweh and Israel and that Deuteronomy anticipates and fully expects Israel to be faithless.

2004 / 1-84227-226-8 / xxii + 270pp

Jonathan F. Bayes
The Weakness of the Law
God's Law and the Christian in New Testament Perspective

A study of the four New Testament books which refer to the law as weak (Acts, Romans, Galatians, Hebrews) leads to a defence of the third use in the Reformed debate about the law in the life of the believer.

2000 / 0-85364-957-X / xii + 244pp

July 2005

Mark Bonnington

The Antioch Episode of Galatians 2:11-14 in Historical and Cultural Context

The Galatians 2 'incident' in Antioch over table-fellowship suggests significant disagreement between the leading apostles. This book analyses the background to the disagreement by locating the incident within the dynamics of social interaction between Jews and Gentiles. It proposes a new way of understanding the relationship between the individuals and issues involved.

***2005** / 1-84227-050-8 / approx. 350pp*

David Bostock

A Portrayal of Trust

The Theme of Faith in the Hezekiah Narratives

This study provides detailed and sensitive readings of the Hezekiah narratives (2 Kings 18–20 and Isaiah 36–39) from a theological perspective. It concentrates on the theme of faith, using narrative criticism as its methodology. Attention is paid especially to setting, plot, point of view and characterization within the narratives. A largely positive portrayal of Hezekiah emerges that underlines the importance and relevance of scripture.

***2005** / 1-84227-314-0 / approx. 300pp*

Mark Bredin

Jesus, Revolutionary of Peace

A Non-violent Christology in the Book of Revelation

This book aims to demonstrate that the figure of Jesus in the Book of Revelation can best be understood as an active non-violent revolutionary.

2003 / 1-84227-153-9 / xviii + 262pp

Robinson Butarbutar

Paul and Conflict Resolution

An Exegetical Study of Paul's Apostolic Paradigm in 1 Corinthians 9

The author sees the apostolic paradigm in 1 Corinthians 9 as part of Paul's unified arguments in 1 Corinthians 8–10 in which he seeks to mediate in the dispute over the issue of food offered to idols. The book also sees its relevance for dispute-resolution today, taking the conflict within the author's church as an example.

***2006** / 1-84227-315-9 / approx. 280pp*

Daniel J-S Chae

Paul as Apostle to the Gentiles

His Apostolic Self-awareness and its Influence on the Soteriological Argument in Romans

Opposing 'the post-Holocaust interpretation of Romans', Daniel Chae competently demonstrates that Paul argues for the equality of Jew and Gentile in Romans. Chae's fresh exegetical interpretation is academically outstanding and spiritually encouraging.

1997 / 0-85364-829-8 / xiv + 378pp

Luke L. Cheung

The Genre, Composition and Hermeneutics of the Epistle of James

The present work examines the employment of the wisdom genre with a certain compositional structure and the interpretation of the law through the Jesus tradition of the double love command by the author of the Epistle of James to serve his purpose in promoting perfection and warning against doubleness among the eschatologically renewed people of God in the Diaspora.

2003 / 1-84227-062-1 / xvi + 372pp

Youngmo Cho

Spirit and Kingdom in the Writings of Luke and Paul

The relationship between Spirit and Kingdom is a relatively unexplored area in Lukan and Pauline studies. This book offers a fresh perspective of two biblical writers on the subject. It explores the difference between Luke's and Paul's understanding of the Spirit by examining the specific question of the relationship of the concept of the Spirit to the concept of the Kingdom of God in each writer.

***2005** / 1-84227-316-7 / approx. 270pp*

Andrew C. Clark

Parallel Lives

The Relation of Paul to the Apostles in the Lucan Perspective

This study of the Peter-Paul parallels in Acts argues that their purpose was to emphasize the themes of continuity in salvation history and the unity of the Jewish and Gentile missions. New light is shed on Luke's literary techniques, partly through a comparison with Plutarch.

2001 / 1-84227-035-4 / xviii + 386pp

Andrew D. Clarke

Secular and Christian Leadership in Corinth

A Socio-Historical and Exegetical Study of 1 Corinthians 1–6

This volume is an investigation into the leadership structures and dynamics of first-century Roman Corinth. These are compared with the practice of leadership in the Corinthian Christian community which are reflected in 1 Corinthians 1–6, and contrasted with Paul's own principles of Christian leadership.

***2005** / 1-84227-229-2 / 200pp*

Stephen Finamore

God, Order and Chaos

René Girard and the Apocalypse

Readers are often disturbed by the images of destruction in the book of Revelation and unsure why they are unleashed after the exaltation of Jesus. This book examines past approaches to these texts and uses René Girard's theories to revive some old ideas and propose some new ones.

***2005** / 1-84227-197-0 / approx. 344pp*

David G. Firth

Surrendering Retribution in the Psalms

Responses to Violence in the Individual Complaints

In *Surrendering Retribution in the Psalms*, David Firth examines the ways in which the book of Psalms inculcates a model response to violence through the repetition of standard patterns of prayer. Rather than seeking justification for retributive violence, Psalms encourages not only a surrender of the right of retribution to Yahweh, but also sets limits on the retribution that can be sought in imprecations. Arising initially from the author's experience in South Africa, the possibilities of this model to a particular context of violence is then briefly explored.

***2005** / 1-84227-337-X / xviii + 154pp*

Scott J. Hafemann

Suffering and Ministry in the Spirit

Paul's Defence of His Ministry in II Corinthians 2:14–3:3

Shedding new light on the way Paul defended his apostleship, the author offers a careful, detailed study of 2 Corinthians 2:14–3:3 linked with other key passages throughout 1 and 2 Corinthians. Demonstrating the unity and coherence of Paul's argument in this passage, the author shows that Paul's suffering served as the vehicle for revealing God's power and glory through the Spirit.

2000 / 0-85364-967-7 / xiv + 262pp

Scott J. Hafemann

Paul, Moses and the History of Israel

The Letter/Spirit Contrast and the Argument from Scripture in 2 Corinthians 3

An exegetical study of the call of Moses, the second giving of the Law (Exodus 32–34), the new covenant, and the prophetic understanding of the history of Israel in 2 Corinthians 3. Hafemann's work demonstrates Paul's contextual use of the Old Testament and the essential unity between the Law and the Gospel within the context of the distinctive ministries of Moses and Paul.

2005 / 1-84227-317-5 / xii + 498pp

Douglas S. McComiskey

Lukan Theology in the Light of the Gospel's Literary Structure

Luke's Gospel was purposefully written with theology embedded in its patterned literary structure. A critical analysis of this cyclical structure provides new windows into Luke's interpretation of the individual pericopes comprising the Gospel and illuminates several of his theological interests.

2004 / 1-84227-148-2 / xviii + 388pp

Stephen Motyer

Your Father the Devil?

A New Approach to John and 'The Jews'

Who are 'the Jews' in John's Gospel? Defending John against the charge of antisemitism, Motyer argues that, far from demonising the Jews, the Gospel seeks to present Jesus as 'Good News for Jews' in a late first century setting.

1997 / 0-85364-832-8 / xiv + 260pp

Esther Ng

Reconstructing Christian Origins?

The Feminist Theology of Elizabeth Schüssler Fiorenza: An Evaluation

In a detailed evaluation, the author challenges Elizabeth Schüssler Fiorenza's reconstruction of early Christian origins and her underlying presuppositions. The author also presents her own views on women's roles both then and now.

2002 / 1-84227-055-9 / xxiv + 468pp

July 2005

Robin Parry

Old Testament Story and Christian Ethics

The Rape of Dinah as a Case Study

What is the role of story in ethics and, more particularly, what is the role of Old Testament story in Christian ethics? This book, drawing on the work of contemporary philosophers, argues that narrative is crucial in the ethical shaping of people and, drawing on the work of contemporary Old Testament scholars, that story plays a key role in Old Testament ethics. Parry then argues that when situated in canonical context Old Testament stories can be reappropriated by Christian readers in their own ethical formation. The shocking story of the rape of Dinah and the massacre of the Shechemites provides a fascinating case study for exploring the parameters within which Christian ethical appropriations of Old Testament stories can live.

2004 / 1-84227-210-1 / xx + 350pp

Ian Paul

Power to See the World Anew

The Value of Paul Ricoeur's Hermeneutic of Metaphor in Interpreting the Symbolism of Revelation 12 and 13

This book is a study of the hermeneutics of metaphor of Paul Ricoeur, one of the most important writers on hermeneutics and metaphor of the last century. It sets out the key points of his theory, important criticisms of his work, and how his approach, modified in the light of these criticisms, offers a methodological framework for reading apocalyptic texts.

2006 */ 1-84227-056-7 / approx. 350pp*

Robert L. Plummer

Paul's Understanding of the Church's Mission

Did the Apostle Paul Expect the Early Christian Communities to Evangelize?

This book engages in a careful study of Paul's letters to determine if the apostle expected the communities to which he wrote to engage in missionary activity. It helpfully summarizes the discussion on this debated issue, judiciously handling contested texts, and provides a way forward in addressing this critical question. While admitting that Paul rarely explicitly commands the communities he founded to evangelize, Plummer amasses significant incidental data to provide a convincing case that Paul did indeed expect his churches to engage in mission activity. Throughout the study, Plummer progressively builds a theological basis for the church's mission that is both distinctively Pauline and compelling.

2006 */ 1-84227-333-7 / approx. 324pp*

July 2005

David Powys

'Hell': A Hard Look at a Hard Question

The Fate of the Unrighteous in New Testament Thought

This comprehensive treatment seeks to unlock the original meaning of terms and phrases long thought to support the traditional doctrine of hell. It concludes that there is an alternative—one which is more biblical, and which can positively revive the rationale for Christian mission.

1997 / 0-85364-831-X / xxii + 478pp

Sorin Sabou

Between Horror and Hope

Paul's Metaphorical Language of Death in Romans 6.1-11

This book argues that Paul's metaphorical language of death in Romans 6.1-11 conveys two aspects: horror and hope. The 'horror' aspect is conveyed by the 'crucifixion' language, and the 'hope' aspect by 'burial' language. The life of the Christian believer is understood, as relationship with sin is concerned ('death to sin'), between these two realities: horror and hope.

***2005** / 1-84227-322-1 / approx. 224pp*

Rosalind Selby

The Comical Doctrine

The Epistemology of New Testament Hermeneutics

This book argues that the gospel breaks through postmodernity's critique of truth and the referential possibilities of textuality with its gift of grace. With a rigorous, philosophical challenge to modernist and postmodernist assumptions, Selby offers an alternative epistemology to all who would still read with faith *and* with academic credibility.

***2005** / 1-84227-212-8 / approx. 350pp*

Kiwoong Son

Zion Symbolism in Hebrews

Hebrews 12.18-24 as a Hermeneutical Key to the Epistle

This book challenges the general tendency of understanding the Epistle to the Hebrews against a Hellenistic background and suggests that the Epistle should be understood in the light of the Jewish apocalyptic tradition. The author especially argues for the importance of the theological symbolism of Sinai and Zion (Heb. 12:18-24) as it provides the Epistle's theological background as well as the rhetorical basis of the superiority motif of Jesus throughout the Epistle.

***2005** / 1-84227-368-X / approx. 280pp*

July 2005

Kevin Walton

Thou Traveller Unknown

The Presence and Absence of God in the Jacob Narrative

The author offers a fresh reading of the story of Jacob in the book of Genesis through the paradox of divine presence and absence. The work also seeks to make a contribution to Pentateuchal studies by bringing together a close reading of the final text with historical critical insights, doing justice to the text's historical depth, final form and canonical status.

2003 / 1-84227-059-1 / xvi + 238pp

George M. Wieland

The Significance of Salvation

A Study of Salvation Language in the Pastoral Epistles

The language and ideas of salvation pervade the three Pastoral Epistles. This study offers a close examination of their soteriological statements. In all three letters the idea of salvation is found to play a vital paraenetic role, but each also exhibits distinctive soteriological emphases. The results challenge common assumptions about the Pastoral Epistles as a corpus.

***2005** / 1-84227-257-8 / approx. 324pp*

Alistair Wilson

When Will These Things Happen?

A Study of Jesus as Judge in Matthew 21–25

This study seeks to allow Matthew's carefully constructed presentation of Jesus to be given full weight in the modern evaluation of Jesus' eschatology. Careful analysis of the text of Matthew 21–25 reveals Jesus to be standing firmly in the Jewish prophetic and wisdom traditions as he proclaims and enacts imminent judgement on the Jewish authorities then boldly claims the central role in the final and universal judgement.

2004 / 1-84227-146-6 / xxii + 272pp

Lindsay Wilson

Joseph Wise and Otherwise

The Intersection of Covenant and Wisdom in Genesis 37–50

This book offers a careful literary reading of Genesis 37–50 that argues that the Joseph story contains both strong covenant themes and many wisdom-like elements. The connections between the two helps to explore how covenant and wisdom might intersect in an integrated biblical theology.

2004 / 1-84227-140-7 / xvi + 340pp

July 2005

Stephen I. Wright

The Voice of Jesus

Studies in the Interpretation of Six Gospel Parables

This literary study considers how the 'voice' of Jesus has been heard in different periods of parable interpretation, and how the categories of figure and trope may help us towards a sensitive reading of the parables today.

2000 / 0-85364-975-8 / xiv + 280pp

July 2005

Paternoster Theological Monographs

(All titles uniform with this volume)
Dates in bold are of projected publication

Emil Bartos
Deification in Eastern Orthodox Theology
An Evaluation and Critique of the Theology of Dumitru Staniloae

Bartos studies a fundamental yet neglected aspect of Orthodox theology: deification. By examining the doctrines of anthropology, christology, soteriology and ecclesiology as they relate to deification, he provides an important contribution to contemporary dialogue between Eastern and Western theologians.

1999 / 0-85364-956-1 / xii + 370pp

Graham Buxton
The Trinity, Creation and Pastoral Ministry
Imaging the Perichoretic God

In this book the author proposes a three-way conversation between theology, science and pastoral ministry. His approach draws on a Trinitarian understanding of God as a relational being of love, whose life 'spills over' into all created reality, human and non-human. By locating human meaning and purpose within God's 'creation-community' this book offers the possibility of a transforming engagement between those in pastoral ministry and the scientific community.

***2005** / 1-84227-369-8 / approx. 380 pp*

Iain D. Campbell
Fixing the Indemnity
The Life and Work of George Adam Smith

When Old Testament scholar George Adam Smith (1856–1942) delivered the Lyman Beecher lectures at Yale University in 1899, he confidently declared that 'modern criticism has won its war against traditional theories. It only remains to fix the amount of the indemnity.' In this biography, Iain D. Campbell assesses Smith's critical approach to the Old Testament and evaluates its consequences, showing that Smith's life and work still raises questions about the relationship between biblical scholarship and evangelical faith.

2004 / 1-84227-228-4 / xx + 256pp

July 2005

Tim Chester

Mission and the Coming of God

Eschatology, the Trinity and Mission in the Theology of Jürgen Moltmann

This book explores the theology and missiology of the influential contemporary theologian, Jürgen Moltmann. It highlights the important contribution Moltmann has made while offering a critique of his thought from an evangelical perspective. In so doing, it touches on pertinent issues for evangelical missiology. The conclusion takes Calvin as a starting point, proposing 'an eschatology of the cross' which offers a critique of the over-realised eschatologies in liberation theology and certain forms of evangelicalism.

2006 */ 1-84227-320-5 / approx. 224pp*

Sylvia Wilkey Collinson

Making Disciples

The Significance of Jesus' Educational Strategy for Today's Church

This study examines the biblical practice of discipling, formulates a definition, and makes comparisons with modern models of education. A recommendation is made for greater attention to its practice today.

2004 / 1-84227-116-4 / xiv + 278pp

Darrell Cosden

A Theology of Work

Work and the New Creation

Through dialogue with Moltmann, Pope John Paul II and others, this book develops a genitive 'theology of work', presenting a theological definition of work and a model for a theological ethics of work that shows work's nature, value and meaning now and eschatologically. Work is shown to be a transformative activity consisting of three dynamically inter-related dimensions: the instrumental, relational and ontological.

2005 / 1-84227-332-9 / xvi + 208pp

Stephen M. Dunning

The Crisis and the Quest

A Kierkegaardian Reading of Charles Williams

Employing Kierkegaardian categories and analysis, this study investigates both the central crisis in Charles Williams's authorship between hermetism and Christianity (Kierkegaard's Religions A and B), and the quest to resolve this crisis, a quest that ultimately presses the bounds of orthodoxy.

2000 / 0-85364-985-5 / xxiv + 254pp

Keith Ferdinando

The Triumph of Christ in African Perspective

A Study of Demonology and Redemption in the African Context

The book explores the implications of the gospel for traditional African fears of occult aggression. It analyses such traditional approaches to suffering and biblical responses to fears of demonic evil, concluding with an evaluation of African beliefs from the perspective of the gospel.

1999 / 0-85364-830-1 / xviii + 450pp

Andrew Goddard

Living the Word, Resisting the World

The Life and Thought of Jacques Ellul

This work offers a definitive study of both the life and thought of the French Reformed thinker Jacques Ellul (1912-1994). It will prove an indispensable resource for those interested in this influential theologian and sociologist and for Christian ethics and political thought generally.

2002 / 1-84227-053-2 / xxiv + 378pp

David Hilborn

The Words of our Lips

Language-Use in Free Church Worship

Studies of liturgical language have tended to focus on the written canons of Roman Catholic and Anglican communities. By contrast, David Hilborn analyses the more extemporary approach of English Nonconformity. Drawing on recent developments in linguistic pragmatics, he explores similarities and differences between 'fixed' and 'free' worship, and argues for the interdependence of each.

2006 */ 0-85364-977-4 / approx. 350pp*

Roger Hitching

The Church and Deaf People

A Study of Identity, Communication and Relationships with Special Reference to the Ecclesiology of Jürgen Moltmann

In *The Church and Deaf People* Roger Hitching sensitively examines the history and present experience of deaf people and finds similarities between aspects of sign language and Moltmann's theological method that 'open up' new ways of understanding theological concepts.

2003 / 1-84227-222-5 / xxii + 236pp

John G. Kelly

One God, One People

The Differentiated Unity of the People of God in the Theology of Jürgen Moltmann

The author expounds and critiques Moltmann's doctrine of God and highlights the systematic connections between it and Moltmann's influential discussion of Israel. He then proposes a fresh approach to Jewish–Christian relations building on Moltmann's work using insights from Habermas and Rawls.

2005 */ 0-85346-969-3 / approx. 350pp*

Mark F.W. Lovatt

Confronting the Will-to-Power

A Reconsideration of the Theology of Reinhold Niebuhr

Confronting the Will-to-Power is an analysis of the theology of Reinhold Niebuhr, arguing that his work is an attempt to identify, and provide a practical theological answer to, the existence and nature of human evil.

2001 / 1-84227-054-0 / xviii + 216pp

Neil B. MacDonald

Karl Barth and the Strange New World within the Bible

Barth, Wittgenstein, and the Metadilemmas of the Enlightenment

Barth's discovery of the strange new world within the Bible is examined in the context of Kant, Hume, Overbeck, and, most importantly, Wittgenstein. MacDonald covers some fundamental issues in theology today: epistemology, the final form of the text and biblical truth-claims.

2000 / 0-85364-970-7 / xxvi + 374pp

Keith A. Mascord

Alvin Plantinga and Christian Apologetics

This book draws together the contributions of the philosopher Alvin Plantinga to the major contemporary challenges to Christian belief, highlighting in particular his ground-breaking work in epistemology and the problem of evil. Plantinga's theory that both theistic and Christian belief is warrantedly basic is explored and critiqued, and an assessment offered as to the significance of his work for apologetic theory and practice.

2005 */ 1-84227-256-X / approx. 304pp*

July 2005

Hazel Sherman

Reading Zechariah

The Allegorical Tradition of Biblical Interpretation through the Commentary of Didymus the Blind and Theodore of Mopsuestia

A close reading of the commentary on Zechariah by Didymus the Blind alongside that of Theodore of Mopsuestia suggests that popular categorising of Antiochene and Alexandrian biblical exegesis as 'historical' or 'allegorical' is inadequate and misleading.

2005 */ 1-84227-213-6 / approx. 280pp*

Andrew Sloane

On Being a Christian in the Academy

Nicholas Wolterstorff and the Practice of Christian Scholarship

An exposition and critical appraisal of Nicholas Wolterstorff's epistemology in the light of the philosophy of science, and an application of his thought to the practice of Christian scholarship.

2003 / 1-84227-058-3 / xvi + 274pp

Damon W.K. So

Jesus' Revelation of His Father

A Narrative-Conceptual Study of the Trinity with Special Reference to Karl Barth

This book explores the trinitarian dynamics in the context of Jesus' revelation of his Father in his earthly ministry with references to key passages in Matthew's Gospel. It develops from the exegeses of these passages a non-linear concept of revelation which links Jesus' communion with his Father to his revelatory words and actions through a nuanced understanding of the Holy Spirit, with references to K. Barth, G.W.H. Lampe, J.D.G. Dunn and E. Irving.

2005 */ 1-84227-323-X / approx. 380pp*

Daniel Strange

The Possibility of Salvation Among the Unevangelised

An Analysis of Inclusivism in Recent Evangelical Theology

For evangelical theologians the 'fate of the unevangelised' impinges upon fundamental tenets of evangelical identity. The position known as 'inclusivism', defined by the belief that the unevangelised can be ontologically saved by Christ whilst being epistemologically unaware of him, has been defended most vigorously by the Canadian evangelical Clark H. Pinnock. Through a detailed analysis and critique of Pinnock's work, this book examines a cluster of issues surrounding the unevangelised and its implications for christology, soteriology and the doctrine of revelation.

2002 / 1-84227-047-8 / xviii + 362pp

Scott Swain

God According to the Gospel

Biblical Narrative and the Identity of God in the Theology of Robert W. Jenson

Robert W. Jenson is one of the leading voices in contemporary Trinitarian theology. His boldest contribution in this area concerns his use of biblical narrative both to ground and explicate the Christian doctrine of God. *God According to the Gospel* critically examines Jenson's proposal and suggests an alternative way of reading the biblical portrayal of the triune God.

***2006** / 1-84227-258-6 / approx. 180pp*

Justyn Terry

The Justifying Judgement of God

A Reassessment of the Place of Judgement in the Saving Work of Christ

The argument of this book is that judgement, understood as the whole process of bringing justice, is the primary metaphor of atonement, with others, such as victory, redemption and sacrifice, subordinate to it. Judgement also provides the proper context for understanding penal substitution and the call to repentance, baptism, eucharist and holiness.

***2005** / 1-84227-370-1 / approx. 274 pp*

Graham Tomlin

The Power of the Cross

Theology and the Death of Christ in Paul, Luther and Pascal

This book explores the theology of the cross in St Paul, Luther and Pascal. It offers new perspectives on the theology of each, and some implications for the nature of power, apologetics, theology and church life in a postmodern context.

1999 / 0-85364-984-7 / xiv + 344pp

Adonis Vidu

Postliberal Theological Method

A Critical Study

The postliberal theology of Hans Frei, George Lindbeck, Ronald Thiemann, John Milbank and others is one of the more influential contemporary options. This book focuses on several aspects pertaining to its theological method, specifically its understanding of background, hermeneutics, epistemic justification, ontology, the nature of doctrine and, finally, Christological method.

***2005** / 1-84227-395-7 / approx. 324pp*

Graham J. Watts

Revelation and the Spirit

A Comparative Study of the Relationship between the Doctrine of Revelation and Pneumatology in the Theology of Eberhard Jüngel and of Wolfhart Pannenberg

The relationship between revelation and pneumatology is relatively unexplored. This approach offers a fresh angle on two important twentieth century theologians and raises pneumatological questions which are theologically crucial and relevant to mission in a postmodern culture.

***2005** / 1-84227-104-0 / xxii + 232pp*

Nigel G. Wright

Disavowing Constantine

Mission, Church and the Social Order in the Theologies of John Howard Yoder and Jürgen Moltmann

This book is a timely restatement of a radical theology of church and state in the Anabaptist and Baptist tradition. Dr Wright constructs his argument in dialogue and debate with Yoder and Moltmann, major contributors to a free church perspective.

2000 / 0-85364-978-2 / xvi + 252pp

Paternoster: thinking faith

Paternoster
9 Holdom Avenue,
Bletchley,
Milton Keynes MK1 1QR,
United Kingdom
Web: www.authenticmedia.co.uk/paternoster

July 2005